MORNING, NOON, AND NIGHT

MORNING, NOON & NIGHT

Finding the Meaning
of Life's Stages Through Books

Arnold Weinstein

RANDOM HOUSE

New York

Published in the United States by Random House,
an imprint of The Random House Publishing Group,
a division of Random House, Inc., New York.

RANDOM HOUSE and colophon are registered
trademarks of Random House, Inc.

Permissions acknowledgments can be found on page 441.

LIBRARY OF CONGRESS CATALOGING-IN-PUBLICATION DATA
Weinstein, Arnold L.
Morning, noon, and night: finding the meaning of life's
stages through books/by Arnold Weinstein.
p.   cm.
Includes bibliographical references and index.
ISBN 978-1-4000-6586-8
eBook ISBN 978-0-679-60447-1
1. Life cycle, Human, in literature.   2. Human beings
in literature.   3. Maturation (Psychology) in literature.
4. Aging in literature.   5. Literature, Modern—History
and criticism.   I. Title.
PN56.L52W45 2011
809'.93354—dc22   2010017523

www.atrandom.com

Printed in the United States of America on acid-free paper

2 4 6 8 9 7 5 3 1

FIRST EDITION

Book design by Casey Hampton

To Catherine and Alexander

Contents

GROWING OLD

Preface

This is the most personal book I have written, personal in ways I had not anticipated. For close to three decades I have been teaching a large undergraduate class called "Rites of Passage." In this course I deal with coming-of-age narratives from medieval France up to our own moment, using a mix of famous writers such as Twain and Faulkner, along with other, less known favorites of mine, such as Tarjei Vesaas's *The Ice Palace*. One of my chief reasons for teaching this course is to urge students to realize that their own experience of growing up is—surprisingly, rewardingly—mirrored in books from other times, other places. Exploring such texts with students is gratifying, for they easily see that their own college experience is itself a rite of passage.

Therefore, when I set out to write a book on two major phases of life—growing up and growing old—I figured it would be easy enough to make use of my teaching for the growing-up part, while finding the appropriate books about aging to use as the second part of the diptych. I had never worked with students on issues of growing old—a nonstarter topic, if ever there was one—but I felt confident that I could make a judicious selection of literary materials dealing with that topic, to create a balanced study. This was going to be fun, I felt.

What I failed to realize was the impress of passing time on myself. During the several years I have spent writing this book, I have moved, at a surprising speed, into the territory of old age. And I began to realize that these literary matters were disturbingly existential for me, that I was in effect doing my own crash course in learning about the challenges, travails, surprises, and (hopefully) rewards of growing old. At the far side of this book now, I am a rather different person than I was when I first envisaged this study: closer to retirement, more aware of physical decline, more attuned to my own gathering exit from much I had taken for granted, more certain that I (like peers my age) am increasingly engaged in dodging bullets. My vision has changed. I now see growing up as something far more precious and exposed, more vulnerable and fateful, than I did in the confident, breezy courses I have taught on this topic over the years. And I now feel the awful weight of Freud's words on King Lear: "making friends with the necessity of dying." There is little that is strictly literary in all this.

But literature is what I know best. And I realized that my most intimate feelings about these key matters of entry and exit nonetheless have their source in literature. And, of course, that is what I am arguing in this book: that literature shows us who we are; it never stops doing this. I've posited this view before, but never with quite the personal conviction that you'll see in the pages ahead. This (very likely valedictory) book also constitutes something of a conclusion to my career. The ground I cover—from Sophocles and Shakespeare to Art Spiegelman and Jonathan Safran Foer—represents pretty much a roll call of the works of literature I've dealt with over a lifetime, but I now understand that they illuminate my own lifetime. And the personal voice I've allowed myself throughout this book is a voice that finds both its matter and its manner, its substance and its timbre, in the books I love. I mean this quite literally: literature frees my tongue and imagination, liberates and creates my best thinking, brings to the fore whatever gift I may have, and is arguably what is most social as well as most private about me. Literature, a term derived from the Latin for "letters," feeds my own letter to the world. I have lived a life of privilege in the academy—working year after year with the ever young as I move through time—and this is my way of repaying the debt I owe to the great writers of then and now. At this late stage of my life, it feels like the right thing to do.

MORNING, NOON, AND NIGHT

The Riddle of the Sphinx

"What is the creature that is on four legs in the morning, two legs at noon, three legs at night?" Oedipus answers, "Man." He wins the prize, becomes king, and marries the queen, all because he understood the riddle. It is a story we think we too understand. Four legs means crawling infant; two legs means erect and upright at one's prime; three legs means leaning on a staff or crutch or family member in old age. Man would be the creature whose legs vary in number, whose very locomotion alters, whose hardwired metamorphoses are governed by planetary rules: a morning phase, an evening phase. Only Homo sapiens goes through these transformations. Other species grow up and grow old, but they leave no record of what they encountered.

Oedipus does not say "time"; he does not say "story." Yet that is what the riddle actually signifies: the trip through time, the universal human voyage from morning to noon, from noon to night. Oedipus's own dark fate lies coiled, concealed, in just those passages. So, too, does our own. The human story is rich in testimony about these two central transformations, growing up and growing old, that script so much: not just our lives but our notions about education, love, maturation, wisdom. Here is the trajectory from innocence to experience, the entry/exit scheme, that frames all life. My book takes its lessons from the Sphinx, to explore these fundamental and fateful passages. How much do we actually know about these crucial chapters of our existence? Is your own story a riddle?

On the Move

Our past grows every moment we live—Proust beautifully said that we live on stilts, stilts that get longer each day of our life, stilts from which we must eventually fall—but it also grows further away, seems at once haunting and unreal. We ask: Was that I? Are those scrapbook images real? I know they are accurate, would pass muster in a courtroom, but are they real? Can I still feel the pulsing life in those frozen images? "Old men ought to be explorers, still and still moving," wrote T. S. Eliot. As I move toward my end stage, what purchase can I possibly have on my beginning, my formation? Proust's legendary account of a tired and depressed middle-aged man dipping a pastry, a madeleine, into a teacup and recovering—shimmering, alive, deep inside him but now rising anew, bathed in the air of long ago—his childhood: this beautiful version of retrieval has eluded me personally for some time now, and I fear it may be the same for many of my readers.

If recapturing childhood's form is hard, the experience and story of aging—inevitably upon me, governing my field of vision—are no less resistant to analysis. Yes, I am out of childhood, but then I am in old age and hence blinded to its evolving and defining contours, even if it is the autumnal air I daily breathe. A wrinkle here, a lapse there, a failing system elsewhere: the somatic last chapter has markers. But the aging mind? The soul in its late phase? The ending that must come? The meaning of the circle that is about to close? Who can see his or her own fuller shape with any finality? How would one go about charting these terrains?

My book addresses a poverty so basic, so elemental, that we do not even realize it afflicts us: we do not possess our own lives. The signifying arc through time that each of us lives—how we became who we are, what we are about, where we are headed—that would illuminate our story is elusive indeed. Do our days and years possess a melody? Especially as we near the end, we yearn for a clearer, fuller, more dimensional record of who we are. Where to find it? The story of our lives should be our greatest possession, our central estate; yet we are all too often locked out of it. We know that time is among the grand culprits, steathily eroding event into memory and memory into ashes. But even if you re-called every single act of your life, could call them all up on some kind of screen, would you know how to put them together, what they add up to?

Hence, those are the large issues I am after. Not unlike Thoreau, who elected to live in a hut at Walden Pond in order to grab life by the throat, I seek to get at the pith of things, to take measures. Es-pecially beginnings and endings. Growing up: What can you know about how you became you, about your formative encounters with family, others, and society, about the forces that nourished or stunted you, about the emerging shape of your life? Where would you go to learn this? And then the second half of the diptych: How can one size up the inexorable process of aging, approaching the end of the curve, with all its vexed questions: When does maturity become decline? When does decline become disaster? Does grow-ing old signify gain or loss of worth? Wisdom or obsolescence? Clarity or murk? Again: Where do we find answers?

Neither mirrors nor diaries offer testimony about these inti-mate yet intractable matters, since they are unequipped to capture our becoming or our altering, our dance through time. It is strange, given the information glut of our day, how unprovided we are on this score. Consider, for a moment, Ali Baba. Visualize him at his cave, pronouncing his mantra, "Open Sesame," and then en-tering those precincts to possess his hidden treasure. But what if the treasure is not coins of gold but the cave itself, the possession of one's own voluminous life? Is that not our truest treasure? And is it not hidden? But it can be made visible. For here is the central truth of this book (and of my life): *we can find our form in books.* Yes, in books written by others, about others. Together we will visit—indeed, raid—the huge storehouse of life stories that go by the name of literature. I think we shall realize that *this is our mirror.*

Literature as Estate

It is odd that the testimony of literature is rarely invoked in these terms: as a tool of personal discovery, indeed as a purchase on our own evolving form. Too easily dismissed as something to read and process either in a mandatory way at school or as an escape before going to sleep, a living work of art actually possesses a bare-bones practicality, indeed a *utility*, that we need to recover: it helps us toward a richer grasp of our own estate. What you find inside this mirror of life stories is an inexhaustible treasure house of "might-have-beens" and "might-bes," a repertoire of scenarios showing how one moves through time, how one is made up of forces beyond one's control and ken, how events form and deform us, how one becomes oneself, how that self responds to its pact with time and conducts its pas de deux with entropy and death. This is precious. A novel of two hundred pages may package a life of seventy years; yet a novel of two hundred pages requires a day or so to read, while a seventy-year life requires seventy years. Isn't this one profound reason we read novels? Art makes life visible.

You might ask: How can a work of literature, especially one written centuries ago, possibly shed light on me: my experiences, my formation, my running story? It is a good question, and it has some good answers. Great art lives in a way that transcends its moment, reaching something more universal, gesturing toward life experiences that are at once time-bound and timeless. The proof behind this (ahistorical) assertion is embarrassingly simple: every time you read a book that speaks to you, that engages your mind and feelings, you are encountering the truth of art. This is an exchange of inestimable value: testimony of the past traveling across the bridge of time into you the reader, hence becoming, at some hard-to-define level, your own lived experience. We are a far cry from websites or databases. We are tapping into living scripts that are big with life, into a mother lode that will nourish and grow us.

When a friend of mine was once asked, "Do you know much about Shakespeare?" she answered, "Not as much as he knows about me." Is it possible that the great writers know us better than we know ourselves? Or that their creations might serve as touchstones for our own self-knowledge? Yes, it is possible. Books house home truths. Harold Bloom points out that we know far more about Hamlet than we do about most of our best friends, and the young prince's assertion that theater holds up a mirror to nature also describes the mirror that it holds up to ourselves.

Yet there is also another answer to this question about art's relevance to our self-knowledge, and here I'd want to emphasize the actual historicity of art. What frequently shocks me most in reading older works—the trajectory of Oedipus from infant to old man, the adventures of the *pícaro* in seventeenth-century Spain or the plight of Shakespeare's tragic figures, the protagonists of Balzac and Dickens and the Brontë sisters and Twain in the nineteenth century, the sacrificial victims of Kafka, the doomed ones of Faulkner—is their bite and pungency, their often disturbing relevance for our moment. Oversubscribed to notions of "progress," we too often live with the fantasy that it was all so different then, as well as the conviction that *now* is unique, unforeseen, not prophesied.

But the great stories, the beggar boy and the arrogant king, the young man trying to succeed in Paris or London, the old man abandoned by his grown daughters, the white dropout kid saddled with a runaway slave, even the salesman turned into a bug or the idiot moaning for his long-gone sister: yes, such stories are drenched in specificity and local color and historical density, but they strike a chord in us in the twenty-first century as well, for we see how stubbornly their plots and crises live on in our own time, our own choices, our own dilemmas. The time travel afforded by art—a miraculously user-friendly form of voyaging in today's tourist culture of busy airports and security checks and jet lag—accounts in part for the surprising immediacy of great books, but only in part. For it is also true that these existential depictions of growing up and growing old, whether 2,500 years ago or today, lay bare for us our own murky arrangements, those we've come through as well as those we're headed toward, for it is certain that, absent terrible luck, each of us has grown up and will grow old.

We read books to widen and to deepen our own repertoire, because the performances of others (including fictive others) shed light on our own possibilities and limits. About those possibilities and limits—the self taking form, the figure achieving shape, the shape finally dissolving—we are otherwise, as I've said, strangely in the dark, since our education in school seems oddly outward-directed and generic in nature, anonymous even, unattuned to the ongoing private voyage we are making every minute. (The dazed look of students around the globe confirms this: whatever is happening in the classroom, whatever the subject, is distinctly *not-me*.) In the dark also because of natural incarceration, we are all landlocked creatures, stuck in particular minds and bodies, marooned in our specific time and place; and no matter how much information may come our way by dint of the electronic revolution that puts the world seemingly at our fingertips, only a click away, the austere fact of life is that we live and die within our own shell, doomed to our own perceptual equipment. Our eye can gauge much, but it cannot take the measure of "I."

Literature is the great bridge that enables us to exit our precincts, that enables other places and other lives to come to us, asking us to "try it on," "try it out." Facts, statistics, theorems, and discursive argument address only our reasoning powers. Art operates differently; it is a beckoning mirror. It is, in the poet Baudelaire's terms, an *invitation au voyage*. Put differently, literature grows us, and I am especially drawn to the unfurling organic processes in play here: not just the evolution of "characters" but our own move through time and—no less central—our move into the mirror, into the precious virtuality of art. Given my topic—growing up and growing old, how we enter and how we exit—nothing can possibly compete with literature as our source of illumination. Yes, the educators, psychologists, sociologists, anthropologists, doctors, and philosophers all have their special say about these two key facets of the life curve, but only the work of art treats us to that richer, pulsating, lived experience of what it might feel like to be there, to have been there, whether coming or going or both.

Art is our second life. Scholars frequently warn us not to identify with what we read but always to remember the constructedness and historicity of our materials, so as to acquire a critical stance. A book, we are admonished, is not a mirror but rather a record of the author's time or place or agenda or even benightedness. On this head, our job is to analyze, even to deconstruct, them. Yet at some primitive and vital level, I think the professors have it dead wrong. The act of reading can and should be a more savage and cannibalistic affair than that. We consume books to absorb their nutrients, to turn words into tissue. Our basic encounter with art is outright elemental, akin to a blood transfusion.

Having taught literature for more than four decades, I know full well that books can also bore, even put readers to sleep. But ask yourself: Why do we read novels? What draws us to browse bookstores, to bring home a book, to open its cover and start in on a several-hundred-page trip? Humans read literature in order to live more, to live differently, to have a precious vicarious experience that is available in no other way. In the stories to come you may encounter a form of drastic dislocation, an opening of self like none other. Reading literature puts you there. No other travel plan comes even close.

To be there: Kierkegaard wrote that written history's greatest deception is its (unacknowledged) hindsight, its inevitable status as after the event, after the outcome; if you know the outcome, he said, you no longer understand the event, for you do not know how it feels to be on the front side of it, looking into the abyss, deciding what to do, making your leap or your fall. Literary depictions of growing up and growing old are rich in open-endedness, and thereby lies their authenticity. They possess no documentable truth, no bottom line, no scorekeeping, and hence offer us a taste of the possible. Not an "idea" but a *taste.*

Nor does literature prescribe. No writer worth reading is likely to tell us: here is the best way to grow up, to grow old. Oedipus's life entailed considerable wreckage, but there is no villain, no false step or bad move to point to. Huck Finn ends up "lighting out for the Territory": has he succeeded, has he failed? King Lear is close to annihilated and is plenty arrogant to boot, but we can scarcely look in, point out his errors, and redirect him. Literature records experience—not wisdom or stupidity—and it is for us to gauge what to make of it, what to learn from it. These works of art have no lesson plan, no sermon, nothing remotely resembling a "how-to" (or "how-not-to") payload. Hence, I will not be judgmental in the pages that follow, even though I will be on the lookout for what they might teach us, how they might bear on our own lives. For growing up and growing old do have a generic character, and even the most distant tales shed light on our own doings.

Much changes throughout history, but much remains the same. The story of growing up is always a story of innocence leading to experience, of the acquisition of knowledge (of oneself, of one's world). It is always a story about how to achieve either vision or power, how to enter or exit society, how to take or make one's place on the stage. It is always a story of education, frequently contrasting prior beliefs with hard facts, and it is therefore invariably far-reaching, for its trials shed light on the values (open or hidden) of a culture. And it is ultimately cued to survival: of the body but also of the heart. Hence growing-up stories are about the cost of living, as the young make their way.

The story of growing old also possesses generic features throughout history. The forward drive of the young—the propulsion that fuels their trajectory—undergoes a sea change, since in old age the "territory ahead" is death. Hence, first and foremost would be the challenge to the old of the entropic force of time: one becomes weaker, one must learn to relinquish power (which one has spent a lifetime amassing). The ramifications of this drama at once natural and cultural are immense. What happens to authority? If eros goes, as it eventually must, what follows? Does love age? What have the old built, and will it remain? Are there lessons to be learned? To be taught? Is there ultimately a final harvest? Here too the great writers have much to show us. I repeat: each of us lives once as "ourself"; through art we are repeatedly invited to live as "other."

In the discussions to come, I want to capture that fuller drama recorded by art, making it possible for us to examine the contours of fictional lives, to gauge how characters in books go through their paces, are shaped or altered by events, become who they are, cease to be who they were. In starting out, let us look again at the life and death of Oedipus, the most spectacularly benighted figure of Western culture, the man whose grasp of his plenary form was nil from morning to noon and unbearable from noon to night. Remember the ingredients of growing up and growing old: innocence, experience, entropy, harvest; these are the ingredients of

Sophocles' work, but horribly intertwined. Cast-out infant becomes king. King is cast out again. Undone by exile and age,
cursed old man nonetheless becomes savior. This story of the man
who confronted the Sphinx and answered its riddle limns unforgettably for us, afresh, the contours of the human trajectory
through time.

The Oedipus Cycle: Morning to Noon, Noon to Night

Sophocles' *Oedipus the King* scarcely seems to most of us a work
about childhood. It is usually read as a disquisition on tragedy,
knowledge, fate, irony, you name it. Yet in its account of a young
man finding his place in the world, coming to realize the elusive-
ness of truth and the limits of power, it also does something that
is monumental and scandalous: it speaks out loud for Western culture, as Freud helped us see, the relation between father and son
as homicidal (not to mention what happens between mother and
son; about daughters it says little). Oedipus exits the stage at play's
end, blind, dependent on his two daughters, but his trek is not
over. If we bring the Greek playwright's later *Oedipus at Colonus*
into our discussion as well, so as to perceive a single master narrative, we can see that Sophocles has, cumulatively speaking,
sketched the trajectory of human life: from conception and abandonment on to the threshhold of parricide and incest, thence to
blindness and curse and exile and miserable old age, but closing
with a radiant, socially redemptive death. Here is the fuller arc
that can be said to stamp the concerns and analyses of my book:
growing up and growing old as the two riddling challenges meted
out to us by time.

If we are to understand Oedipus's childhood as echoing, we
must remember that this man who limps off the stage at the end
of *Oedipus the King* has been limping for a long time prior to that,
given that he was cast out as an infant, with pins put into his an-
kles. It is not easy to stomach the brutality of this story: a child
sentenced to death because of a curse, a mother having her infant
torn from her, a shepherd and a messenger swapping this baby
around, so that, perchance, it lives rather than dies. It's a harsh beginning. Can knowledge be made of this? Whereas many of the

books we will study go "inside" a child's life, Sophocles is content to give us only its terrible outline, so as to put into place the *machine infernale* that will twist this life into a horrid pattern. Of a child's consciousness, there is none; Greek tragedy has little interest in the formation of children. But how not to imagine injury here? We certainly register in Jocasta's laments how much damage oracles inflict on mothers. She too is crushed by the machinery: thinking she has experienced the worst—having her infant taken—she is of course destined for still more horror when she learns the child did not die but lived on to become her husband. One is entitled to feel that Sophocles chose perhaps the wrong tragic story to tell here, that Jocasta's fate is more drenched in sorrow than anyone else's. But his sights were on that little boy who survived and grew up to be a man, and then an old man.

To be sure, we never see young Oedipus as such, and from what we know of his story, he was a loving, respectful son who did everything in his earthly power to avoid the parricidal/incest curse attached to him: he fled Corinth and his adoptive parents, thinking that he was thus protecting the man and woman he had every reason to think were his father and mother, all the while running full tilt toward that dreadful crossroads where he struck down a man in anger, having no inkling that he was Laius. Sophocles achieves a mix of tragic irony and cinematic immediacy in Oedipus's account of this faraway moment when he responded to the Oracle's terrible prophecy:

> *I heard all that and ran. I abandoned Corinth,*
> *from that day on I gauged its landfall only*
> *by the stars, running, always running*
> *toward some place where I would never see*
> *the shame of all those oracles come true.*
> *And as I fled I reached that very spot*
> *where the great king, you say, met his death.*
> *Now, Jocasta, I will tell you all.*
> *Making my way toward this triple crossroad*
> *I began to see a herald, then a brace of colts*
> *drawing a wagon, and mounted on the bench ... a man,*
> *just as you've described him, coming face-to-face,*

and the one in the lead and the old man himself
were about to thrust me off the road—brute force—
and the one shouldering me aside, the driver,
I strike him in anger!—and the old man, watching me
coming up along his wheels—he brings down
his prod, two prongs straight at my head!
I paid him back with interest!
Short work, by god—with one blow of the staff
in this right hand I knock him out of his high seat,
roll him out of the wagon, sprawling headlong—
I killed them all—every mother's son!

This sequence makes my heart beat and my skin crawl each time I read it, so magnificent and overdetermined and echoing are its words and images. Running away from fate turns out to be running toward fate. (Good-bye, human volition, human orientation, sweet belief in knowing where you're going.) And then comes the breathless present-tense narration of the encounter itself (yes, the past is present tense, that's the meaning of the story), as it moves inexorably into focus, like an unfurling zoom shot: herald, colts, wagon, and then . . . a man, a man determined to force Oedipus off the road, an old man watching from his higher position in the wagon as his wheels are about to crush Oedipus, an old man assuming his fuller form as he brings down his prod and strikes. One feels that this is the very machinery of destiny: the death battle between old and young, father and son. And so the son commits the species-defining act of libido, as Freud saw it: he slays his father. Again one is stunned by the eloquence: "Short work," Oedipus claims, little knowing that this work will be immortal, framing not only his own entire temporal existence but that of all others to come; "every mother's son," the young killer exults, "I killed them all": how can we fail to see what is damning here, that the fruits of this act will be for Oedipus the son to enter his own mother's bed, something Freud saw as the desire of "every mother's son"?

Yet the ironies are for us, not for Oedipus. Even at play's end, his knowledge would seem to be about men's limits and gods' powers. At no point does he ponder the relationship between father

and son or mother and son, as such. He is crushed by his transgressions, but he can make no sense of them, other than as a curse.
They have for him no logic. True enough, Jocasta tells him it is not
unusual for men to dream of sharing their mother's beds, but she
says nothing to him about murder or parricide. It took Freud, in
The Interpretation of Dreams, to theorize these matters: "It is the
fate of all of us, perhaps, to direct our first sexual impulse towards
our mother and our first hatred and/or first murderous wish
against our father." Yet the image of a wagon with an old man
bearing down on a young one, seeking to remove him from the
road, from life, has a residual power that gives pause, as if to ask:
Who will stay on the road? Who will move forward? Who will give
way? We cannot avoid seeing a generic conflict here about the prerogatives and rights of the young versus the old, and the setting
makes it amply clear that only one of them can maintain his position, can occupy the road. In this regard, final things are on show:
the young must burst through and conquer, the old must yield and
abandon the road. There must be blood. And perhaps motivation
is irrelevant: whether the son thinks himself respectful and pious
or desires murder and power counts somehow less than the bare
facts themselves: yielding or fighting, dying or killing, as the grim
logical outcome of nature's station drama: growing up versus
growing old, coming into strength versus moving out of strength.
All living creatures are primed for this showdown.

And perhaps all young people are doomed to a benightedness
resembling that of Oedipus when it comes to the forces and vectors that rule over life—maybe not to the Sophoclean tune of parricide and incest, but condemned to the murk nonetheless. We the
readers can make this dark fable luminous, can see in it the dreadful work of prophecy and fate, can savor its fierce ironies and
shapely horrors. We are gifted with the vision of Tiresias. But no
child is born with such a gift. *Agency* is what Oedipus—the man
who brilliantly bested the Sphinx, the man who personified the
culture of intellectual daring in Periclean Athens—never has,
never will have. Here is one of the legacies of the play: the imperative of the young to see clear, to understand the workings of their
world. Sophocles is not soothing on this score: yes, Oedipus fully
assumes his fate, his identity, at the play's bloody end, but as for

seeing clear, it is not to be done. Reason—insatiable reason, blind reason—is his sole and grand trump as he moves unstoppably, rashly (as ever) toward the damning light, but truth is doomed to be after the fact, to be ever belated and retrospective.

It has often been argued that the chief values of Western culture are adumbrated in the drive to light that fuels the Oedipus story. Nietzsche saw in this brash young man a culture hero who invaded the secrets of Nature, of the gods. Surely the most admirable feature of the play is the king's own relentless truth seeking. Our modern era prides itself on its Enlightenment legacy of rationality and scientific progress, but no one in the twenty-first century can avoid feeling that this legacy is in horrible trouble. That old Delphic oracle still wields considerable lethal power, it seems to me, even though we tirelessly speak of liberty and agency. Even the new genetic knowledge that we are on the cusp of possessing about the "prophecy" of our bodies—none of this signals especially good things about freedom or seeing clear. Already our diagnostic prowess has outrun our ability to cure. As John Barth wrote, "The wisdom to recognize and halt follows the know-how to pollute past rescue. The treaty's signed, but the cancer ticks in your bones. Until I'd murdered my father and fornicated my mother I wasn't wise enough to see I was Oedipus." Sophocles' play is about sweet reason being a latecomer, about our understanding being always behind the curve, being the plaything of forces beyond our ken. "Be what you want to be! Be fulfilled!" we Americans like to tell our children. Oedipus's fate suggests otherwise. You do not and cannot know who you are, where you are going, or what you have wrought. This is not a happy formula for growing up.

I give Oedipus's story pride of place in this book in order to emphasize the mystery and benightedness that accompany growing up. Frequently I tease my students by urging them to look critically at the résumés they construct with such teleological fervor: From conception on, including my education and each position I've had, life has destined me for . . . (fill in the blank indicating the job applied for). Whereas, I suggest, if you actually remember the true checkered course of your life, you will doubtless find that the youngster at ten, the student at fifteen, the undergraduate at twenty, the professional at thirty, probably didn't have a clue as to what was coming, as to what was being built. Yes, retrospective logic is awfully good at cramming causality and purpose into one's life, thereby transforming the haphazard into pattern. No harm done. But it is tonic to recognize the dosage of deceit in it all. True enough, most of us are unlikely to have the monumental bad luck that Oedipus had. But all of us share in his blindness. He made the moves he thought best—running from his mother and father after learning of the curse, striking the tyrannical old man at the crossroads who wanted to run him down, accepting the crown and the bed of the queen as his rightful due after answering the Riddle of the Sphinx—and he got all of them catastrophically wrong.

But Sophocles has more in store for us as we track this fellow's fate. Blinded, yes, but not out. *Oedipus the King* ends, as the Riddle of the Sphinx predicted, with an old man reduced to child status, walking now on three legs, being helped by his daughters to exit the world. Yet he is not to die but rather to be preserved for some great fate. Sophocles returns to that fate, as if he felt the original story were somehow inconclusive, that self-blinding was but a stage of this man's trajectory, that his actual old age and dying would require another story altogether. Oedipus as old man, as seen in *Oedipus at Colonus,* written at the end of Sophocles' life and the end of Athens's status as the intact and controlling center of Greek culture, is still a proud even if feeble ex-king, but he seems shockingly angrier, less "wise," less reconciled to his fate, than the man we glimpsed at the end of the earlier play. His anger at his sons, his repeated ireful self-defense regarding the transgressions of incest and parricide, make one wonder if "maturation" and "wisdom" are useful terms for gauging this man's long life and trials. Sophocles is unrivaled in depicting creatural indignities: we cringe at the plight of old Oedipus—beggar, outcast, fugitive, ailing, "married to disaster," as he himself says— brought so low, now in rags, with his "ravaged face." The very rendition of the blind and ragged old man, utterly dependent on the help of his daughter Antigone, now coming at long last to his destined burial ground at Colonus, has an unmistakable pathos. But once again destiny is beckoning.

The play moves genuinely toward transcendence and transfiguration at the close, as Oedipus actualizes the gods' final prophecy: his secret burial place at Colonus will be a divine protection for Athens itself. In his dying he will ultimately reclaim, in a different key, the kingly powers he possessed in his prime. At the very portal of death, the miraculous event transpires: the old man rises to his feet, without the help of his children, and begins to move with slow, majestic steps, announcing to us, "I stand revealed at last." When we consider the horrid revelations of the earlier play—the rebuke to human knowledge, the blind committing of incest and parricide—there is something mesmerizing about this final metamorphosis, as if time and suffering and curse were now being reversed, turned into stature and power and regal strength. Of course, prophecy takes some of the credit here, and there is a Greek discourse about shrines and holy sites, but we cannot fail to see a beautiful reversal of time's arrow, a reversal of the physiological calvary that the old must experience if they live long enough.

One recalls Pascal's sinister words *"Le dernier acte est toujours sanglant, quelque belle que soit la comédie en tout le reste."* ("The last act is always bloody, no matter how sweet the comedy is otherwise.") All that is overturned here. At our end we become kings once again. (Ionesco would rework just this conceit 2,400 years later.) It is an arresting yet glorious image of death as our final apotheosis, our final assumption of the form and legacy we leave. I see nothing actually religious here, no prattle about the soul leaving the body and moving heavenward, but rather a decrepit old blind man getting a chance to preen and flex his muscles as exit performance, as savior of Athens. It's a final harvest, a radiant view of the end.

But that is not how most of us remember this play or this story. Oedipus's drawn-out miseries and misfortunes, hauntingly visible when the curtain goes up, are given immortal voice in this play as the inevitable punishment meted out by time. This blind man, who enters the stage leaning on his (death-marked, as we know all too well) daughter Antigone, images for us a destiny that has little to do with transgression or holy shrine and everything to do with the "mortal coil." Sophocles' chorus is worth citing in full:

Show me a man who longs to live a day beyond his time
who turns his back on a decent length of life,
I'll show the world a man who clings to folly.
For the long, looming days lay up a thousand things
closer to pain than pleasure, and the pleasures disappear,
you look and know not where
when a man's outlived his limit, plunged in age
and the good comrade comes who comes at last to all,
not with a wedding-song, no lyre, no singers dancing—
the doom of the Deathgod comes like lightning
always death at the last.
Not to be born is best
when all is reckoned in, but once a man has seen the light
the next best thing, by far, is to go back
back where he came from, quickly as he can.
For once his youth slips by, light on the wing
Lightheaded... what mortal blows can he escape
what griefs won't stalk his days?
Envy and enemies, rage and battles, bloodshed
and last of all despised old age overtakes him,
stripped of power, companions, stripped of love—
the worst this life of pain can offer,
old age our mate at last.
This is the grief he faces—I am not alone—
like some great headland fronting the north
hit by the winter breakers beating down
from every quarter—so he suffers,
terrible blows crashing over him
head to foot, over and over
down from every quarter—
now from the west, the dying sun
now from the first light rising
now from the blazing beams of noon
now from the north engulfed in endless night.

It would be hard to improve on these searing lines about the fate of aging. Sophocles is merciless in his scrutiny: you look for pleasures still, as you have always done—is this not how we live?—but they are shrinking, disappearing altogether, being canceled out by time. This is what must happen if you do not have the wisdom or wit to exit the feast at the right time. It is folly. Not that you are condemned to die alone (as we all imagine); on the contrary, you acquire a grisly final companion for this ultimate phase, the death god, who will be faithful to the very end. The wisest course is not to be born, the chorus says, but none of us has that choice. Being born, our next wisest course would seem to be to go back to where we came from. Where do we come from? Can we return and thus escape the indignities slated for us? Is that perhaps what Oedipus unknowingly sought to do when he coupled with Jocasta?

But he lived on, becoming old and feeble, hobbled with infirmities. The chorus envisions them as a dreadful form of intimacy and disrobing: we are stripped of all that gave value and substance to our existence: power and love; in this naked final state, our last lover, our mate, death, comes. Bereft, without cover, we face the elements that will undo us. The winter breakers crash over and through us, flaunting their vigor and our nullity, as if the entire cosmos were now taking its ultimate revenge on the human creature who has lived too long: the dying sun mocks us from the west, for it will return tomorrow to die again, but we go down only once; the rising sun mocks us from the east, for we will not share in the rebirth of light and life; the noonday taunts us with its heat and vitality, for we are detritus; the north finally cloaks us in our last vestments: eternal night.

That is how it ends.

The Oedipus story stands as the entryway into my book. It presents the life of the young as at once enterprising and blinded, crowned and crushed. We live in the murk. Our trajectory from morning to noon is checkered, and the crossroad we come to has consequences beyond our ken. Answering the Sphinx, becoming a king: here is a luminous parable of growing up, of achieving power. Committing (without knowing it) both parricide and incest: here is the horrific rebuke, as great feats of doing stand revealed as great trials of undoing. And this same story in its later phase, from noon to night, offers a comparably double-edged portrait of old age: suffering the merciless indignities of both entropy and exile while eking away a hard life, yet rising at the very end to recovered kingship and sovereignty. There's a worthy riddle here: does time beat us down or raise us up as we reach the end?

In the pages to come we will look at works of literature (and film) from many different times and places, representing books I know and love, devoted to the trip from morning to noon, and from noon to night. My choices are personal, and other works might come to mind or might have been chosen by other writers. In these stories we will see, once again, the trajectory of the young as they encounter and interpret life's coercions and riddles, and we will examine the plight of the old as they near their end, as they size up their end. Hence the life story of Oedipus—saved but doomed, doing but unknowing, intrepid but undone, decrepit but triumphant—seems exemplary to me as the master narrative for launching our exploration; it will stay with us, casting a long shadow.

GROWING UP

Itinerary:
Morning to Noon

The Language of Childhood

How to write about growing up? As children, especially as young children, we are too busy actually growing up to be able to put this experience into the distanced and interpretive frames of language and narrative. Not only are the great stories about childhood always written by adults looking back, remembering, perhaps inventing, perhaps fantasizing, but childhood itself might best be understood as an adult construct, a retrospective adult project. For starters, what would be the language of childhood? The French writer Georges Bernanos, late in his life, seeking to visualize the entry of his soul into the afterlife, saw himself as child—*"l'enfant que je fus"*—as the deadest of his dead, yet leading the way, even though irretrievable. And on the far side of words. Is it too much to claim that language itself is the price we pay for leaving childhood, the conversion of wonder into grammar? Or could we, alternatively, see language as prize, as central attainment and means of empowerment in the process of growing up?

These matters are at once primitive and abstruse. Anyone who has seen the vibrancy of children at play senses the gap (in beauty and power) between "being" and "speaking." And that may be the least of it, for language also heralds a regime of deferral and translation. The immediacy of experience is exchanged for the mediation of words. We exit the Garden into a realm of signs. Consider, in this regard, the young Jean-Jacques Rousseau, who saw his fundamental life crisis in just these colors. Retelling his life from the vantage point of age and retrospect (in *Les Confessions*), Rousseau recalls the life-altering episode of a stolen comb. *A stolen comb?* Yes, stealing a comb is what the child is wrongly accused of doing, but when he passionately argues that he is innocent, he is not believed. You may ask: Where's the crisis? I repeat: He says he is innocent, he is not believed. This is no less than the entry into language as facticity, language as unreliable conduit. "There ended the serenity of my childish life," he writes; words are a broken bridge, our hearts cannot be read.

But the other side of this equation is no less crucial: language as empowerment, language as means of comprehension and agency, language as indispensable tool for growing up. We will have occasion to see that the most "successful" figures in my study, the ones who manage best to make their way into life, whether it be by overcoming adversity or understanding the nature of culture (the culture that contains them), enlist words as one of their chief resources. We will see this writ large, as it were, in the trials and exploits of figures like the *pícaro* Pablos, Faulkner's Ike McCaslin, and Alice Walker's Celie.

Further, what would we know about the lives of others if it were not for the written record, the vital transcription of experience into language? Our most precious accounts of childhood, of the experience of growing up and making our way, come to us by way of writing. Writing not only ensures the communication of this key phase of life, it is the tool that enables us to give shape and meaning to it, to retrace it, to convert its quicksilver into cadences and form. Writing eludes (as nothing else does) time's entropy and erasure, so that the depicted childhood of, say, Rousseau or Dickens or Proust still shimmers in its immediacy (and in its mix of terrors and errors) while those men's bones moulder in the earth. But that is the least of it: the stories of growing up, bequeathed to us by literature, partake of the miraculous plenitude proper to narrative: they are big with time, awash in culture, so that they yield an echoing script that not only captures the child's experience but also signals much more: the gathered familial and cultural vectors whose weave inhabits the mind of the child and the foreboding temporal curve to come, as the child leaves childhood and enters the adult scheme. Through the narratives of childhood, the accounts of the voyage from morning to noon, we access something no photo, no single utterance can express: at once an unfolding of human potential and a peculiar map of private and public destiny, interwoven.

Childhood: Romantic Construct?

And more still: we see, thanks to the optic of these books, the elemental shock that the adult world, with its peculiar rituals, routinely inflicts on the young, and this is tonic, for it is what we adults have stopped perceiving for some time now. Aided, we now see the ticket we bought long ago for admission to "reality." As readers, as thinkers, as folks with miles to go before we sleep, we're already positioned on the far side of this dividing line, ousted from innocence and locked into experience, as William Blake would have put it, but for a precious while—as we negotiate, say, the poetry of Blake himself or the novels of Dickens, Twain, and Faulkner—we breathe another air and grope toward an earlier self. Literature restores to us the most moving chapter of our life—the truly kinetic time when everything was mobile, the time before things made adult sense, perhaps the only time things actually made real sense.

Or did they? It is well known that our current ideas about childhood as precious are profoundly inflected by the tenets of Romanticism, which did much to single out that special time of life as special: unspoiled, innocent, closer to nature, formative, holding in potential all that we might conceivably become or destroy. This discovery of the purity and preciousness of children is doubtless related as well to the increasing socioeconomic exploitation of them as it occurred in the Industrial Revolution of precisely that time period, as if to show that the value of young lives only becomes visible when those same lives are at risk and under attack.

(Blake provokes along just these lines.) Here would be a belated-ness hardwired into our thinking: it is damage that instructs.

But go further back than nineteenth-century Romanticism, and you find nothing so sweet or so value-laden. There was no mys-tique about children then. Their (virtually invisible) fates could be arduous indeed. As we saw, *Oedipus the King* traces such a fate, but Sophocles is not interested in child measures, only in adult mea-sures. One is struck, in reading literature from antiquity to the nineteenth century, by the harshness and marginality of children's lives, and it seems essential to pay heed, today, to those earlier, sterner accounts. Shakespeare and the authors of the seventeenth-century picaresque and baroque tales and eighteenth-century writ-ers such as Abbé Prévost and Pierre Choderlos de Laclos had little interest (or belief) in angelic children, nor did they believe that the child was "father to the man," as William Wordsworth famously put it in the following century. Even later writers who believed in the sanctity of children—the Brontë sisters, Dickens, Dostoevsky, Twain, Ibsen—surprise us with their findings, not merely about the vicious treatment children often received but also about their liabilities, vices, and blind spots. Of course, moderns such as Kafka, Faulkner, Ralph Ellison, and Toni Morrison and figures of our own moment are acutely aware of the ideological forces that not only beset children but also "compose" them, bleed into them as the work of culture, thus making us see that the consciousness of chil-dren is inflected by all manner of things beyond their ken.

Age of Children

In examining the suite of growing-up stories to come, many of them brutal and dark, I am concerned with illuminating the coming-of-age drama that each contains. Coming of age is of course a conceptual as well as somatic or temporal proposition, and we rightly see it as a kind of education, a movement toward understanding and maturity. What kind of education, under-standing, and maturity? That is what these materials so richly dis-play. Let me first clarify that my terms "childhood" and "old age" are not strictly age-specific. Faulkner's Benjy (in *The Sound and the Fury*) is only a few years younger (thirty-three) than Joyce's

Leopold Bloom (in *Ulysses*), who is all of thirty-eight, yet I regard Benjy as a child and Bloom as man growing old. My reasons are simple: Benjy is constructed as an idiot who possesses no powers of ratiocination and is thus permanently infantilized, but Bloom sees himself as crucially past his prime, mindful of a more vibrant but long-gone past, obliged to find gratification via substitution. Each depiction is wise in lessons for us, regarding how life is parsed at distinct phases of our trajectory. Indeed, each is cued to a past that cannot be recaptured, but Benjy does not know this and Bloom does. One is permanently arrested on the front side of life, whereas the other reflects incessantly on his belatedness. We see (frozen) childhood and (reflective) old age in these postures.

Yet I am all too aware that growing up and growing old can— indeed, must—coexist in each of us, and that sense of tandem has a special pathos of its own as we go through life remembering and experiencing and taking stock. Finally, many of us who get to old age may find that we are still children or, worse, made into children, infantilized, either by culture or by senility. So if childhood is not a calendar truth, what is it? What follows are some of the generic features that shape and cohere the story of growing up.

Rubrics for the Narrative of Growing Up

Innocence (and Experience)

William Blake titled two major poetry collections *Songs of Innocence* and *Songs of Experience*, and nothing, I believe, stamps the perceptual drama of growing up more profoundly than this crucial binary. These two radically different lenses make visible how fatefully perspective shapes what we make of our lives. One thinks, initially, that we all move from innocence to experience (with whatever happy or catastrophic results that may occur), but it is no less true that we move from experience to innocence, inasmuch as experience alone makes prior innocence visible. Yet innocence also makes visible, which is what Blake's greatest poems show us. "Out of the Mouths of Babes" is, like its folkloric sibling, "The Emperor's New Clothes," a window onto human foible and distortion or masquerade. It cannot surprise us that many of the books we most love move along such axes, often signaling in both directions: the child records more than he or she can know, while the sense-making of retrospect sifts and takes measures of what has occurred. Maybe that old Sphinx who tested Oedipus knew that every life is ultimately on four feet, two feet, and three feet, *at the same time.*

If Blake's disturbing poems exploit innocence as optic, the great German novel of the seventeenth century, Hans Jakob Christoffel von Grimmelshausen's *Simplicissimus,* appearing more than a century before Romantic conceptions of childhood set in, is still more brutal in its use of naiveté as lens. Once again the optics are double—the book counts on us to "know" what its character does not—but this earlier text widens the stage immeasurably beyond Blake's late-eighteenth-century London, giving us a rare sense of what "history" (bloody history) might look like at "ground zero," prior to all abstractions. This shattering account of a simpleton's experience of the Thirty Years' War, written by a man who was there, reads almost like an allegory of the soul: how can it preserve its purity and integrity in a time of horror? The novel's punch comes from its angle of vision: to render the convulsive antics of a world out of control, as perceived by an unknowing victim.

We continue our investigation of innocence as lens with Twain's much-beloved *Huckleberry Finn.* Twain enlists the vision and voice of a school dropout, an uneducated boy with zero cultural capital, to tell the story at hand. What would slavery look like to such a person? The novel's grandeur is to be found in the evolving moral education of Huckleberry Finn as he gradually, fitfully, registers the humanity of Jim, the runaway slave whom he is helping to free, who becomes his figurative father. Huck faces a shockingly modern dilemma, a dilemma no child escapes: can one possibly get clear of the dictates of mainstream ideology, especially if those dictates are lodged inside one's head and go by the name of conscience?

Faulkner's Benjy is my next and, arguably, supreme instance of innocence as vision. *The Sound and the Fury* obliges us to negotiate the jumbled perceptions of a mind that is completed unfurnished, along cognitive lines, while the emotions rise and fall and careen in roller-coaster fashion, as he responds to the sole and enduring tragedy of his life: Caddy (his sister) is not there (in reality) but is always there (in his heart). Benjy is one of the grand readerly challenges in modern literature, but this is not some intellectual puzzle; rather, his responses to life write large for us the fate of love: our need, its beauty, its loss.

I want to conclude this discussion of childhood innocence by examining one of the most endearing characters of contemporary literature, the little girl Marjane, the protagonist of Marjane Satrapi's poignant graphic novel *Persepolis,* which depicts a female child's coming-of-age drama in Tehran in the fateful years between the shah's expulsion and the beginning reign of the ayatollahs. A daughter of privilege, good-hearted but politically unaware, Marjane not only registers the Iranian change of regime but also embodies the dynamic of a young girl moving toward adolescence, and this combination of forces at once personal and ideological achieves a surprising pathos and poetry in the graphic format.

In all five instances—Blake, Grimmelshausen, Twain, Faulkner, Satrapi—the eyes and voice of the unknowing child become our conduit toward knowledge, toward a shock of recognition: this, we understand, is what exploitation, war, racism, terrorism, and even love actually look like, feel like. We may have known those terms forever, but we have never envisioned the world from this angle, never put on these particular glasses, never inhabited this position. A curtain goes up, and the innocent child is our teacher.

Experience (and Innocence)

Experience is the name we give to what life either shows us or does to us. At the opposite pole from *innocence,* it is the tally sheet that records our actual passing through, and as such, it is in frequent warfare with the expectations of innocence. All coming-of-age stories negotiate these two poles, as if they made up a magnetic field that the young traverse. Experience almost always has a pedagogical tinge to it—"this is what life has taught me" or "this is what it *really* was like"—and its greatest virtue is its open-eyed, unflinching acknowledgment of things as they are, rather than as they might or should be. In this light, it will be seen that our greatest works of art record the gradual accumulation of experience on the part of the young, as if the task of narrative were to put them on time's treadmill and then show what they encounter and how they alter. Here is the schooling of life itself, an education often at odds with the precepts that are drilled into us by culture.

One of the chief aims of this book is to see how that story of coming of age alters over time and space. We begin with one of the oldest narratives we have: the anonymous *Lazarillo de Tormes* of 1550. This brief picaresque tale records a young boy's brutal entry into a hard life, and it is thus a fable about adaptation, about the school of hard knocks. We already glimpse an ethos coming into focus: success, survival, i.e., what it takes not to die. Which in turn means what is needed not to starve. The first school lesson meted out by life is: fill the belly. We speak to our children about "fulfillment," but we are rarely literal about this: *fill full.* You won't grow up if you have no food.

A seventeenth-century, more sophisticated installment in this genre is Francisco de Quevedo's *The Swindler,* which tracks the adventures and misadventures of Pablos, en route to becoming a consummate con man (after painful stints with starvation and abuse). The pedagogical lessons of *Lazarillo* are expanded. Larded with puns and wordplay (as well as considerable filth), Quevedo's book makes the monumental discovery that wit and language can be enlisted as trumps in life's game and that you might recoup verbally what you lose materially. We are not far from a street-smart philosophy of survival via cunning, of artistry redefined as performativity, and we recognize Pablos's maneuvers as a tool kit for hard times, as a way of getting ahead when you have neither rank nor funds.

Our next book of experience, Balzac's masterpiece of 1835, *Père Goriot,* graphs an exemplary capitalist education via the career of the law student Rastignac as he moves from the provinces to Paris. In this novel of would-be mentors advising a student, blood ties yield to the cash nexus, and selling out is the order of the day. Can you serve God and Mammon at the same time? I see this story's daunting challenge writ large each year as my under-graduates head off to law school or business school, trying to gauge the potential trade-offs between "success" and "con-science."

If Balzac initiates the genre of "success" as loss of ideals, Dickens amplifies and deepens it still further in *Great Expectations*. Pip's trajectory from blacksmith to snob, from country boy to Londoner, is a more ambitious and layered affair, cued to the Balza-cian model of selling out but also concealing copious amounts of rage and resentment that have no course but to go underground or to be sprinkled into the margins of the story. Pip's life is a muffled one, since there is so much in it that can never acknowledge the light of day, but great writing illuminates such matters by track-ing libidinal energy in all its guises, as if to say that there can be a psychic cost to material success, and though the retina cannot per-ceive it, art brings it to visibility.

Visibility: the novel of experience invariably sheds light on the actual—as opposed to the touted—laws that govern society and inform human consciousness. This is what Lazarillo, Pablos, Rastignac, and Pip found. It is the education and evolution that the young everywhere are destined to undergo, no matter how dis-tant it may be from the teachings of school or Church. Recogniz-ing the requirements of "the system" is no less central in the experiential education of my next protagonist, Ralph Ellison's In-visible Man. Ellison inverts Twain: instead of the serenely racist Huck, who comes to understand Jim's humanity, the Invisible Man must discover how power truly operates in mid-twentieth-century America and what stratagems a man with black skin needs to employ if he is to succeed. At issue is the same epistemo-logical question: Can you see the operative laws of the culture you inhabit? And if you do see them, what next?

In all these texts innocence is exposed as naiveté, as gullibility, while experience opens your eyes. This, one might demur, we al-ready knew. But literature's illumination of these matters creates surprising new vistas, brings to visibility the workings of culture in a way that few of us know. Through the perception of innocent children an eerie, unsettling world comes into focus: the young, we realize, often serve as fodder for the institutions of power, whether they be called Church, Throne, War, or Race. Belief undergirds power. Such are the gift and price of innocence.

Through the actions (and reactions) of the young entering culture and responding to its laws and challenges, we register a spectrum of survival skills, many of them coming at a high moral cost, as they negotiate a world they never made, trying to fathom its operation, so as to succeed. Their successes range from not starving to hustling to getting rich to opting out. They have learned. Such is the gift/price of experience.

Love

If the journey of growing up can be fruitfully understood as the journey from innocence to experience, with all the complications that entails, we have yet to discuss head-on a prime motor force that fuels humans (both young and old) in their onward march: love. By love, I mean a wide spectrum of feelings and pulsions, replete with diverse actors and positions, ranging from the familial to the sexual, from desire to abuse, from gift to wound, from sustenance to sacrifice, from individual relationship to collective experience. One can scarcely talk about human striving without bringing love into the equation, as the lives and needs of figures such as Blake's chimney sweep, Balzac's Rastignac, Dickens's Pip, and Faulkner's Benjy, discussed earlier, make clear. But in this chapter we will focus on love explicitly as the key to young destiny, whether ecstatic romance or lacerating abuse or familial injury to social and national nightmare. What is sweetest and what is most toxic about growing up is cued to the fate of love.

Falling in Love

Falling in love is scarcely the exclusive prerogative of the young—some people experience it all their lives, some never—but it will be admitted that it is often regarded as the most glorious discovery of youth, the galvanizing, life-altering threshold over which the young leap or plunge to enter into the affairs of the heart. The verb "fall" tells us that this experience costs you your balance and stability and says something as well about young love's suddenness, its throbbing power, yet raises questions as to whether such passion can last. Great literary texts on this topic frequently display a mix of ecstasy and anxiety, for love catalyzes the life of the young, opens the door to feelings of an intensity hitherto unknown, but also alters—indeed, wrecks—prior notions of contours and consciousness. Subjectivity is jolted, personal longing may collide with social barriers or even with the otherness of the loved one, bringing to life and urgency much that had been quiescent or invisible, such as private wants or class lines or racial taboos, fatefully forcing the lover into a broader awareness of difference. Here begins an education for the young that is like no other.

The text I begin with is perhaps the most famous work in the Western world when it comes to young love: Shakespeare's *Romeo and Juliet*. Shakespeare's lyricism and poetic flights chart the terrain of love in unforgettable fashion: we see it allied to light and fire; we see how inflammatory beauty and desire are, how they transfigure the human subject, turning star-crossed lovers into new beings. But the darkness of Shakespeare's tragedy is also central to our understanding of young love: it cannot be denied, but it cannot be fulfilled. Behind this story of parental feuding, we must recognize that the forces of death and extinction seem hardwired in the genesis and flowering of love, and that perception governs many of the great romance texts we know.

If Shakespeare's play is known the world over, the same cannot quite be said for the French novel *Manon Lescaut*, published in 1731, and that is a pity. Abbé Prévost's short, pithy account of a young nobleman's infatuation with a girl of loose morals displays the "suddenness" of young love in all its destabilizing, indeed transmogrifying power: the young man, Des Grieux, becomes in short order a cheat, pander, and murderer in order to maintain his liaison with Manon. This book registers the fault lines of a culture that will explode in 1789, and it does so through the uncomprehending eyes and feelings of a young man whose love campaign is doomed to failure. Individual consciousness itself is on the docket here, as a medium of love but also as a carceral condition of subjectivity.

I then discuss two of our most canonical nineteenth-century

versions of romantic love, written by two sisters: Emily Brontë's
Wuthering Heights and Charlotte Brontë's *Jane Eyre*. The love between Catherine and Heathcliff begins virtually in the cradle, as
the deep and unbreakable bond between two lonely children—
one privileged, one an orphan—and it goes on to reach a crescendo
of passion, madness, death, and revenge that no reader easily for-
gets. Their oceanic connection is tinged with hysteria and violence, suggesting that "absolute" young love—love understood as
fusion of beings—can produce a wreckage as fatal as anything ordered by the Oracle. Jane Eyre is also rightly understood as utterly
marked by love—she claims it as her due from childhood on,
when there is none to be had—and this rich novel tracks her quest
for romantic fulfillment through a complex series of relationships, centering on the mysterious Byronic man with a secret, Edward Rochester, but also including the handsome yet cold and
demanding St. John Rivers. *Jane Eyre* closes with a marriage, but
much darkness, injury, discovery, and alteration are required to
get there. And in both Brontës the demands of class and money
possess a kind of gravity, a kind of countertug, that love must
somehow contend with. Finally, in keeping with our theme, there
may be reason to believe that the hurting child of each book's beginning never quite disappears from view.

My final love text, Marguerite Duras's *The Lover* (1984), seems
a book cued to our postcolonial awareness. Over and over, this
story returns to the liminal moment when the fifteen-year-old
French girl on the ferry returning to Hanoi is seen, approached,
and drawn into a torrid love affair by the wealthy young Chinese
man who is smitten by her. What fascinates in *The Lover* is its
postmodern rupture of all familiar frames—not just racial or atti-
tudinal but narrative and libidinal—so that an entire life seems
contained in embryo in this sexual initiation, so that our notion of
"young love" opens out onto something immeasurably large, inflected by feelings and sensations of every stripe that bleed together into a panoramic evocation of existence where everything,
like the Mekong Delta that is its locale, is in flux. It's a story of
transgression and rupture for our time: West, East, taboo, flowing
feeling, love, self.

These five cardinal works of literature do justice to the sheer power and beauty of young love. Each sketches a rebirth of sorts, a molting of self that changes everything that came before while at the same time propelling the young into the oldest rhythms, gestures, and sensations known to our species. Seen together, however, Shakespeare, Prévost, the Brontës, and Duras illuminate a world that is also molting: the movement of texts from a sixteenth-century culture of honor and obedience to a mercantile exchange ethos of love in eighteenth-century Paris on to a nineteenth-century class-and-property-inflected British marriage scheme to close with an anonymous regime of pleasure in a racially conflicted twentieth-century colonial setting is a trajectory of uncommon social density. But even beyond the sharply etched societal crises looms the massive existential one: what happens to the self when it first encounters young love? Literature—given its unique capacity to write diverse subjectivities and to represent the interaction between self and setting—helps us answer that question.

Love's Failures: Abuse

All of us know that love can damage as well as delight. Like all love, young love always entails vulnerability, sometimes even bondage, and the great love stories do not minimize the loss of agency that passionate love brings, a loss that may extend to life itself. Romeo, Juliet, Des Grieux, Manon, Catherine, Heathcliff, Jane, Rochester, Duras's narrator: all would agree. But if love may wreck us through its intensity, it may injure us still worse through its absence or its twistedness. We simply have no way of gauging the amount of suffering, horror, and evil that has resulted from love's failures, but I suspect that much of what we take to be "history," both private and social, has its etiology in love gone wrong. It thus follows that cruelty, sadism, exploitation, and other manifestations of feeling and power that we term "abuse" are to be logically understood in relation to love.

Yet child abuse presents challenges that are perceptual as well as ethical. It is devilishly hard for outsiders to see or measure, but it possesses an astounding potency of its own, frequently scripting the emotional life of its victims. Some writers on this topic, such

as Dostoevsky, are in your face, and Ivan Karamazov offers us
some chilling and unforgettable pages about such transgressions.
But in many well-known literary works we have to read against
the grain, peer into corners, if we are to get a fix on abuse; I'd
argue that literature resembles life in this regard, by keeping its
poison and garbage in cellars and closets, and it seems fair to
say that reading becomes an ethical as well as cognitive activity,
obliging us to parse and gauge much that is quite unaccented in
the fiction. Texts by Laclos, James, and Mann will be studied in
this fashion, each circling about damaged or threatened children,
often obscured in the margins, as if to dare us: can you see what is
actually going on here?

But the most unforgettable abuse narratives validate fully my
thesis about love gone wrong. Hence we will return to those two
famous nineteenth-century stories of breathless love, *Wuthering
Heights* and *Jane Eyre,* but now with a different perspective, cued
this time to injury, and we may be surprised by what we discover.
Heathcliff is the most obvious subject of our analysis, for the
novel depicts what happens when oceanic love fails (or is thought
to fail): it produces a monster who can never forgive or forget and
who must take it out on the next generation of children. But Jane
Eyre also qualifies fully (even if surprisingly) as an unloved and
abused child, and even though she ends up inheriting money and
marrying Rochester by book's end, many (feminist) readers today
see her repressed ongoing rage displaced onto the figure of Bertha
Mason Rochester, the novel's "madwoman in the attic," now seen
as Jane's necessary alter ego. Take a step back from these two famous love stories, and you encounter a cartography of other libidinal forces altogether, bent on expression, wreaking havoc,
displaying the "forking path" of feeling denied or killed.

My study of abused children closes with Jean Rhys's remarkable *Wide Sargasso Sea* (1966), which is nothing less than a "prequel" to *Jane Eyre* but ups the ante on Brontë (and the feminist
reading of Bertha as Jane's double) by reimagining Bertha's story
altogether. Bertha is termed "bad, mad and embruted" in *Jane
Eyre,* but Rhys presents her as tragically damaged goods: hungry
for love, rejected or betrayed by all those she needs, victimized by
racial prejudice and coldness of heart, finally imprisoned in En-

gland. Abuse can deform you forever. Unlike CAT scans, which offer depth readings of the body, literature works to give us soul readings of this stripe, to image for us a causal emotional and psychological chain that no retina perceives.

Familial Sacrifice and Kindermord

When children die in literature, an authorial will is in play, requiring such deaths. In works by several of our most remarkable writers—Dickens, Ibsen, Kafka, and Faulkner—we see children being murdered (authorially) in quasi-systemic fashion. One is obliged to ask: What kind of psychic economy requires such sacrifice? Is it an anti–Oedipal impulse in the old that quashes the young in order to preserve its own hegemony? Or is there a dark lesson here about the threats to growing up? About the forces arrayed against the young?

We begin with Jo, the illiterate child of the slums in *Bleak House*. Without the tiniest scrap of agency, Jo is perhaps the exemplary child victim of my book, yet Dickens has the genius to make him the carrier of disease; he possesses nothing (or "nothink," as he would say)—neither family nor money nor even the ability to read—but he spells death. *Kindermord* means "child murder"; Jo works that phrase both ways. Dickens has amplified his victimhood still further by cutting him off from language as well as love, and we read his fate systemically, virtually as ritual sacrifice. No love here. The London machine devours children.

The Norwegian playwright Henrik Ibsen is known as one of Western literature's fiercest champions of human rights, especially when it comes to the plight of women. Hence it is with shock that one encounters all the child cadavers that litter his plays. Here is the grim underside of the playwright's emancipation scenarios: for a character to become fully adult, it appears (over and over) that a child must die. Why? Could the journey to adulthood have a built-in sacrificial mandate? At whose behest?

Child murder is still more central and pivotal in the tortured fables of Franz Kafka. Kafka himself was notoriously bullied by his father, yet he devised an artistic creed out of his low place in the food chain: the victim-son writes his demise at the hands of ogre-dad. Both "The Judgment" and "The Metamorphosis" are keyed to these infanticidal energies, where family relations turn on murder. What kind of ballet or pas de deux is this? They are extremist stories, perhaps, but they operate according to a lethal principle that warrants our study.

My final sacrificed child is Quentin Compson of *The Sound and the Fury*. A student at Harvard with intolerable memories—Father's drinking, Mother's coldness, above all the quasi-incestuous bond with his vibrant and feisty sister, Caddy—he chooses death by drowning. All of Faulkner's brilliance and pathos are on show in the writing itself, for the stream-of-consciousness narration disgorges entire chunks of family history, of remembered conversations, of manifold instances of failure—this is what inhabits Quentin on the inside—and we realize this to be a death sentence.

These dark stories fascinate as well as disturb, for they point to a powerful systemic logic that damns the young, and they situate this logic frequently in the very heart and pulse of family. Once again we measure the horrific failure of love—or perhaps the still more horrific cost of love: the nest you are to exit is toxic, so you do not exit; the bonds you have will strangle you, for you are entrapped in their mesh. These materials tell us something we are often reluctant to recognize: that growing up takes place against a human backdrop that got there first, that can be rife with injury, even lethal.

Systemwide Sacrifice: Children and the Nightmare of History

All of the varieties of coming of age discussed up to now centralize the encounter between the young and culture—innocence to experience, love, abuse—but could there be instances when culture itself exits, is destroyed? Instances where love's absence produces slaughter and genocide? I have elected to close my account of sacrificed children by examining the "delayed reactions" to such upheaval: not the immediate child victims but rather the inheritors of destruction, the children who grow up among ruins either real or figurative. The outright number of destroyed children pales when we compare it to the still greater number of those who do not experience such horrors firsthand but have to live with and through them secondhand, trying to make sense of things.

I turn to World War II, in which real Holocaust occurred, and my text is the stunning graphic novel Art Spiegelman's *Maus,* which depicts the difficult efforts of Artie, the son of Vladek, a Holocaust survivor, to find a form for this horrendous chapter in our history. Spiegelman confronts a radical double challenge: how to understand Father? and how to represent the historical nightmare that (de)formed Father? "My Father Bleeds History" is Spiegelman's subtitle, and it points to the awful learning experience inflicted on the young when the world seems to come apart.

My last book of sacrifice, Jonathan Safran Foer's *Extremely Loud and Incredibly Close,* focuses on the downing of the World Trade Center on September 11, 2001, and on a grieving child who must come to terms with it. History again bled. Several thousand people died almost at once in that catastrophe, but many more thousands were threatened with dying more slowly, with being undone by the loss of a parent, spouse, or child. In linking his story of the American disaster to the Dresden firebombing of 1945, Foer shows us what growing up can be like, as the sky falls in on the heads and hearts of our children.

The Wild Child: Saying No to Culture

If the literature about growing up is a barometer of sorts, which gauges the "cultural weather" and measures the absorption of the young into the adult society that awaits and confronts them, the question arises: Can one say no? Can you "refuse the ticket," as Ivan Karamazov proclaimed one should? We all know about Thoreau's idyll at Walden Pond, and there is something deeply seductive about finding a "free space" beyond culture. For many of us, childhood itself may seem bathed in just such colors.

Implicit in my last paragraph is the conviction that society is at once flawed and escapable and that nature is our true home. But there are darker and more unsettling views of these matters, and there exists a handful of books that look unflinchingly at the consequences of "rejecting" society—or the even more disturbing consequences of obeying nature. I begin with the story of Lena Grove and Joe Christmas, Faulkner's protagonists of *Light in August* (1932), one nine months pregnant without a ring and serenely happy, the other living out the sacrificial fate coded in his name. Thinking he has "a little nigger blood" in him, at war with "natural" processes such as food and sex, Christmas the ungrounded, cast-out child rewrites the story of Oedipus in violent racial terms, doomed to misfit and calvary.

Two very pure and brave narratives about the child who says no appeared in 1963 and 1973: the Norwegian Tarjei Vesaas's *Ice Palace* and Toni Morrison's *Sula*. Not only does each offer girl protagonists, but each uses the strategy of paired girls, one "straight," one wild, one committed to life, the other to death, so as to derive maximum contrast from the topic. The tonalities are different—Vesaas's mysterious Unn elects to exit the human realm and enter nature's dance through her death in the Ice Palace, whereas Morrison's "experimental" Sula is the most untamable and hell-bent-for-freedom figure of this study—but each leaves us with a profound grasp of natural and social law: what it costs to obey it, what it costs to deny it.

Success

If you can read these lines, it means you have grown up. Most of us do. It would seem to be the plan of both nature and culture. What measures do we have for doing it well?

I want to close my treatment of growing up by looking at two rich twentieth-century narratives that are unflinching in their account of the obstacles that beset children, yet bequeath a vision of complex yet successful maturation: Faulkner's *Go Down, Moses* and Alice Walker's *The Color Purple*. We will see that these two narratives are profoundly cued to the phases and rubrics that structure my book: innocence, experience, love, abuse, sacrifice, freedom. Each is invested as well in an exploration of history, race, gender, and empowerment, as they inform the course of growing up and taking—or not taking—one's place in society. Finally, each has the merit of following its protagonists from childhood—sheltered in one instance, abusive in the other—all the way to old age, thereby setting the stage for the second half of my study, which is devoted to growing old.

We begin with Ike McCaslin, the young/old protagonist of Faulkner's autumnal *Go Down, Moses* (1942). Given the quasi-sacrificial fates of Benjy and Quentin Compson and Joe Christmas, it is fascinating to see a wider-angled view now of growing up. Faulkner moves toward myth: the myth of the hunt, of the immortal wilderness, into which Ike is to be initiated. But we soon realize that the initiation—so similar to that of tribal cultures in form, so opposed in consequence, for it leads to exit rather than incorporation—brings to Ike a terrible knowledge of his own society's racial and gender fault lines, inscribed in his own family history. But it is knowledge nonetheless, construed in the key figure of reading: reading the forest as hunter, reading the South as culture. Here is a luminous model for education, for literature.

I close my study of growing up with a narrative that manages to create eventual but lasting uplift out of early horror: Walker's *The Color Purple*. Celie is the most victimized figure of my entire study: impregnated by the man she takes to be her father, robbed of her loving sister and her two children, married off to another man who beats her, finally loved but ultimately rejected (erotically) by the book's femme fatale, Shug Avery. Yet this story shimmers with self-flowering as it chronicles Celie's hard-earned ascent into selfhood and authority, an ascent allied to resiliency, self-affirmation, empowerment through language, and triumph of love. Walker's pain-larded novel affirms something wonderful: strong children can work through trauma and injury; human growth is real and triumphant. Love, volition, and life have their say; the Oedipal saga of blindness and coercion can be overcome.

The Uses of Innocence

William Blake's Chimney Sweeps

William Blake's *Songs of Innocence* (1789) and *Songs of Experience* (1794) arguably present the quintessential binary that governs our perceptions and underwrites any notion we might have of education or maturation. Blake himself was rather supple about his categories, and he juggled a number of pieces from one collection to the other over time. If we approach these poems with the Romantic conception of the "child as father to the man" or with a view of childhood as the bliss we seek throughout life to recover, I think we go seriously astray. Blake is tougher, more countercultural, more destabilizing than that. It will be seen that these two modes, innocence and experience, are at once perspectival and time-drenched. They have everything to do with *when* we examine the affairs of our life—"we" of the poem, but also "we" as readers, since a second or third (or fiftieth) reading of these poems is no longer "innocent" but rather "experienced"—and how our understanding of things hinges on just this.

To see how this works, I want to discuss his two famous accounts of chimney sweeps, one published in each cycle. We are about to take a course in optics: what will the condition of chimney sweep look like from each of these perspectives? The poet focuses on one of the great ills of late-eighteenth-century London life: the use of young boys (and girls), aged between four and seven, sent up into the London chimneys and destined for a life of almost incredible hardship and pain. It is known that some died in the chimneys (when fires were lit with the chimney sweep still there) and that many developed skin cancers, due to the fact that they often worked naked, so as to spare the cost of replacing ruined clothes.

What is breathtaking (and heartbreaking) about these poems is what they teach us about acculturation, about the the shaping and importance of values. Hence, the "Innocence" and "Experience" poems can be read in some sense as before and after, inasmuch as the poet often seeks to render the child's "uncritical" angle of vision in the first set, whereas the tone of the second set is likely to be much more judgmental. In so doing, Blake wants to expose the forming and working of ideology. This is crucial, since ideology is exactly what none of us can see, for it is the air we breathe and the soup we swim in. But it might indeed come to vision, using a consort of innocence and experience, enabling us to get a sighting on how we are both formed and deformed as creatures of culture. For all these reasons, it makes sense to look first at the later poem, the rendition of the chimney sweep in *Songs of Experience:*

A little black thing in the snow,
Crying "weep! weep!" in notes of woe!
"Where are thy father and mother? Say?"—
"They are both gone up to the church to pray.

"Because I was happy upon the heath,
And smil'd among the winter's snow,
They clothed me in the clothes of death,
And taught me to sing the notes of woe.

"And because I am happy and dance and sing,
They think they have done me no injury,
And are gone to praise God and his priest and king,
Who make up a heaven of our misery."

There is nothing difficult at all here. The poem is a broadside against the gross exploitation of children, all the grosser by being trumped up in the clothes of piety. The retrospective voice of the child is experienced, and it speaks clearly its victimization: reduced to a "thing in the snow," with only "weep" as language, it spells out its lesson of violation and victimization. Clothed for death, uncomplaining, it is sacrificed by its parents to the spurious claims of both Church and Throne. The equation could not be more obvious, and Blake ends with a fine spatial, even artisanal, metaphor: the "heaven" posed/constructed by that (vicious) trio of God, priest, and king is made up, literally composed, of children's misery. Most shocking of all, perhaps, is the "innocence" of the parents themselves, who think they've done the child no injury. Anyone reading this poem sees it as a clear indictment, expressed by the comprehending victim, of a religious and political order that manifestly commoditizes its children.

Now, "knowing" (from the later poem) that chimney sweeps are victims of abuse at the hands of family, Church, and state, we are in a position to read the earlier poem with the same motif, but seen from the optic of innocence:

When my mother died I was very young,
And my father sold me while yet my tongue
Could scarcely cry 'weep! 'weep! 'weep! 'weep!
So your chimneys I sweep, and in soot I sleep.

There's little Tom Dacre, who cried when his head,
That curled like a lamb's back, was shav'd: so I said,
"Hush, Tom! never mind it, for when your head's bare,
You know that the soot cannot spoil your white hair."

And so he was quiet; & that very night,
As Tom was a-sleeping, he had such a sight!
That thousands of sweepers, Dick, Joe, Ned, & Jack,
Were all of them lock'd up in coffins of black.

And by came an Angel who had a bright key,
And he opened the coffins and set them all free;

Then down a green plain leaping, laughing, they run,
And wash in a river, and shine in the sun.

Then naked & white, all their bags left behind,
They rise upon clouds and sport in the wind;
And the Angel told Tom, if he'd be a good boy,
He'd have God for his father, & never want joy.

And so Tom awoke; and we rose in the dark,
And got with our bags & our brushes to work.
Tho' the morning was cold, Tom was happy & warm;
So if all do their duty they need not fear harm.

Few poems in the English canon move me as much as this one. At first we see the resemblances with the later, overtly critical piece: the child's only words are the telltale " 'weep! 'weep! 'weep!"—the child's garbled version of "sweep"? or the natural language of pain?—but the parental arrangements are more severe: the mother is dead, and the child has been sold into servitude, to sleep in soot. One next expects—"one" being a reader with some sense of justice and some belief in children's rights— a tirade lambasting such treatment, but instead our child speaker tells us of his comrade Tom Dacre's experience. Little Tom's head was shaved, but he was comforted by our speaker, who explained the advantages of such a procedure to Tom, namely that his white hair could no longer be soiled. Comforted, Tom dreams and has a vision. It is a vision of liberation and purity: all the sweeps (there are thousands of them now) are rescued from the black coffins where they are locked up (hardly a metaphor, this, if you think of them dying in the chimneys), and the rescuer is an Angel with a "bright key." Free at last, the children run and laugh and play on the green plain, and wash in the river and shine in the sun. It is a chimney sweep's vision not only of paradise, but also of resurrection itself: to move from life in death to joy in Heaven. And their pleasures grow: naked (no longer a hazard), free of their bags, they rise to the clouds and "sport in the wind." Further, they now have a kind Father to look after them and keep them in this state of happiness, requiring only that they be "a good boy."

How does one go about being a good boy? The final stanza answers that (unposed) question by returning us to the waking world of reality—dark, cold, replete with bags and brushes and work: exactly what one had been freed from by the good graces of the Angel—with a strategy for happiness: do your duty, and you need fear no harm. We realize, of course, that duty consists of going back (forever) into chimneys, but now armed with a vision of beatitude. And that is where the poem leaves it. But where does it leave us?

In my view, Blake has reprised the oldest and most potent political critique of the Church known to civilization: its delicious promise of salvation, its solemn pledge of an afterlife, and its clear exhortation to accept current conditions as they are, to do your duty, as the ticket to that radiant afterlife. For we cannot fail to see that the vision of happiness, gaiety, and freedom is a dream, a vision, and that it accords smoothly with a sociopolitical order that requires children in chimneys. The pathos of the poem stems from our sentiment that the great joys of this paradisal vision—running, laughing, playing, washing in the river, shining in the sun—should be available to children in reality, not merely in dream. And Blake's terms prefigure our own more cynical discourse, for how can we not see that the miraculous washing at the core of this beatific vision (miraculous for chimney sweeps, shorn and sleeping in soot) is a version of brainwashing? Brainwashing means altering someone's moral perspective to suit the needs of power. Brainwashing means that one's moral perspective is actually alterable, and power knows how to do it. Brainwashing is Blake's tragic yet profound view of growing up.

Why is none of this critique I've elaborated stated in the poem? Because it is a poem of innocence. And here we approach what is most sublime in this short poem: the radical distinction between what we see and what the child sees. And more still: the world-altering power of innocence. We see in this poem a portrait of victimization, carried all the way into the soul. But that is not what the child speaker sees. He sees a radiant dream of purity and salvation and bliss, and that dream is enough to carry him through the darkness of his life as chimney sweep. He is warmed by his vision of radiance, by the promise of joy to come. And that is why no

easy final verdict is possible here. One does not know whether to
pity or to envy this child. What, after all, is the ideal mind-set of a
chimney sweep? To want to take to the barricades and tear down
the system? Or to do one's duty, with the ardent conviction that it
will lead to final bliss? It is seductively easy, I think, to come down
hard, as I have to believe Blake himself did, because an ideologically savvy twenty-first-century reader is likely to see exploitation
in every word of this poem. But I am no less stunned by the wisdom of innocence, for make no mistake about it: it pays its way, it
warms the child, it generates the energies needed to live a life of
toil.

Growing up, for Blake, at least in this poem, is shown to be a
tragic operation, for it signifies a kind of ideological brainwashing, whereby the power culture permeates your very dreams, constructs your subjectivity, makes you who you are, makes you into
an accepting social subject. Blake announces Freud a century in
advance, for he understands that consciousness is a hivelike discourse of voices and injunctions that wash into you without your
knowing. He prefigures the French theorist Louis Althusser, who
would erect an entire system based on such views, claiming that
ideology is utterly invisible, that our enmeshment within it is profoundly if unknowingly consensual. Blake's most explosive formula is found in his poem "London," when he states what he
hears on every street of the city: "mind forged manacles." It can't
be better said: the true incarceration, the true penal work of culture, is an inside job, done every day one lives. In Blake you hear it.

Writing of this stamp proves, as nothing else can, why we
need to consult literature if we are to understand what it means
to grow up. Written in the mode of innocence, "The Chimney
Sweeper" yields a rich and echoing double script: it tells a story
of victimization and of belief, of coercion and of escape, of reality and of dream. It makes us want to change the cruel world, yet
it makes us realize that faith is a great (if blinding) armor. It displays the extraordinarily sinuous workings of power. Blake uti-
lizes the angelic vision of innocence to bring to light the drama
of ideological formation, of how the mind and the soul become
what they do. Whereas Blake is brief, almost lapidary, in his account of the child's innocent vision, other writers unpack the

deep and rich human consequences—ethical, perceptual, political, emotional, even comical—of such a vision. Hans Jakob von Grimmelshausen, writing more than a century before Blake, and Mark Twain, William Faulkner, and Marjane Satrapi, coming in the centuries afterward, are among them.

Innocence and Growing Up in the Thirty Years' War: Simplicissimus

Hans Jakob Christoffel von Grimmelshausen is not a household name for many readers today, and that is at once a great pity and a great injustice. The author of two seminal works in the seventeenth century—*Der Abentheuerliche Simplicissimus* and *Die Lanstörtzerin Courage*—he is the greatest German writer of his time and on a plane with Rabelais and Cervantes as a founding figure in the development of the novel. Bertolt Brecht, who brilliantly pastiched so many earlier authors, wrote what is arguably his greatest play, *Mother Courage* (to be discussed later in this book), by rewriting Grimmelshausen. In *Simplicissimus,* a hurdy-gurdy, carnivalesque account of life during the Thirty Years' War (1618–48), Grimmelshausen's central figure, Simplicius, is a tabula rasa on whom experience writes its lessons.

Living as shepherd in the woods with his father, his *Knan,* Simplicius is told of only one real threat to be on the lookout for: the wolf; should the wolf come, play your bagpipe, he is told. Okay. But there is one problem: what is a wolf? He hears figures approaching, and he plays the bagpipe for all he is worth, which brings the soldiers—for that is what they are—right to him. Soldier to us, wolf to him: " 'Aha,' I thought to myself, 'so here we are! These must be the four-legged rogues and thieves my Dad told me of.' " Men on horses look to him like four-legged creatures. No mortars or shells or overhead planes are needed here, since this Thirty Years' War turns life itself inside out, brings marauding soldiers from village to village, drinking, gambling, whoring, torturing, beating, "nothing but hurting and harming and being, in their turn hurt and harmed," whether they be Protestant or Catholic, Swedes or Austrians. (Note the chiastic construction Grimmelshausen uses: all those "ing" verbs denote, first, what you do, and, second, what is done to you: utterly egalitarian, like a boomerang.)

Horrors abound, but *horrors* is an adult word, an adult notion even, in this text, so that raping the hired girl, pouring liquid manure down the serving man's mouth via wedge and pail, brutalizing even parents and sister, all are recounted as flatly as changing wallpaper, as set design, as moving stage, as "things that happen." It would be hard to overstate the pith and reach of this condition whereby one inhabits a toppling, tumbling world of moving pictures, shifting shapes.

These wolf creatures destroy the child's home in short order, and he escapes into the wilderness, only to come upon another strange figure: a man with long hair, tangled beard, heavy chain, and "a huge crucifix, some six feet high, which he clasped to his breast." Again he thinks: wolf. Given the conventions of seventeenth-century literature, we are not surprised to learn later that this hermit is actually the boy's real father, but what most strikes us is Grimmelshausen's use of naive perspective, of innocence as point of view. It can be a devastating point of view. The child at one point looks into a large house and sees "men and women twirling and swirling around . . . stamping and bawling" with sweat pouring out of them and breathing noisily. What can this be? They are dancing. How strange the signs of pleasure must be if you do not know them. Farther down this road, he observes a pair in a goose shed, hears noises, and sees strange postures, but then the boards "began to creak and groan, and the girl to moan as if in pain," and he thinks they are like the maniacs who tried to stamp through the floor, that they might next come out and attack him too, as part of their campaign of destruction. Again, as with Blake's chimney sweep, the "experienced" reader fills in the blanks, translates into the adult code.

Simplicius is captured many times, and his captors are always unsure whether he is a simpleton or a spy, so they test him: by giving him drugs, by displacing him into staged settings, by trying to destroy his reason. The parade of masks now begins: Simplicius is sequentially disguised as a calf, as a woman, as a devil, as an actor and gigolo in Paris, as a quack doctor, as a pilgrim, as a farmer, as a nobleman, as an underwater visitor to the Mummelsee kingdom. The kaleidoscopic nature of this novel is its enduring truth: life is a merry-go-round; one goes through a repertoire of roles; the world is crawling with wolves, hermits, and madmen, as well as soldiers and captors. We hear stories of mania: someone thinking he'd become an earthenware jug and would be broken, another thinking he was a rooster, another convinced that his nose trailed on the ground. Languages swirl too: as gigolo, Simplicius calls himself the *"beau Alman"* (handsome German) and sings French songs (which he does not understand) to the Parisian women who purchase, groupwise, his services in the dark. The boy's most triumphant role is as the Huntsman of Soest, the quasi-mythic figure whose finest trick is the creation of shoes that point both ways, that leave no reliable tracks, that render you untraceable, anonymous, no one.

The fuller novel is far more complex than I have suggested, with a serious spiritual vision, but its view of growing up should now be fairly clear: maturation is not possible in this topsy-turvy world. Holding on to one's soul, so that it can be nurtured, is next to impossible in a situation where one lives in drag, ingests strange chemicals, vomits out one's insides, has nothing to hold on to or nurture: Thirty Years' War. For most of us living today in industrialized societies, learning about war through news clips on the TV or via the Internet, it is hard to imagine existing for three long decades in a swirling regime of capsizing forms and figures. It is an education in morphology, in the deceitfulness of stable appearances, in the roller-coaster nature of perception and identity.

Simplicissimus above all deserves recognition because it is our premier European story about growing up in war, forcing us to realize that most of our notions of growing up are peacetime notions, presupposing a huge measure of stability, so that a young person can make his or her choices in life and move through it with some composure and directionality. Put more bluntly, our concept of coming of age assumes (without ever realizing it) that the world itself stands still, that the human subject is the moving figure, and that the stage remains immobile. But if you are born into a raging war, if the terrain where you live is invaded and reinvaded continuously by soldiers and pillagers and scavengers of all stripes, if you yourself are picked up and packed off as a child, a thing moved from one place to another, well, then, any ideas about a stable, unmoving reality go up in smoke.

We do not sufficiently measure or appreciate our debt to stability and sameness—one expects one's room and one's body to be the same tomorrow, just as one expects one's loved ones to retain their shape—and we ignore thereby our royal good luck when things actually stay still around us, when we as humans have some kind of agency or maneuvering room, when sweet notions such as *ours* (our money, our house, our body, our life) with their proprietary promise seem to make sense. Children in war zones have none of this. War's violence and disruptive power extend well beyond weaponry's impact; they upend the world, make it into a place where things jump out of their skin, where ownership (including of self) disappears.

Grimmelshausen's war novel would be prodigiously fertile for Western literature, even if no direct lineage is invoked. The adventures of Simplicius already beckon to the experience of Stendhal's Fabrice del Dongo as he encounters unreadable pandemonium on a field called Waterloo; Tolstoy will pick up the same threads in *War and Peace* as Prince Andrei is initiated into battle, discovering how divorced real combat is from all the labels and frames we have for it. Stephen Crane's *The Red Badge of Courage* takes these matters still further, offering us a galvanizing, capsizing, impressionist account of military action. The list goes on. Hemingway's war stories toil in the same vineyard, and Nick Adams emerges as a young man nearly undone by what he has seen of violence and anarchy; Frederic Henry, in *A Farewell to Arms*, experiences the obscene fictiveness of all our docile labels and Big Words for saying "war." Norman Mailer's *The Naked and the Dead,* Joseph Heller's *Catch-22,* and Tim O'Brien's *The Things They Carried* are later installments in the same genre, bringing us news from the front, refracting this news through the vision and response of the young themselves, trying to make sense of the horrors and absurdities coming their way. Is it too much to say that the project at hand here is to transport us to ground zero so that we realize the bankruptcy of our notional world when it comes to measuring chaos?

At his most pungent, Grimmelshausen calls the bluff on us, much as Galileo did when he asserted, contrary to received views and retinal evidence, that *it moves*. He was referring to the planet itself, but texts of innocence school us in metamorphosis and whisper to us that our notions of fixity and sameness are just that: notions. Just take a longitudinal look at your own life, and you will find swirling forms: the cells live and die, the body marches on its treadmill, desires and fears and relationships and careers have no truck with stability, perhaps not even with pattern, try though we may (via résumés and the like) to domesticate such matters and pin them down in some permanent form. *Growing up:* the very term testifies to a kinetic regime, to life on the move. Art restores this mercurial scheme to our vision.

Growing Up as Huckleberry Finn

Two of America's most famous children's books are Mark Twain's *The Adventures of Tom Sawyer* and *The Adventures of Huckleberry Finn*. Tom Sawyer is etched deeply in the American imagination: a lovable, hooky-playing rascal who sneaks out to smoke and who is a consummate con man, as evidenced by the splendid fence-whitewashing episode. Tom loves games: pirate games, magic treasure, getting all his friends to play along. In this respect, he is our child version of Don Quixote, scrupulously modeling his escapades according to the rules laid down in the adventure stories he has read. He is also our Peter Pan, the child who never grows up. At the end of the story devoted to him, Twain does imply, through the words of Colonel Thatcher, a future for this clever, bold young man as a lawyer. That story is not written, but it is not far-fetched to imagine, down the road, young man Sawyer, credentialed, in a suit, arranging significant deals, good with gab and spin, in the swim. Bear this in mind.

Tom reappears in the second book, *The Adventures of Huckleberry Finn*, and he is true to form: assessing life according to the prescriptive laws of the adventure tales he has absorbed and being willing to go all out, to live up to this deeply bookish code. All serious readers of *Huckleberry Finn* must indeed wish that Tom Sawyer had never gotten into the second book, given that he does his level best to ruin it by transforming its profound moral vision into a kindergarten fantasy of disguise, high jinks, doing it by the book. The "it" that is done (in) by the book is, of course, nothing less than its moral heart: Huck's nascent and difficult awareness of his culture's ills regarding racism and dehumanization, which recedes from the picture, replaced by Twain's stock resource whenever in a pinch, fun and games. Even Jim, who had his moments of great dignity, seems transformed into a one-dimensional minstrel-show figure by book's end.

Yet *Huckleberry Finn* remains a stupendous account of growing up, no matter how deeply botched its close may be. Electing to tell Huck's story in Huck's own voice must be accounted as one of the most brilliant narrative choices in the history of fiction. If Tom Sawyer is glib, smooth, and destined for success, Huck is, in every respect, his opposite number: orphan, from the wrong side of the tracks, dropout, uncharismatic, zero cultural capital. Huck is not headed to law school at book's end. Huck, innocent though he is, is a pragmatist, and he actually tests out some of Tom's pet theories and finds that they don't add up. No Spaniards, no A-rabs, no camels, no elephants; not even a genie, no matter how hard you rub the old tin lamp. Huck's verdict is swift and profound: "It had all the marks of a Sunday school." (Once you get your head around that phrase, you begin to appreciate both the Blakean Twain, the man who knows the insidious reach of ideology, and the Nietzschean Twain, the man who deconstructs.)

Yet it won't do, either, to consider Huck as the prosaic counterpart to the "poetic" Tom, since much of the novel's extraordinary beauty is to be found in "Huck-speak," an unlettered vernacular discourse that can be lyrical and haunting. A storm comes upon Huck and Jim camping out in the woods, and Twain writes it like this:

> It would get so dark that it looked all blue-black outside, and lovely; and the rain would thrash along by so thick that the trees off a little ways looked dim and spider-webby; and here would come a blast of wind that would bend the trees down and turn up the pale underside of the leaves; and then a perfect ripper of a gust would follow along and set the branches to tossing their arms as if they was just wild; and next, when it was just about the bluest and blackest—*fst!* It was as bright

as glory and you'd have a little glimpse of tree-tops a-plunging about, away off yonder in the storm, hundreds of yards further than you could see before; dark as sin again in a second, and now you'd hear the thunder let go with an awful crash and then go rumbling, grumbling, tumbling down the sky towards the under side of the world, like rolling empty barrels down stairs, where it's long stairs and they bounce a good deal, you know.

You'll not find this awe and immediacy in *Tom Sawyer,* and it bids to introduce a pungent native eloquence into American prose that rivals what Whitman had done, a few decades earlier, for poetry. Twain wants to bring you directly into the roiling spectacle of natural forces, and his homegrown metaphors and similes— spider-webby, like rolling empty barrels down stairs—make us sit up and take notice. This is *son et lumière,* as witnessed by a fourteen-year-old boy, yielding a bristling, pulsing vision of the natural world before it disappeared into our adult frames of reference. There is a grandeur here that is quite different from the pathos we saw in Simplicius's notations of war or Blake's account of the chimney sweep's vision. Yet it is also, despite the bursts of light, often dark and grisly and outright death-inflected, as we see in the kinds of stories and lies that Huck routinely tells. From his early mention of being "so lonesome I most wished I was dead" and hearing the faraway owls "who-whooing about somebody that was dead, and a whippowill and a dog crying about somebody that was going to die" on to his theatricalized death (in order to escape Pap) and his throwaway fabrications about his sister, Mary Ann, "run off and never was heard of no more, and Bill went to hunt them and he warnt heard of no more, and Tom and Mort died, and then there warn't nobody but just me and pap left," we understand Huck to be a plenty disturbed boy, and one wants to agree with Toni Morrison's brilliant observation that Huck needs Jim more than Jim needs Huck, in order to be saved from terror, melancholy, and suicide.

Yet my interest is not in putting Huck on a couch but rather in measuring the stunning moral (and ideological) education he undergoes. Twain's genius, as always in this text, lies in writing from

Huck's angle of vision. Hence, although the novel was written in the 1880s, well after the Civil War, its setting is the 1840s, and Twain wants us to ask ourselves: what did the great questions of race and slavery look like to a dropout kid from Missouri at that time? They don't look like great questions at all. Huck is, albeit decent, as serenely racist as everyone else around him. Jim, though likable and sweet, must needs be a not-fully-human creature, not fully evolved, given to extravagant fantasies and folk beliefs, in short: a fellow Huck enjoys laughing at.

Sometimes the laughing is quite nasty, as in the bald-faced lie Huck tells Jim regarding their getting lost in the fog. The sudden fog makes vision impossible, and all Huck's efforts to use the canoe and secure the raft fail, so that not only are he and Jim separated, but he is "shot out into the solid white fog ... with no more idea which way I was going than a dead man." We have a surreal scene of a literally unmoored Huck, flying around in the fog, hearing "whoops" coming from all sides, losing all directionality. *Losing all directionality.* This is a bad day for the fixed, anchored self. Grimmelshausen's Simplicius found himself on a moving stage set in motion by war. Huck experiences a comparably unhinged setting, but it is located in nature itself, in the majestic river that is a vortex of forces bidding to undo the human subject. Orphaned in every sense, Huck is booming down the river, seeing "smoky ghosts of big trees," then comes to an eddy, utterly lost, and addresses the reader directly: "If you think it ain't dismal and lonesome out in a fog that way, by yourself, in the night, you try it once—you'll see." He whoops for a while, hears and then loses sounds, ends up on open river, and goes to sleep. When he wakes up, it is nighttime, with shining stars, and sure enough, he sights the raft, makes to it, sees it has been badly damaged and covered with litter and trash; he climbs on it, sees Jim sitting there with his head between his knees, asleep; and he lies down "under Jim's nose."

Jim wakes up, sees Huck, and explodes with joy that the boy is alive, "back agin, 'live en soun', jis de same ole Huck—de same ole Huck." At this point the same old Huck asks Jim if he's been drinking, since his talk is so wild and makes so little sense. He assures Jim he never left the raft in the first place, so he could scarcely have come back. Jim is rocked by this assertion, cannot square it with what he's been through, and asks some of the novel's greatest existential questions: "Is I *me*, or who *is* I? Is I heah, or whah *is* I?" Huck plays it to the hilt: Jim's a fool, there never was a fog, Jim's conviction that he and Huck were separated, that he almost drowned, all this is said by Huck to be dreams. Jim remains silent for five minutes, observes that he's never before had a dream that so exhausted him, sets about offering an elaborate allegorical interpretation of the dream, but is then stopped in his tracks by the sly Huck, who finally points to the evidence of reality, the leaves and rubbish on the raft, and sweetly asks Jim: "What does *these* things stand for?" It is an elaborate con game, a one-upmanship performance worthy of Tom Sawyer. Jim's answer ranks among the most noble things in the book:

> "What do dey stan' for? I's gwyne to tell you. When I got all wore out wid work, en wid de callin' for you, en went to sleep, my heart wuz mos' broke bekase you wuz los', en I didn' k'yer no mo' what become er me en de raf'. En when I wake up en fine you back agin', all safe en soun', de tears come en I could a got down on my knees en kiss' yo' foot I's so thankful. En all you wuz thinkin' 'bout wuz how you could make a fool uv ole Jim wid a lie. Dat truck dah is *trash;* en trash is what people is dat puts dirt on de head or dey fren's en makes 'em ashamed."

Huck's reaction to this indictment is justly famous: "It was fifteen minutes before I could work myself up to go and humble myself to a nigger—but I done it, and I warn't ever sorry for it afterwards, neither." By setting this entire sequence under the aegis of *fog*—collapse of contours, inability to see clear, undoing of "I"—Twain is depicting a disoriented white boy under siege, letting go of received ideas, beginning to measure the dignity and humanity of a black man. The pathos of these pages resides in their grudging generosity, since nothing in Huck's makeup or background could have prepared him for such a perception. On the contrary, not only is Jim still, even in this passage, a "nigger"—how could he be anything else for Huck?—but Huck is routinely astonished by Jim's humanity. Seeing Jim homesick,

Huck knows that he misses his wife and children, that he'd never been away from home in his life, and again he registers one of the novel's lovely discoveries: "I do believe he cared just as much for his people as white folks does for their'n. It don't seem natural, but I reckon it's so." Is this not what brainwashing looks like? *It don't seem natural.* This is what Twain has signed on for in this book: to take an unschooled boy—hence a barometric figure, a kind of random sampling of how a culture thinks—and give him a set of adventures that scrambles his received views, that goes counter to what is "natural." For that is what ideology is: the natural, the obvious, the transparent. All of which, for Huck Finn, mean: Jim as less than human, Jim as "nigger." There is something very fine, but also very revolutionary, in moments like this, when the big protocols start to waver, to show as constructs, to lose their governing authority. Beyond even Grimmelshausen and Blake, Twain uses the lens of innocence as a window onto identity formation and the struggle needed to resist it.

The book's final third is an embarassing mishmash of Tom Sawyer tricks, transforming the moral center of the novel—the recognition of Jim's humanity, the emancipation of Jim from slavery—into a nauseating, spiraling series of fun and games. More distressingly, Huck experiences genuine pangs of conscience at what he is doing: freeing a "nigger." Here is where the "natural" does its dirty business again, for how can this child view his acts as other than seditious, outright evil? "It would get around that Huck Finn helped a nigger to get his freedom." The more Huck thinks about this, "the more my conscience went to grinding me, and the more wicked and low-down and ornery I got to be feeling." Tom Sawyer's games were seen by Huck as smacking of Sunday school; but Twain, like Blake before him, knows that Sunday school is lodged deep inside the human being. How, the boy asks himself, can he justify "stealing a poor old woman's nigger that hadn't ever done me no harm"? Providence is watching him, he feels; wickedness such as this will be punished; he's headed for the "everlasting fire." Culture is speaking.

Anguished by such thoughts of his sins, Huck writes a note to Miss Watson, telling her where Jim is. And he feels great relief: "all washed clean of sin for the first time I had ever felt so in my

life." Again the biblical language testifies to the stubborn and enduring pact with culture, even in a seeming disbeliever. Huck reflects back on how close he has come to being lost and going to
Hell. But reflection is a double-edged sword, and, in quasi-
Proustian fashion, it brings the human Jim of these past adventures terribly, wonderfully, to life, so that Huck sees Jim before
him "all the time, in the day, and in the night-time, sometimes
moonlight, sometimes storms, and we a floating along, talking,
and singing, and laughing." (Jim is virtually storming Huck;
Twain understands the vagaries of consciousness, how helpless we
are when it gets riled up, how we can be victimized by what is
best, as well as worst, in us.) Huck knows he is morally obliged to
turn Jim in, but the Jim he sees is kind and generous and loving:
he "would always call me honey, and pet me, and do everything he
could think of for me, and how good he always was." Remembering Jim saying "I was the best friend old Jim ever had in the
world," Huck opens his eyes, looks around, and sees the note to
Miss Watson. The moment of spiritual truth is here:

> It was a close place. I took it up, and held it in my hand. I was
> trembling, because I'd got to decide, forever, betwixt two
> things, and I knowed it. I studied a minute, sort of holding my
> breath, and then says to myself:
> "All right, then I'll *go* to hell,"—and tore it up.

Twain's page or so on the (penal) working of conscience and the
courage required to leap clear are worth reams of theoretical pronouncements about the operation of ideology. "All right, then I'll
go to hell" is arguably the most luminous utterance in nineteenth-
century literature. I cannot imagine a book that brings out more
forcefully, more unhingingly, what we have to gain by reading
about the experience of growing up. Huck Finn's gradual but inexorable recognition of Jim's humanity, and therefore of his own existential choice, writes large for us how we might move from
darkness to light, from the lawfulness of prior arrangements to a
shimmering moment of freedom. Nothing is easy here. Huck is
prepared to pay the full price he's been told he'll have to pay. That
is what gives this scene, and this novel, its astonishing gravity.

Twain creates here a fleeting glimpse of truth, of seeing through the constructs that we've taken for real, of the challenge that life metes out to us as unaccommodated mapless spiritual creatures with living responsibilities, regardless of fog.

I find it especially sad that Twain's novel has become a battleground for what is sayable or not, offensive or not, when it comes to race in America. I do not think Twain can be absolved of his own racist assumptions, so that the intermittent characterization of Jim as minstrel-show figure has its undeniable ugly truth. Yet the book's very failures speak to us about the racial fault lines of our society. The book wants to adjudicate who is to be Huck's "father": Pap or the Widow and the Judge? But whoever reads Twain's novel has seen that the father in this story is Jim: a man of deep feelings who misses his wife and loves his children, as is exquisitely shown when he tells Huck about having struck his child for disobeying, not realizing the girl was deaf; Twain's genius is on show on the next page, where Jim is decked out by the King and the Duke as King Lear. No commentary is given, and none is needed. Both texts are about blind fathers, but Jim's remorse in that instance illuminates the whole man for us. And that is what Huck painfully remembers when he is on the verge of turning him in: kindness, tenderness, generosity, love, meted out to a boy who has seen precious little of them in his life.

That love is what makes this novel so moving. That it has nowhere to go, that both the novel and Huck will "forget" about Jim and his plight, is a heartbreaking commentary on what Martha Nussbaum has called "the fragility of goodness." Toni Morrison has rightly said that every reader knows that "no enduring adult fraternity will emerge" in *The Adventures of Huckleberry Finn*. Human nature is fickle, the flights of the soul are hard to sustain, racism is real, America is a hard place. Huck himself lights out for the Territory at novel's end, and it does not seem far-fetched to see him as a lost boy, someone rudderless and destined to be manipulated, despite his good heart and decent soul. We know that Twain was haunted by the magic he had— momentarily, all too briefly—achieved in this novel and that he returned to Huck and Jim in later life, in sequels and drafts, yet never succeeded in finding a future for the white boy and the black father. It is not entirely unlike the dream of childhood itself: unforgettable, unrecoverable.

The Idiot's Tale: William Faulkner's Benjy

Mark Twain seemed to have virtually stumbled into the richness and beauty and edge that might result from a vision that is radically unschooled. One returns to *Huckleberry Finn* for its inexhaustible freshness and poetry, and it is hard to disagree with Hemingway's assessment that all American literature stems from this vernacular account of an uneducated child's adventures. For that matter, to present the wonder (and horror) of the world by refracting it through the lens of innocence and simplicity is a writerly injunction that we find even earlier, in Grimmelshausen's seventeenth-century *Simplicissimus* and Blake's poems of the 1790s, as we have seen. But it remained for William Faulkner in 1929 to introduce into American literature the voice of the idiot. Benjy Compson, the leadoff "speaker" in *The Sound and the Fury*, is unmistakably Faulkner's response to Shakespeare, whose famous lines in *Macbeth* equate all of life with the vision of the idiot: "a tale told by an idiot, full of sound and fury, signifying nothing." Yet we will see that Faulkner's sights have little to do with the nihilism expressed in Shakespeare; on the contrary, he intuits that the idiot's tale can be unbearably rich and full, as well as being a unique conduit for conveying radical innocence. With Benjy, we move a quantum leap beyond the unschooled Huck: we encounter a vision arrested in infancy, doomed to infancy. Never before had innocence been put to such use.

The first page of *The Sound and the Fury* is justly famous for its rendition of Benjy's retarded vision: looking "through the fence," he tells us of people hitting, hitting repeatedly, coming forward, of hunting in the grass, of a flag taken out and then later put back, of hitting again, of people going on, of hunting again in the grass; this soundless notation is capped by two spoken words: "Here caddie." Faulkner then writes, "He hit. They went away across the pasture. I held to the fence and watched them going away." Such prose, oddly blinkered, is trouble for most readers, yet its most obvious secret is easily found out: the scene being described is a golf course. We know this. The innocent Benjy does not know this; all he knows is hitting and flags. Once we realize it is a golf course, we see "Here caddie" as a logical expression, but at this point the rules of the game appear to have changed, because we now understand, from the spoken words of his keeper, Luster, that Benjy is moaning.

"We now understand," I wrote. But why is he crying? To understand, we must look again at what is in plain sight: "They went away across the pasture." Plain sight on the page, perhaps, but in our minds it is a golf course. What's going on? In due time—after a few pages, perhaps after reading the entire novel, perhaps never?—we should realize that this golf course is indeed a pasture for Benjy: it was the family pasture (now sold, now become a golf course, but not for Benjy). This is the fence where he has always gone to wait, ever since childhood, for the return homeward of his sister, Caddy—*Caddy*, indistinguishable orally from *caddie*—from school, bringing him the only love he has ever known. Once we know this, things become rather clearer, and the most crystalline utterance of the book, we now see, is "Here caddie," or rather "Here Caddy," a phrase as freighted with significance as the sounds of the Delphic oracle. In two simple words it expresses the living tragedy of Benjy Compson's life: Caddy is not here, Caddy is gone, love won't return. Benjy will never go past this rupture; instead he is fated to rehearse it continually, because every event in his experience seems marked "Caddy": the voice heard on the golf course, the remembered sight of his niece Miss Quentin sitting on a swing with her beau (recalling Caddy on a swing), the sight of some girls walking home after school, walking by the fence as a daily dare, to watch the strange man inside it respond by running along its edge, moved, desperate.

The novel's most heartbreaking episode occurs on the fateful day, long past, when the girls came by and Benjy went beyond holding to the gate; he got out:

They came on. I opened the gate and they stopped, turning. I was trying to say, and I caught her, trying to say, and she screamed and I was trying to say and trying and the bright shapes began to stop and I tried to get out. I tried to get it off my face, but the bright shapes were going again. They were going up the hill to where it fell away and I tried to cry. But when I breathed in, I couldn't breathe out again to cry, and I tried to keep from falling off the hill and I fell off the hill into the bright, whirling shapes.

As Benjy's desire to embrace Caddy/the girls—for we realize they are for him versions of each other—fuses with the forced anesthesia given to him prior to castration (for that is what is happening), we may measure a number of things: not only the (surgical, sexual) closure that life has meted out to him but also the incomparable power and poignancy of an "innocent vision." We readers parse Benjy Compson's life of injury, and we see that the absent Caddy—run away, married because pregnant, long gone—courses through his memories in passages that can break your heart: Caddy feeding Benjy, Caddy explaining "ice" to Benjy, Caddy holding Benjy, Caddy taking Benjy for a walk, Caddy giving up perfume because it makes Benjy cry, Caddy resisting the very march of time so as to remain the loving sister her brother needs, so as to be forever the Caddy "who smells like trees."

We will never fully know what it felt like to be Caddy. Yet she remains, for me, one of Faulkner's most beautiful characters: generous, loving, feisty, loyal, irrepressible, true. Her story is never told as such—and Faulkner has been roundly chastised for representing her largely through the eyes of her hungry brothers—but she is the book's living heart, the life principle that the male siblings, especially Benjy and Quentin, cannot survive without. Would she be as moving if she had been granted a chapter of her own? I somehow doubt it. Faulkner loved her, referred to her as "my heart's darling," and must have sensed that she would move us most if refracted through her brothers' eyes. Her own tragic tale of growing up is brutally compacted by the book we have, leaving us to imagine the terrible hand that life dealt her: loveless mother, alcoholic father, two insatiable brothers, Don Juan lover, unwanted pregancy, desperate marriage, plunge into dishonor, separation from child, permanent final residence beyond the pale; a story never quite written.

What we do know is that Benjy never grows past his almost animal need for her: at every point in his trajectory, she is the compass, the source of love, the horizon of living. We the adult readers see all too clearly the sweeping curve of time that bathes Compson lives, we see Caddy grow into adolescence and rebellion and finally exile. We see the monstrousness of a thirty-three-year-old man with the mind of a three-year-old. But Benjy himself seems to exist entirely outside of time, as we measure it. We distort the novel if we say that Benjy remembers Caddy; you must forget in order to remember, and he cannot forget. I cannot think of any fate more awful. Time heals nothing for him. Every day he goes to the fence, awaiting her return. Every gesture is capable of making her present to his awful hunger. Any event can signal to him the love he once had, a loss that he now recovers with all its immediacy and hurt.

Benjy is frozen in time, and in that regard he is deprived of the essential learning process that life confers on the living. Innocence and experience were Blake's grand terms. The chimney sweep of the "Experience" poem grasps in retrospect what has been done to him, in the name of Church and king. Huckleberry Finn comes gradually to understand that Jim is a human being with dignity and feeling, no matter how "unnatural" it might appear in his environment, indeed to his customary way of thinking. But Benjy realizes nothing. Huck, at book's close, lights out for the Territory, ahead of the others. Benjy has no place to go. He cannot outgrow his hurt. He cannot turn it into wisdom. He cannot mature. Such permanent stasis is tragic. And perhaps that is the secret strength that fuels human development: to get past injury, to work through it, to find ways to go beyond it, to learn how to deal with the irremediable, the unacceptable.

Benjy is at once the most poignant and resourceless figure of my book. I do not want to make him emblematic. We have seen coping and surviving aplenty among even the most innocent children up to now: Blake's chimney sweep, Simplicius, Huck, and still more to come. But no figure in literature is as unfurnished as Benjy, and no figure in literature lives quite the daily calvary that he does. Faulkner's genius is to write Benjy in such a way that we—the schooled, the thinking, the privileged—experience vicariously this boy/man's incessant hurt. When you finish *The*

Sound and the Fury, you will never be able to hear those two simple words "Here caddie" in the same way, given their awful, freighted significance in the life of Benjy Compson. The stream-of-consciousness narration hurls us (without guideposts) into his sensations, and I can think of no nobler reason for having art than to provide us with experiences of this sort.

What does this tale of an idiot teach us about growing up? I have emphasized all that Benjy has lost and continues to lose every day. Is there anything gained? Not for him, that is certain, but for us? The answer is yes: his uncomprehending vision of things, his to-the-death fidelity to his sister, both convey to us in words an immediate luminous fragrant noisy poignant unlabeled world we have long ago exited. We could not return even if we wished to. Yet I believe that at some primitive level of psyche—a level prior to all the abstractions we adults live among—this is how it once was for all of us: an incessant craving for love, a total helplessness, an unfiltered picture of bright shining shapes that rush upon us, an existence parsed only by crying or not crying.

The Little Princess: Marjane Satrapi's Marjane

Little Marjane, the child heroine of the graphic novel *Persepolis* (2003), is doubtless based on the real life of the author, Marjane Satrapi, herself distantly related to an earlier shah of Persia (1848–1896). This matters a great deal, for Marjane's perspective is indeed that of a privileged child, even if she and her family are targeted by the regime. She is privileged but also perky, feisty, and irresistibly winning as she offers her little testimony of the events in Tehran from 1979 to 1982: events of enormous political moment, as the (current) shah loses his grip on power and is replaced by the Ayatollah Khomeini, who installs a no less repressive order of militant Islam and militant communism. But it is also a time of enormous personal change, as Marjane moves from childhood into adolescence, identifying ever more closely with the seductive Western culture that is demonized by the (new) forces that be. This is a potent artistic mix, and the force of this memoir stems unmistakably from an innocent child's evolving angle of vision.

Blessed with the temporal reach of all narrative, *Persepolis* is not confined to its three-year central drama but contains a number of haunting episodes from the more distant past, as Marjane learns about her family origins, especially about the princely identity of her dead grandfather (as the text has it). This sequence illustrates to perfection how Satrapi makes use of her graphic language and child perspective. At first the child is simply thrilled to learn that her grandfather was royal, and we see an image of a gentleman with a crown astride an elephant, in charge of his domains. Then we see the shah confiscating all his possessions, only to ask him, in a later frame, to serve as prime minister. At this point Mother—the blood daughter of the prince—takes over the storytelling and evokes, in a few harrowing frames, the punishments meted out to her father because of his Marxist leanings: frequent arrests, frequent prison sentences, torture via water cell, rheumatism, ruined health. But because this is a graphic text, we now see the mother as child, as uncomprehending as Marjane herself is, visiting her father, leaping and riding on his (damaged) back. Most striking here are the images of the innocent Marjane's open-eyed bewilderment, the blankness of her face as she receives this political and familial education. She had earlier asked to play Monopoly but is now so dazed that she wants only to take a bath, "a really long bath." The penultimate frame shows her, still vacant-eyed, lying in the tub while conversing with God, who has been a frequent nightly visitor of hers; He sits next to the tub and seems manifestly unequal to the task. The last frame of this episode displays the naked little girl, having exited the tub, standing in a small puddle of water, examining her hands intently. The caption reads, "My hands were wrinkled when I came out, like Grandpa's."

Granted, this is scarcely a version of Huck's "All right, then I'll *go* to hell," but it shares something of the same generosity and moral growth. Perhaps this is how political understanding is born, in low-to-the-ground moments when a ten-year-old girl tries to feel the torture inflicted on her grandfather. What is certain is that Satrapi's clean, almost bare images seem like the perfect conduit for news of this sort. And it is news, for we have few lights on the ways in which we come to maturity, of the moments when we suddenly realize the density and preciousness of others' lives, of that otherwise unrecorded little odyssey that gives a drastically new meaning to the word "water." One cannot easily imagine this sequence having the same power had it been consigned entirely to language. The graphic novel's very means of expression possesses a kind of conceptual innocence, prior to ratiocination and cognitive argument, cued to elemental insights.

Satrapi is wonderfully faithful to the child's bewilderment at adult realities. In one early episode, we witness, through the father's accounting, a dead young martyr being carried to the cemetery; this is followed by an angry crowd with yet another dead victim, protesting the repressive violence of the shah's police, but then we see an old woman trying to stop them, explaining that her husband died of cancer. Satrapi offers us an astonishing frame of confused adults holding a dead body whose upside-down face stares out at us; the crowd decides that this cancer victim is still a hero, that the king is a killer, and then the widow actually joins in the fracas. Mother and Father find the irony of this tale too delicious not to laugh at it, and so too does Grandmother, who now realizes that she'll be a martyr no matter how she dies. But Marjane is befuddled, and we see a small frame with her sweet, puzzled face trying to process all this. The caption goes "Something escaped me," then "Cadaver, cancer, death, murderer," then "Laughter?" In the next frame, little Marjane trots out her new wisdom by going to her parents and grandmother and laughing as hard as she can: "Ha! Ha! Ha! Ha! Ha! Ha!" They are now bewildered. The next frame shows Marjane poring over a book with the title *The Reasons for the Revolution.* The caption reads, "I realized then that I didn't understand anything. I read all the books I could."

I didn't understand anything. Do you? What we do grasp—what Grandmother grasped—is something of the cheapness and one-size-fits-all nature of the term that used to be used sparingly: "martyr." And this is a sobering lesson, since in many parts of today's world there are huge marketing campaigns for turning "martyr" into a household expression denoting sanctification at bargain rates, while opening the door to dying made easy. And we (in the West) have no clue as to how to discredit it. The graphic text is very eloquent when it comes to the reign of slogans. And children are no less eloquent when it comes to the gap between slogan and reality.

Now, these are adult matters. So, true to form, Marjane does not subject them to ideological analysis. Instead, as the tempo of political violence and murder—by the shah's army and police, then by the fundamentalists who succeeded them in power, finally by the still-larger-scale catastrophe that was the invasion of Iran by Saddam Hussein's Iraq—escalates and heats up further and further, we begin to see cadavers piling up in unprecedented numbers, as if martyrdom were the common fate. As a logical complement to this turn of events, we see that instruction in the schools has altered dramatically: separation of the sexes, covered hair, scarves, black uniforms, and so on. Even self-flagellation in the streets occurs. Yet, predictably enough, the children see clear, and do what children have always done: they make fun of the pieties being imposed on them. One frame shows them hysterically laughing and shouting "The martyrs! The martyrs!" The next one shows two girls grinning from ear to ear as the third one, Marjane, lies on the floor with her feet pumping up, imploring "Kill me!" Their teacher arrives, asks Marjane what she's doing, and gets this answer from the supine child, who seems to be winking at us: "I'm suffering, can't you see?"

Here is the second shoe dropping. Marjane learns to empathize with those she knows and loves—Grandfather, her extended family, her friends—but finds the ethos of wholesale martyrdom and suffering in God's name simply incredible, hence puffed up, hence a subject for laughter and histrionics. "Out of the mouths of babes," we sometimes say when they puncture some of the inflated ideological bubbles that so many cultures send out into the air. Puncturing bubbles. In some odd way, the graphic novel—with its one-liners, its simple drawings, its embubbled electric lights to signal "thinking"—is ideally suited to conveying the reductive jingoism of modern life, alive and well in the West as well as in the Middle East, where monosyllabic abbreviations take the measure of politics, morality, religion, and behavior, all in one fell swoop.

Persepolis centers, I think, on the issues of violence, rhetoric, and childlike perception that I've discussed. Its most endearing feature is its principled retention of the child's vision, its refusal to get lost in politics or ideology, its quiet insistence on keeping score as rhetoric moves ever farther from reality. Hence, one of the heartbreaking episodes depicts the response of the state to its swelling number of martyrs: it hands out keys (plastic, painted gold) to young boys at school before conscripting them as cannon fodder for Saddam Hussein's superior firepower, but the keys are magic, we gather, for if "they were lucky enough to die, this key would get them into heaven."

We actually see this special key: it is lying on the palm of the Satrapis' maid's hand, the last connection she has with her son, who is off to war. The Satrapis ask the maid what her son thought of this "exchange," and he apparently reported to her that he was content, that he had been promised "food, women and houses made of gold and diamonds." "Women?" Marjane's mother inquires, confused. "Yeah, well, he's fourteen years old. That's exciting," the maid replies. Marjane is intrigued. Is that what fourteen-year-olds are excited by? She herself is not far from fourteen. She wants to question her cousin Peyman about these matters, and he responds by inviting her to a party. Her first party. We then see a few frames depicting busloads of young boys from the country, poor and uneducated, who are, in the words of the text, "hypnotized" and "tossed into battle."

The next page is staggering. We are, as it were, "blown away." There are two frames only, sharing the space. The first one shows us children exploding into the sky, each with a key attached to his neck. They are presumably entering Paradise, but these careening, flying bodies have all too earthly a feel to them. We are not all that far, conceptually, from the logic of William Blake, whose chimney sweep was also brainwashed into service and death, while being told that this was the high road to Heaven. No expressions are visible in this piece—the bodies are all in black—so we cannot know what they feel at their dying. But the frame underneath shows us another set of children, their faces filled with ecstatic joy as their bodies leap and cavort to the music of punk rock. This is the "first party." Marjane herself fills one-third of the frame, her hair flowing upward, her eyes wide in excitement, her mouth open in sheer pleasure; the final caption reads, "I was looking sharp."

THE KEY TO PARADISE WAS FOR POOR PEOPLE. THOUSANDS OF YOUNG KIDS, PROMISED A BETTER LIFE, EXPLODED ON THE MINEFIELDS WITH THEIR KEYS AROUND THEIR NECKS.

MRS. NASRINE'S SON MANAGED TO AVOID THAT FATE, BUT LOTS OF OTHER KIDS FROM HIS NEIGHBORHOOD DIDN'T.

MEANWHILE, I GOT TO GO TO MY FIRST PARTY. NOT ONLY DID MY MOM LET ME GO, SHE ALSO KNITTED ME A SWEATER FULL OF HOLES AND MADE ME A NECKLACE WITH CHAINS AND NAILS. PUNK ROCK WAS IN.

I WAS LOOKING SHARP.

Perhaps this is what a new Blake might look like today. Perhaps this is the very character of innocence: children in adolescence dancing wildly to punk rock. Much of the integrity of *Persepolis* is on show here: children remain children, Marjane is, yes, unhappy that so many young boys (with keys to Paradise) became martyrs and were blown sky-high by the minefields, but we mustn't forget that this is her first party. It is as if Satrapi were remembering Natasha's first great ball in *War and Peace,* another text that relishes the juxtaposition of the social and the lethal. Desire has its own fierceness, and it is right to see that it can exist even in the Tehran of the ayatollahs' reign, at least among the children of Marjane's class. Stories about growing up remind us that we were once young, that all the horrors of the world, black though they are, coexist with moments of pleasure.

After all, this is a rites-of-passage tale of sorts, and this little girl is on the somatic and hormonal treadmill that all living creatures are on when young. The poor boys' dreams of Paradise (with its goodies) and the well-to-do little girl's thrills at her first party share the same basic human and animal wants. But it is here that Satrapi's art proves its mettle: the boys are dead, and the girl is living. It makes a difference. And we see it with shocking clarity when we look at this page as a single page, thus noticing the horrible similarities between the two frames: writhing bodies of children, flying through the air. One set has been blown up by mines; the other is responding to punk rock. The order and rationale of art are visible here, via this conjunction of bodies and fates. This conflation of images is luminous, begs (and beggars) commentary. Pages of ideological sermonizing or theorizing would not come close, in my view, to the grisly eloquence of those two juxtaposed frames in a graphic novel.

Much more might be said of this fetching and hard-to-put-down novel. The privileged Marjane, en route to adolescence, is drawn ever more strongly into the orbit of Western rituals and pleasures: a culture of cigarettes, wine, rock music. But we also see the effects of war ever more powerfully, as the house next door, the home of a dear friend, is bombed to smithereens. We had earlier heard of another friend, Niloufar, who had Communist sympathies and was executed, but now the details start to come in, namely that Niloufar was first raped and then executed, since Islamic law proscribes the execution of virgins. After this lesson in hard facts, Marjane lies in bed pondering the phrase so favored by the regime, "To die a martyr is to inject blood into the veins of society," and she realizes that Niloufar is indeed a martyr by a standard we may well call "double." (One wonders whether Marjane herself, at fourteen, may have a special understanding of a girl's bleeding. Much can be packed into a graphic text.) At just this juncture Marjane's parents present the plan for her exit from Iran to Austria. The education story is almost over. It closes with the girl spending one last night with Grandmother, hearing once again that her fine breasts remain round because she soaks them in ice water twice a day, and then leaving her parents at the airport, looking back in horror at the black figure of her father holding her mother, who has collapsed.

She leaves. She is ready to go. She is not far from being a woman. She has had her Iranian education. It is time to go west. (My analysis stays with the first volume of *Persepolis;* its successor—outlining Marjane's adventures in Austria and her return to Iran—has little to teach us about childhood.) In reading—*seeing*—her story, we understand once again the trumps of art, the way it has depicted at once a life in progress and the otherwise invisible exchange between self and setting, between a child's wants and the mobile, careening political stage where her life is playing out. Many directionalities come into visibility: Marjane's trek toward understanding, maturity, and freedom, and the lurching political evolution of Iran itself. In the tradition of Grimmelshausen, Blake, Twain, and Faulkner, Satrapi has deepened our grasp of what it means to grow up and make the move from innocence to experience. And she has, like them, shown us that innocence as lens brings an entire culture's beliefs—hidden as well as enforced—into shocking visibility. Finally, this graphic text, with its sweet and ungussied images of children going through their paces, coming headlong into contact with adult rites and laws, is an appropriately bare aesthetic form for completing our discussion of innocence. Seen against the increasingly inward renditions of psyche that reach their culmination in Faulkner's Benjy, Satrapi's little princess, drawn and spoken with utmost simplicity, acquires thereby a pathos we do not easily forget, as we ponder the story of growing up.

The Lessons of Experience

Experience lessons: that is the inescapable law of life, the secret of both survival and success. Experience is the crucial education that very frequently dwarfs the formal schooling we receive. In so doing, in displaying how different the world actually is, in contrast to the world one either expected or fantasized, texts about experience possess a powerful economy: they show the incompatibility between our notions and our lived life. Can we be surprised that Dickens called his great novel of growing up *Great Expectations* or that Balzac's supreme opus in this vein is titled *Illusions perdues*? There is something profoundly utilitarian about such art, for it goes about the principal business of our species: finding what will do, discarding what will not, figuring out how to live.

The following studies interrogate works of art from the sixteenth century to our own moment, yielding a rich historical curve, obliging us to see just how variously experience can be defined, how arduous the search for both truth and the "right path" can be. Each of these novels is larded with collisions as the hard world breaks into the young, smashing their assumptions, delivering its educational payload. I who teach at a university marvel at the sheer pedagogical verve of these narratives, how brilliantly they shine their beam of light on the adapting human response—for good, for evil—to circumstance. When one considers the institutions in place for teaching the young how to live—family, school, Church, state—it is surprising to me that "art" never shows up in the equation. But art and literature are all too often misconstrued as frills, as marginal to the nitty-gritty basics that must be taught; yet such a view has it backward. Here is perhaps the most pragmatic reason we consult literature: as a way of adding to our tool kit, as that special mirror that shows us both how others have come through and how we might learn from them.

Lazarillo de Tormes: *The Hungry Child*

How apt it is that the sixteenth-century anonymous *Lazarillo de Tormes*—often credited as being the first true narrative in Western literature because it renders the consciousness of an "I" responding to the experiences that beset it—tells the story of a hungry beggar child making his way through the school of hard knocks, learning from adversity, becoming a person. At story's end, the child is Lázaro, an established figure, a town crier, married to a woman who is the archpriest's "maid" (with all that implies) and sure at last of solid meals every day. It was not always so.

The *"fortunas y adversidades"* of Lazarillo tell a double story, focusing on the material poverty and brutal conditions that assault the child but adumbrating an even more severe fable about the extinction of spirit and inwardness in the barter world of sixteenth-century Spain. Lazarillo becomes Lázaro through a rigorous education: he learns that fulfillment is a literal concept—filling the belly full—but its figurative dimensions come at too high a price and must disappear from the equation. Here is a freighted story, a classic drama of selling out, written centuries before Balzac and Dickens came to the theme, and it serves as a bitter lesson about the realities of survival, about what life teaches us.

The most persistent and frightening note of this early fiction is its fierce rendition of hunger as the primary sensation and need of life. A glance at the animal world of creatures clamoring for sustenance—baby birds in their nest with beaks open, desperate; babies of all species who will die unless fed—confirms this un-yielding material view of life's requirements. Lazarillo's story obeys similar laws, but there is no mother bird to supply him with his wants: he must use his wits if he is to eat. We are treated to a number of hallucinatory scenes where the pleasures of food and drink are cut with violence and cruelty. An early notation involves the child sneaking wine from his first master, the blind man: face turned to the sky, eyes closed, savoring the precious liquid, Lazarillo is struck brutally by his master, who takes the jug and smashes it against the boy's face with all his strength. This passage is written in apocalyptic terms—"So it seemed like the sky and everything in it had really fallen down on top of me"—and the reference seems just: gratification makes you vulnerable, the hard world can fall on you, destroy you. At another juncture the blind man asks the boy to put his ear next to the statue of a bull, to hear what is inside, but when the child obeys, the adult doubles up his fist and knocks the boy's head into the stone statue with all his might. It's the same lesson: the world is a hard surface; going "in-side" is risky business. "Wake up!" the boy says to himself. To what? we wonder.

The most surreal moment of this sometimes grisly tale comes when Lazarillo has stolen and wolfed down some black sausage; the blind man suspects as much, grabs the child tight, opens the boy's mouth, and inserts his own nose inside, so as to smell the sausage that lurks down below. It's a dicey move, it turns out. The pointy nose of the master hits the boy in the throat, and the vis-ceral response comes at once: "before the blind man could take his beak out of my mouth, my stomach got so upset that it hit his nose with what I had stolen. So his nose and the black, half-chewed sausage both left my mouth at the same time." What is one to make of this savage warfare, traffic going into and out of the body? It conveys to us what a world of pure somatic hunger might look like: corporeal passageways with traffic in both directions. There is something tonic as well as chilling about the primitive conflicts and needs depicted in this story: later fictions will be psy-chologically subtle, will ponder a great deal about that other (more modern) meaning of fulfillment, about how to live right, how to be happy in love or career, but this lean tale has no truck with such frills. Instead, it sticks with the basics: how to eat and drink enough to survive.

As mentioned, Lazarillo succeeds; he survives to tell the story. What is fascinating about the narrative, however, is that its protagonist fudges more and more as he grows older and finds his place. The brutal episodes of hunger and punishment are a lead-in to more sophisticated accounts of subsequent masters, with a dosage of satirical observation about the workings of the world. But the Lázaro who emerges as town crier has lost all authenticity as speaker, covers up the dirty bargains he has had to make with experience. Such a transformation, never acknowledged but shimmering on the page, tells us, as nothing else could, what the price of growing up might be: the loss of one's integrity, one's commitment to truth, one's ability to face the truth. There is a grim but coherent social parable on show here: let circumstances be punitive enough and the soul goes out of business, is tossed out because it is no longer affordable or bearable.

Lazarillo is the child hero of hunger. There is no anguish or breast-beating in this slim piece from more than four centuries ago. We cannot even see in him anything that might go by the name of "innocence." He brings no doctrines, no expectations with him. Yet his alteration by life is eloquent. *He adapts.* He has seen what must be done to get by, and he does it. His hunger will live on in literature: it will become a richer and more figurative affair—no more pointy noses and black sausages—encompassing the erotic needs of some, the emotional needs of others, the economic and political designs of still others. The young are born hungry. What must they do or pay to satisfy their needs?

Picaresque Wisdom: The Swindler

We know that *Lazarillo* begat an entire genre of seventeenth- and eighteenth-century fiction called the *picaresque,* devoted to the lives of rascals, down-and-outers, often children at the margins of society surviving through their wits, often becoming tricksters or con men. An argument can be made that this tradition remains vital throughout the history of the novel: we see it in such well-known later books as Dickens's *Oliver Twist,* Twain's *Huckleberry Finn*, Mann's *Confessions of Felix Krull, Confidence Man*, Bellow's *The Adventures of Augie March*, Ellison's *Invisible Man*, Grass's *The Tin Drum.* We would be well served to recover some of this fare, because its pedagogical verve and acuity, its fascination with "getting by" (against harsh odds), are essential to the story of growing up, no matter when or where.

Francisco de Quevedo is largely known as a poet, yet his single venture into the picaresque, *Historia de la vida del Buscón (The Swindler)*, published in the 1620s but written earlier, is an exemplary tale of education—a young boy's development into con man and trickster—like *Lazarillo,* yet with a playfulness and verbal brio that we identify with Shakespeare and Donne. The book insists on the dichotomy of a mean and tawdry world on the one hand (the *pícaro's* setting), and the magisterial transformations afforded by language and wit on the other. I call this text modern because it is wise about "street smarts," about the multiple avenues of disguise and invention open to someone with sufficient ingenuity and chutzpah. One might not go far afield in referencing today's rap culture; it too is a heady verbal thing, concerned with getting by through performance.

Quevedo's protagonist, Pablos, is subject to miseries beyond even those experienced by Lazarillo, and they invariably highlight the vulnerability and shamefulness of the body: he is spat on, peed on, and shat on. Perhaps the book's most poignant scene comes when the boy, crouched under his covers, fearing that the older schoolboys wish him harm, falls asleep and dreams of his family but wakes up to see brutal whippings being carried out. He hides under the bed, but while he is there, "the bastard who slept next to me got into my bed, crapped in it and covered the mess up." Pablos returns to his bed, twists and turns in his sleep, and wakes up "smothered in shit." It is essential to see the punitive dimension of these indignities: in bed, dreaming of kin, you are most vulnerable, and that is when you will be initiated into the regime of shit. For it is an initiation and a regime, depicting the final stage of both hunger and ingestion, depicting a caricatural model of human creativity, input and output. At some level this text seems to be asking: do we ever get past shit? Excrement is the base

currency of the bare, forked creature's life. The body's frailties
loom large in this text: we hear of starvation, diarrhea, farting,
hernias, sodomy, and finally cannibalism. Flesh is heir to so many
disasters in *The Swindler* that many readers find it too filthy to
enjoy.

Yet it is a text for our time. Lazarillo learned duplicity. Pablos
goes much further: he sees that poverty and stinking flesh can be
offset by wit, language, and art. For purposes of education, this
constitutes a quantum leap, from the animal to the human. Hence
the novel is stamped by a delirious kind of aesthetic vision, so a
scene of starvation becomes a threshold for verbal fiat: "Then our
masters ate an infinite meal, by which I mean it had no beginning
and no end." One needs to consider the peculiar equilibrium of
that phrase, the manner in which the savvy wordplay counterbal-
ances the needs of the gut. Might there be a real dialectic here?
Pablos encounters a series of fascinating lunatics: one would capture Ostend by sucking up the sea with sponges; another claims to
be a swordsman but mouths only complex geometric formulas;
another tries to pass a plague scar for a military wound but then
finds that his "papers" are construed as toilet paper. All of these
instances involve shape shifting, implying that the hard world
might be alterable, that "things" might yield to "words."

The prizewinner is one Magazo: "he'd been a soldier, in a play,
and fought the Moors, in a dance. When he spoke to men who had
been in Flanders he said he'd been in China, and he told the China
veterans he'd been in Flanders. . . . He was always going on about
Turks, galleons and captains, but he got it all from a few songs
about them. He didn't know a single thing about the sea; the only
naval thing he knew was navel oranges." One is humbled, I think,
by the transposition of realms parading in this spoof, as if verbal
clout were enough to replace actual doing. Note the lovely ongoing tit for tat: to be a soldier/in a play; to fight the Moors/in a
dance; naval ships/navel oranges. An entire ballet is on show here,
dishing up for us the supreme trump of language as reality making. To dismiss this performance as a mere lie is to close one's eyes
to the metamorphic power on display. All writers, all speakers,
play this game. From eloquence to outright lying, words are our
weapons. Quevedo is shining his light on the oldest sleight of

hand in history, and he has the genius to posit this kind of skill as a tool kit for a child.

We tend to think of the "saving virtues of language" as a late-stage acquisition, the sort of thing someone well advanced into life might finally come to enjoy in some bittersweet fashion, as compensation for losses; but Quevedo makes us consider childhood itself, especially disadvantaged childhood, as a kind of linguistic playground, a site where verbal prowess might stand in for material deficits. Pablos encounters a world of wordsmen, and we realize that this is an education in itself, for he is discovering how peculiarly egalitarian life just might be, how you might, if you were clever enough, pass off the word for the thing. With this in mind, consider the games children play, the extraordinary power granted to virtuality in children's lives, as they point fingers and go "Pow!" or make salubrious signs and piqued expressions. Children are not outfitted (yet) with muscles or money or weapons, so they make do with simulacra, facsimiles, representations; they become experts at displacement and magic; they believe in the living extensions of the words that leave their mouths. They reimagine power. To use a figure that is at the heart of this story, they reclothe themselves in garments of their own making.

On this front, *The Swindler* is wildly vestimentiary, paying extravagant attention to clothes and uniforms and medals and saddles and horses, all implements of station. We know that the Spanish notion of *quedar bien* ("looking right") governs much of the postures and impostures of these denizens, but in Quevedo's hands, the artisanal rises to something more dizzying and empowered. At one point, the boy Pablos joins up with a group of "gentlemen thieves" who are masters of make-believe, covering their bare asses with cloaks, covering holes in their clothes with capes, meticulously picking their teeth in public even though they've eaten nothing. Pablos tries his own hand at disguise: donning elegant chothes, giving himself a pretentious name, going through the various paces that denote the behavior of a gentleman (mounting an "available" horse and pretending to your aristocratic acquaintances that it is yours, walking behind servants in the street so as to pretend they are your own pages). With a sure hand, Quevedo brings his episodic plot home by having Pablos give his greatest performance in counterfeit and disguise in front of no less than Don Diego, the true aristocrat whom he served as a child. Here is the book's high noon: Will Don Diego recognize Pablos, or will the swindler's art carry the day? Can wit trump reality?

Strictly speaking, the comic logic of exposure seems to win out. Pablos is recognized and is severely punished: he is beaten up and slashed from ear to ear, his face cut in half. One does not escape one's past, Quevedo appears to be saying. Make-believe can go only so far. Here would be the confirmation of traditional values, of a preexisting reality base that no amount of tricks will alter. Except that the story does not end there. Your face is cut in half? Well, sew it back together. Skin is not so different from cloth. And then up again, and into the fray. Pablos continues his career, leaves Spain for the New World (after a few more criminal deeds, including murder), and that is where Quevedo leaves him.

What does this tale tell us about growing up in the twenty-first century? Much, in my opinion, that Francisco de Quevedo could have neither seen nor intended but that art nonetheless makes visible. Wit—not the wit of the court, but that of the street—turns out to be a genuine resource, an incomparable tool of persuasion and success. Wit has clear siblings in this seventeenth-century text: lying, disguise, conning, creating one's own persona. It's not pretty, I agree. But after all, does truth really have much of a track record, when it comes to gauging how we make our way in the world? (I write these words at a time of Ponzi schemes and credit default swaps, at a time when blogospheres house truths and Wikipedia vouches for them.) *The Swindler* is one of our great tales about performativity as the force that generates success. Pablos has no cultural capital to begin with and must figure out what his weapons are to be if the world is to do his bidding. Wit is the trump card that people without trumps nonetheless may possess. The people we encounter in life do not have X-ray vision; if we are sufficiently good at producing ourselves, we are likely to carry the day. Who knows—indeed, who cares—what you are *really* like? It has been argued that Pablos actually has an inferiority complex, that he is ashamed of his parentage, his origins. But such reasoning goes in the wrong direction, backward toward origin rather than forward toward performance, and it thereby misses the vitality, gaiety, and joy—and wisdom—of this prancing tale about a poor boy's exploits.

And it misses perhaps what counts most for our purposes: the career of the *pícaro*, Pablos, is a parable about education, about learning what you need in order to get ahead. In this instance, there is nothing very distinguished or elevated in sight: no diploma, no professional horizons, and absolutely no implantation of sonorous moral principles that would earn him our respect or a ticket to the afterlife. On the contrary, Pablos has done graduate work in the field of self-production and deceit. He has realized that the world is a gullible place, that folks without credentials still have the option of manufacturing their credentials. (In our age of computerized identity theft, he looks nostalgically like the genuine article, an artisan/artist of identity snatching rather than a mere technician.) What I have called *wit* has little to do with clever words or metaphysical conceits but denotes instead a willingness to reshape both self and events to carry the day.

That is what amazes: that both self and events are subject to reshaping, repackaging. One does not learn these things in any school, but life teaches them nonetheless. Pablos sees, early on, the immense cleavage between high-sounding principles and the actual talents needed to get by, to achieve mastery. His hunger is very different from that of Lazarillo: one feels that his greatest joy comes in exploiting the marvelous resources of his intellectual and artistic equipment. Quevedo's pungent narrative deserves a modern audience. The tale measures, without ever saying much about it, the abyss between professed ideals and the actual carnival in front of our eyes. It is in this sense that it is luminous as a parable of education, because it calls the great bluff that has ever characterized our schools: what they teach has little to do with reality; what you need for success is something else altogether; what you actually encounter in life has nothing to do with adages and pieties. Some of our great rites-of-passage stories of the nineteenth century will pick up where the picaresque left off, adding more depth and pathos to this cynical wisdom, but few will possess the sheer verbal exuberance of Quevedo's romp.

Honoré de Balzac's **Père** Goriot: *A Capitalist Education*

Balzac is the giant who presides over much of nineteenth-century fiction, yet he seems little read today, despite the fact that his legacy shines in the work of writers as different as Tom Wolfe and Don DeLillo. *Père Goriot,* his early masterpiece of 1835, has a place of pride in this study of growing up and growing old, because it presents an unforgettable picture of both sides of the equation: the young man from the country, Rastignac, comes to Paris to study law but receives a radically new education; and the old Goriot, Balzac's candidate for King Lear, being bled dry by his two ambitious daughters, ranks among our most compelling images of fathers run amok, of the horrible finishes that are possible.

I will discuss Goriot later in this study, but Rastignac's exemplary nineteenth-century "career" in the big city can be meaningfully investigated as an extension of the picaresque adventures of an earlier epoch. To link Balzac to the picaresque would surprise many literary historians, since he is usually situated within the Bildungsroman tradition, and a word is in order. Inaugurated by Goethe at the beginning of the nineteenth century with his account of Wilhelm Meister's adventures, the Bildungsroman—the novel of "formation"—stamps a good deal of that century's fiction, as it tells the story of the young seeking their place in society. This focus on the choices available to the young sounds the modern note, since it is their story, their engagement with a rapidly changing world, that most deeply engages the writer. This is not innocent. Why centralize the story of the young? One answer is that they are peculiarly barometric figures, displaying at once the adequacy and inadequacy of their "formation" (a word still used in Europe to indicate education itself), i.e., bringing to light the clash of generations and the shifting values and upheavals in culture.

In a well-known passage, Balzac explicitly contrasted the challenges faced by Rastignac with the idealistic historical narratives of Walter Scott, and he sounded the modern note by claiming that the contemporary story that mattered was a story of selling out, a kind of dance whereby young men with principles, encountering in the city a culture driven by the cash nexus, must decide whether to save their souls or to plow ahead at all costs and succeed. *Parvenir*—"Succeed!"—is the battle cry. It is the battle cry today as well, I believe. In some restricted sense, it was the call heard by Lazarillo and Pablos, even though their circumstances were radically straitened when compared to those of the Parisian law student. Equipped with notions of honor and integrity, outfitted with a distinguished name, Rastignac arrives at a Parisian boarding-house, the Maison Vauquer, and from that point on, the original game plan of legal study and hard work is increasingly thrown into doubt. This happens because the moral world he had thought to be permanent and true, the moral world he assumed was conquerable by dint of diligence and drive, is shown, via what he encounters in Paris, to be something else entirely, to be collapsing like a house of cards.

What does he encounter? The spectacle of three figures of stature, indeed three potential mentors, spiritual advisers, caught in the Parisian rat race, each one either suffering or exposing the ethical bankruptcy of his time. The title figure, Goriot, functions as a living allegory of what happens to fathers in this culture. Having enriched himself through shrewd and murky dealings during the Revolutionary period, Goriot came to the boarding-house a wealthy man, but by the time of Rastignac's arrival, he is a broken figure of ridicule, living in a garret. There is talk of his being visited by beautiful young women, but soon enough we realize that they are his married daughters: one squanders her money on her conniving lover, the other is unhappily wed to the book's venture capitalist, and each comes repeatedly, insatiably, to the father for more and ever more money. Rastignac is stunned by Goriot's almost bestial love for his daughters and sees that they are eating him alive. The second mentor is the student's elegant *grande dame* cousin, Mme. de Beauséant, a queen of society but unknowingly on the verge of a ruthless betrayal by her lover; she gives her country cousin unillusioned instructions about how to succeed in Paris: use others like packhorses, and if ever you feel true sentiment for someone, keep it a secret, never expose your heart.

The third mentor, Vautrin, almost runs away with the book. A master criminal in disguise, possessed of qualities at once satanic and seductive, frightening and irresistible, Vautrin comes to us as the book's great Sphinx: the man who sees through everything (people's secrets, Parisian mores, what-have-you) but is himself impenetrable. Rastignac is irritated by his manners, and it appears as though the two might end up in a duel, but instead Balzac delivers himself of one of the greatest scenes in nineteenth-century fiction as the older man takes the student aside and gives him a grand lesson in Parisian life management. Vautrin is the narrative's Nietzschean superman figure—amoral, fearless, at once amused and contemptuous—who shows Rastignac exactly (as if it were a computer printout) what his chances are if he sticks to the straight and narrow, completes his law degree, tries to make a career. Rarely has the "sweat ethic" been given such a cuffing. A life of honest hard work will yield . . . yes . . . a life of honest hard work . . . although both the work and staying honest will be harder than imagined. And that's it. Four or five pages of brilliant, insolent, mesmerizing social analysis, a countercultural almanac in brief compass, that you will not easily forget.

It is worth pausing over these three mentor roles for a moment. This book exists for me as a mirror for the struggles of my university students in the twenty-first century, trying their very hardest to do the practical and moral calculus necessary to determine what is needed to *parvenir*, to get ahead. Law school or not? Business school? And what about your major at college? Be careful of too much humanities, since everyone knows it won't get you to the next stage. And what use are the arts, after all? In my humanistic corner of an institution, where it costs well upward of six figures to get a degree, I too wonder, as they do, what the right course is. What is missing, truly missing, however, is mentors. Today we call them "deans" or the occasional friendly professor who is willing to listen and to advise. But even at its very best, with an apparatus of informed and committed administrators and teachers, my university will never come up with a Vautrin, much less a Mme. de Beauséant or an old Goriot. Balzac's novel etches the generational hurdle with great clarity and force: three figures, each destined to finish rather strangely, each representing a code of values and behavior, each available to Rastignac. Yet Vautrin alone possesses a systemic vision of how the game is composed and played.

One of the supreme ironies here is that the novel itself (as genre, as institution) enjoys a kind of moral and pedagogical authority in the nineteenth century that is long gone today. Back then, there was no competing art form, and certainly no media such as TV or the Internet, where the young might go to find out about the culture they're soon to enter. Back then, Parisians read Balzac to better understand the city they lived in, just as Londoners read Dickens and denizens of Saint Petersburg pored over the books of Gogol and Dostoevsky. But Balzac's authorial voice outsounds all of them. His Vautrin is a master of the game.

Whatever his initial sentiments of suspicion might be regarding the sarcastic Vautrin, Rastignac starts to listen up when the older man takes him aside and spells out his chances as an eventual lawyer in Paris. I am reducing this exchange to its core, but in the novel itself we are treated to vivid, authoritative detail regarding every prospective avenue that lawyer-Rastignac might take, replete with exactly the revenue to be received and the (human) price paid. Much sweat and hardship, little money or happiness. But why go that route? If life as a lawyer can't make you rich, what can? Crime, for starters, explains Vautrin—every fortune in France rests on a concealed crime, he informs us—but he knows that the student has no stomach for something quite so vigorous.

Yet it turns out that there is a solution much closer to hand. There happens to be a young girl, Victorine—also in the boardinghouse, impoverished because her wealthy father prefers his son, taken in hand by her aunt—who has been making eyes at the handsome Rastignac ever since he arrived. It is really quite simple: Rastignac must woo Victorine now, because soon (very soon) she will be rich, because her father is going to give her all his money, because her brother is going to be dead, because Vautrin is going to see to it that he is murdered in what looks like a legitimate duel (but is really an assassination). No problem, Papa Vautrin will take care of everything.

Well, there is a problem. Rastignac thinks he's enamored of

Goriot's daughter Delphine (the one married to the fat financier Nucingen), and he's not one to redirect or sell his affections. Still, Victorine is awfully sweet. And she is making eyes at him. We can feel the net closing in. With the little lucidness remaining to him, he asks Vautrin why he's looking out for him in this way and what would be in it for him. What's in it for Vautrin is spelled out: a portion of the huge fortune that will be Rastignac's wife's, so that a chunk of land in the American South can be bought, enabling Vautrin to live there with a goodly number of black slaves. Why is only hinted at; Vautrin coyly says he'll whisper it in Rastignac's ear one day. (Later we are actually told that Vautrin doesn't like women.) The student is stunned by this bold proposition for immediate wealth, and so is the reader. And the wheels of the plot start to turn as Vautrin sets his scheme into motion.

I have been describing these events as drama, but it is patently clear that they constitute a significant piece of the education that Rastignac is undergoing, a series of lessons and principles that are not to be found in any of his lawbooks or lecture halls. But Balzac has more in store for Rastignac. The student's growing affection for both Delphine and her father, Père Goriot, bring him ever more deeply into the growing family tragedy at hand: namely that the decrepit old man is feverishly, indeed suicidally, trying to gather funds to help out his two daughters, most especially Anastasie (who, though married to an aristocrat, is channeling money non-stop to her lover). The social game is now being played at both ends: Rastignac is making his entry, while Goriot is moving toward exit.

This side of the novel is far more complex than I have indicated, but the upshot of it is that the egocentric wishes of the two daughters are going to become ultimately a death sentence for the old father, who has given them everything they ever wanted, who has nothing left except his febrile schemes for pawning his few remaining furnishings and somehow getting hold of more francs. As Goriot becomes increasingly desperate and moves from sick and miserable to intermittently comatose and finally dying, Balzac's *machine infernale* rachets up its speed. The great late scene in the novel is Mme. de Beauséant's reception—filled with false friends who are there to witness her being betrayed by her lover, not unlike a public execution—to which Delphine insists on going with Rastignac, since it marks her upward rise in high society.

Unfortunately her father is dying at exactly this time—dying and wanting nothing more than to have his two daughters at his bedside. And this too is an education: a Parisian education. Rastignac acquires an almost hallucinatory sense of Parisian values as he looks at all the (specious, morally empty) finery and riches at the Beauséant reception and sees—simultaneously, retinally, it would seem—through it to the squalid garret where Goriot lies dying, abandoned by his daughters. He sees, as it were, the cost of living in Paris. None of his law books has this kind of information in it. Not even Vautrin hinted at quite this. Here is the deeper vision of the novel, and the reader comes to it as one comes to a three-dimensional film: the text confers on you the red and blue lenses that convert what seemed flat into something bristling, with heights and depths, yielding an unforgettable larger picture. It all fits together. Something vital (if tragic) is being learned.

The novel ends with the funeral of Goriot. It is a funeral procession attended by empty coaches bearing the insignia of his daughters' married names. (Empty coaches: an emblem for this text.) The only living friend who is there is Rastignac: too poor even to pay for the service, sickened by what he has witnessed of betrayal and coldness of heart, now agonizingly aware of what it takes to succeed in Paris. One senses that more than Goriot's body is being buried in this scene. An entire cluster of ideals and principles is on the block. The final lines of the novel depict the law student standing at the cemetery overlooking the city of Paris and issuing his famous words of defiance: *"À nous deux, maintenant!"* Balzac writes that the student's first insurrectionary act was to accept an invitation and go to dinner with Delphine. Lazarillo and Pablos had learned to play the game by dint of wits; Rastignac realizes something further: love must be cashiered. The sellout is complete; he has learned his lesson.

Have we learned ours? Vautrin is arrested, Victorine is made rich, Mme. de Beauséant cloisters herself in the country, and Rastignac moves into a life of Parisian conniving, of doing as his cousin recommended: hiding the heart. To be sure, this much is clear. But ultimate meanings in both life and art are more complex than my equation suggests. Reading *Père Goriot* constitutes, I believe, an ethical experience of its own, one that goes counter to the cynical wisdom of some of its players, complicating the moral import of what has been witnessed. The most powerful scenes in this novel depict close human encounters: between Rastignac and Vautrin, Rastignac and Mme. de Beauséant, and Rastignac and Goriot. In particular, the many pages devoted to the misery and dying of Goriot are, in every sense of the word, the book's heart. Yes, the old man is delirious, shrieking for his two daughters, dying alone. It makes for hard reading.

But that is just it: he does not die alone. The reason we have the story at all is that he is attended by Rastignac (and by his friend at the boardinghouse, Bianchon the medical student). The tenderest notation of the novel comes when the two boys minister to the dying man's needs, staying in his miserable room, helping him when he cries out, writing letters home and studying their books when he sleeps or is unconscious. I call this "tender" because it is the very pulse of family, of human connection. Increasingly, in those pages, Rastignac calls Goriot "Papa." With considerable panache, Balzac writes the actual moment of death as a moment of sublime error: the old man, held up by the two students, clutches at their hair and murmurs, *"Mes anges!"* The novel then says that Goriot was foiled yet one final time, thinking the boys were his daughters. But the deeper reality of this scene is what it shows, not what it says, and we see a scene of family-making, a scene of poignant substitution, as the two young boys lovingly help this man in his exit from life. In a way that literature alone documents, they have become his children.

I want to close my discussion of growing up by insisting that the lessons of this book are richer and deeper than first appear. Goriot's actual dying makes it onto the page only because two young students are there to care for him and soften his exit. That we would see this thicker story of allegiance subtending betrayal is a tribute to the resources of literature. After the old man's death, one of the boarders at the Maison Vauquer quips that it is high time to stop talking about Goriot, that one of the virtues of living in the great city of Paris is *anonymity*. You can live and you can die, and nobody notices, thank God.

But the law of art goes the other way. This novel tells us to attend to Goriot, care about his emblematic life and fate, see how the student experiences his destiny, see how the human heart lives as well as dies. What Rastignac is to make of this is an open question. What my own students (who are poised to confront their own Balzacian dilemmas) make of it, or of their own looming choices, is unknown to me. They do not tell me; they do not even know. But a novel published almost two centuries ago does indeed refract their own lives. That is what it means to say that art mirrors nature, and that is how books live.

Charles Dickens's Pip: Haunted and Homeless

Near the very end of *Great Expectations*, Dickens's tragicomic masterpiece about a young boy whose trip from childhood to maturity, from blacksmith to gentleman, is all too easily read as social allegory, the ever-mysterious lawyer Jaggers—a man who knows everyone's dirty secret but who is himself inscrutable, calling to mind Balzac's Vautrin in a different key—discloses one of the novel's key secrets: his role in saving the child who grew up to be Estella.

> "Put the case that he lived in an atmosphere of evil, and that all he saw of children was, their being generated in great numbers for certain destruction. Put the case that he often saw children solemnly tried at a criminal bar, where they were held up to be seen; put the case that he habitually knew of their being imprisoned, whipped, transported, neglected, cast out, qualified in all ways for the hangman, and growing up to be hanged. Put the case that pretty nigh all the children he saw in his daily business life, he had reason to look upon as so much spawn, to develop into the fish that were to come to his net—to be prosecuted, defended, forsworn, made orphans, bedevilled somehow."

"I follow you, sir."

"Put the case, Pip, that here was one pretty little child out of the heap who could be saved; whom the father believed dead, and dared make no stir about; as to whom, over the mother, the legal adviser had this power."

With some license I would claim that Jaggers lays bare the generic conditions besetting children in Dickens: grisly, tending toward misery, death, or the gallows. It is against this that Jaggers has acted. But it seems crucial to recognize that Jaggers's heroic gesture has met with dubious results, to say the least. Yes, the child was saved, but the person it became—the cold and beautiful Estella, molded by the vengeful Miss Havisham to break men's hearts—is scarcely a success story. We are hard put not to see in her evolution from child to adult the same tragic pattern that Pip's trajectory reveals: failure of feeling, failure of judgment. One sought to be a gentleman; the other was raised as a gentlewoman. Each transgressed against the heart. In some disturbing sense, this ill-fated couple deserves each other, even though the narrative suasion of the novel seeks to persuade us of Pip's moral superiority over the insentient girl he worships. Is this the cost of experience? To deny human feeling? To realize it only late in life?

One pretty little child out of the heap who could be saved. Yes or no? To answer this question we turn, of course, to Pip, the child whose maturation seems so allegorical to us, readable as the fate of a boy who tackled caste and class in order to lift himself (or be lifted), as we Americans might say, by his bootstraps from blacksmith to gentleman. Remember that Balzac's Rastignac comes from a noble family; Pip, however, has no cultural capital, no manners, no ease. We already see Fitzgerald's Gatsby in the wings, even though Pip's rise is cued more to mysterious dark dealings by the fates, rather than titanic energy or some "green light." The social ramifications of this fable are not hard to grasp; one saw them in caricatural form in Quevedo's seventeenth-century story of Pablos, for whom border crossing is a comic convention, but the rising middle class (and its tidal swell) is no longer a subject for simple caricature in mid-nineteenth-century England. It is a fact—a fact that Charles Dickens himself lived out, in all its complexity, from drudge to world-famous author. He knew something about that journey.

What makes *Great Expectations* unforgettable is its rendition of Pip's tortured psyche. All of the wonderful touches of humor that Dickens can muster—the depictions of Pumblechook and Wopsle, the routines of Mrs. Joe, Joe's own sweet mannerisms, the touching relations between Wemmick and the Aged P, the fawning efforts of the female Pockets to pocket Havisham money—light up this story at the edges but do little to soften its dark center. Our abiding feeling from this novel stems from our conversance with Pip himself: genial, capable of wry humor and self-reflection, downright philosophical at times, yet deeply and incurably wounded from the outset and continuously injured as the book goes forward. Can it be an accident that the novel opens in a cemetery set among the marshes? Pip is there looking at the gravestones of his father, mother, and siblings, doing his countdown, trying to understand "the identity of things." Getting clear of the dead may not be easy.

The elements themselves rule here, more potent than the buried humans, more active in their role as impossible site, as ground zero for all human doing. The marshes are where Pip returns for many key encounters—sometimes figurative, as when Herbert begs him to give up Estella and Dickens writes, "I turned my head aside, for, with a rush and a sweep, like the old marsh winds coming up from the sea"; sometimes associatively, as Pip wonders why his entire past seems tainted by a mix of "prison and crime" forever bound to "lonely marshes on a winter evening"; sometimes invading London itself with their penetrating wind and rain, as when the long-lost convict makes his way into Pip's elegant lodgings to deliver his tidings, "Look'ee here, Pip. I'm your second father. You're my son—more to me nor any son"; reappearing as "stagnation and mud" and sheer primal ooze in the failed effort to escape by boat with Magwitch; and finally present as literal fate, as when the burned Pip makes his way back onto the selfsame marshes to the selfsame lime kiln, where he meets the crazed Orlick and comes close to meeting his death. The marshes parse his affective life.

Nonetheless, the marshes in *Great Expectations* constitute a dreadful mockery of *Heimat,* a place of raw inhuman corrosive energy where you cannot live but from which you cannot escape. They are "the identity of things." It is in this sense that Dickens's novel is more than a social parable about the price paid for becoming a "gentleman." More profoundly, it tells the story of a young boy whose only pact is with the marshes. To see Pip as moving from "grounded" blacksmith to "alienated" gentleman gets this book wrong, because its starkest testimony is in front of our eyes on the first page as we see Pip interrogating the gravestones and then meeting the convict. The little boy is lifted up violently by the convict and turned upside down—all with a kind of immediacy reminiscent of Grimmelshausen and announcing Faulkner—and we are to understand that the solid world can be turned upside down, might be just a stage set. Pip is, in some final way, homeless from the outset. Standing outside the forge, as a mere child, he looks up at the stars and considers "how awful it would be for a man to turn his face up to them as he froze to death, and see no help or pity in all the glittering multitude." He is looking at his fate: not just Estella (as the star imagery suggests), but the entire about-to-unfurl scenario of life with Miss Havisham and Co., then life in London.

Later in the novel, after Magwitch has returned and announced himself the source of the great expectations, Pip is mightily concerned to see that his benefactor eludes those tracking him: the law (which has no choice but to hang the returned criminal if it finds him), but especially Compeyson, the fiend of the book. All the pieces of the puzzle are beginning to assume their dark, damning coherence. Pip is returning home, tired, after a depressing visit with Miss Havisham and an Estella set upon a loveless marriage, but when he gets to Whitefriars Gate, he is handed a scribbled note with these fateful words: "Don't Go Home." Pip, unable to sleep in a strange lodging he's had to find, parses this injunction in every possible way: "Do not thou go home, let him not go home, let us not go home, do not ye or you go home, let not them go home. Then potentially: I may not and I cannot go home; and I might not, could not, would not, and should not go home." Wemmick has written this warning to signal trouble coming in the form of Compeyson, but we cannot escape the feeling that it broadcasts the novel's larger theme: there is no home to go to. There is no ground to stand on. Perhaps worst of all: there is no firm self to hold on to.

I am not suggesting that Dickens's Pip is already a random unbounded figure such as we find in Kafka, Beckett, or Camus. But I do want to say that this story of moral promiscuity, of molded and deformed children, of losing one's soul while seeking one's fortune, is cued to the elemental restlessness and miasma of the marshes, to a psychic mobility that will not be easily corralled into characterological form. Pip's relation to Joe and Biddy has the markings of a ballet: as the boy grows up under the shadow of his expectations, they recede, recede existentially, become unreachable. This is of course social: Pip the snob is ashamed of (what he sees as) their coarseness. But Dickens derives a painful poetry out of it, as in the late sequence when Pip is alone in London, but injured and delirious with fever, and Joe comes to nurse him. We see a heartbreaking return to childhood—Joe ministers to the boy, carries him, feeds him, nurses him—that cannot be sustained, and we watch Joe's manners become ever more stilted and "contrefait" as Pip regains strength. You can't go home. When Pip does go home, at novel's end, all prepared to ask Biddy to marry him, he relearns the same lesson: it is always/already too late, Biddy is marrying Joe, Pip is doomed to be alone. And strangely alien to himself. Even in sequences that seem entirely sociological, such as Pip's crushing awareness of his commonness in the eyes of Estella, one senses a disconnect that is also existential: "I was a common labouring-boy . . . my hands were coarse . . . my boots were thick . . . I was much more ignorant than I had considered myself last night . . . I was in a low-lived bad way." He is discovering that he is not who he thought he was.

Dickens's great genius as a writer is to convey to us this same kind of discovery. Philip Pirrip Esq. is a strange bird. There is much that Pip can see clearly: he intuits the identity of Estella, figures out who her parents are, fathoms the role of Compeyson in Miss Havisham's undoing, turns much mystery into fact. But the darkness at the core remains: I cannot see I. The most grotesque instance of the masquerade is the episode with Trabb's boy: Pip, demonstrably well heeled, saunters back to his village, receives the dripping homage of Pumblechook, but then encounters the fabulous treble mockery of Trabb's boy, who goes through an elaborate triple series of baroque gestures of bogus fealty, closing with just the right refrain: "Don't know yah, don't know yah, pon my soul don't know yah!" Comedy? Or central misprision? Do not forget the opening page: a child in a cemetery reading gravestones, trying to pin himself down, slated for upheaval and murk.

This young boy who discovered he was in a "low-lived bad way" is also haunted by guilt: guilt at helping the convict, guilt at being a blacksmith in training, guilt at becoming a snob. One might think that guilt is a solid feature of self, but Pip's guilt is of a different sort, shadowy and ungraspable, pointing to reaches in his makeup that are entirely beyond his ken or scrutiny. He can be other unto himself. We see this perhaps most pointedly in the early pages of the book, the so-called idyllic time, the time of the sweet childhood innocence that is (said) to be cashiered by his great expectations. Or so the story goes in traditional readings. But take a closer look: the early, bucolic Pip is already a tortured fellow. He may look back to this time as one of peace, but we can see it as one of strife and injury. All the colorful "types" that Dickens surrounds Pip with—Pumblechook, Wopsle, and most especially his own sister, Mrs. Joe—are an impossible lot to live with. Pip can never tell us this, but he cannot avoid showing us. Hence, as Mrs. Joe gives her recital of Pip's misdemeanors, the boy looks at Wopsle's Roman nose and confides to us "that I should have liked to pull it until he howled." Pumblechook is of course larger game, and when he pours himself a brandy that is actually half tar, Pip is certain that he "had murdered him somehow." By novel's end, Pumblechook comes to resemble Flaubert's Homais as a monstrous creature who invents his own fables and then imposes them on the community, in this case the fable of being Pip's true, genuine sponsor; and this moves from being comic to something darker and deeper, as Pip realizes that Pumblechook's deceit actually slanders Joe: "I had never been struck at so keenly, for my thanklessness to Joe, as through the brazen impostor Pumblechook. The falser he, the truer Joe; the meaner he, the nobler Joe." How not to see the true casualty here, the book's central impostor: Pip himself? Might not have been so bad to have "murdered him somehow," old Pumblechook, as a way of getting rid of the evidence.

My point is that Dickens is doing something quite radical in this novel: he is writing Pip all over this text, displaying his darker, unavowable wants in the text's nooks and crannies—and sometimes right out in the open, if we could but see. I am thinking of the key melodramatic scene of Miss Havisham's burning. Here is the book's sole moment of fierce somatic violence, and it takes place right where it should: on the floor, with the maggot-filled wedding cake on top of the players, accompanied doubtless by the spiders and beetles and rats whose home the cake has been. And who are the players? Pip and the old lady he's (wrongly, tragically) thought to be his benefactress. A man and a woman, body to body. On the surface, this is a heroic gesture on Pip's part: to try to save the life of this bitter old woman who has recognized her sins, and to do so at considerable personal cost (serious burning). But Dickens's language gets our attention here, makes us wonder if something else is also transpiring: "we were on the ground struggling like desperate enemies . . . the closer I covered her, the more wildly she shrieked and tried to free herself." Critics who have seen a form of sublimated sexual violence here, bordering on rape, are onto something, I believe, and it has to do with the layers of Pip's smoldering psyche that lie beneath his consciousness but that are now coming to expression. For this old woman is indeed the novel's witch: it is she who has introduced him to the cold Estella, made him think he was destined to marry the princess, led him on in exactly that delusion for years and years. How could he not—in some place deep inside—hate her? How could he ever admit it?

But the most sensational indictment of Pip as Other requires no textual sleuthing on our part: it comes via the good services of Orlick, who is hell-bent on murdering Pip to avenge himself for all the problems Pip has caused him earlier. *"Moi?"* Pip demurely asks. And we need to remember that Orlick courted Biddy, but that was cut short by Master Pip; and that Orlick was working at Miss Havisham's, until that too was cut short by our young man. Orlick's revenge comes in two installments, separated over time: he murders Mrs. Joe, and now, many years later, he is about to

murder Pip. Beyond even the motive of lost jobs is his undying hatred for the little boy who was favored, who basked in the affections of the blacksmith, who occupied the sole place in the sun. He
was loved, I was not: so goes Orlick's plaint.

But that is the least of it. Orlick murdered Mrs. Joe on Pip's orders: "Wolf . . . Old Orlick's a going to tell you somethink. It was
you as did for your shrew sister." Now, at last, the evil story of envy
and murder is out in the open:

> "I tell you it was your doing—I tell you it was done through
> you . . . I come upon her from behind, as I come upon you to-
> night. I giv' it her! I left her for dead, and, if there had been a
> limekiln as nigh her as there is now nigh you, she shouldn't
> have come to life again. But it warn't Old Orlick as did it; it
> was you. You was favoured, and he was bullied and beat. Old
> Orlick bullied and beat, eh? Now you pays for it. You done it;
> now you pays for it."

Dickensian mysteries lead to murk as well as to light. Orlick
says far more than he knows. He is functioning here, as he has in
the past, as Pip's alter ego, as the unsayable enraged side of Pip.
Hence we are obliged to ponder just how "favoured" Pip was, and
just why being favored would somehow bring about murder: "It
was you as did for your shrew sister." And we remember all those
apparently comic touches about being brought up by hand, about
being reminded of every small misdemeanor, of being incessantly
hounded throughout one's childhood, and we conclude: Can one
get past injury? Could Orlick's words have their psychic truth? The
figurative rape of Miss Havisham and the figurative murder of
Mrs. Joe weigh heavy in the docket against Philip Pirrip Esq., demanding that we incorporate their affective tidings into our
emerging portrait. They confirm him as a citizen of the marshes.
Not that they make him a villain—he remains decent, and he remains our essential conduit for the story, our own surrogate—but
they testify to the indelible stain of human experience, to the reality of emotional damage and psychic injury. They give this
beloved book a Dostoevskian tinge.

Above all, they limn a portrait of childhood that is arguably richer than any other of the nineteenth century, for it registers the actual slings and arrows that Pip has suffered, slings and arrows that make it through the genial comic defenses of the novel and point to its costs. Pip is the lonely fellow whose graveyard tears open the book, who is terrified by his complicity with the convict, who is riddled with guilt, who is heir to visions (he repeatedly sees Miss Havisham hanging), who has a good bit of garbage in him. He is haunted forever by returnees from the past: Magwitch, Compeyson, Orlick, Mrs. Joe. He can neither return nor exit. Homeless (both inwardly and outwardly), haunted (both inwardly and outwardly), Pip is the caught child. Experience will exercise his ghosts, but it will not exorcise them. This is why the book finishes perfectly, whichever ending one prefers, because both endings are twilight endings, chastened endings, endings to lives that have been misspent and error-driven, prey to spirits and pulsions beyond his ken. Lazarillo, Pablos, and Rastignac completed their education by learning how their respective cultures operate and then devising their own coping strategy. For the lacerated Pip, it is tougher going, mistakes are made, self-knowledge is hard to come by, no one gets clear, the ghosts are on the inside; he finishes as he began, injured. He is testimony to bad news that we do not expect from a seemingly sentimental writer: that growing up is hard to do.

Understanding Power: Growing Up as the Invisible Man

Balzac's Vautrin dreamed, in the early nineteenth century, of finishing his days in America as "Mr. Four-Millions," surrounded by black slaves to do his bidding. Racial business as usual in America, Vautrin has to have thought. But of course we in latter-day America know that these arrangements were and are anything but neutral. Major white and black writers have tackled these matters: one thinks of Faulkner, Zora Neale Hurston, Richard Wright. But Ralph Ellison's *Invisible Man* stands especially in our minds as a stunning mid-twentieth-century installment of the Bildungsroman, approaching race through a prism quite different from those of any of his predecessors, while also committed to a remarkable investigation of the workings of power and how it impacts the story of growing up. Ellison had his debts to the great modernists James Joyce and T. S. Eliot, and he sought to create a playful, improvisational account of a young man's difficult education, reminiscent of the techniques of jazz and the blues. But I cannot help seeing the shadow of Balzac in this novel, especially the Balzac who is on show in the figure of Vautrin; Ellison is not going to give us a comparably omniscient figure with a blueprint, but his aims are the same: to explore the huge gap between polite versions of how society operates, on the one hand, and the grisly yet systemic nastiness underneath, on the other. It seems fair to say that the protagonist negotiates this crucial divide his entire life. Like Lazarillo and Pablos, he needs to wake up to how things actually work, so that he can finally take charge of his own life. That will not be easy. But once again, experience is to be the teacher.

In a way that echoes *Père Goriot, Great Expectations,* and *Huckleberry Finn,* Ellison's novel is in search of fathers, but the results are going to be dire. We follow the protagonist's slow, seemingly dense, certainly arduous transformation from docile believer in Booker T. Washington's doctrine of uplift via humility and submission on to increasingly violent and picaresque adventures in New York, most notably his long stint with the Brotherhood, a Marxist collective aimed at altering society through strict application of dogma, and finally on to the spectacular close in the famous Harlem race riots, after which our man assumes his key position underground. At issue in each of these ventures is the burning desire to see clear, to devise a strategy and a posture for effecting genuine social change.

At its best, *Invisible Man* is an incandescent fiction, larded with startling, over-the-top episodes that are luminous, even surreal, in their workings, even if mystifying to the protagonist. These episodes carry the book's abiding vision of power, its vision of what you must know in order to grow up. The *you* referred to is not merely the hero of the fiction; it is also today's reader, for whom this story of growing racial awareness, although more than a half century behind us, still writes large a number of key, scary, not easily forgettable dictates in American culture.

Let's start with the first failed initiation: the Battle Royal. Here is the book's first ugly piece of business: black youths are invited to a white smoker, and our protagonist, the class valedictorian, is eagerly awaiting his opportunity to give his speech to this assembled group. Expecting an opportunity to display his earnestness and oratory, he has failed to ponder just why he and his cohort would be told to put on their boxing togs. Half-naked, in a ballroom filled with half-drunk bankers, judges, doctors, and the like, he and his cohort now see the other attraction: a naked blonde doing a slow, writhing dance, arousing the elders, arousing also the young blacks (whose erections are all too visible). As the woman goes through her bump and grind, the men lose control, start to grab her, but order is established by launching into the next number: putting the black boys, blindfolded, into the ring. The crowd's frenzy grows greater still as the black youths are ordered to strike one another, blindly, with increasing panic and ferocity. All the while our boy is wondering when he'll give his speech, even though blows are landing on him constantly. Finally the boys are invited to come up and receive their money, placed on a rug, but the rug is electrified, it turns out, creating a spectacle of wet, twitching, jerking bodies whose every contact with the money violently jolts them with flowing current.

There is something spellbinding in Ellison's lurid depiction of racist fun and games: the leering and drunk white power brokers, aroused by both the naked white woman and the jolted, contorted young black male bodies, seem like a textbook exercise of displaced energies, of obscene puns such as current/currency. And we also register some very old racist clichés about black people— they have rhythm, they can dance—by noting how gruesomely Ellison has updated them, put them into electric shock form, turned them into torture.

Against this anarchic backdrop the protagonist tries manfully to deliver his speech, trips up in saying "social equality" instead of "social responsibility," is chastised for his error, but is at the end of the day rewarded for his dutiful performance: he receives a calfskin briefcase. This briefcase is to be one of the chief icons of the novel, and it will accompany the boy right through his adventures and trials, up to the final moment when he jettisons it. But already now, that briefcase reveals its potent message via the dream the boy has that night: he's in a circus with his grandfather—a man who has offered his wisdom to the family in the guise of "yessing" white folks until they either vomit or bust wide open—who insists that he open the briefcase, and inside it he finds this message: "To Whom It May Concern: Keep This Nigger-Boy Running." Here is a formula for the entire novel, it seems to me, as well as a disillusioned picture of racial arrangements in twentieth-century America. Given the way Ellison has packaged this venom—a script hidden in a briefcase as fantasized in a dream but later to be actualized when the boy finally sees the diabolical contents of the letter of introduction he is carrying from his college to various job interviews—we begin to grasp how slippery things are going to be here, how arduous it might be to get underneath the surface of things.

We move from the Battle Royal to the university, where our protagonist has a leadership position but is, once again, poised for a disaster he will fail to interpret. It comes in the shape of chauffeuring Mr. Norton, the philanthropic white trustee (who is mourning, in Poe-like libidinal terms, the death of his daughter). The student and trustee come across Jim Trueblood. What white Norton has dreamed and repressed, black Trueblood has enacted, but done so in hallucinatory fashion. This black farmer has sired a baby on his own daughter and has become something of a minor tourist attraction of the area. Not unlike the Ancient Mariner, Trueblood has a story to deliver himself of, and once again, it will be enacted in dreams, as if only this oneiric discourse allowed Ellison to bring into his text the powerful and poetic cargo it needs.

Trueblood and his wife share their bed with his eldest daughter, we learn; the girl sleeps in the middle. It is pitch dark; mother and daughter sleep, father feels keenly the presence and smell of the girl, hears her say "Daddy" in her sleep, begins to reminisce about his salad days, feels Matty Lou start to squirm against him, and then commences to dream. What a dream it is. It centers on going to see (white) Mr. Broadnax looking for "fat meat," going through the front door, finding no one, going through the bedroom door, smelling "woman," hearing and seeing a grandfather clock strike, seeing a white lady step out of the glass door, clad in a silky nightgown with nothing else on, wanting to run but having no exit (except the clock door), being grabbed around the neck and held tight by the woman, being kept out of the clock, flinging her onto the bed, seeing little white geese come out of the bed, hearing a door open with Mr. Broadnax saying "They just nig-guhs, leave 'em do it," trying again to exit via the clock door, get-ting inside and finding it hot and dark, going up a dark tunnel, approaching the machinery that is making all that noise (resem-bling the power plant by the school), feeling it get hotter and hot-ter, running, then flying, then sailing, yet always in the tunnel, finally spying a bright light that bursts "like a great big electric light in my eyes," feeling scalded, yet finally outside and in the cool daylight again. (I have chosen to write this oneiric sequence as one long, unbroken, breathless sentence, so as to convey its utter authority.)

Sequences like the Battle Royal and Trueblood's dream an-nounce that we are in modern territory, faced with a kind of writ-ing that is wildly emancipated, possessed of a poetic logic that cries out for interpretation: the sort of thing unavailable to and unimaginable by novelists of earlier times. A quantum leap be-yond even the displacements on show in Dickens's portrayal of Pip, Ellison's growing-up story now comes to us as an urgent psy-chic phenomenon of remarkable density, pointing toward layers of affect, desire, and censorship that might well have subtended the affairs of Lazarillo or Pablos or Rastignac but that only now make it into writing.

Back to Trueblood. Not knowing how to make amends for his incestuous behavior (even though hit with an ax by his wife), Trueblood eventually ends up singing the blues. *Singing the blues.* At this point we realize how self-aware this fiction is, how even its most primitive scenes of violence and transgression eventuate into art, into form. One feels that Ellison's entire novel is obeying this injunction.

I rehearse this astonishing episode in detail to convey how compelling and dictatorial it is, how it is hell-bent on utterance, on finding a language for libido's dance, no matter how much it interrupts and makes a mockery out of any docile plot scheme. This material wants out. Above all, Ellison is offering us a code language for the way power is conceived in this book. For we can scarcely fail to see that the woman's body and the sexual drive are inseparable from the heat and noise of machinery, imaged in the clock and the glass door but also referenced in the power plant near the school. There is much to ponder here. Body/clock/machine/power plant emerges as a gestalt, a cluster of seemingly distinct things now united as carriers of energy, gesturing toward an entire discourse of occulted power. Displacement reigns everywhere in the strange world that Ellison is charting: a place of liminality, transgressions, imperious circuits, and raw hunger, a glowing map of how power is always disguised, lives in dreams and drag, operates behind the scenes, makes all people do its bidding, resists the light of day and the clarity of design.

I have intentionally played the professor here by insisting long and loudly on the figurative connections and emerging coherence of Ellison's prose. But please note: the protagonist himself—an unfathoming witness—understands nothing, nothing whatsoever. Hence he is doomed to endless repetition: he will encounter still further enactments of this same systemic force, coming at him in repeated episodes of trauma and lunacy but never turned into personal knowledge. And here is one key interpretation of the book's title: not only are black people invisible to white, but it is the very nature of ideology—what levers and forces actually govern the world you inhabit—to be invisible to its adherents. Ellison's novel may well frustrate today's readers, because it seems as though it takes an awfully long time for its young hero truly to catch on, to grasp the actual meaning of what is befalling him. "Don't you realize? Don't you get it?" we want to scold him.

But hold on. The body grows up a lot quicker than the mind does. Maybe we're always playing catch-up (at best) or blindman's bluff (at worst) with the ideological makeup of our condition; maybe we're always as benighted as this young man is. Oedipus never saw clear until late, late in the game. Remember the innocence of Blake's chimney sweep: he never did get it right either, never did lay bare the sources of power that consign him to living death in chimneys. Maybe the integrity of *Invisible Man* lies just here. The Vautrins who offer a printout of society, who take the young aside and show them exactly what is to come—such figures may exist in literature but never in life. Deans and professors, as I said, fail at this task, for they are as much cogs in the machine, victims of the "murky mirror," as students are. Maybe all of us are caught up in the midst of arrangements whose logic we can never make out, even though it governs our lives both inwardly and outwardly. Do you really know what is in that briefcase you're carrying through your life?

At his best, Ellison goes about this gulf between event and explanation like a poet, like a writer who composes musically, with a certain number of motifs that are going to be sounded and resounded, even if in different contexts and with seemingly different colorations. Hence, after the utter fiasco with Mr. Norton—the episode with Trueblood is followed by a still more manic incident, this time at the Golden Day (bar and brothel), where we see a mix of madmen and damaged veterans engaged in bouts of violence and philosophical speculation about the evils of race in America—the protagonist is called in to the formidable head of the school, Mr. Bledsoe, to get some much-needed reality lessons. Bledsoe cannot believe that our man has been idiot enough to take Norton to Trueblood's farm, and he wants the boy to understand that he, Bledsoe, is not going to put up with such idiocy. Like so many of Ellison's characters, he then launches into his own tirade about the absolute control he exercises in the school: "I's big and black and I say 'Yes, suh' as loudly as any burrhead when it's convenient, but I'm still the king down here. I don't care how much it appears otherwise. Power doesn't have to show off." (One remembers the grandfather's "yes strategy.") This is followed by a prophetic piece of advice: "You let the white folks worry about pride and dignity—you learn where you are and get yourself power, influence, contacts with powerful and influential people—then stay in the dark and use it!"

For my money, this is what Balzac's Vautrin would sound like in an American racial setting. We are not far, here, from a dialectics of invisibility: if you want control, you exercise it hidden. Bledsoe, the theorist of operating in the dark, it turns out, is as good as his word: he sends the boy out into the world with sealed, poisonous letters of introduction tucked away in his precious briefcase. Poor hero: blindsighted in every direction, misreading what has happened to him, being set up for further misadventures—more in the line of Simplicius or a chimney sweep than Lazarillo or Pablos or Rastignac.

How would you write a novel and chart an education, following this vision of occulted power? As I said, Ellison's protagonist is excruciatingly slow on the uptake, finding himself in crisis after crisis, where others are doing the controlling and he is playing the marionette. The crescendo arrives when our man takes on a job at Liberty Paints, where his task is to assist in the production of its great specialty paint, Optic White, "the purest white that can be found," a white that is used to paint national monuments. Our first surprise here is the discovery that white may be no more than an optic. (Toni Morrison would take this perception a good bit further in her book *Playing in the Dark*.) To the protagonist's amazement, the fellow responsible for producing Optic White is a surly, uneducated, little old black man, working some three levels underneath the main factory, named Lucius Brockway. He, and only he, has the secret. He is the power magnate. All the others, the whites, the so-called engineers and trained folks, "they just mixes in the color, make it look pretty. Right down here is where the real paint is made." Brockway divulges the core truth: "we the machines inside the machine." It is the yearned-for wisdom of this novel, even if expressed in an industrial figure: Bledsoe and Brockway embody it; can the protagonist get there? Lazarillo and Rastignac saw into the machinery of their world; can Ellison's hero do as much?

Brockway, being utterly paranoid about being replaced by the young, thinks the protagonist is a spy, and very quickly things spiral out of control, producing a homicidal battle between these two figures, with distinct Oedipal implications. At this point, nourished by resentments building ever since Battle Royal and Bledsoe, our man (brought up to respect his elders) finally pops, and another battle royal takes place. The two start to tear each other apart, no holds barred, but the stronger boy overcomes the old man. (At some primitive level, this is what must darkly fuel the story of both growing up and growing old; we will see more of its threatening power in the second half of this study.) However, in the process the gauges—the gauges! don't forget: we're in a factory—have been ignored, and the machines, as if cued to the manic humans, go haywire. Gauges swing madly, needles dance, wheels resist, goo covers hands, and it all closes with an explosion: "I seemed to run swiftly up an incline and shot forward with sudden acceleration into a wet blast of black emptiness that was somehow a bath of whiteness." Everything comes together, we realize: the clock door, the heat, the violence, the pulsions, the machinery, the power plant. These are the icons of the system, and they are grinding the protagonist to bits.

"Shot forward," Ellison writes; a rebirth is about to happen. The hero will wake up in a clinical setting, reduced to zero, not knowing who he is, turned utterly malleable, fodder for an experiment, faced with mocking white-coated figures who intend to make him anew. This black youth's growing-up story is pathologized, enters the medical regime, showing us that victimization takes on new guises in the twentieth century. Our man lies there, paralyzed, now the perfect specimen for behavioral engineering. In a book filled with violence, this almost refrigerated scene is the scariest. The critical step through the clock door seems to have been taken. He is *in the machine*—but as cog, not as controller. Machines hum, voices are heard as he is prepped, then there is a whirring "that snapped and cracked with static, and suddenly I seemed to be crushed between floor and ceiling. . . . I was pounded between crushing electrical pressures; pumped between live electrodes like an accordion between a player's hands." The musical image is telling: the entire quest of this book is to move from being "played on" to becoming a "player." There is much cruelty in this sequence as the personnel shoot current into him, make his body dance (blacks do have rhythm, they remark), his teeth chatter, his mouth fill up with blood. The treatment is supposed to erase all prior identity markings, and it does: he is now a blank sheet. Only one faint memory stays: that of Buckeye the Rabbit, blending with Br'er Rabbit, creatures of black folklore, as if to say, here is the permanent residue of race and it will not go away.

The book is now poised to complete the learning curve, via the protagonist's long stint with the Brotherhood, acting as its agent in Harlem. The story of maturation has acquired its defining contours. After all, he has been turned invisible and let loose, quasi-lobotomized. He has yet to act on the key principle that invisibility is the precondition of power if you know how to harness the system, to operate the machinery (rather than being operated by it). The long political education that constitutes the book's second half is stamped by the hero's growing awareness of being used (again) by others. He gradually realizes that he is a pawn of the Brotherhood; he also comes to understand that its ideology is utterly unequipped to take the measure of race as the dominant factor in the social misery that needs changing.

And, reminiscent of both *Père Goriot* and *Great Expectations*, the novel reworks its family tropes, redefines the unit that matters, makes us rethink notions of both family and community, so that the young man increasingly realizes that his search for "fathers" must yield to a recognition of his true "brothers," brothers with no connection to the Brotherhood. Rastignac had to choose between Goriot and Vautrin; Pip has to recognize that Magwitch is his figurative father. Ellison's protagonist, at book's end, has to define himself against a cluster of black brothers: Tod Clifton the Jesus figure, who is shot down by the police; Raz the Exhorter, who wants to jolt Harlem into militant action against white folks; and most mysterious of all, Rinehart the numbers runner and ladies' man, with whom our protagonist is significantly mistaken. All three of these "brothers" are figures of racial reaction. One is sacrificed, one preaches war, and the third works via mask and cunning. Together they constitute a weave of black positions, all geared to a central awareness of race as the governing principle of behavior. The protagonist elects at the end to take on their collective mantle, via his move to the underground, living in a blaze of electric lightbulbs, thinking through his next moves, and telling his story.

Invisible Man, despite its sound and fury, can often allow the protagonist himself to remain marginal to events, including events where he is at center stage. One feels that the fellows administering the electric shock treatment may have succeeded in emptying the protagonist, in making him a cipher. He is muffled throughout, from the thick incomprehension displayed at the Battle Royal on through his encounters with power figures who know how to work the system: Bledsoe, Brockway, folks applying electrodes, Brotherhood chiefs, and finally the triad of black brothers who represent the possibilities of taking a genuine existential stand. What is to be his stand? How will he go about altering society? By going underground. By assuming the mantle of invisibility. By entering the machinery. He reminds me a great deal of Rastignac at the close of *Père Goriot:* the law student makes his fateful choice of living masked, of hiding the heart. And perhaps that is the grimmer truth that shines through this long novel. Purposive behavior goes out of business. Social change remains beyond the pale. Ellison has limned a portrait of a man responding to the system by virtually disappearing, by being almost erased.

But not entirely. He has not lit out for the Territory, he is not dead, he is not living in a cave in Crete. He lodges quite comfortably, thank you, in his extravagantly well-lit laboratory, taking current from the system without paying for it, thinking through his options, recognizing his place in a long line of American thinker-tinkers, beginning with Franklin and Edison. He has come a long way. And, like the Ancient Mariner, he has a tale to deliver himself of, a story about race in America and how hard it is to see clear. Ellison's chastened protagonist, so unequal to circumstances throughout his picaresque adventures, evinces considerable wisdom in his final parting shot: "Who knows, but that, on the lower frequencies, I speak for you?"

And he does. I'd suggest that we live in a time when the curse of invisibility—so long a trope of science fiction—bids to become the ideological truth of our own dark age, stamping not merely racial differences but economic, class, religious, ethnic, tribal, and national differences. His arduous journey toward light, so triumphantly and literally enacted at the book's klieglike shiny close, reads like a modern-day Ibsen tale of maturation and seeing clear. With considerable pizzazz and brio, Ellison has written this odyssey in musical fashion, giving us a rhythmic, often dazzling spectacle of figure and mask, of the paths to self-enactment as motifs in a score, as improvisational riffs in a performance. It is a provocative model, for it transforms what is hardest about the weight of facts and experience—the hardness of the jug or statue that Lazarillo's head collided with, the hardness of racism in mid-twentieth-century America—into something malleable, musical, and even masterable.

The noted scholar Henry Louis Gates has posited "signifyin' " as the central strategy of much African-American literature, by which he means that the freedom of the oppressed lies in their ability to rework and twist and put to their own uses the forms handed down by the oppressor. It is a handsome thesis, at once creative and unillusioned, and perhaps it gestures toward a can-do-ism that is broadly American and not exclusive to black artists, for perhaps we are always doomed to fashion whatever freedoms and fictions we can out of the facts that hold us in bondage. Lazarillo finishes as town crier, Pablos as con man, Rastignac as someone poised to sell out, Pip as chastened young man. They do not change the world. So it is that the Invisible Man liberates no one—certainly not the oppressed of Harlem—other than himself. But all of them live to tell the tale. Perhaps the story of experience can go no further than that.

Love

Roughly a third of the way into Laurence Sterne's brilliant eighteenth-century narrative potpourri, *Tristram Shandy*, the author informs us that it is time to write his preface. Hence, well into my account of the business of childhood, the trip from morning to noon, I now come to the central, abiding life force that reigns over the experience of growing up, often determining whether it is even-keeled, nurtured, ecstatic, deprived, or destroyed: love. Happy love, sad love, twisted love, abusive love, no love: surely our trajectory through childhood (and life itself) is deeply, crucially enabled or disabled by this basic motor force. Whether it be the role of family, the discovery of passion, the treatment of peers, the victimization by society, or the grieving for the dead, the young are formed and deformed by their apprenticeship with this primal feeling in all its many guises.

One reason I place this topic so late in the book is that I've been talking about love all along, since there is no way to imagine growing up without referencing it or its lack. Blake's innocent chimney sweep is at once deprived of love and overflowing with it, as he comforts and counsels little Tom Dacre. What Huckleberry Finn feels deep inside him, so deep that it is at war with all the received views of his culture (including the voice of conscience), is a tender, abiding emotional attachment for an escaped slave, an attachment that is profoundly familial, for Jim emerges as Huck's figurative father. Given the racism of the culture, it is indeed a love that dare not speak its name. The *pícaros* Lazarillo and Pablos seem untouched by love—it would seem an incredible luxury item as well as a vulnerability in their straitened affairs—but the same cannot be said for Rastignac, whose affection for Delphine is real and whose beautiful ministrations for Goriot constitute whatever "heart" Balzac's novel has. Pip's entire life can be seen as parsed by the presence, absence, construing, and misconstruing of love: hopelessly pining for the cold and haughty Estella, painfully recognizing the humanity and tenderness of Magwitch the convict, realizing too late that Joe and Biddy offered him the true kindness, nurturance, and affection that can never be regained.

How do we measure the love we receive or lack? Neither science nor psychology can give us a definitive answer, for neither empirical research nor sustained introspection yields a bottom line. Many of us spend our entire lives trying to get a fix on this elusive equation, and we do so because we realize it is the factor most responsible for determining who we are, who we've become. Yet just as we cannot see the oxygen we must inhale in order to breathe and live, we cannot easily gauge the lines of force that are so regnant in our development over time. In that regard literature can be invaluable to us as a map of human feelings, a curious map that writes large what must forever elude our retina: the reality of connection, the linkages we seek or suffer, the relationships that nurture or coerce the self we take ourselves to be. Novels offer a strange cartography along just these lines, for they are perforce ecosystems, charting the individual's comings and goings within a mesh that contains others: loved others, hated others, ignored others, sometimes fatal others. Still more remarkably, these categories do not rule one another out: the story of love invariably runs the gamut of all these poles and positions, for they constitute its force field. What is love, if not the elemental opening of self onto something larger, whether it calls itself parents, lovers, society, country, even God? That crucial opening is the precondition of our moral and emotional growth, but it is also the threshold stage that exposes us to hurt as well as ecstasy, to injury or death as well as fulfillment and happiness. These are the inevitable, generic conditions of growing up.

In the pages ahead, we will examine love's place in the story of growing up by discussing four distinct areas of human experience: falling in love, suffering abuse, being sacrificed, coming to terms with the nightmare of history. As different as these may appear, their significance in the development of young people is cued directly to the basic need for love and the consequences thereof. Literature gifts us with a sighting on these matters and thereby helps us to a clearer understanding of where we ourselves have been and what has happened to us on our journey.

Falling in Love

Falling in love is the glorious, liminal experience that so many of us place at the center of growing up. It does not seem exaggerated to regard it as the greatest show on earth, as the defining adventure of growing up, as the primordial challenge to both identity and society, for it bids to alter both. I would hope that anyone reading these pages has some firsthand knowledge of the topic. But it is also true that much of what we know about this crucial phase in human life comes to us from books. Don Quixote was doomed to see the world through the prism of courtly romances; Emma Bovary went into adulthood nourished (blinded) by the love stories she had read in the convent. Well before puberty all of us are acculterated into notions of love, notions we inevitably (even if unknowingly) bring to our love life. It can seem strange that love—seemingly the most intimate and personal of human experiences—is also something of a readymade, something molded and pre-contoured in our minds and hearts well before we try it out in reality. Time for a closer look. I want now to tackle this rich, explosive theme head-on by looking at a sequence of ex-

emplary texts about such matters that might serve as a baseline
for our understanding of what young love means.

William Shakespeare's Romeo and Juliet

Who does not know the story of the star-crossed lovers from
Verona? "Romeo" has passed, *as name*, into the popular culture,
designating a "lover-boy." Love may be born inside the human
heart, but it quickly extends, via Shakespeare's lyricism, into the
firmament, displaying its fuller cosmic dimensions. Here is a form
of emotional space travel antedating by many centuries our scientific era but possessed of comparable boosting power. Romeo, hidden, is mesmerized by the sight of the fair Juliet on her balcony,
and he proffers the well-known Petrarchan comparison of eyes to
stars, feeling that the heavenly stars "entreat her eyes / To twin-
kle in their spheres." Love makes curious as well as tender: he
takes his own metaphor seriously and asks, "What if her eyes were
there, they in her head?" To this fine query comes an answer, and
what was a cliché explodes into something far richer: "The
brightness of her cheek would shame those stars / As daylight
doth a lamp; her eyes in heaven / Would through the airy region
stream so bright / That birds would sing and think it were not
night."

There we have it: love propels the loved one into the heavenly
bodies, but as a force of transfiguration and power, deifying the
human while refiguring the natural order, so that human beauty
"shames" that of the heavens and Juliet's radiance becomes outright demiurgic, turning night into light, tricking the birds and
triggering their song. Young love alters all givens, redistributes
light and dark, sound and silence, makes a world of its own.
"Brave new world," Miranda will say in *The Tempest*, announcing
the core truth about love's explosive, quasi-colonializing power, inserting the human into a richer, grander world than before, put
there as monarch. Each love text we will study reaffirms this elemental fact: love rebirths us, gifts us with a new homeland. (There
can be terror as well as beauty in these arrangements.)

Later in the play, married but not yet "enjoyed" (as she puts it),
Juliet wonderfully reverses the radiance scenario imagined by

Romeo, for she awaits her lover/husband. And again the cosmos is refigured: "Come, gentle Night, come, loving, black-browed Night, / Give me my Romeo, and when I shall die, / Take him and cut him out in little stars, / And he will make the face of heaven so fine / That all the world will be in love with night / And pay no worship to the garish sun." Night, gentle and dark, is the time for lovemaking. But we can scarcely fail to note what is more broadly dark in her words: her death leading to a dead Romeo, cut into little stars, even if still so entrancing that he will overtrump the sun and command the love of all.

The laws of gravity also yield to love's indwelling power. Romeo asserts to Juliet that love endowed him with wings, and the Friar informs us that "A lover may bestride the gossamers [spiderweb] / That idles in the wanton summer air, / And yet not fall," displaying yet again love's unique vehicular power. But leaping over walls, leaping even into the firmament, implies feeling's outward reach; Shakespeare is no less concerned to speak of its inward weight and measure, and there are few domestic notations in literature that match Romeo's exquisite desire, when he is transfixed by her on the balcony, to touch Juliet's face: "O that I were a glove upon that hand, / That I might touch that cheek." The playwright's large-souled register comes into view here: among the stars, bestriding spiderwebs, becoming a glove, all this writes large the mix of ecstasy (propelling outward) and intimacy (flesh to flesh) that charts love's course. This is exquisite: young love thrusts us into new precincts, so that body and universe intermingle, each empowering the other.

"Stony limits cannot hold love out," Romeo declares, and the phrase has a carceral feel to it: walls cannot contain this newborn desire of ours, and much of the tragedy's pathos has to do with those walls, which can indeed be glimpsed in the obstacles of the story: the feud between the Montagues and the Capulets, the curse even of name itself, as suggested by Juliet's immortal lines "What's in a name? that which we call a rose / By any other word would smell as sweet." There is something quite modern in these two young lovers' awareness of their entrapment in a nominal scheme that has nothing to do with the exalted feeling that courses through them, making them feel that love is, or should be, a territory of its own, free of the laws that otherwise govern our affairs. Romeo and Juliet's courage in defying family prohibition is on the order of a declaration of independence.

Love remakes the young, recomposes them, gives them dimensions they did not have before. Juliet, though she is not yet fourteen, displays a sublime generosity along just these lines, telling us that her love for Romeo mocks all measures: "My bounty is as boundless as the sea, / My love as deep; the more I give to thee, / The more I have, for both are infinite." If I had to single out a line from this play that spoke most perfectly the miracle of young love, it would be those words. Loss, gain, and the entire zero-sum logic of our finite dealings—I give you this, and I no longer have it—are cashiered in this beautiful utterance. Brave new world—a new physics, a new metaphysics. One cannot easily imagine older, more experienced lovers feeling quite this way.

But it is not to be. Their love will be consummated—at least they have that—but it will have no future. Why? Some have felt that the parents are fully to blame, and of course the feud is a crucial piece of the puzzle, not to mention old Capulet's choleric rants. Others have said that society is at fault, and that too has its truth. And it has been claimed that they simply have rotten luck, also unarguable, for the final scene with Juliet waking up after Romeo has swallowed the poison, culminating in a double death because the postal service failed, well, that is hard to take. *If only*, we say to ourselves, thinking: Why must cousin Tybalt cross paths with Mercutio? Why must Romeo return just in time for avenging his death? Why must Romeo be unapprised of the Friar's fake poison scheme? Why must Balthasar tell Romeo that Juliet is now dead? Above all: Why must poor Romeo arrive in the tomb exactly at the moment he does, since a mere few extra minutes would have cleared up all errors? *Then*, we think: love could have had a chance.

But perhaps Shakespeare is reaching deeper than all this in his severe plot. One of the most endearing aspects of the play (which makes it irresistible onstage) is the sheer exuberance and impatience of these two young people. One remembers the scene where the Nurse returns to Juliet out of breath and toying with her young charge before giving her the report she is so desperate to have: that Romeo is prepared to marry her at once. We identify with such scenes, even if we are old and gray, for love boiled in our veins long ago, and we can remember the urgency of it all. Out of breath the Nurse is, and we laugh; out of breath, permanently, both lovers will be, at play's close, and we weep. This love story is indeed breathless, in a rush, urgent. But can time be bent to one's ends? Can pulsing blood be a fault?

Even Juliet cautions her lover not to move so quickly: "It is too rash, too unadvised, too sudden, / Too like the lightning, which does cease to be / Ere one can say, 'It lightens.' " Does lightning make durable light? *Son et lumière:* the sound of the thunder and the brilliance of the light, yes, these are the markers of ecstatic love, but can such a spectacle last? The Friar pronounces similar words to Romeo in an effort to slow him down: "These violent delights have violent ends / And in their triumph die like fire and powder, / Which as they kiss consume. The sweetest honey / Is loathsome in his own deliciousness, / And in the taste confounds the appetite. / Therefore love moderately, long love doth so; / Too swift arrives as tardy as too slow." I think Shakespeare is not simply peddling the wisdom of graybeards but rather telling us something about the makeup and fate of desire itself, of ecstasy itself. The Friar's figures are arresting: desire is destroyed by consummation, just as fire and powder end in explosion and quiescence. The sweetest things can be taken only in moderation, else they turn loathsome by excess. Is fiery young love sustainable?

Romeo and Juliet is certainly not a cautionary fable. And both Romeo and Juliet grow and mature in front of our eyes, as they take the measure of their new selves and new responsibilities toward love, toward each other. But who can fail to see that its view of pleasure and delight is shadowed by death and destruction? Over and over, death is figured as the ultimate lover, the one destined for Juliet—she says it more than once, her mother and her father both say it, in heat but also in prophecy—the one we see at play's end, when Romeo himself thinks her dead in the tomb and swears to stay with her, to prevent the "lean abhorrèd monster" from being her "paramour." And even in the play's vitals, in its evocation of vibrant physical love, in the very caresses between two young people infatuated with each other, we are invited to see something darker. I am thinking of the lovely initial encounter between Romeo and Juliet with its elaborate wordplay on pilgrims, praying, hands, and lips, closing with the young man twice pressing his lips to hers, invoking the language of religion and sweetly inverting it into that of love: "Sin from my lips? O trespass sweetly urged! / Give me my sin again." How ominous all this looks at play's end, when each of the lovers has experimented with poisons—Juliet's temporary, Romeo's permanent— and each, seeing the supine body of the loved one, proffers a final kiss. Listen to Juliet: "I will kiss thy lips, / Haply some poison yet doth hang on them, / To make me die with a restorative." It does not work; Juliet dies by stabbing herself with a dagger.

But how can we not glimpse a grisly poetic truth here: that kissing is venomous as well as ecstatic, that it can transport us out of life entirely? This immortal story of impatient pure beautiful young love is saturated with duels and poisons—sword fights litter the stage with cadavers (Mercutio, Tybalt, Paris), Juliet's mother wants nothing more than to have Romeo poisoned abroad; Juliet offers to give him the poison herself in a savage line of erotic violence, "To wreak the love I bore my cousin [Tybalt] / Upon his body [Romeo's] that hath slaughtered him"—and we are obliged to ask if they are not, in the final analysis, versions of each other. There is nothing cynical or morbid in such a view; on the contrary, Shakespeare has remained true to this vision of ecstatic young love as an exit from all the precincts that formerly contained us. All of us have heard that the French call orgasm *"la petite mort"*; Shakespeare has wanted to celebrate the wonder and beauty of first love, capable of reordering the world and transcending all limits. Except death's, which is of the party from curtain up to curtain down.

Abbé Prévost's Manon Lescaut

Romeo and Juliet may be star-crossed, but they are not classcrossed; Montagues and Capulets are equal, but we cannot imagine Romeo falling in love with a servant girl. The Chevalier des Grieux, the young, aristocratic, sensitive protagonist of Prévost's novel of 1731, destined for a high rank in the Church, comes across the ravishing Manon, a girl of lower station being packed off to a convent as a curb to her love of pleasure, and he is altered forever. He runs the gamut of the coming-of-age tales I have outlined. He is innocent (hasn't noticed the difference between the sexes up to now, he tells us) and will become dreadfully experienced (coping with the trials entailed by his tumultuous love affair with Manon). Hence he will be as transformed as Romeo and Juliet, but this time the "rebirth" brought on by love has a darker hue, for it wrecks all prior identity and hurtles the young lover into an outright war with the authorities of his time. This volatile yet tragic story of young love in the eighteenth century is prismatic: it instructs us about not only the intricacies of the human heart but also those of the *ancien régime* and the hustling Parisian culture, where sexual favors can be bought but class lines cannot be crossed. What I am terming "instruction" in the affairs of both heart and society comes across in the novel as a series of bewildering collisions, conferring on this story a sense of breathlessness and even trauma.

Smitten by her beauty, Des Grieux abandons his religious path, saves Manon from the convent, and the two of them elope. Burning with sexual hunger, they make love already in the carriage bringing them to Paris. Des Grieux is initiated into pleasure. But the little money he has cannot last long in the big city, and very soon he encounters the first betrayal: Manon seems melancholy at supper, there is a knock on the door, he is hauled off by three men whom he recognizes as his father's lackeys, his older brother awaits him in a carriage, he is returned home to Father. Only there does he learn that Manon has acquired an older, wealthy suitor and that she was party to his abduction. His father chastises him for his simplicity, even offers to buy him a pretty woman, but the wound is too deep. The young man is angry, hurt, brokenhearted, but this quasi-penal stint at home for six months reorients him toward spiritual horizons, and after much diligence the great day comes when he is to make his public oration at the Sorbonne in recognition of his ecclesiastical gifts and vocation.

You know what has to happen. Manon has heard of the event, comes to hear him, and then asks to have a few words with him in private in the parlor of Saint-Sulpice. *Coup de foudre.* They are inflamed with each other, he again bolts from the Church, they launch again into their tempestuous love life, a life always doomed by the same recurring fate: when money is short, separation will occur. That is the very structure of the novel: the young man's desperate efforts to keep his mistress with him, undone over and over, often enough by fate and bad luck, sometimes by the girl's own machinations. The beautiful Manon always lands on her feet: both older and younger men covet her, bid for her favors, and she knows her market value. At one point, after leaving him for an older man, she assures Des Grieux in a letter that she loves him, that she will return to him, but says, "But don't you see, my poor darling, that loyalty [*la fidélité* is Prévost's term] is a silly virtue in the pass we are in? Do you really think we can love each other with nothing to eat?" It is, in a sense, the novel's most revolutionary perception: matter trumps all. She seems born knowing this.

The wellborn Des Grieux cannot fathom such materialist logic. He repeatedly explodes with wrath, jealousy, and tears, so much so that others are often stunned by his performance. One sees a clear pattern: happiness, shortage of funds, betrayal, rage and misery, reunion. The young man's affective fireworks constitute perhaps the novel's most dramatic movements: the heart is a powder keg, a volcano, a transformative force that nothing else in life rivals. The very plot of the narrative, keyed to separation, ensures these eruptions at a regular clip. Young love is taking a beating, for it is under constant attack. And Des Grieux routinely casts oaths against the very heavens, claiming that love is the noblest feeling on Earth, that his father is an ogre for not allowing him to marry Manon, that the world is a corrupt place, and so on. But he never stops loving her.

I have taught this novel for more than four decades, and my students are always impatient with the poor Chevalier. Why doesn't he get a job? they ask. He can't, I reply, since his social station prevents it. (By the way, how does he get the funds he has? He learns to be a professional cardsharp, and he later justifies this to his father by claiming that many of the highest-born young people in France do the same thing.) Above all, my students are mystified that the Chevalier stays with his paramour. Given that she routinely cheats on him, why doesn't he break off the relationship? "Addiction" is frequently the trope they invoke for understanding this tortured love affair; he is besotted with her, he has lost all judgment, he is sick, he is bent on self-destruction. I see with great clarity that undergraduates in the twenty-first century are not likely to emulate the Chevalier des Grieux when it comes to their love life. And I wonder what has happened to passionate young love, to the sort of tempestuous thing that sweeps Romeo, Juliet, and Des Grieux right off their feet and wrecks their lives.

Manon Lescaut is a classic in French literature in part because it conveys with great power the turbulence, intensity, and life-altering character of love, of sexual passion. Prévost is unrivaled when it comes to writing the shock and vehemence of infatuation, when it comes to showing how feeble a thing willpower is when desire and irresistible pleasure are in the mix. Des Grieux is one of literature's most mercurial figures: he waxes lyrical when he has Manon to himself, and he rages like a hurricane when she is taken from him. He himself senses that love may bring ecstatic feelings to you but that it also robs you of your core identity. Early on, in the seminary, when Manon came to him after months of separation, he realized that his life was no longer under his control; he puts it like this:

> I was horror-stricken at the contrast between the serenity of
> but a few moments ago and the wild stirrings of desire I could
> already feel within me. I was shuddering as you do when you
> find yourself alone at night on some desolate moorland, when
> all familiar bearings are lost and a panic fear comes over you
> that you can dispel only by calmly studying all the landmarks.

This is, I submit, the landscape of passionate first love: a place of abduction, an oneiric place akin to nightmare, where you have no bearings, no control, no freedom. You are a hostage. For all the sentimentality one may find in this tale, such passages announce something dark and unwelcome about the tyranny of feeling. It is, with its dreamscape, a kind of awful awakening, an initiation into a new regime. Addiction, my students say; "terrorism" would be just as apt a term. Volition has no place here, and I suspect that is one reason my students don't like it.

One reason I myself love this book is because of the blindness at its core. Des Grieux is a self-proclaimed apostle of love, but he never for a moment suspects his own hypocrisy: he cadges money from his best friend, he lies incessantly to get it from others, he cheats at cards but claims it's a peccadillo, he even shoots a guard when he breaks out of the prison where he has been put (for theft and other little infractions, committed in the name of love). Yet there is not a whiff of guilt about him. On the contrary, he virtually preens with pride over the intensity of his feelings for Manon. There is something astonishing about a novel using a flawed hero to fight a just war. For the war is just: love should be a noble passion, and the barter culture of quasi prostitution that Des Grieux battles is a philistine culture indeed. The young man finds himself repeatedly (and literally) imprisoned by the structures of authority (family, Church, prison), and one cannot miss the Oedipal dimensions of this plot. Romeo and Juliet faced a family feud; Des Grieux is battling the entire system.

But this is literature, not sociology, and Prévost gives us in the portrait of Des Grieux a remarkable psychological confection, replete with longings and fears beyond the scrutiny of his consciousness. As said, his self-image remains blithely intact, even as we watch him sink into the mire of deception and self-deception. But there is a splendid network of images to convey insecurity and anxiety underneath his rhetoric and bravado, especially along sexual lines. For do not forget: he is a sexual champion of sorts, for the bliss he works feverishly to maintain is the sexual union with Manon (and we have textual evidence to suggest that she finds him an unparalleled lover); when you see that pattern, you realize that all the scenes of forced separation—many of them yanking the two of them directly out of bed—are virtually a form of coitus interruptus. Society does not want those two together.

The supreme moment of (textual) sexual trouble comes when Des Grieux and a friend are trying to rescue Manon from the dreaded prison L'Hôpital. Getting into her cell requires *"une clef d'une grandeur effroyable"* (a frighteningly huge key), eh, but once there, the intended disguise scheme—they will dress up Manon as a man in the clothing they've smuggled in—is in trouble, for they forgot to bring pants for her. No problem, we're told.

"However, there was only one thing to be done, and that was for me to leave my own breeches for Manon and get out somehow without them. My cloak was very long, and thanks to the help of a pin here and there I was fit to pass through the door with the decencies preserved." Yes, the decencies are preserved, but one need not be a card-carrying Freudian to wonder at what is going on here: a man giving up his pants to his mistress, a man walking out of a prison with no pants on, a man exposed in his genitals (cloak or no cloak). Prévost's story is an echoing one: it outfits its swooning oratorical hero with a plot and textual details (a gun that seems both loaded and not loaded, a sword that breaks, etc.) that call into question precisely the erotic battle against the fathers that is at its core.

Growing up is invariably about the young discovering and assuming power, and it is naive not to think about these matters sexually as well as physically, cognitively, and economically. Erotic war between father and son is at the core of *Oedipus,* and its familial frame tells us that the ascent of the young may well be inseparable from the vanquishing of the old. It will be seen, in the second half of this book, that the story of growing old is crucially inflected by these issues as the young challenge the power of the old in every domain, including the sexual. What is fascinating in *Manon Lescaut,* however, is the sneaky recognition that the young might also be an anxious lot, however much bravado they display. It is not clear to me that Prévost intended to signal such uncertainty in the role of Des Grieux, but the great beauty of art is that it always exceeds the intentions of the artist, so that we are justified in weighting these textualized moments of figurative anxiety to get a fuller picture of how complicated the trip from morning to noon can be. Art's testimony about life is special in just this sense.

But I want to conclude my discussion of young love by returning to two of the motifs I've already emphasized: love itself as a surreal nightmare setting and the generalized problem of blindness. The strange new world that Des Grieux is obliged to chart and negotiate is more than Paris's mercantile ethos. Of course, he fails utterly to see that money is the key to his systemic troubles, that all his talk about fate and the gods is twaddle: his love affair with Manon needs money just as a fire needs oxygen. But that is the least of it. The world he repeatedly collides with is Manon Lescaut. His high-flying rhetorical love code is not only maladapted to the Parisian culture of his moment but is alien, unattuned to the very woman he loves. Remember her words: "Do you really think we can love each other with nothing to eat?" Des Grieux is shocked by her vulgarity, but we who have read Marx and know that there is a material substratum to even the most ethereal pursuits must understand that she has a point. At another juncture, she tells him that the fidelity she expects of him is the fidelity of the heart. What is the fidelity of the heart? It denotes a view of love that can see beyond sexual possession. Des Grieux can make nothing of it.

What is a gal to do? Is that not the quintessential (unstated, unexplored) dilemma of Manon Lescaut? Des Grieux comes from a noble family, and he easily enough finds people to support his cause. He has cultural capital even if he is short of funds. He is the book's first person, its impassioned speaker, conferring on this subversive novel an emotional immediacy of great power. Manon has only one thing: her beauty, her body. That is her currency. Hence she uses it every time she has to, to make her way in a setting that reifies her, that classifies her as sexual merchandise.

Lazarillo, Pablos, Huck, Rastignac, and the Invisible Man used wit and cunning to make their way. Manon's assets are of a different stripe, but she understands their market value in a patriarchal society. So too does her anxious lover, a lover bent on staving off all male rivals. What is most cunning about *Manon Lescaut* is how much we have to work at it to understand Manon Lescaut; our work consists in taking her seriously as a person with her own values and formation, rather than judging her exclusively by Des Grieux's exalted love code. This is not easy, for his is the eloquent hungry grandiose voice of possessive male desire, and his needs are indeed real.

So too are hers. And that is perhaps what we most need to take from the literature of young love: that each of the lovers is real, that each has wants, that the story of human relations is a perspectival story that mandates generosity everywhere, on the part of its characters and even its readers. Romeo and Juliet squabbled about larks versus nightingales. This young couple has considerably more to óvercome than warring families, but perhaps their greatest problems lie closer to home, in the very makeup of consciousness and its inevitable blindsightedness, its constitutive myopia. Written long before Marx and the materialist philosophers challenged the tenets of idealism, written long before feminists fought to establish the rights of women, this brief tale, written so long ago, is much more than the account of a lover's infatuation. It is an exploration of subjectivity itself, as well as an anatomy of its time, and it shows us that young love brings, as nothing else can, the complex forces and vectors of ourselves and our world into focus. The experience of love has caused both to grow, but there is little to celebrate and no diplomas are in sight. At story's end, Manon, though reformed, dies, and Des Grieux, old beyond his years, is penitent. We do not know what they have learned. It is for us the readers to grasp the painful wisdom of this short novel: young love is grand, but it is also blind. Conflict, misunderstanding, and benightedness—about ourselves, our lovers, and our world—are constituent elements of the story of growing up.

Emily Brontë's Wuthering Heights

Wuthering Heights (1848) is one of the most powerful and heartwrenching love stories ever written. It is also among the most primitive, savage, and frightening. Catherine Earnshaw, the spoiled and impetuous daughter of a prominent family, and the mysterious Heathcliff, a gypsylike orphan found in the Liverpool slums and adopted into the Earnshaw household, create in earliest childhood a bond that is indissoluble, that will turn out to be fateful for both of them. As tyrannical as the love potion that Tristan and Ysolde innocently swallow, the linkage between these two children fuses them—psychically, emotionally—into one being, and the novel helps us to see that a love of this sort is as much a curse as a blessing, for it erodes the contours of the two young people—they are still children—in such a way that each is permanently "inhabited" by the other.

At a pivotal moment in the novel, Catherine explains to Nelly, the shrewd housekeeper, that she is indeed fond of the genteel

Edgar Linton, who courts her, but that her feelings for the lowly Heathcliff are of a different stamp altogether:

> "What were the use of my creation if I were entirely contained here? My great miseries in this world have been Heathcliff's miseries, and I have watched and felt each from the beginning; my great thought in living is himself. If all else perished, and *he* remained, I should still continue to be; and, if all else remained, and he were annihilated, the Universe would turn to a mighty stranger. I should not seem a part of it. My love for Linton is like the foliage in the woods. Time will change it, I'm well aware, as winter changes the trees. My love for Heathcliff resembles the eternal rocks beneath—a source of little visible delight, but necessary. Nelly, I *am* Heathcliff—he's always, always in my mind—not as a pleasure, any more than I am always a pleasure to myself—but as my own being—so, don't talk of our separation again."

Brontë finds here a language for love that rivals the glory of Shakespeare. There are no references to the stars, nor to gloves or kisses, but the natural world is invoked with a rare pith and beauty, providing a code for what is transient and what is permanent, what is peripheral and what is essential. If Shakespeare and Prévost emphasized the ecstatic thrill of young love, Brontë bypasses pleasure altogether in order to speak of more basic and elemental things: "I *am* Heathcliff." It is an astonishing statement, and there is nothing romantic about it. Further, Heathcliff could have said it about Catherine. Each contains the other, as "core" of identity, as fused subject. Desire has no role to play here. Love, at the level Brontë is articulating it, is a morphological truth, a redefinition of who and what you are, prior to sentiment or even cognition. Brontë's oceanic depiction of young love is staggering in its implications, for it spells the end of individual agency and offers a view of human connection as structural, as if the loved one were an implant, were lodged inside oneself. Subjectivity seems overcome, and a new double creature, an amalgam of Catherine and Heathcliff, shimmers in front of our eyes. Such a view of human connection is, in my view, terrifying, on the order of a genetic liability rather than a glorious choice, and *Wuthering Heights* goes a long way toward measuring the horror that may result from such a scheme.

I call this scene pivotal because Heathcliff has overheard only Catherine's initial remarks to Nelly about his being too low and degrading to be married and thus exited the house for good before those beautiful words are spoken, not to return for many years. The entire revenge plot hinges on this *malentendu:* Catherine will indeed marry Edgar, thinking Heathcliff is gone forever. But the rest of the novel will show us, in the most extraordinary and painstaking detail, just how sublime, awful, and true Catherine's words are. When Heathcliff later returns—man-grown, distinguished, and powerful-looking, even rich—all hell breaks loose. He despises Edgar as too wimpish and unmanly for Catherine, is ready to throttle him, chastises Catherine viciously for her choice; Catherine herself senses that a storm is now coming that is beyond anyone's control, that the raving Heathcliff is both demonic and correct, that her proper marriage will never withstand this violence, that her mental composure is beginning to come apart. And we see a sort of meltdown as the demons, the psychic forces let loose by human feeling, run their course, leading to a collapse that finishes in her death. As she is dying, Heathcliff, still hounding her, has the temerity to tell her that he can forgive her the homicidal injury to himself but not the suicidal one to her. And he is right; her marriage to Edgar is not far from a double murder. Her death maims him forever even though it does not kill him. She dies and he will live on, to enact his revenge. Love shines here in all its glory and horror. It looks more than a little psychotic.

How on earth can one imagine a successful growing-up model here? Catherine and Heathcliff are tormented, possessed creatures, as paralyzed and fixated on each other as the idiot Benjy on his lost Caddy. Des Grieux looks like a free agent by contrast. Later I will discuss in more detail the unprecedented violence, ferocity, and abuse of *Wuthering Heights,* but it is clear to me that Brontë's creation is a profoundly ambiguous one: the Edenic fusion between these two young people has a beauty we are not likely to forget, but it is steeped in a kind of libidinal frenzy that must somehow be mellowed if life is to continue. And that is how one makes sense of the generational plot: the children of these plot-crossed lovers will be called upon to reorient things, to insert some degree of measure and rationality into these affairs. It is a brave effort in the right direction, but it can scarcely make us forget the Gothic to-the-death version of maniacal young love at the core of the book. The sick and sheltered Emily Brontë, who had seen so little of the large world, delivered herself of a primitive tale that seems to hark all the way back to Greek tragedy, a world where the gods sliced and diced, handing out to mortals whatever manias they felt like distributing, yielding a view of humans beset/composed by demonic forces beyond anyone's control. We would not hesitate to pathologize such a scheme today and seek medical redress. Growing up finds itself in a tight corner.

One might argue that we should turn our sights backward toward the actual marriage between Catherine and Edgar, a happy enough little union until it is wrecked by Heathcliff's return. The entire novel is framed by the contrast between the "proper" world of Linton's Thrushcross Grange and the savage fierceness of Wuthering Heights, the abode of the Earnshaws and Heathcliff. At times the book reads like a Lévi-Strauss experiment that contrasts the "raw" with the "cooked," as if Brontë were desperately trying to find a way to get the genie back into the bottle in the name of "civilization" and to conclude with some kind of social cohesion and development. These matters impinge fully on the theme of growing up. The entire rites-of-passage model, as well as the implied ethos of the Bildungsroman, is oriented toward an outcome of marriage and social adaptation. From an anthropological perspective, marriage and adaptation signal the young's entry into society, into the human dance. But I invoke these concepts in order to question their validity in literature, not only in *Wuthering Heights* but in so much of what we have seen: Romeo, Juliet, Lazarillo, Pablos, Simplicius, Des Grieux, Manon, Rastignac, Pip, Huck, Benjy, and the Invisible Man have no wedding bells ringing for them, nor do they receive a regular paycheck as proper citizens doing their bit to uphold the social contract.

Could it be that great literature is always cautionary? Even countercultural? Or that the poet, as Blake said of Milton, is always of the Devil's party? One thing seems to be sure: the old adage that "happy love has no history" seems to possess a kind of rock-bottom artistic truth, for the great works of art are invariably keyed to the problems and complexities of culture, what Freud rightly called civilization's "discontents." It is worth pausing a bit over this rather dark view of literature's tidings. We will see that even books about love that finish "well"—and the next one we'll discuss, Charlotte Brontë's *Jane Eyre*, does indeed finish well— can be fiendishly illuminating about the obstacle course, indeed the roller-coaster ride, needed to get to that "positive" finish line.

Charlotte Brontë's Jane Eyre

Jane Eyre, Charlotte Brontë's grand story of a young girl's struggles for love, recognition, and authority, is one of the most famous "success stories" in English literature. Unlike in the world of Emily's *Wuthering Heights*, manners, rules, and conventions have a real presence, as do social institutions, so that we can track Jane's arduous path from misery to happiness and power; it is virtually a station drama, as well as an ongoing education. Jane is, as she herself says to her cold aunt Reed, desperate for love, for no human being can live without it. We see her experience an angelic version of such a bond at Lowood School, where she meets and adores the saintly, older Helen Burns, destined to die. Here Jane sees what goodness looks like, yet she cannot help noting that Helen dies as the victim of a cruel institutional culture, and the little girl determines to fight for what she wants. She then becomes a teacher in her own right, still yearning for happiness and fuller self-realization.

The crowning moment for love comes when she encounters Edward Rochester: an older man, haughty and virile, a wounded warrior with a secret. Brontë has cast their romance in quasi-mythic terms: she the elf creature, he the Gytrash of legend; she the spirit who will save him, he the proud male who must command. The scenes between these two people are wonderful reading: Rochester teases and taunts Jane, tests her; she responds in kind, timidly at first but increasingly spiritedly and feistily. Rochester's pride, intellect, and forthrightness are what she has yearned to meet and worship all her life. Their exchanges have a zest and bite that jump out at us from the page, no matter how many times we've read this novel. We are very far from the raw savagery of *Wuthering Heights;* Charlotte is unrivaled in showing us how wit, nerves, intelligence, and feeling do their finest dance when two people probe each other in a drawing room, moving ever closer. We know they are falling in love well before the topic is openly discussed, and we sense also the distinction and superiority of each of them, the clear-eyed, unillusioned view of behavior and world that is being sounded. There is a wonderful freshness here, like a window being opened, causing us to realize just how mannered and stifling the rules of decorum in British high culture have to have been. For Jane, of course, such a love is unthinkable, given the social barriers between governess and gentleman; for Rochester, one senses a mix of yearning and anxiety, as if this grizzled man knows he has found something perfect yet is bound by some constraint that remains unvoiced.

But things are less simple than I have indicated (as readers of the novel know). Not merely are there some huge unwelcome surprises and secrets out there, waiting to explode, but the actual texture of the Jane/Rochester relationship merits a closer look. Charlotte Brontë is more akin to Dostoevsky than we realize, for her view of human affection is, at some profound level, keyed to insult and injury. I say this because there is more than a little sadism on show here: Rochester does not hesitate to sing the charms of his buxom (wellborn) fiancée, Blanche Ingram, to the little wrenlike governess Jane, telling her of his (bogus) plans for marrying the full-bodied Blanche, of his determination to send governess Jane away to Ireland to work in another family. He asks Jane to be ready to sit up with him the night before his marriage (to Blanche), so that he can expatiate on Blanche's beauty:

> "To you I can talk of my lovely one: for now you have seen her and know her."
>   "Yes, sir."
>   "She's a rare one, is she not, Jane?"
>   "Yes, sir."
>   "A strapper—a real strapper, Jane: big, brown and buxom."

I confess to seeing in these lines—do not forget: Jane is tiny, poor, and *plain;* this matters—a kind of sadistic cruelty that fully matches the more sensational stuff found in *Wuthering Heights.* Growing up—the education of the heart—entails lessons of this stripe also. Rochester intentionally brings her to tears more than once. He bullies her, taunts her, toys with her, all with the intention of finding out what she is truly made of. He is no snob, but he is indeed her moneyed, propertied employer, and we are never allowed to forget the social hierarchy that is in place. (Consider those "Yes, sir" replies of Jane's and tell yourself that these two people are falling in love: this is one way of gauging the depth of class structure in mid-nineteenth-century England; Rochester's later marriage proposal is no less hierarchical in its manner.)

And Jane? When she's not crying, she's loving it. She fantasizes surveying him, mastering him, even "penetrating" him (as the text's metaphor "looking into the abyss at her leisure" has it). She prefers him to more insipid fare, likening his saltiness to a ragout. Moreover, once he has come clean about the Blanche charade and announced his desire to marry her, she also starts to dish it out. She upbraids him for his grandiose wedding plans, for his extravagant gifts and language. She won't be dresssed like a doll; she won't be part of his seraglio. She dismantles an entire Romantic construct of gallantry and effusive love. She is prickly, briny, vinegary. She plays with him. These exchanges are also delicious, in my view, especially if we think back to Romeo and Juliet or Des Grieux and Manon and wonder where the irony was, where the kidding was. Love has many tonalities, and the spirited mixing it up between this young girl and older man—she snappish, he not minding it—ranks high on my list as a persuasive account of how would-be lovers might talk.

But as all readers know, this love story will be interrupted by the discovery of a first wife locked in the attic, Bertha Mason Rochester, a corpulent, bestial madwoman bent on destroying Rochester if she possibly can. Yet Jane's lessons in love continue. Rochester pleads with her to stay with him, but she will not compromise her integrity; she bolts, leaves Thornhill, loses the little money she possesses, begs for food, for garbage. Almost dead from starvation, she is at last taken in by the Rivers family, where soon enough she receives the attentions of St. John Rivers, a would-be missionary who flexes his muscles as well, trying to subdue her into becoming his wife and accompanying him to India, albeit sans passion. Again she is tempted. Force seduces, mesmerizes. But in extremis she hears the voice of Rochester calling, leaves Rivers, returns to find Thornhill burned down, Bertha Mason Rochester dead, and Rochester himself blind and missing a hand. He has been, as they say in the military, "softened." He can now be married.

Did I mention that Jane has conveniently inherited a deal of money in the interim? Brontë is keeping her books, and it is clear that Jane is to be catapulted into power, just as Rochester is to relinquish a good bit of his, so that a marriage can finally take place. I have wanted to trace the stages of this famous love story in order to emphasize the marathon course of little Jane Eyre. There's no gouging here, as in Emily's novel, but a cult of power and an underlay of brutality nonetheless. Jane Eyre's story has elements of a "pilgrim's progress" in it, for she encounters and overcomes obstacle after obstacle in her search for love and self-affirmation. But the arduous journey makes us realize that "falling in love" is a dicey and reductive term for gauging the affairs of the heart, even with the young. Each of the texts we've looked at is larded with time and conflict, and each traces an evolution in human feeling, a schooling of self through the experience of love. Because this is a nineteenth-century novel written by the daughter of a reverend, it ends, as it must, with a marriage. I ask my students, when I teach *Jane Eyre,* whether such an outcome makes sense to them in the twenty-first century. One wonders: could the discovery of passionate love lead elsewhere altogether?

Marguerite Duras's The Lover

And modern love? Love across borders? Marguerite Duras's signature would seem to be racially crossed lovemaking—understood as social taboo and erotic stimulant—as is evident in her classic film *Hiroshima Mon Amour,* in which a Frenchwoman has torrid sex with her Japanese lover while remembering her tragic affair with a German soldier during the Second World War; sexual desire moves from somatic to ideological event, and we are meant to ponder how "difference" attracts and repels, how the murderous violence of war might yield to the interactions of bodies on a bed. We are a far cry from the love plots seen up to now: beyond feuding families or class differences within a culture, the love story now reaches across continents and oceans, bridging races, spanning great divides.

Duras's acclaimed novel of 1984, *The Lover*, seems at once to be working those issues, while also constituting a modern installment of the themes from *Romeo and Juliet*, *Manon Lescaut*, *Wuthering Heights*, and *Jane Eyre:* star-crossed, class-crossed young lovers now recast as a fifteen-and-a-half-year-old French girl who has a love affair with a man from north China. Hence the private love story is contextualized in a new way, with broad ideological ramifications: the (mis)fortunes of a modest French family in Indochina, the exoticism of a colonial regime entering its death throes, the deep-seated prejudices regulating the reciprocal views of the French and the Chinese, and the experience of sexual initiation as the life-altering liminal adventure of a young woman soon to leave the colonies for France.

And there are superbly wrought scenes of both erotic intimacy and familial tumult. The accounts of lovemaking between the young girl and her Chinese lover have a sensual pith that make the lush rhetoric of both Shakespeare and Prévost, as well as the Brontë sisters, seem operatic and overblown, for the physical rules supreme in this book, and the great metaphysical flights of the earlier texts have no place in this spare but intense encounter of bodies. Duras stands out for her unblinking focus on how bodies interact, how they live a life of their own, how they trigger sensations and thoughts, how all-powerful this can be, how different it is from received views of "love." There is nothing here about stars or birds or lightning or love being an innocent passion. Nor is there anything about blinding beauty or ravishing appeal. Jane Eyre's sense of her obligations to herself is reprised by Duras but reoriented drastically in the direction of a libidinal personal awakening that has no truck with fond notions of relationship and marriage.

Further, we soon learn how deep the contempt for the Other

goes when it comes to erotic matters. Loving "in the wrong direction"—at the core of each text we've seen—is a crash course in xenophobia. One does not easily forget the evocations of meals in extravagant Chinese restaurants, offered and paid for by a lover whom neither of the French brothers, gorging themselves with food, will even speak to. The girl herself turns silent, shares momentarily in the absolute contempt of her delicate lover. It goes without saying that the girl's family treats her as a whore, leading to scenes where the mother beats her brutally while the older brother stands, listening, on the other side of the door. But then, the book is democratic in its view of prejudice, and we know that the Chinese lover's rich father has the same contempt as the French do, is certain that the girl is indeed a whore, interested only in getting to the lover's money. (Parallels between the Chinese father and Des Grieux's father are not lacking: each old man is outraged by the sluttish choices of the son, each holds on to the purse strings.)

Yet everything I have written thus far about *The Lover* is misleading. To see it as a frank, uncensored account of young love in a colonial setting, to see it as the clash of generations or of cultures, is not so much wrong as it is peripheral. Those features of the narrative are real enough, but they do not explain the book's disturbing power. To begin with, it breaks all traditional rules of storytelling. There is no real chronology. Over and over, the narrative returns to the key event of the (now-old) narrator's life: the ferry crossing when she was fifteen and a half, when she was approached by a wealthy Chinese man who is transfixed at the sight of her, with her gold lamé high heels and her man's flat-brimmed hat, a brownish pink fedora with a broad black ribbon. (Here is this girl's own adolescent perspective on a threshold moment, inseparable from her clothes—the sort of thing unimaginable in Shakespeare and unimagined in Prévost and the Brontës.) At any moment this scene returns, and the old narrator knows that it somehow contains within it her entire life to be. About the adult life that followed, we get virtually no coherent information, just scrambled tidbits: a career, a drinking problem, intellectual circles in Paris, mention of a dead child, a deported husband, a father's death, but thrown in as trifles, weightless, not related to the Main Event.

Linear plot does not behave this way—Shakespeare, Prévost, and the Brontë sisters graph with great care the unfurling and developing of young love as linear event—but perhaps the psyche operates according to different rules and directionalities, perhaps it returns to its seminal data to make ever more sense of it, to unpack it, to make it yield its secret. Duras's story is *remembered;* is that not, at some level, the right, the only, "tense" for approaching young love? In this light, growing up is not simply the early-stage journey we've studied but also the later processes of recollection and interpretation, the crucial labor required to possess one's own story, to grasp one's own formation. Unlike the other texts under discussion, *The Lover* is built of this ceaseless two-way traffic, the narrating and remembering a liminal event of sexual initiation, and it makes one wonder if threshold experiences are ever truly over. Do we ever stop growing up?

The frozen, pirouetted, ever-entrancing scene of the girl on the ferryboat leads, as it must, to the sexual initiation that is, in many respects, the novel's heart. Juliet asks for the darkness of night to receive her lover, but Shakespeare does not go to their bed; Prévost snatches his lovers out of bed when the forces of order appear, but he does not focus on what was going on in the bedroom. Both Brontës, writing in mid-nineteenth-century Britain, are predictably close-lipped about such intimate matters. We are now in modern territory, and Duras writes young love—young lovemaking—with candor, tact, and beauty. The girl repeatedly asks the man to do to her what he does to other women he brings to his flat. But soon enough it is she who takes the lead, undresses him, guides him. Her education has begun:

The skin is sumptously soft. The body. The body is thin, lacking in strength, in muscle, he may have been ill, may be convalescent, he's hairless, nothing masculine about him but his sex, he's weak, probably a helpless prey to insult, vulnerable. She doesn't look him in the face. Doesn't look at him at all. She touches him. Touches the softness of his sex, his skin, caresses his goldenness, the strange novelty. He moans, weeps. In dreadful love.

And, weeping, he makes love. At first, pain. And then the

pain is possessed in its turn, changed, slowly drawn away, borne toward pleasure, clasped to it.

The sea, formless, simply beyond compare.

Here is her entry into pleasure, and it is written with a modicum of details—certainly nothing pornographic, even if deeply sensual—that limn the particulars of the Chinese lover (thin, hairless, weak, vulnerable) but are insistently generic in their notations of touch, body, and pleasure. Personality, intimacy, emotion, sentiment—the constituents of what we think of as "love"—seem banished here, so that the dance of the body may receive the attention it deserves. Orgasm takes the metaphor often ascribed to it, "the sea," but in this text, with its rains, rivers, and ocean, with its insistence on a powerful current that drives all human affairs, sweeping up belongings and animals and persons, such a notation seems right and in its place. There is no moralizing, no verbiage, no tender words between lovers.

At about this point most readers of the novel begin to understand why Duras has titled her book so impersonally: *The Lover.* Sexual desire, copulation, pleasure, orgasm: these are anonymous forces that have no proper names attached to them; they are the mating rituals of the species, possessed of a force and magic on the far side of all notions, including the one we call love. The man tells her he knew she'd love love, that she is made for it; she concentrates entirely on his expert hands, on what he does to her body, on what it then feels. He curses her, is violent, she asks him to do it again and again, he does. Her body, she says, is seeking and finding and taking what it likes. All is right.

Despite the sharply focused particulars of this love affair, it comes across as profoundly impersonal, even anonymous. What they do together has a riveting intensity, but our familiar "domesticating" labels have no purchase. At one point she actually wonders if she ever loved him, and the reader wonders too; they talk very little, and when they do, what they say is immaterial. Yet there is something truly undying about this liaison, for it is still hypnotic and beckoning all these years later, still asking to be interpreted, still promising to contain, coiled inside it, her whole life to come. Young love comes across as the core riddle of our lives, the central event to which all refers, the origin that must be sought and wooed through memory and language.

There is nothing technical about Duras's novel; it is no primer on ways of making love or awakening the body to pleasure. Even in its erotic professionalism—the girl is being initiated, is initiating herself, into the mysteries and science of *jouissance*—it gestures to larger patterns. "Love" would seem to be the name we give to the opening of self that lovemaking engenders. *Growing up:* love grows us. There is nothing reassuring about this model, no heightening of our moral sensibilities, but nonetheless a broadening of our forces and strengths, an extending of our reach. Experiencing orgasm, the girl now realizes that her mother—the woman whose misery parses so much of this book and this child's psyche—has never known pleasure. Love teaches. Still more astounding, more unsettling, is the way in which love coheres us, brings the disparate elements of our far-flung lives into relation, into fusion. Hence the girl comes to understand that her deep and occulted feelings for her two brothers—her hatred of the older one, the bully, the night hunter, the one loved by the mother, the one who amounted to nothing while eating up the resources of the family, and her twisted desire for the younger one, the weaker, more beautiful, more sensitive one who died in his forties, who shared something primitive and perhaps sexual with her in the past, whose death sealed off her family affections altogether— somehow course together into the relation with the Chinese lover, as if this sexual liaison incorporated all the libidinal pulsions of her existence into one sweeping current.

And it does not stop here. Arguably the most mesmerizing pages of this novel depict the girl's violent erotic attachment to her school friend Hélène Lagonelle, the friend with the luscious, unbearably enticing breasts, the friend unaware of her own ripe body, which obsesses the girl and possesses a kind of sexual potency far beyond that of the male lover. Again, it all comes together, as if the love affair with the Chinese man were not only inseparable from her lust for Hélène but these passions feed each other, enable each other, substitute for each other, require each other:

I am worn out with desire.

I want to take Hélène Lagonelle with me to where every evening, my eyes shut, I have imparted to me the pleasure that makes you cry out. I'd like to give Hélène Lagonelle to the man who does that to me, so he may do it in turn to her. I want it to happen in my presence, I want her to do it as I wish, I want her to give herself where I give myself. It's via Hélène Lagonelle's body, through it, that the ultimate pleasure would pass from him to me.

A pleasure unto death.

A new map of the human subject is coming into view here. The initiation into sexual pleasure is the entry into a territory, a libidinal cartography that links all its key players via desired and imagined couplings. Substitution is the order of the day, for desire works along these pulsing lines, and there is something at once delirious and grand in this yearned-for sexual triangle, in which what is done to you is what most inflames me, charting a kind of exponential libidinal playground, a field picture of "love." *The Lover* seems to me most astounding along just these lines, for it dares to reimagine the company we keep, the invisible currents that link and arouse and gratify us, the broader erotic topography in which single lives are placed and play out. And it can move beyond the erotic altogether. The most hallucinatory passages in the novel graph something like an epidemic of outpouring feelings and "secret sharing," yielding a universe charged with "sisters" who are crazed versions of the protagonist, such as the madwoman of Vinh Long who pursues the girl in her fantasy, or the beggar woman who moves through the Mekong en route to Calcutta, "tending her foot eaten up with maggots and covered with flies," carrying the dead little girl with her, or the Lady whose lover commits suicide, Lady as the girl's alter ego, described as "alone, queenlike," each possessed of bodies made for love, "consigned to the infamy of a pleasure unto death." These are all versions of the protagonist, reflected images of whom she desires, what she is or might become: a pluralist view of the self.

All this is contained in the scene of the fifteen-and-a-half-year-old girl on the ferryboat, poised to step into her future, fecund with life and love and sorrow to come. Young love is the embryo of all this. We are meant to take it seriously when Duras writes that the Chinese lover loves her as a child: "He plays with his child's body, turns it over, covers his face with it, his lips, his eyes." Yes, we know that these notations evoke incest and abuse. Yet that is not how they come across in this novel, as if Duras wanted to explode all our registers for understanding sexuality and desire, as if she wanted to make us understand that "young love" is the incandescent crystallization of all the desire we'll ever have, that it inflames both lover and loved one, that it haunts forever the minds of those on time's treadmill. To somehow possess this magic moment would be tantamount to possessing all the promise of one's life. Thus the novel closes perfectly with the phone call from the (married) Chinese lover, now in Paris many many decades later, telling the protagonist that "it was as before, that he still loved her, he could never stop loving her, that he'd love her until death." A supreme fantasy on the part of the old, ravaged woman whose story this is? Or a supreme feat of self-appropriation through writing, across time, enlisting young love as the focal point of existence?

Young love thrusts us into our larger selves as well as into the world. Even though injury and sometimes death press closely in our five love texts, we remember them most for the birth of self they seem to inaugurate. Even the problems and obstacles they highlight serve as grist for their mill, incite love to live on and go further, feed the fire. Romeo and Juliet die, but they have flowered. Des Grieux is fated to lose Manon, but one feels that the substance of this man's life (what he was capable of) is cargoed in his tumultous affair with Manon. Catherine and Heathcliff experience from earliest childhood an absolute link, on the order of an umbilical cord, that can never be severed, and this is their energy source, even if it leads to early death for one and implacable revenge for the other. Jane's entire growth saga revolves around evaluating different forms of love: Helen Burns, Edward Rochester, St. John Rivers; each of these figures contributes vitally to her education as well as to her feelings. Duras's old woman's project of retrieval seems especially geared to self-birthing, to taking the measure of the unique moment when it all began, to decoding her own formative

riddle. All these texts contain heartache, but they present it ultimately as growth, as development, as the stuff of maturation. This,
we think, is nature's plan. The same photosynthesis that transforms the energy of the sun into the life of plants seems also to rule
over human affairs. Our stories of young love perhaps dazzle most
via the sheer vibrancy, strength, and intensity of feeling that they
celebrate, that love catalyzes, then actualizes. This would be our
dance.

Love Gone Wrong: The Story of Abuse

Young love, as we have seen, must often do battle with culture. Romeo and Juliet die, but no reader would go on to fault their love as inherently flawed. Des Grieux's passion for Manon brings him great pain, but the novel stands as an early testament to the power of romantic passion, even when it is blind. Things become more ambiguous once we get to *Wuthering Heights*, for we begin to see the disturbing kinship among love, vulnerability, injury, and violence. Jane Eyre and Duras's narrator seem to me to be ultimately victorious in love as maturation, as they acquire ever more self-knowledge, yet their stories echo in ways that get our attention: we see the punishment meted out to Jane, even by those who "love" her, and Duras's girl figure inhabits an affective familial world of great discord and misery, no matter how intense and transformative her sexual education is.

But none of these narratives directly indicts love itself, even if each measures its dangers. Yet what happens when love fails? When it turns to hatred, when it freezes into indifference, when it becomes something monstrous by reveling in its power? Or simply when its hunger for possession turns vicious and crippling? I am the first to admit that the literary fare presented up to now has not been shy about pain and injury. But there is a real distinction between the hard knocks of education—the things experienced by Lazarillo, Pablos, Rastignac, and the Invisible Man, as they slammed into a world so alien to their needs, as they sought to develop the vision or skills needed to negotiate that world—and what I want to call *abuse*, love gone wrong. As my title suggests, abuse is indeed a story. The damage it causes all too often has a tenacious life of its own, for it operates much like trauma, as violent injury that not only shocks our system but also releases its venom in us over time. It seems fair to ask: is it even possible to grow up without being exposed to injuries of this stripe? We need not be of a psychoanalytical bent to accept the notion that we are, all of us, working through the forces and conditions of our childhood, some of our making, others inflicted on us without our knowing.

I want to borrow the wonderful phrase used by Borges—"a forking path"—to characterize the trajectory of abuse. Borges himself wrote elegant parables in which the human subject goes through its strange permutations, but I believe that full-scale novels are still more illustrative when it comes to tracking our trajectory through time. Novels are singularly eloquent in "speaking" abuse; i.e., in displaying its long, forking, sinuous life. We the readers, who have absorbed stimuli and perhaps injury during each and every one of our days and years, cannot easily espy such a form, such a coming into focus of what was sown in us and that we only later reap. Mind you, we doubtless "enact" our injuries incessantly, but whereas the somatic ones are visible—a limp, a stiffness, a stutter—the psychic ones remain beyond our scrutiny, even if they script our moves.

If we are in the dark when it comes to measuring what is cooking inside us—not so much tumors or aneurysms but the fixed yet evolving emotional patterns we are acting out—literature can be helpful in getting a sighting. But literature is not graffiti: it does not shriek out its significance on every page. Often enough, literature requires that we ourselves perform an interpretive labor that goes well beyond just making out the story: we need to read ethically as well as cognitively, in the sense of espying damage or abuse even when it is not signaled. This is not easy, in art or in life. Just as no one I have ever known carries a sign indicating the injuries he or she has received, so too do characters in literature go about their lives, feeling, thinking, speaking, acting, but often enough leaving it up to us to gauge the deeper impact of what has been done to them. In this segment of my book, focusing on stories of abuse, our work can be downright diagnostic. This amounts to an ethics of reading, and it seems particularly mandated when discussing the fates of children, who may possess precious little agency or not even garner much attention in the stories in which they appear.

Fyodor Dostoevsky

Some writers put child abuse up front. One of the most painful set pieces in Dostoevsky's *The Brothers Karamazov* is when Ivan speaks of the torture of children. Dostoevskian psychology in general is cued to insult and injury, and most of the relationships depicted in the novel have their share of gleefully inflicted pain. But nothing compares with the list of horrors that Ivan recounts, horrors that make (for him) any notion of God unacceptable (not incredible, just unacceptable): I will return the ticket, he says; no amount of later forgiveness or justice can eradicate the damage done to children as children. We learn of Turks ripping fetuses out of their mothers' wombs and catching them on bayonets for the visual pleasure of the dying mothers; of the child Richard, brought up by shepherds, who was not even given pig mash to eat but beaten when he stole it; of an intelligent lady and gentleman who flog their seven-year-old daughter with ever more zest to arouse themselves; of a five-year-old girl flogged, kicked, and locked out all night in the outhouse, face smeared with excrement, forced by her mother to eat excrement; of an eight-year-old boy guilty of hurting the paw of a general's hound and therefore made into the object of the hunt: undressed, hunted down in front of his mother's eyes, torn to pieces by the dogs. (Note the twisted role of the caregivers in several of these anecdotes.)

Dostoevsky's main story does not shy away from such abuse either, and we see an attenuated version of it in the fate of Ilyusha, the child who witnessed the angry Dmitri's prolonged and vicious humiliation of the child's father. The novel seems to want to measure how much damage children can stomach without dying. Ilyusha actually does die, but his father—buffoon though he is—recounts to Alyosha just how much torture the boy went through, making us realize that emotional pain beggars physical hurt: the hurt child—by having seen his father brutally taken down, literally pulled by his beard; our worst injuries can come to us via looking—is desperate for revenge, promises even to slay Dmitri when he grows up, then asks his father how much it costs to move, if they might move, if somehow, through spatial distance, one could find a way to erase what happened. These pages are hard going, as Dostoevsky explores vulnerability, showing it to be a huge country of its own, making us understand how bruising life in a family can and must be, how powerless children (and even their parents) are in a hierarchical culture. *The Brothers Karamazov* has more curiosity than any other novel written in the nineteenth century, and very much of it is cued to injured children.

And, still more awful, to *injuring children*. We see, for starters, the gang of children taunting Ilyusha, stoning him. But the pièce de résistance is to be found in the depiction of Lise, the partially crippled girl whom Alyosha will later marry: in a scene that defies comprehension or digestion, she reveals to her saintly older beau her fascination with torture, recounting the story of a Jew who captured a Christian child and tortured him to death for four hours. These four hours seem to her "delicious" in their slowness. They come close, in inflicted pain, to a crucifixion, but a crucifixion that provides virtually orgiastic pleasure for its onlookers and executioners. This sumptuous confection of horror reaches its pinnacle as Lise tells Alyosha that it would be capped off by her eating pineapple compote while watching the show. We have no maps for measuring such moves of the heart, such strange hungers, but any normative view of childhood is simply undone by such evocations. I believe that Lise's recital of wonders is meant to send us back to Ivan's proud view that God—even if he exists—must be rejected, given not only the world of executioners and victims he has bequeathed us but also the vile snake pit he placed deep inside us regarding pleasure and pain. Childcrucifiers ingesting pineapple compote as accompaniment would seem to be the ne plus ultra of crossed wires, of an abuse-world we cannot afford to believe in.

But think, for a moment, backward to what we've seen. Lazarillo, Pablos, and Simplicius were exposed to routine violence: nose in the throat, spat on and beshat, drugged and experimented with. Blake's chimney sweep told us that "God and his priest and king, / ... make up a heaven of our misery." Remember Orlick's venomous envy of Pip, which caused one, and almost two, murders. Or the treatment meted out (by other children as well as adults) to the orphan Heathcliff and the little Jane Eyre. Or even sweet Huck's mockery of Jim in the fog episode. Or Ellison's strapped-down boy receiving electric shocks. Dostoevsky's pineapple compote takes us farther into the pit than many of us are prepared to go, but the heart has dark recesses, and the slaughter of the innocent takes place every day.

What role is there for art, even for journalism, here? Can these faces be looked at? Susan Sontag's last book deals with our terrible complicity with suffering, our dreadful readiness as witnesses, willing and able (and desirous?) to take into us the vilest that life offers. Sontag poses a very severe question, it seems to me: does our apprehension of horror and abuse ever lead to social change? One knows that the photographs of the My Lai massacre in Vietnam did actually play a role in changing Americans' attitudes toward that war, just as the photographs of torture in Abu Ghraib have altered Americans' thinking about the Iraq war. Nonetheless, I think back to Rousseau's troubling essay in the mid–eighteenth century against building a theater in Geneva: art's representations, he argued, do nothing whatsoever to improve moral behavior. We weep at suffering in the theater and then walk serenely past the beggar outside, having already paid our dues, as it were. Can the story of abuse make a difference?

Stories of Abuse: In the Margins

Dostoevsky's broadside about injured and injuring children is in your face. But I have tried to argue that literature is often more indirect in its portrayals, hence requiring that we readers espy and measure the damage threatening children. Consider, for example, Thomas Mann's celebrated *Death in Venice*, which charts the fascination/undoing of the writer, Aschenbach (a model of discipline and form), who sees in Venice a fleshly embodiment of the beauty he has always worshipped, but now in the form of the exquisite Polish boy Tadzio, with whom he falls tempestuously in love. About Aschenbach's ensuing downfall, the textual evidence is in, but about Tadzio himself we know very little indeed—we see how his family, siblings, and friends treat him, we note his shimmering beauty—and I wonder what *his* story might look like, how it might feel to be this boy on vacation in Venice on the receiving end of Aschenbach's desire.

Tadzio is the object of someone's appetite, and we simply do not know how to measure these things. In every sense of the term: measure their ethical significance, measure them at all. Ponder this: What if appetite were visible? What if affect had a color? What if my lust or revulsion for you or anyone in the crowd were a Technicolor affair, a bright umbilical cord extending from me to my "target"—or had a smell like a fart—so that it would be known to all? Brave new world, indeed. Perhaps we should be grateful that we see through a glass darkly. In life, others' motives are invisible, but in art it is different. Yet even there we are on the line, having to grasp what "Here caddie" actually means.

I am not asking that we always read against the grain, but that we read generously, that we widen our sense of the moral life, extending it to minor as well as major players. Minor versus major players: the egocentric nature of subjectivity mandates that each of us is the major player of his or her life, but are we not the minor players in the lives around us, the lives of those we love, those we hate, those we touch, those we ignore? So the pressing question is: can imagination get us beyond our own precincts? We again bump into the general utility of literature: it schools us in feeling, sometimes around corners (where we are likely to be most deficient), by asking us to take seriously—as real—the fates and feelings of the people it presents, especially when they are children growing up.

Consider, in this regard, what is in store for little Miles and Flora in Henry James's masterpiece "The Turn of the Screw."

Given that the story is (brilliantly) refracted through the lenses of the governess, what we most see in this fiction is her valiant and arduous and nonstop effort to protect her young charges from evil, namely from what she perceives ever more clearly as the sinister designs of the "dead" ghosts, Quint and Jessel, who seem to her bent on initiating the angelic little ones into some kind of awful sexual complicity. But here too, if you take a step back from this piece and give your head a good shake, so as to free it from the tug of the governess's angle of vision, you see two children exposed to the increasingly passionate wants of the woman who is supposed to be protecting them, and one feels that these wants have a libidinal character of their own. The story climaxes with the exit of the injured girl, Flora, and the death of the boy, Miles; I cannot help ultimately viewing him as a victim of the governess's appetites, even though her conscious motives are noble. Miles does not grow up. He dies at/in the hands of his caregiver. James never even whispers to us to pass judgment, but I sometimes feel that Jamesian indirection may tell us more about the muffled, actual character and nature of abuse than Dostoevskian pineapple compote does.

In this vein of bringing occulted things to the light, let me now address "the saga of Cécile Volanges." I suspect that most readers will have no clue as to whom I am referring to. Cécile Volanges is a somewhat minor character in the elegant but deadly eighteenth-century French epistolary novel *Les liaisons dangereuses* by Pierre Choderlos de Laclos, a text devoted largely to showcasing the astonishing erotic campaigns of the two key seducers at the core of the novel: the Vicomte de Valmont and Mme. de Merteuil. The novel is complex, but essentially two major relationships—or liaisons—remain embedded in our minds long after we've read the book (or seen any of the fine films made of it): the front-and-center seduction plot involving Valmont's increasingly desperate courtship of the virtuous Mme. de Tourvel and the more occluded but ultimately more fascinating and venomous relationship between Valmont and Merteuil themselves, which progresses in the novel from a strategic partnership to a fatal libidinal war of two. As for Cécile Volanges, she is, as it were, the cannon fodder of the novel: the convent-educated, utterly naive daughter of Mme. de

Volanges who is in love with the equally naive music teacher Danceny. She becomes cannon fodder by falling into the clutches and designs of Valmont and Merteuil.

Initially the perfidious Mme. de Merteuil—seen by all as virtuous, in the confidence of both Mme. de Volanges and Cécile—seeks to help Cécile and Danceny acknowledge (and perhaps consummate) their mutual affection, but soon enough things change. Valmont becomes apprised of the fact that Mme. de Volanges is cautioning Mme. de Tourvel to have nothing to do with him, given his reputation as a world-class rake, and his furious reaction is to take sexual revenge, not by attacking the old mother (no sexual payoff there) but by seducing the young daughter (while pretending to be furthering her relationship with Danceny). All this takes place, as so much eighteenth-century fiction does, in a country house, where Valmont's aunt Mme. de Rosemonde has invited her friends for a visit: Mme. de Tourvel, Cécile and her mother, and of course her dashing nephew Valmont. Our seducer goes to work by arranging to get himself into Cécile's bedroom at night, ostensibly to speak to her of Danceny—remember her naiveté—and he successfully initiates her into the erotic life, at first by bullying and soon enough in a consensual manner. She is a good student.

A not pretty, but not unfamiliar, story, you might think. But it acquires some spice thanks to Valmont's manner of going about his business. First of all, Cécile is a sufficiently silly goose—sexually hungry though she is—to believe that what she is doing with Valmont has no relevance to her continued devotion to the sweet Danceny (who is told by Valmont that he, Valmont, is working hard for his young friend, to bring the two young ones together). Second, as part of his revenge strategy, Valmont has decided to corrupt Cécile by trying out all forms of sexual coupling, by equipping the young girl with an erudite technical vocabulary for the postures they are assuming (a vocabulary calculated to produce some shock on the wedding night for whoever marries the virtuous Cécile). Third, Valmont regales the young girl with stories (when he is not fornicating with her), and these stories are filled with dirt about her own mother, about Mother's putative earlier sexual escapades (suavely invented by Valmont). But his most productive move of all is that he has systematically avoided taking any precautions in his intercourse with Cécile.

As you might expect, this cannot end well. Cécile becomes pregnant and miscarries, without even knowing exactly what her body has conceived and is now expelling. The young girl nonetheless realizes that her life has gone terribly amok and asks her mother to be sent to a convent to finish out her days. Mother understands nothing and is miserable at this outcome, is now prepared even to let her daughter marry the penniless Danceny, but when she asks Mme. de Rosemonde for advice here, the old lady—who has learned of the manifold deceptions carried out in her house by her nephew—advises the mother to consent to her daughter's request and never to ask why. There is much pathos here: lose your daughter forever, never ask why. The old Mme. de Rosemonde functions virtually as the container of the novel, the residual recipient of all its horrors, and she feels personally defiled at book's end, sickened by what has been possible in her house and family (Valmont is her favorite), by what predators can do to children.

And more explosions occur. Mme. de Tourvel, having yielded to Valmont out of passionate love, realizes with horror that she is sport for him and goes mad out of self-hatred and pain; in a scene of surreal beauty, she hallucinates Valmont's ghostly penetration everywhere as he crashes through walls, fiendishly bent on finding her, both desiring and hating her, torturing her right up to the end. Valmont himself, vain though he is, dimly understands that in losing Tourvel, he, not unlike Othello, has sacrificed (to Merteuil) what was most dear to him and therefore allows himself to be vanquished by the young Danceny in a duel, the young man having been told, as well, of the horrors that took place in the country house. The corpses are piling up. For his closing shot, the author Laclos endows the most demonic but fascinating figure of the book, Mme. de Merteuil, with smallpox, as if it were the only resource he had left to bring this Nietzschean character back under control.

But what I'd like to close with is the image of the ruined Cécile Volanges in a convent, permanently lost to her mother, to the world, and to herself (she has no religious calling whatsoever).

Some editors take the view that Laclos envisioned a Cécile sequel that would get her out of the convent and back into action; for me this is a nonstarter, since her ruin has been so utterly imagined and executed. Earlier in the story, Merteuil and Valmont banter about the malleable young girl at their disposition, terming her *"une machine à plaisir,"* "a pleasure machine," at which point Merteuil points out that sooner or later everyone learns how to operate such a machine, so the best course for them is to use her, break her, and discard the pieces. Which is what they do. This elegant if cruel novel has a lesson to teach us, and it is embodied in its title, *Les liaisons dangereuses.* All liaisons are dangerous. Cécile Volanges is a prime exhibit of children being abused and undone through the will to power of adults, a hunger that is gratified only by the manipulation of others. Cécile, the novel's innocent virgin, has zero status in its scheme of things; she is straightaway reified (*"une machine à plaisir"*), and her body serves as a currency for the grown-up fun and games at hand.

Protecting anyone against predators is hard. "Safe sex" has a meaning; "safe love," "safe desire," have none. But seeing children exposed to such designs as these is rough indeed. Tadzio, Miles, now Cécile Volanges: targets of appetite with nowhere to hide. Is there a lesson for us? I wonder if we might not consult the very form of this fiction for some reply. The epistolary convention itself—the entire book is a series of exchanged letters; even the innocent Cécile is "spread out" letterwise—has stunning parallels with today's culture not only of e-mail but of its more advanced and troubling progeny, such as Facebook, MySpace, Twitter, Craigslist, and the like: arenas where the young enter into a circulation they cannot always measure and achieve a visibility and vulnerability whose consequences are not easily charted. It seems to me that Laclos, the grand strategist of military and amorous relations, tried to chart them more than two centuries ago. *Les liaisons dangereuses* is one of our greatest "ecological" fictions, and it calls the bluff on the muscular, even deified individual—which is what Valmont and Merteuil think they are: gods taking others apart—by meshing all its players together, by highlighting the very traffic of human relations. What are Facebook and MySpace if not traffic systems, sites of exposure, settings where "I" enters a web not of its making, on show, readable, and even reachable. Look at the fate of Cécile Volanges, and you will see a child caught in—then undone from—a mesh it could not see.

I have wanted to reference Cécile Volanges's story in order to make us better readers, to sensitize us to the nasty events unfurling often enough in the dark corners of our canonical literature. Laclos is, of course, the contemporary of the Marquis de Sade, and many scholars of the period have pointed to the parallels between their respective works, seeing in them a cult of cruelty and principled exploitation that is almost Luciferian in character. After all, Sade's admirers argue, his stature derives from the incessant warfare he posits between human desire and all forms of morality and constraint. Is that not what "love gone wrong" means, appetite liberated from all constraints? From our vantage point in this book, however, or from our vantage point perhaps as parents, it is hard to look past the horrendous price that is paid for such a cult of freedom at all costs, especially if our children are instrumentalized in the venture, as objects to be toyed with, perhaps abused, perhaps destroyed.

Wuthering Heights *Redux*

For the most part, enduring literature rarely paints pictures of quite the victimization we see in Cécile Volanges. But a number of our most revered love stories are remarkably hard going, once our eyes are focused on the amount of abuse that either fuels them or is carried in their wake. I can think of no better way to measure what happens when love goes wrong than to return to the Brontë sisters and take a second look at their remarkable narratives in order to get a better fix on the abusive violence they contain concerning injured children. Emily Brontë's *Wuthering Heights* ushers its readers from the get-go into the realm of tortured children: the initial narrator, the overcivilized fop, Lockwood, has a visionary encounter with a ghostly child who wants in. A guest at Wuthering Heights, hearing a rapping on the window in the middle of the night and seeing a spectral child figure, Lockwood, terrified, pulls the child's wrist onto the broken windowpane, and "rubbed it to and fro till the blood ran down and soaked the bedclothes; still it wailed, 'Let me in!' and maintained its tenacious gripe, almost maddening me with fear." Mind you, "to and fro," not just a single swipe. One has trouble keeping this moment in focus, it is simply too sadistic. Brontë is showing her cards (as well as her teeth), setting the stage for a host of horrors meted out to children, as if to say that not only is growing up a time of punishment but the tortured child remains forever there, frozen in time, seeking entry, subject to endless laceration.

The book's unforgettable male protagonist, the Byronic Heathcliff, provides the fullest portrait of what abuse is and does. Routinely mistreated by Hindley, Catherine's brother, after old Earnshaw dies, Heathcliff would be the tortured/torturing *thing* of the novel, if it weren't for his extraordinary love for/kinship with Catherine. As we've noted, that Edenic bond, unseverable, spells fate for both of them. But he misconstrues her love, he leaves, she marries the genteel Edgar, he returns: the *machine infernale* goes into gear. Deprived of Catherine (while bound to her, soulwise, for eternity), wounded at the core, doomed to live after she dies, Heathcliff can respond only by abuse and revenge. And we will see that abuse and revenge are self-nourishing passions, unstillable, unquenchable, prior even to volition or design; one feels that Heathcliff is himself the victim of his rage, for that is what love's residue has become.

Arguably the most shocking feature of this savage novel is its unremitting general violence—hanging dogs is routine, beating and kicking and slapping and gouging are par for the course, and the sadistic treatment of those who are weaker (of whatever age or gender, but especially children) seems present on every page— and therefore Heathcliff's nonstop brutality toward everyone once he is in power appears horribly natural. It is especially the vicious circle that matters: treat someone like a dog, and they will do it in kind when they have a chance. Perhaps violence refashions our appetites, as when Heathcliff observes that the more brutally he humiliates the genteel Isabella, the more she comes back for more. As for the torturer, he is following a program: "I have no pity! I have no pity! The more the worms writhe, the more I yearn to crush out their entrails! It is a moral teething, and I grind with greater energy, in proportion to the increase in pain."

Heathcliff disturbs most via his torture of the novel's children, those who represent perhaps a chance for redressing things. We see him repeatedly thrashing Hindley (who'd abused him as a child), but also, as tit for tat, Hindley's son, Hareton, kept wild and unschooled, replaying Heathcliff's history; more unnerving are the scenes where he physically assaults and beats Catherine's daughter, little Cathy, and imprisons her in his house while Edgar, the child's father, is dying. (At one point she tries to embrace Heathcliff, but he throws her down, saying he'd rather be hugged by a snake.) But perhaps the nadir of his behavior is seen in his Machiavellian treatment of his own son, the sickly Linton, whom he uses as bait to ensnare young Cathy, arranging their marriage while knowing the boy is soon to die. Much has been made of the economic motive in play here: Heathcliff, spurned and brutalized as a poor orphan, is set upon gaining control of the Earnshaw and Linton properties, which he effectively does. But in my view the financial rationale is dwarfed by the sheer elemental rage that this man feels toward the children put into his care or within his reach. Hurt as a child, he is at war with children. I see no vice, no pineapple compote here, just a sullen to-the-death tyranny over the young, meted out as punishment for what he himself has had to endure.

Many of us will want to remember Heathcliff as the star-crossed lover, as the young boy whom Catherine loved so utterly that she could tell her housekeeper, "Nelly, I *am* Heathcliff." But to see Heathcliff's program of torture for all who go on living after Catherine dies as the response of a jilted lover is only to add to the horror. Loss of love is an abuse as deep as inflicted blows, for at bottom they are alike. Yet even if we assent to this quid-pro-quo model of love/loss/rage, we are accustomed to psychologizing such matters, assuming they apply to feelings only. But the behavior in *Wuthering Heights* is shockingly uncensored and unrestrained, and therefore feelings are immediately and explosively acted upon, conferring on this dark book an aura of affect run wild, of a scheme entirely without discipline or control.

Brontë's abuse-filled novel can be read as a dark version of growing up, if indeed growing up ever occurs. Most of its key figures— Heathcliff, Catherine, Hindley, Hareton—are twisted creatures, driven by fierce pulsions of rage and want, falling repeatedly into veritable tantrums of violence and fury, as if they were condemned to remain infantile all their lives. There is something shocking about these fully grown folks continuing to kick, bite, and hit, to trade blow for blow, right on past the gates of death. Brontë brings a second generation of children into the mix—they too are hounded and persecuted by Heathcliff—as the only way of calming the storm and yielding a semblance of peace. At book's end, we see, in the coming union of the daughter Cathy with the Caliban-like Hareton, an old comic rhythm of marriage and regeneration, yet the final image of the book is of the two tormented souls of Heathcliff and Catherine, seeking each other *d'outre-tombe,* in the entrails of the earth. The very concept of maturation is alien, more than a little quaint, in this tempestuous scheme where time does not leaven and injury is not forgotten.

A disturbing notion, this: time does not leaven, and injury is not forgotten. Look around and ask yourself how many of the grown-ups you know have remained angry, unforgiving, still hurting children. Emily Brontë's nineteenth-century Yorkshire wilds is a place for literalizing these matters, but modern life is no less violent toward its young even if the appearances are more seemly. We possess no affective MRIs, no magic scans that can display the scars and lesions on the soul, make visible to us the hurt that was done and that will not die. A dose of *Wuthering Heights* strikes me as tonic, as a reminder that bodies and hearts hurt and bleed for a long, long time when they are injured. Remember the ghostlike wraith with the bleeding wrists, begging (forever) to come in: it would be hard to find a better emblem of abuse.

Jane Eyre *Redux*

Emily's sister Charlotte seems to be a far more civilized type, and *Jane Eyre* has none of the outright hangings and beatings of *Wuthering Heights.* It stays in the minds of many of us as a moving tribute to pluck and character, as Jane arduously makes her way through thick and thin. But its story of abuse is no less horrid for all that. I have already mentioned Rochester's own sadistic toying with Jane, but she is bullied well before that. Young Jane is systematically injured and damaged while living with the Reeds at the book's beginning, and one is free to read the entire novel in the light of the abuse she receives as a child. The pièce de résistance of such an interpretation is of course the scene in the Red Room, where little Jane is imprisoned (after being battered by John Reed and chastised by her aunt) with no company but ghosts: the ghost of the dead patriarch whose body lay in state there and the still more frightening winged creatures that seem to arise to invade her (for good), yielding a shriek that knocks her insensible.

Brontë writes this spirit attack in virtually clinical fashion: "My heart beat thick, my head grew hot; a sound filled my ears, which I deemed the rushing of wings; something seemed near me; I was oppressed, suffocated: endurance broke down." There is a good bit of traffic registered here, and the child's psyche cannot hold its own in this affective storm, indeed storming. "Abuse" is a familiar term, yet who among us would know how to chart or graph its actual impact, the actual dynamics of injury? Most insidious, I think, is the intimation that something *living* is bearing down on Jane, violating, forcing its entry. Moreover, this scene has been cunningly arranged with a mirror (rightly termed a "visionary hollow") as its central furnishing, enabling us to construe all the Gothic traffic and wailing spirits as elements of the injured Jane's psyche, as "fellow-travelers" on the itinerary she is embarked on.

That itinerary and the wonderfully reasoning voice of Jane that accompanies it confer on this novel a pattern of rational deliberation and upward march toward ever-fuller self-possession, against all obstacles: the initial bullying at Lowood; further bullying by the handsome, rugged Rochester; a major setback in the form of an earlier Mrs. Rochester in the person of the ghoulish Bertha as madwoman in the attic; the final testing at the hands of the cold and compelling St. John Rivers, who (lovelessly) wants her to accompany him as helpmeet in his missionary efforts in India. Jane emerges triumphant from each of these contests and ends the novel with the trophy she deserves: the compliant Rochester, softened by blindness and maiming, readied at last for the novel's preening victory announcement: "Reader, I married him."

But a generation of feminist criticism has taught us to take a closer look at this marathon of achievement—Jane crossing hurdle after hurdle on her way to the finish line—and to interpret the novel's features in a far more ambiguous and disturbing way. Namely, we are asked to see in the figure of the monstrous Bertha Mason Rochester—bestial, violent, full of oaths, corpulent, sexually overflowing—an alter ego of the little, wrenlike Jane Eyre, a displaced double that seems to tell us: what you chase out the door may come back in through the window. Bertha can be read as a portrait of Jane's repressed appetites and desires. Every time she breaks into the narrative—and her strange laugh seems indeed to punctuate things—she tells us about the dynamics of child abuse, about the story of child abuse, given that she is its result. Remember *Wuthering Heights:* punish Heathcliff enough, and you produce an ogre who will punish everything in sight. Can we not say as much here: punish Jane enough and you produce Bertha? For she is the very spirit of revenge, going into action whenever Rochester's bullying and toying become unbearable, by mounting a counterattack: trying to burn him alive in his bed, tearing up her wedding veil in front of the horrified Jane so as to warn her of ever becoming Mrs. Rochester, and ultimately settling scores with the patriarch at book's end by torching the castle and doing her best to dismember its owner, costing him an eye and a hand.

How does one get a bottom line on this kind of fissured fiction, with its play of shadows and roaming spirits? How to measure this coming of age, given that Jane now seems spread out in multiple fashion? At first blush, on a straight, univocal reading—the reading the book always gets initially—Jane seems a winner, a plucky, feisty survivor who indeed overcame rough odds and finished by getting what she wanted. This remains true at second blush as well, with Bertha as her double, but it is considerably more complicated and offers us a radically more vexed and fascinating notion of maturation: namely, that it is never a simple sprint to the finish line, that each step of its trajectory is likely to leave traces in the psyche, that one's own story is inevitably a murky collective affair, filled to the brim with other figures who swim in one's orbit, who seem to mingle in one's blood, who might be alternate faces. And here would be the prize that literature itself offers us: that

fuller reading, the assessment that measures both surface achievement and the depth charges underneath. "Reader, I married him"
is no less stunning a statement in both versions, but it has the feeling of an earned, suffered, and painfully just reward in the more
spectral reading of the novel, for it writes large what our so-called
victories consist of, which may often include blood, tears, scars,
and assorted ghosts to boot. *Jane Eyre* asks us to rethink—to think
more deeply—how we got to where we are, how we became who
we are.

Jean Rhys's Wide Sargasso Sea

Not all readers are prepared to read Bertha as Jane's displaced
rage. Some will hold on to their more congenial views of the feisty
Jane making her way through thick and thin, without needing a
ghostly double. Others, of a more postcolonial bent, have argued
that it won't do to reduce Bertha (from the colonies) to some kind
of "return of the repressed" for the nice white girl, that Bertha is
entitled to her own history. More than a century later, Jean Rhys
succeeded brilliantly in writing just that history. *Wide Sargasso
Sea* (1966) is the haunting prequel to *Jane Eyre,* and it teaches us
everything we could wish to know about the making of monsters,
about how you end up being Bertha Mason Rochester. Its heroine,
Antoinette, is formed and deformed in front of our eyes: (heartbreakingly) deprived of love and tenderness by her mother, incessantly "othered" by her peers (not white enough for the blacks,
not English enough for the whites), haunted by the memory of
her ancestral house set on fire by angry natives (the very ones who
call her "white cockroach"), permanently frightened by the conditions of her life, Antoinette desperately seeks what she is to
know of happiness in her union with the handsome, sick, manipulated Edward Rochester, come to Dominica to find a wife.

It is a catastrophic marriage, written with remarkable acuity
on the part of Rhys, for they are all victims. Rochester longs for
parental approval, knows he is being used (as a pawn for his father
and brother's interests) in wedding Antoinette, is initially intoxi-
cated with desire on their honeymoon. Yet things go too far; he
risks, in their besotted and ungovernable sexual encounters, losing

himself and all boundaries, so he soon comes to fear and to hate this alien woman with her terrors and needs and strange skin and stranger eyes. One might argue that sexuality itself is being deconstructed here, that it wrecks definitions and parameters, that it is unownable. The entire colonial project is cued to secure ownership, and Rhys's plot is to obey exactly that logic: Antoinette in a cage, brought to England. (Rhys originally wrote Rochester more simply but then realized that this young couple had to have had its moment of magic and that that sexual magic could be the ultimate trigger of the male anxieties and cruelties to come. This is brilliant and beyond what would have been thinkable for Brontë.)

The price must be paid. Rochester is told (by a jealous relative, another unloved son) that Antoinette is unchaste, has lovers (which may be true); he realizes he can never understand her, can never make his peace with these primitive people and their exotic voodoo customs, so different from England. If he cannot have her to himself—it is the ultimate colonial dream: to possess the very jewel of the culture one expropriates—he has no choice but to punish her, destroy her. Thus we are witness to a grotesque building project: the fashioning of a monster, the making of a coarse, foulmouthed, murderous creature whose fate will be to be locked up on the third floor of Thornfield Hall, while waiting for the propitious moment to set fire to it, as a repeat version of the fire that annihilated her Edenic home. The career of Antoinette Bertha Mason Rochester is an exemplary tale of growing up into horror.

It is also artisanal in the worst sense. Monsters are not born but made. Antoinette's childhood of deprivation and fear segues into a passionate but desperate relationship with a man who sequentially courts, desires, uses, fears, and destroys her. (He also takes her fortune.) It is the Frankenstein story recast as love story. He caps her education into horror, step by step, from the Caribbean on to jolly old England and the third floor of Thornfield Hall. He is no Gothic monster but an all-too-anxious male, also deprived of tenderness, alienated by these dark-skinned creatures who are not English, trapped into a fiery conjunction that will destroy him if he does not destroy it first. So he does, with grisly thoroughness, beginning with (noisily) fornicating the servant girl and closing with the removal of the dazed Antoinette marionette to a ship sailing for the pasteboard England that can never be home. Rochester leaves a host of cadavers in his wake: Christophina, Antoinette's marvelous black nurse, is slated for arrest; the servants are disbanded; and the trophy wife is taken back home as a beautiful, kept-behind-bars ghoul. As said, we've been taught recently to code this fable as "colonialist," as a testament to the European exploitation of the non-West; but it is useful also to see it as a nightmarish version of human development gone amok, as a case study of what love gone wrong can produce, as outright proof of how malleable a human being is, as a laboratory experiment in deformation.

Let me add still a further note here. Rhys, experiencing herself as a maladapted transplant her entire life, shows an extraordinary kind of imaginative generosity in reprising Brontë's novel, in "making a life for the poor ghost" she saw in Bertha Mason Rochester. Rhys started with the posited monstrous adult—the obscene Bertha of Brontë's devising—and wrote her backward into the past, intuited that a great deal of earlier horror had to subtend, to "finance," the performance shown in the English text. What you know us to be is not so much what we are but what we have become, what life has made of us. And that development is no natural process: it is a saga of human and ideological (and racial) forces, of vectors crossing, of wires crossing, of the constitutive work of time. Could we see this had Rhys not shown us?

One final word about *Wide Sargasso Sea:* I have come to see it as the saddest book in my teaching repertoire. It is not as tragic or profound, perhaps, as my favorite modernists such as Proust and Woolf and Faulkner, but it hits me—me the professor of comparative literature who lives in three countries, speaks a batch of languages, and routinely teaches literature from all across the Western canon—where it hurts: it exposes the myth of cross-cultural understanding. What aches most about this awful story is the neediness and vulnerability of both Antoinette and Rochester, and one wants—I want—their relationship to be possible. Rhys refuses to demonize Rochester but sees him as an unloved son, just as Antoinette is an unloved daughter. There lies the first, perhaps unsurvivable, abuse. Then comes the second pitfall, the one that makes me unhappy: they cannot bridge their cultures. Rochester cannot will himself into believing that people from the colonies, most especially the beautiful one with the strange eyes whom he has married, are quite real. Antoinette suffers the same failure of vision, feeling that the England of her new husband is but a cardboard world, without resonance, even though it is the prison in which she is destined to finish her days. Yes, they have their moment of ecstasy in the Garden, and this too poisons their life, since the Eurocentric Rochester cannot abide the sexual fury she awakens in him.

Since the beginning of my career, I have been advising people to learn other languages and to live and study abroad, as well as read books from many different cultures. It is, I feel, the great model for education, the only way of widening your view of the human, of fathoming that others from faraway places and times (encountered in print as well as in person) are real. Exposure to other cultures is the royal way to become truly civilized. It is the growing-up formula in which I have invested my own life as teacher. And as writer: this book, like all my books, is written in exactly that spirit. Why else do comparative literature? The path to understanding (and peace) goes across the bridge from home to abroad. Jean Rhys's beautiful but heartbreaking book suggests otherwise: the Sargasso Sea that separates Rochester from Antoinette, me from you, is too large to be crossed.

Familial Sacrifice:
Kindermord

We know that children die. Not only do they die of disease and other ills that remain with us, but some of them seem outright sacrificed either by their culture's arrangements or, closer to home, by the toxic, life-sapping impact of family itself. The nest can kill. This takes us a step beyond what we've seen up to now, for even the abuse story is strangely a testament to human resilience as well as vulnerability: Cathy and Hareton survive to marry at the close of *Wuthering Heights;* Jane acquires money, family, and husband by the end of her trajectory; Antoinette/Bertha's case is grimmer, but she lives on to become an avenging angel. Yet growing up damaged is not the same thing as being wiped out altogether, as if according to a systemic logic that rids the world of children, through either intention or no less lethal neglect.

Pat Barker's fine, quasi-documentary novel about shell shock in World War I, *Regeneration,* develops this sacrificial view with considerable eloquence, and the chief protagonist, W. H. Rivers, espies here the oldest dirty trick in human history, with us from Abraham's willingess to sacrifice Isaac all the way to present-day politics: the old ask the young to show their obedience by being willing to die, and those who live will in turn move into this same august position of power when they become old and require it of their own children. It is as if civilization tirelessly sought to invert the Oedipal story by having the fathers crush their progeny. We'll see more of this in the latter part of this study.

Barker is writing about the horrors of war. But we can find evidence of such a dystopian vision in works of literature that have nothing to do with battle or the power of the nation-state. Such works are, in some ways, still more disturbing, because they seem to point to a more primitive kind of bargain that has been reached concerning the rights and prospects of children. Let us look at several radically different versions of "murdered children" in texts by Dickens, Ibsen, Kafka, and Faulkner. We will want to ponder: What is the operative logic here? What order—political, economic, moral, libidinal—requires this sacrifice?

Charles Dickens

No novelist is more identified with sacrificed children than Dickens. Many of his young characters come through alive, even if damaged. As far back as *Oliver Twist* we have the spectacle of children being exploited by the new urban order, even though Oliver comes through unscathed. Dickens later learned to write this story with ever more power and reach. David Copperfield's manifold struggles against adversity rehearse much of the deprivation and heartache that young Dickens himself experienced. I have already discussed the injured Pip of *Great Expectations*, and a good number of the great late novels toil in this vineyard, yielding figures such as Esther Summerson of *Bleak House* and Little Dorrit of the book bearing her name, each persevering against considerable odds: illegitimacy in one instance, poverty in the other. These are among Dickens's finest and most complex portrayals of children.

But the death of children exerts a sometimes morbid fascination for Dickens, as if he were staging the outcome he himself most feared while growing up, using the novel form as a kind of affective workout to rehearse/avoid such a fate. Readers wept at Little Nell's death; and one remembers little Paul Dombey's demise. Such pathos-loaded scenes may come across as sentimental today, especially given how angelic and innocent the little ones are, how undeserving they are of their fate. But Dickens can be tougher than this, and I want to turn my sights to the figure who is arguably the most victimized in the whole of Dickens: Jo the orphan boy in *Bleak House.*

This rich, elephantine novel is studded with figures of damaged children, and, for the most part, theirs are stories Dickens can tell. Ada and Rick's is a touching if tragic love story, and it closes with the birth of Ada's child and Rick's death. Esther, the central heroine of the narrative, enacts a tale of maturation and understanding, one that flirts with bad outcomes but finally closes with marriage and happiness ever after. But Jo, the marginal figure I want to emphasize, does not have a story. He does not even have a last name. He is the exemplary creature of the great London slum Tom-all-alone's, yet it might be claimed that he is the book's most potent and influential figure: he alters lives. The recipient of nonstop harassment, told incessantly to "move on," sick, Jo does move on, hides out at Bleak House, is cared for by Charley (Esther's maid), infects Charley with his smallpox, and ultimately infects Esther, whose face will be permanently scarred because of this human encounter.

Potent, influential, but without a story, he dies later in the book, but we know nothing of his parents or his background and little even of his feelings. *He does not grow up;* by this I mean that there is no cultural plot available to him, no trajectory imaginable. Jo's actual death, late in the novel, is presented with the pathos one expects from Dickens, as the dying boy repeats, in the manner of a countdown, the words of the Lord's Prayer. But we can scarcely miss the fact that this child's death has a coherence and symbolism even beyond the coping strategies of the book's surviving children. Parentless, he is the creature, indeed the offspring, of the pestilent slum Tom-all-alone's, figured as an omnipotent "miasmic" force that out-trumps even Chancery in determining human fate. Jo—without resources, contaminated by the city's filth and disease, unsavable—is the living proof that nineteenth-century urban and social arrangements ground up children. His bereftness exposes, with an embarrassment Dickens could not have intended, just how lucky Esther, Rick, and Ada are from a material point of view. Those children have their own obstacle course, but they benefit from Dickensian paternalism at its most heightened: the rich John Jarndyce steps in to adopt and save all of them. I mentioned earlier that few young people in college today receive the omniscient counsel of a Vautrin; even fewer real abandoned children receive the helping hand of a "rich uncle" who wants to save them from ruin.

To have conceived of Jo as illiterate is a mark of Dickens's genius, for it takes his victim status a quantum leap further, disempowers him still more radically. Dickens wants us to measure just what it might feel like to be a stranger to written language. Jo's recurrent phrase throughout the novel is "I don't know nothink." The (intended?) pun is telling: being shut off from words is to be shut off from thinking, to be exiled from what is most human about the human community. He sees a world of utter, complete mystery—a mystery far beyond that of unsolved crimes, a mystery of blankness and absurdity, as if he were an alien from another planet—and he has no connection to it:

> To shuffle through the streets, unfamiliar with the shapes, and in utter darkness as to the meaning, of those mysterious symbols, so abundant over the shops, and at the corners of streets, and on doors, and in the windows! To see people read, and to see people write, and to see the postmen deliver letters, and not to have the least idea of all that language—to be, every scrap of it, stone blind and dumb! . . . what does it all mean, and if it means anything to anybody, how comes it that it means nothing to me? To be hustled, and jostled, and moved on; and really to feel that it would appear to be perfectly true that I have no business, here, or there, or anywhere; and yet to be perplexed by the consideration that I *am* here somehow, too.

Jo's estrangement is total. Even the Dickensian prose that conveys his lostness is doubtless articulated and nuanced in ways far beyond Jo's own ken, for the novelist can only point toward the black hole that is this boy, the daily discovery of his nothingness in the larger scheme. He is toolless. Beyond even the material abuse he suffers, he moves us most by his islanded state, his doom as a stranded figure of another species, abject, reified, turned into the book's carrier of disease, its walking time bomb. We need to see that language can be as great an asset as money when it comes to the story of growing up. Already in the exploits of Pablos we noted that verbal prowess can be a mighty resource in redressing material circumstances. And in studies still to come, language will play a still greater role in self-empowerment, enabling the young to comprehend ever more fully the culture they inhabit, the history that precedes them, so as to complete their journey to adulthood. Jo has none of this. In his disenfranchisement he looks horribly forward to Kafka's sacrificial stories of exiting-the-human.

Henrik Ibsen

Childhood is a state that matters for Henrik Ibsen. *A Doll House,* his breakthrough play of 1879, unforgettably stages the drama of Nora's recognition that she has never left childhood, that she is still inhabiting a dollhouse, even though she is married and the mother of two children. Infantilized by her father, then by her husband, Torvald, defined as the property of males, Nora comes increasingly to understand that she has never developed any full sense of selfhood or agency. How to emancipate oneself? We know that Nora's own solution—to exit this bad marriage, leaving her children with her husband, in search of herself, en route to becoming fully, genuinely "adult"—utterly shocked nineteenth-century audiences, who could not believe that a decent woman could behave in this fashion.

Little license is needed to see growing up as the central drama that Ibsen writes over and over. Sometimes this process comes late in life: Helene Alving (in *Ghosts*) is a widow with a grown child before she fully gauges the injuries inflicted on her as a young girl, the coercions she experienced and even handed on, due to the repressive conditions in which she was brought up. A later heroine, Hedda Gabler, comes to a comparable discovery, as she desperately tries to find stimuli and freedom in the caged life she has bought into, as the wife of the dull Tesman, as a proper bourgeoise who is being asphyxiated by the air she breathes, by the walls that are closing in on her. Ibsen's men are not immune from these dilemmas, even if the coloration is different, since their penal condition is of another stripe, voluntary rather than male-imposed; I'm thinking of the two male protagonists of *The Wild Duck*, the neurotic, indeed fanatic, idealist Gregers and the pampered, self-deluded, soi-disant "inventor" Hjalmar, each of whom is hopelessly egocentric and infantile in his behavior and blindness, each of whom contributes to the death of the child Hedvig.

Hedvig dies, the doomed plaything of the two puffed-up males arguing over principles. So too dies Oswald Alving, Helene Alving's talented artist-son, who has inherited syphilis from his dead, dissolute father, who returned to Norway from Paris to die because his brain was turning to mush. And there are other dead children in Ibsen: the little twin boys in *The Master Builder* who had to die, it seems, so that Solness could somehow be liberated to do his great work (before he too goes on the block, escorted out of the play by its child-executioner, Hilde). The most poignant of these victims is Eyolf, the title figure of *Little Eyolf*, crippled at birth because of his parents' neglect (and sexuality), destined to death by drowning at the end of Act I, so that the adults on the scene can settle their scores and begin to see clear in their own arrangements.

There are lots of dead children littering the stage of these plays or buried behind the scenes. We can scarcely avoid perceiving a rather grisly coherence, a pattern being worked out on the loom: namely, that the moral emancipation of adults is darkly cued to the sacrifice of children. These plays seem to obey a zero-sum logic, according to which the price of my freedom is yours. There is also an anti-Oedipal impulse of considerable force here, condemning the next generation to death as their elders make their way toward light and clarity. The grand paradox is that Ibsen's energies are profoundly liberal in character; his protagonists are all moving toward a greater sense of agency and self-knowledge. These plays are about education. It is all the more awful, therefore, that the young themselves fare so badly, end up sacrificed. "I refuse the ticket," Ivan Karamazov proclaimed when he realized that accepting God also meant accepting the torture of children; in Ibsen, all too often, the children *are* the ticket for whatever emancipation is to be achieved.

The most surprising feature of Ibsen's work is how occulted this business of systemic child sacrifice is, how you have to take a step back from these plays of adult emancipation in order to see the disturbing machinery that lies behind it. We know that Ibsen himself had an unhappy childhood, replete with parental financial ruin, and that he remembered himself as undersized and underendowed. That hurting child would become the Great Man of nineteenth-century European theater, who rang a death knell for what was culturally ossified around him. In looking at the compromised adult Norwegian society around him, he fastened onto Truth and Light as his two authority principles. His grown-ups make their way circuitously but unstoppably toward this luminous horizon, yet, as we've seen, the children seem shunted into the dark, slated for destruction.

There seems to be a kind of libidinal unfinished business that whips and goads Ibsen's psyche, meting out punishment and death to children. The persistence of outright or veiled infanticide in these plays speaks of the gruesome price that might be exacted if one is to grow up. Becoming adult is inseparable from *Kindermord.* Is that what successful maturation means: the destruction of the child oneself was? What gears need to be shifted, for all of us, to cross over the gulf from child to adult? Did Ibsen have to "off," in play after play, a "child self" that could not live? A child that had to be sacrificed precisely because growing up and adult success required it? The moves I have traced in this book from innocence to experience to love's successes and failures: what do they spell for the child we were? Might the familiar cliché "one's inner child"—a notion that conjures up a vital infant still living within us, with its own needs and values—be a fantasy that cloaks something much grislier: a corpse? Rethink your own life: no cadavers? no early self put to death so you could become you?

Going Under in Franz Kafka

One of Franz Kafka's most beautiful utterances is "Art is the ax that chops through our frozen sea." It's a forbidding statement, perhaps, but also uplifting when one construes it as a recognition of the murk and torpor that routinely characterize our psyche and our sentiments, while positing art as the cutting edge that makes its way into us, awakens us, arouses us to life. But of course the phrase is edgy in more ways than one, since it figures this awakening as a wound, as a potentially violent, potentially lethal entry into both mind and body. I am also struck by the verticality of the metaphor, its way of representing our interior as dead depths, its implication that art might be akin to trauma in its penetration of our surface, its rupturing entry into our all-too-insentient reaches. If we view art as a kind of depth charge, we begin to sketch the landscape of Kafka's strange world, a place of surfaces that are at once real and penetrable, a material scheme that is at once solid and oddly porous, yet haunted and infected by the "immaterial," thereby generating the key metaphors of his work: the radiance of truth that shimmers behind a series of closed and guarded doors; the routine failure of protagonists to get past obstacles or find their way; the figurative landscape of a writer trapped in the phenomenal scheme of flesh and matter while hungering for something beyond them.

Kafka once expressed admiration for Flaubert's declared envy at the sight of low-to-the-ground, simple people anchored in their reality: *"Ils sont dans le vrai,"* sighed the French novelist. It seems to me that Kafka imagines functional adulthood in terms of a sought-after stability, a fit within the system, an at-homeness in flesh and world, an incorporation of the deep rhythms of life and love. The pathos of his work is that children rarely make it this far. One does not grow up in Kafka; one goes under. Kafka's *Letter to the Father* offers a richly articulated account of a failed childhood, an experience of growing up as constant injury and humiliation. But the famous fictions go even further in their account of children going under.

One could claim that Georg Bendemann, the protagonist of "The Judgment," is not a child. After all, he is taking care of his infirm father, is ready to take over the family business, has a fiancée, is poised to move securely into the stream of life. Except, as we will see, that this cannot happen, cannot be allowed to happen. Kafka regarded this short story, written frenetically in one fell swoop at the very onset of his career, as a breakthrough, describing it as a mucus-covered fetus emerging from the womb, a "birthing" text for his coming work. Very curious: Franz is to be born as writer via the account of Georg's being arrested as a child.

For that is what will transpire. Georg seems initially to be an anchored figure, reliably informing us of his prospects and responsibilities: readying himself for marriage to his fiancée, corresponding with his faraway, self-exiled friend in Russia, and moving more and more centrally into managing the affairs of the business, given his father's evident decline. We have no reason to doubt any of these statements, since they behave just as literary utterance always has, nailing down a person's situation and thoughts in language. Hence we anticipate nothing more than a mild exchange of views when Georg at last enters his father's darkened bedroom to have a look at him; Georg fills in his father on matters relating to fiancée and friend, yet is struck by the enfeeblement he now perceives, worries that he has neglected the old man for far too long. Georg goes on to lift his bedridden father up so as to better arrange his covers. "Am I well covered up?" asks the old man. *"Bin ich gut zugedeckt?"* Can fathers ever be under cover?

One has to be a veteran Kafka reader to hear the ticking bomb that *must* accompany such seemingly innocuous notations. For there is an explosion. It is Father exploding, Father rising and deploying his gathered energy, Father preparing himself to pronounce judgment on his hapless son, Georg. Little in literature matches this moment of upheaval and transformation: we suddenly realize that nothing is what it seemed to be, that the relation between these two figures is loaded in ways we hadn't seen, and that the text is in the process of turning it all inside out. Father now revisits Georg's little agenda items: fiancée, friend in Russia, general prospects of taking over. Of becoming the man in the house. And we are stunned by the virulent, withering indictment we now hear: Georg is accused of role playing, of plotting, of make-believe, of disloyalty and betrayal. There is no friend in Russia, Father says; then, a minute later, yes, there is a friend in Russia, but he is Father's friend, not Georg's. As for the fiancée, this cheap little trick, this pathetic effort at sexual assertion, is nipped in the bud, recast as vulgar titillation, as defiling of the dead mother, as inconsequential.

Every first-time reader wonders: what's going on here? If what Father is saying is right, everything Georg told us is wrong, false. What, we also wonder, is Georg's response going to be to these vicious, hallucinatory accusations? Which one is nuts? Initially, Georg treats Father's diatribe as a sign of his disturbed senses, but very soon, all too soon, the Father's declarations start to usurp the field, to acquire in front of our eyes a dreadful kind of authority and power, as if the words were generating their own truth as they issued from Father's mouth. Georg, wounded in his very reality, backs up further and further, seems to be shrinking in authority, seems slated for some horrible kind of erasure. And sure enough, it comes. Father speaks: Georg, you seemed like a good child, but in reality you've always been a devilish creature, and now I pronounce your judgment: death by drowning. And lo and behold, it will happen. Georg accepts the death sentence—it is a genuine death sentence since each word is imbued with lethal power—and Kafka virtually lifts/sweeps/sucks him out of the story (and out of life) in the last sentence of the story: Georg is literally propelled out of the apartment, down the stairs, onto the street, up onto the bridge, and over the bridge into the water to his death, all the while intoning "Dear parents, I always loved you." He goes under.

What is one to make of this surreal exercise? We say to ourselves: life isn't like this, even the most despicably bullying parents do not act like this, even the most victimized child does not exit like this. No, this is not a "slice of life" notation that obeys daytime logic. But as nightmare, as fantasy, indeed as deep-seated truth about the tyrannical power of the father and the helplessness of the son, this will do quite nicely indeed. The reader's commonsensical questions as to why this happens and what it means simply have no purchase, no traction. No explanation is offered, but the sacrificial message is clear: one does not grow up in Kafka.

Georg Bendemann's fate is repeated in even more monstrous fashion in the famous story of Gregor Samsa, the equally docile good little son—the breadwinner this time—who has the misfortune to wake up one morning as an insect. Much can be, and has been, said about "The Metamorphosis," but its anti-Oedipal punch is unmistakably one of the things we most remember. But note how much further Kafka has taken it: the child will not only be prevented from making his way, he will be transmogrified.

Gregor does not quite pose the threat that Georg Bendemann did—he's not preparing to get married, and it would seem that he's already replaced Dad as provider—but the bill comes anyway: he is to be undone. *Undone.* When we remember that the etymology of the Bildungsroman is "formation," we understand better the morphological fantasia on show in this story: a person is to be deformed, re-formed, unformed. Poor Gregor goes through his calvary of being systematically weaned from humanity—his body is now that of a beetle, he can no longer speak (other than to us), his human habitation is transformed into a lair, and finally he dies of starvation (after being wounded by the apples thrown at him by his father)—without ever proffering a word of anger against his progenitors, just like Georg. Yet at story's end the dead beetle will have invigorated and rejuvenated his entire family: his mother and father are brought back into circulation, turned vital, and his sister, Grete, is seen stretching her nubile body in the last line of the narrative. I can scarcely imagine a more brutal reversal to the story of growing up: instead of evolving and maturing, one is metamorphosed and put slowly to death, in order to seed change for others.

Einstein is said, perhaps apocryphally, to have read this story with astonishment that the human brain could be that complex, and I think I share the physicist's stunned admiration for the weird processes of loss and gain, displacement, and empowerment enacted by the narrative. For somewhere in this food chain, there is one Franz Kafka, the "injured" son-writer, busily composing devious fables of son sacrifice; this Kafka lives and grows by sentencing to death his alter egos in story after story. If growing up means entering the adult world of marriage and responsibility, of entering *"dans le vrai,"* Kafka's message seems clear: you can't get there from here. But keep your eye on the ball: Kafka did indeed get somewhere: into world literature, into our minds, into our nightmares. He found a way to transform his sense of (permanent) injury and arrestedness and fear into an art form that is as supple, indeed muscular and vital, as that of sister Grete, whose nubile, outstretched body is the last image we see in "The Metamorphosis." But maybe what we are supposed to remember is not the swept-away, dried-up beetle carcass of Gregor Samsa but the flowering body of the sister who lives, who has made it through from cramped nightmare to fresh air. We'd have to be blind not to see that there is indeed a passage to life encoded here. But—a sacrifice is needed for it to happen.

Ibsen and Kafka: both place children "in the penal colony" (as Kafka might have said); both devise a logic that requires children to die. But note: in both cases, they serve as sacrificial, enabling figures. "I died so that you might live." It is a phrase—indeed, a view of life—that we have heard before. The master narrative of Christianity requires a son's death, and the amount of sacrifice demanded in other, older traditions—remember Iphigenia and Isaac—is substantial. To propitiate the gods, someone or something must be slain. There is a disturbing coherence on show here, a machinery of power that seems to announce that the affairs of the adults—indeed, of the community—need a young corpse if they are to prosper. One wonders how far we have come, in modern times, from these infanticidal injunctions. Doesn't war itself exact its portion of child blood? Aren't children the first and foremost casualties in famine and disaster? Is it only because they are weak? Or is there something ghastlier still at work in this ancient sacrificial covenant? It's a conundrum worth pondering.

William Faulkner's Quentin Compson

If Dickens, Ibsen, and Kafka offer us the anatomy of child sacrifice—a repeating plot of done-in children, seen as offerings to propitiate either economic order or family—Faulkner has left us perhaps the most moving account of how it might feel on the inside, to *know* one is slated for going under. I return to *The Sound and the Fury*, to Quentin Compson, the boy who will commit suicide. Unlike his brother Benjy, Quentin has hyperkeen neural and intellectual equipment, is all too able to make knowledge of his injuries, and hence he evolves. After all, he got out of the South and is now at Harvard; it almost looks like an advertisement for freedom. But the exit from Yoknapatawpha is only apparent, for he is as stuck in time as his idiot brother, even more so, since time itself looms impossibly large in his consciousness as a ticking, indicting sentence: the hands of his watch, the position of shadows, the obsessive sense of leading a mummer's life at Harvard, outwardly free but inwardly cued forever to the damning family history back home: sold pasture, dysfunctional family, frigid mother, alcoholic father, helpless brother, and above all, as the very figure of doom: Caddy. He loves her as maniacally as Benjy does but with more punitive twists, since he is expected to protect her honor (ha), whereas the nasty truth is that he himself is the virgin (ha ha), failing in every department: fearful of sex (rendered in the novel as asphyxiating honeysuckle), jealous of her lover, impotent (in all senses) in measuring up to the code he's inherited.

Faulkner's rendition of Quentin Compson's final day in life is a tour de force in modernist writing: his psychic equipment resembles that of his brother, so the memory of Caddy not only is plastered everywhere but is subject at any moment, via any stimulus whatsoever, to burst into his mind and take over. Mixed up with his life in Cambridge and his exchanges with his roommate and others are whole conversations of the past still playing out in his consciousness, leaving us with the sense of a human being who is damned, who is drenched (on the inside) with lethal material. One feels that one is looking at a psychic X-ray, so that the still-upright surface figure we (and all his peers) see is horridly hollowed out and honeycombed by the noxious living residue of the past, a past that pulsates and speaks and usurps everything. Kafka's children are executed, but we are never told why; Quentin's descent into death is horribly illuminated from the inside, showing us how and why at every juncture.

Nowhere is this entrapment more spectacular than in the Kafkaesque episode in which Quentin makes a last pathetic bid for freedom by taking a tram outside Cambridge—as if any tram could transport him out of himself—where his stroll leads him into a bakery where he encounters the little Italian girl who spells fate. "Hello, sister," he says when he first sees her. The child cannot speak English, carries a phallic-looking loaf of bread, becomes glued to the young man, cannot be sprung loose. Trouble. In come

honeysuckle and more damning memories of sex disarray: the recall of a man who castrated himself, of himself wrestling with
Caddy, all leading to upsurging chunks of narrative, vomited onto
the page, relating Quentin's fiascos with Caddy (who'll make love
with him if he wants), as well as his shameful showing with her
lover Dalton Ames, when he faints while trying to fight. The version I have just presented of these materials is accurate as far as
Quentin's psychic story goes, but it is flagrantly wrong in one key
respect: it's all psychodrama; Quentin is reliving all this in his
mind, while at the same time, in the public arena, going through
the last stages of the little-girl imbroglio outside Cambridge,
which closes with his being quasi-arrested and then, as grand fi-
nale, duking it out with the Harvard Lothario Gerald Bland and
being bloodied up in the process. Quentin has disappeared into his
past. Thinking he's hitting Dalton Ames, Caddy's lover, he is in
fact being pummeled by Gerald Bland. I do not know of a fiercer
way of choreographing someone's exit from the stage, someone's
final, definitive succumbing to ghosts.

Each of us arguably jousts with ghosts on a permanent basis.
Perhaps we do more of it asleep than awake. The balancing act
consists of compartmentalizing, forgetting, locking up, burying,
plugging one's ears: so many different strategies for saying yes to
life as it comes, to ourselves as works in progress, to freedom as
conceivable, to growing up. Faulkner's young people fail at tuning
out the past. There are in real life no cameras or speakers to represent this intercourse that takes place on the inside, that is cued
to a there and then that is invisible and inaudible to our fellows.
Faulkner writes as no one else ever has exactly this dialogic dance
of death, and Quentin Compson is its purest incarnation. *The
Sound and the Fury* has the rigor and horror of a scientific experiment in which the toxins of the past are uncontainable, im-
mutable, and therefore free to assert their absolute reign. It is a
ballet of takeover. One's family, one's memories, one's feelings,
one's entire past, all cohere into a gathering scene of execution.

Yet it has its severe beauty. It is worth remembering that
Quentin elects to commit suicide in order to reject the "temporary" philosophy of his father, a philosophy doubtless shared by
all of us who survive and subscribe to the adage that time heals.

That, Quentin realizes, is what cannot be brooked: that he will heal, that he will get over Caddy, that he will go on to live. I call this beautiful inasmuch as it is a radical choice: he refuses change, refuses the forking path that marks all unfurling lives, and instead fastens onto his past as the self that cannot be let go. It is, in its way, a permanent endorsement of childhood—no matter that that childhood contained so much suffering—for that is where he found himself in his entirety, and he will not debase it/himself by moving into a future where he will be different. He commits suicide not as an escape but as a self-enactment, as a Pyrrhic victory over time. Something in this story whispers to us that growing up is a form of betrayal, an abandonment, perhaps a desecration of the child we once were. This may not resemble the ticket of complicity that Ivan Karamazov refused, but it is a ticket nonetheless, and Quentin Compson refuses it.

Systemwide Sacrifice:
Children and the
Nightmare of History

In my account of Grimmelshausen's *Simplicissimus*, I focused on a subject that is all too real to us, century after century: children victimized, deranged, destroyed by war. There has been no war that has not had this impact, and we have a memorable literature—often written by the survivors themselves, grown to adulthood, delivering their testimony, often simply imagined by those who were not there—devoted to this topic. Crane's *The Red Badge of Courage* does not lose any of its power when we learn that Crane was "only" a journalist, that he did not experience the chaos of war firsthand as a combatant. On the other hand, Hemingway encountered much of war's carnage as an ambulance driver in World War I, and his Nick Adams has an apprenticeship with the dissolution caused by the horrors of combat—bodies rotting, forms altering, things returning to the primal ooze—that is doubtless traceable to the author's experience.

But what if you were at once there and not there? What of the children who themselves either saw nothing firsthand or understood nothing of what they saw, but who nonetheless grew up absorbing war, absorbing Holocaust, as their sole diet of childhood, whether they were living securely in another country or somehow shielded at home? We have no statistics for measuring such a group, but it must be a staggering population. In phrasing it this way, I am trying to sketch something of the horrid dimensions of this issue: how far war goes, temporally; how many victims it claims, even long after it is over; how the concentric circles never stop spreading, as if all wars, even the most primitive ones fought with swords and arrows, are actually, ultimately, nuclear events, toxic events, leaving a radioactive legacy that is generational in character, that has a half-life that can continue almost forever.

That is not all. As we have seen so often in this study, much that we think we know appears Other when reflected and refracted through the eyes and hearts of children. Not only are children stamped—sometimes stamped out—by the upheavals of history and calamity, but they are often our most shocking guides to the horrors of the past, because their vantage point brings home to us, as nothing else can, the human cost of events that are all too easily defanged when presented to us as the cold data of our chronicles and archives. They teach us how to see.

Art Spiegelman's Maus

With this remark, I wish now to fast-forward to a later age, in order to explore two narratives dealing with massive destruction—the Holocaust and 9/11—and focusing on a child's effort to come to terms with the incomprehensible, whether it be the genocidal events suffered long ago by one's parents or the disappearance of a father in the World Trade Center. *To come to terms:* that is precisely what Art Spiegelman has done in *Maus* by creating a new language altogether—a graphic visual language of remarkable eloquence—to convey what he inherited and what he made of it for us to see. I think that *Maus* is stunningly successful on just that front: as a new optic, as a privileged medium for conveying with unprecedented pathos what it means when the parents' world is racked by convulsions and the child picks up the pieces long afterward.

Art Spiegelman's two volumes of *Maus*, published in their entirety in 1986 and 1991, created the moment when many of us realized that this so-called children's genre was capable of a pathos and ethicopolitical payload that traditional prose fiction could not easily match. Spiegelman, albeit American-born, is a child of the Holocaust, and it is the determining event of his life. What is darkly beautiful here is that it ultimately drove him to find a mode of expression that would somehow convert this corrosive legacy into something luminous and heart-wrenching for readers throughout the world who had no connection at all with the six million Jews who died.

This did not happen easily or quickly. In fact, Spiegelman himself—Artie, as he is called in the books—rarely appears textually as a child but rather as a young married man with a most difficult father. About the child's own experiences, we get very little other than a tiny prologue dated 1958, taking place in Rego Park, New York, where young Artie is playing with his friends Howie and Steve, only to be left behind when his skate comes loose; it does not take more to hurt a child, and he goes sobbing home to his father, Vladek, who informs him that the test of real friendship would be to lock them together in a room with no food for a week, and "THEN you could see what it is, friends." And with that the prologue closes. When we turn to the opening chapter, little Artie has disappeared: he is now grown-up Artie, who has come to get from Vladek the story of his life.

Yet the truth is that Artie is still working through these issues, all during childhood, all during adulthood, and probably right on through his life today and continuing on to his future death. There are many reminders in the text that these matters do not admit of closure. This is not happy news, and it suggests that all the child stories discussed in this book—the material of growing up—are inevitably positioned on a temporal treadmill that moves right through life, mocking any clean boundary lines. Perhaps we never stop growing up. Contrary to all calendar proofs of birth and death, the old continue to inhabit the young, the young remain inscribed in the lives of the old, and each group seems to go through its paces forever. My mother saw me as a child up to her dying day (when I was in my sixties), and my grown-up children still live for me as infants. (How I live for and inside them is not for me to know, but it surely exists.) But catastrophe marks its victims still more profoundly: parents never heal from it, and children are forever processing the results. The wreckage can play out over entire generations.

Inserted within the larger saga of Vladek's Holocaust experience is a story within a story entitled "Prisoner on the Hell Planet," an actual graphic text published by Spiegelman in 1972, depicting Anja, the mother's, suicide as well as the boatload of guilt and rage experienced by Art, the "failed" son released from the state mental hospital, spewing considerable venom as response to the family he inherited. These few pages are in a 1960s graphic style utterly unlike that of *Maus,* and we learn (in sweet postmodern fashion as the book mirrors its own processes) that Vladek has in fact discovered this early published expression of Art's views. But what most stamps this little vignette is the affective material at its core: the last living image of Anja as a disheveled woman coming into her son's bedroom late at night, asking him, "Artie . . . you . . . still . . . love . . . me . . . don't you?" Turned away to the wall, unwilling to look her in the face, full of resentment, the son utters the last words his mother will ever hear from him: "Sure, Ma!"

I don't think it excessive to say that the origin of *Maus* lies as much in this little episode as it does in the "grander" tableau of Vladek's experiences in Poland and Auschwitz. Not unlike Stephen Dedalus, whose pride prevented him from praying at his mother's deathbed and who periodically chokes on this throughout James Joyce's *Ulysses,* Artie himself is a bleeding figure, haunted by his own transgressions, even if he subtitled his first volume *My Father Bleeds History* and presented himself as intact. Do all of us bleed history? Is that perhaps the truest image of history's hold on us: that it lies in our blood, that it is unstillable, that it makes its liquid way out all through our lives? Arguably the sharpest exchange of the book is when Artie, learning that Vladek has actually burned Anja's diaries (which would have been the sources he needs for his book, as well as perhaps the forgiveness he needs even more for his peace and sanity), mutters to himself his judgment of his father upon exit: "Murderer." It's a word that has a funny, almost surreal ring to it, given what Vladek has gone through.

But in a crucial artistic sense, this inserted story of young Artie is stillborn, because the larger testimony, the testimony of a convulsive moment in human history that subtends this young man's relation to both mother and father, moves from parental background to something far more vital: a historical catastrophe that needs a child's vision to bring it to life. This narrative can assume its proper proportions (and liberate its child captive) only when Spiegelman creates *Maus*, when Spiegelman realizes that his inherited story of genocide mandates a radical graphic strategy: namely, to see all the players as different species: the Jews as mice, the Germans as cats, the Poles as pigs, the Americans as dogs, the French as frogs. Perhaps taking his cues from Orwell, with a malicious salute to Disney, Spiegelman has found a way of saying/ showing the pseudo-speciation that finances systemic slaughter. And he has used a child's palette to do so. One is stunned by the primitive eloquence of Spiegelman's animal farm: we repeatedly see German cats and Polish pigs brutalizing Jewish mice, hitting them, kicking them, shooting them, burning them, gassing them, hanging them—indeed, treating them like vermin, like a lower species. I actually think the horrors of this moment in history come through to us more keenly and laceratingly because of the animal figures, as if we were obliged to recognize that notions such as morality, kindness, dignity, and respect had no play in the animal kingdom and were perhaps always quaint fictions in the human kingdom.

Thus Art the child does what few children ever accomplish: he takes the measure of his father's life because it is key to his own existence. This is not easy. In fact, Vladek is impossible to live with: he is hard on Mala, his second wife (also from the camps), and he has been permanently shaped—deformed?—by his experiences. Physically a wreck (diabetes, two earlier heart attacks, popping pills incessantly, afflicted by glaucoma and cataracts, spending a good bit of time on his exercise machine so that his circulation will let him sleep), Vladek is quite recognizable as a survivor with tics: he wastes nothing, saves on wooden matches, cannot spend a dime (although he has substantial funds in the bank), refuses to pay for household help, is ingenious at getting bargains and never paying extra; he seems even to Mala (who comes from the same background) a monster who cares more about things than people. His son, Artie, remembers being forced to clean his plate, muses that his father is a caricature of the miserly Jew. (And he's racist to boot.) Perhaps all of us know of older people like this—or at least *knew* them. My (long-deceased) Yiddish-speaking grandmother from Poland who fled from there in 1907 had a number of Vladek's traits, and I can scarcely claim that they endeared her to me.

Yet one look at Vladek-maus utterly dispels the view I've sketched. He looks pretty good, right to the end, pills, exercise machines and all. Spiegelman's mouse figures are wonderfully immune to the ravages of time. They can be unbearably eloquent figures of torture and suffering, as we see in a number of hallucinatory frames of hanged mice, shrieking mice, mice undergoing virtual crucifixion. But mouse faces have little register. Vladek looks good. And he was good: physically good, so good that he survived (survived what killed most people) and is now able to tell the tale to his uncomprehending son. Hence we start with a vital Vladek, called "the sheik," a Valentino-maus, attractive to women, good with his hands, supple, a quick study, a quick tongue, able to withstand punishment, really quite an Odyssean figure. The two volumes follow him—via his storytelling to Artie—through all the ghastly chapters of his hellish life (right on through Auschwitz), and we see him come through again and again. He is Homeric, even if in mouse form: wily, resourceful, cunning. (Small wonder that his son feels throughout his life that he cannot compete with him; or that the only commensurate countermove is the one we see happening textually: the son creates the images of the father's tale. Shades of Kafka.)

The dance between Vladek and the nightmare of history that befalls him—the coming of Hitler, the persecution of the Jews, the countless close escapes from death, the internment at Auschwitz, all bathed within a richly articulated family story of in-laws and cousins and friends—coexists with a second, less overt but no-less-central dance, that between teller and scribe, father and son. Artie, who could not say more than "Sure, Ma" to his about-to-die mother, creates for us the full-blown life of Vladek, finds images for Vladek's words, offers us a man in his prime whom the son never knew, paints a portrait of survival. Yes, Vladek is in many respects impossible to live with, but there is the rub: this is what his life has made of him. Spiegelman remains wonderfully honest here, reminding us that survivors are an almost impossible species in themselves, and Artie's grudging tone, his impatience with Vladek, his repeated sense of being put upon, all this endows this story with considerable integrity.

And muscularity. The saga of the past has no pills or exercise machines in sight. Vladek had to be a man for all seasons—agile, observant, good at hiding, quick-tongued, a wearer of masks, a speaker of languages, an unyielding survivor of starvation and typhus and much else—and one comes out of this book with a terrifying sense of what it took not to die, of how many skills and how much tenacity it required not to go under or to be broken beyond measure. But the muscularity goes beyond this. There is a narrative and pictorial generosity of the first rank here, as Vladek goes through his marathon in Hell. Other writers would have given us the roiling psychological depths of this story, its cargo of sound and fury. Spiegelman does something just as fine: in his maus figures he shows us not only the crucifixion scenario we know but also the canny moves of life as it opposes death, and he makes us see how smart life is, how cued we are to living, how the forces of destiny are lodged inside the little creatures as well as in the great death machines that seek to exterminate them.

But he also shows us, utterly without fanfare, what cannot be borne: his cousin Tosha, who, in the face of the gas chambers, elected to poison herself and the three children in her care, one of them being Richieu Spiegelman, Artie's older brother, the other dead corpse (along with Anja) that "finances" this story, by haunting those who survived with its awful legacy.

Many of these frames are surpassingly eloquent in juxtaposing survival with horror, as in the image of Vladek sitting by the window with little Richieu playing with dolls, but all of them dwarfed by the huge, distorted visages of the hanged mice, twisting on the gallows on Modrzejowska Street, there to advertise German policy, sowing terror in Vladek, for he can't stop thinking that they may have informed on him before dying, that he may be the next to go. We realize that the graphic frame can have the same reach as Faulknerian italics or a Joycean/Woolfian stream of consciousness, for it can convey the traffic between event and soul without ever pronouncing any of the big words. In like manner, *Maus* shows us the brittleness of morality, the ways in which virtue requires material support if it is to be real, so that friendship and help must be lubricated by money and food if they are to be reliable, and they may not be reliable even then, as so many Jews seeking assistance from "friends" learned to their horror. Artie the American son is repeatedly dumbfounded by Vladek's unillusioned equanimity, as if paying and bribing people to help you stay alive were the most obvious thing in the world, something Vladek seems almost to have been born knowing. It is an education in survival. There was no Vautrin, no Bledsoe, no mentor or wise man in sight to steer Vladek: just grit, a father's grit being imagined by his son.

In a striking sequence in the second volume, we come upon an Artie with writer's block. He's already published the first volume and has become famous, with film offers and entrepreneurs seeking him out, but he can't go on with this and seeks the aid of a psychiatrist. We see Artie regressing even in size, becoming a shrinking maus, needing Mommie, unequal to the circumstances, in trouble. And we see the trouble itself in one unforgettable frame: the world-famous writer wearing his maus mask—all identity is mask, he suggests—sits at his drawing desk, telling us about foreign editions and film and TV offers, reminding us as well that Mother killed herself in 1968, letting us know he's feeling depressed, but the floor of this frame is littered with maus cadavers, with naked maus bodies, such as the ones that littered the camps and became the awful photographs that all of us have seen. And we understand the paralysis of the writer: *this is his material.* It is as if he were a vampire or a ghoul, feeding on corpses. Maybe that is what it means when the son writes the life of a dying father: feasting on the dead.

That is the fate of the children of the Holocaust. They find themselves, without ever having experienced any of the horrors firsthand, filled with corpses nonetheless. And so one begins where one always begins, knowingly or not, with the corpse closest to home, the cantankerous old man who cannot be lived with

but who cannot be allowed to be forgotten. How to get his story? How to get it right? By finding images for the reign of systemic, dismembering sacrifice that preceded you, you elect to remember, to do homage to the lifeline that stayed intact. Maybe then you could spring clear, exit the pit.

Thus you realize, as an opening gambit, the incipit to the cathartic work to come, that the world is to be shown as multi-specied. You will also be dealing with the fact (demonstrated every day) that fathers and sons constitute different species as well and that your book is the only way possible—conversation won't do it—to bring these different creatures from the same family together. Thus it will turn out that the final link between living beings is a narrative link: the son-scribe creates the life story of the father-survivor. It is exhausting labor for both son and father. Vladek asks, at story's end, to stop the tape recorder, saying that he's tired from talking. And he calls Artie "Richieu," saying "it's *enough* stories for now." The story has been told, the dead son and the living son merge. The last frame shows the Spiegelman grave, listing the birth and death dates of Vladek and Anja. Perhaps the ghosts are at rest now, thanks to the labors of the American son.

Many of us, most of us, will be called upon to bury our parents. Artie does a good bit more: he births them in literature. Maybe this, too, is how one grows up.

Jonathan Safran Foer's Extremely Loud and Incredibly Close

For many Americans September 11, 2001, was the day mass death came to our shores, and it seems fair to say that we are still working our way through this tragedy, which altered our country forever. *Extremely Loud and Incredibly Close,* which appeared in 2005, the second novel of the extravagantly talented Jonathan Safran Foer, offers us a child's view of this apocalyptic event but does so in a zany, sometimes manic, sometimes pretentious postmodern style, a freewheeling circuslike account of Oskar Schell's coming to terms with the death of his father, Thomas, in the Twin Towers.

Oskar can seem cloying, with his white clothes and tambourine, his mix of nerdhood and scientific genius, his peculiar habit of telling women how beautiful they are and writing letters to worthies such as Stephen Hawking, but he is there to bear witness. Foer's story of 9/11 is systematically cut with that of the Dresden firebombing and even Hiroshima, reminding us that disaster regularly parses human history and that children are its most poignant victims. (Kurt Vonnegut's *Slaughterhouse-Five* and Günter Grass's *The Tin Drum* are evident models here.) Finally, the book is larded with high jinks: typographic liberties, blank pages, bizarre photographs, morphing print, the incorporation of seemingly banal images such as keys, doorknobs, and other realia that undergird Oskar's quest narrative, and, as an unforgettable closing suite, the graphic reversal of time, space, gravity, and death whereby the (multipixeled) falling body *rises,* page by page, back into the very tower that is being undoomed in front of our eyes. (Another salute to Vonnegut.) Yet this is a book that will endure. Even its wildest posturings make a strange sort of sense when it comes to measuring the immeasurable, making sense of the absurd.

Foer's *Extremely Loud and Incredibly Close* presents mass destruction as the jagged, never-to-be-repaired wrenching apart of the human family. Oskar Schell stays in our mind as one of the walking wounded, and Foer makes us understand that an injured but gifted child is an astonishing lens through which to revisit horror. This hurt child is bubbling over with inventions for making the world better—he cooks them up at night when he can't sleep, which is often—and they display something of this book's luminousness: hearts that talk directly to one (requiring only microphones and speakers), skin that changes color to announce what it's feeling underneath, "Nature Hike Anklets" that leave a trail of bright dye so you would never get lost, ambulances that broadcast (for everyone to hear) how the injured party inside is faring, skyscrapers that move up and down while elevators stay in place, "because if you're on the ninety-fifth floor, and a plane hits below you, the building could take you to the ground, and everyone could be safe."

There's nothing easy about the fantasy in play here. His bright, meliorist recipes have blood on them. History changes us, pain teaches, disaster spawns creativity, but the entire consort is death-driven. Oskar's responses are not limited to the ludic inventions I've listed. He is hurt in far more familiar ways. He refuses to take public transit because it is "an obvious target." He becomes a specialist in how other species react to trauma and death, informing us that a cat falling from the twentieth floor of a building has a better chance of survival than one thrown from the eighth, because it takes eight floors for the animal to realize what's happening and to position itself. He is interested in the legendary memory of elephants and speaks of researchers playing the call of a dead elephant to its family members, resulting in the elephants approaching ever closer. He takes to school a recorded interview with a Hiroshima survivor, a mother who looked everywhere for her lost daughter and found her with her skin peeling off, maggots everywhere in her wounds. That gruesome account is followed by the reactions of Oskar's classmates: the girls weep, the boys make "funny barfing noises." Foer does not let us forget that most kids have no stomach for horror—except those whom it has wrecked.

The novel's basic plot consists of Oskar's far-flung search for the truth of Dad's death, a truth that might set his son free:

If I could know how he died, exactly how he died, I wouldn't have to invent him dying inside an elevator that was stuck between floors, which happened to some people, and I wouldn't have to imagine him trying to crawl down the outside of the building, which I saw a video of one person doing on a Polish site, or trying to use a tablecloth as a parachute, like some of the people who were in Windows on the World actually did. There were so many ways to die, and I just need to know which was his.

This is almost Conradian or Faulknerian in its sense of alternate possibilities, yet it captures the tortured imagination of the children of disaster, doomed to act out (inwardly) whatever new data about cataclysm come their way, thanks to the prodigious information output made possible in our time. When three thousand people die, many scenarios become available for haunting the living. Uncertainty spawns plots, whether they be those of jealousy or of grieving.

Oskar's most preciously guarded secret—the one that is causing him the most misery—is the series of phone calls that Dad made in the last hour of his life, calls that only Oskar knows about, because he had returned home to their apartment and listened to them. Arriving at 10:22, he listened to five earlier messages—from 8:52, 9:12, 9:31, 9:46, and 10:04, each from Dad saying "I'm still okay, things will work out"—and at 10:26:47 the phone rang again: it was Dad's last call, and Oskar could not take it. He listened to the answering machine, heard Dad's voice asking over and over "Are you there? Are you there? Are you there?" and couldn't pick up the phone. At 10:28 the phone went silent, for that was when the building went down; then Oskar took the phone, wrapped it up and hid it, and replaced it with a similar one, cleansed of the terrible tidings. He wonders if there can be forgiveness for this failure of nerve, heart, and love.

Hence the precious precocious prattle of Oskar Schell, the white-clothed, smart aleck, genius-nerd, covers some basic home truths. Some of them are familiar. Mom's relationship with her new friend Ron, her effort to get past the tragedy, is unforgivable, and the grieving Hamlet-like son lets her know it, over and over,

even to the tune of putting the knife in as deeply as he knows how
when he informs her, "If I could have chosen, I would have chosen you." Ground zero: you should have died, not Dad. Yes, he regrets this, yet it is only fair, since he also suspects that Mom
harbors the same horrible thought: "If she could have chosen, it
would have been my funeral we were driving to." Tit for tat. Lives
lost acquire a heinous market value: yours is worth less than his,
mine should have been the lost one. That is what happens when a
family is riven. Wires get crossed, guilt can be neither expressed
nor overcome, one can't get clear. Dr. Fein, the psychiatrist on the
case, tries his level best, and Oskar gives him an earful: his emotions are going haywire, he's panicky away from Mom, he's not
good with people, his insides and his outsides (Oskar's own terms)
don't match up. Dr. Fein, Freudian that he is, wonders if puberty
might be involved, but the boy has a different theory: "It's because
my dad died the most horrible death that anyone ever could invent." Still trying, the good doctor asks if something good might
come of Dad's death; Foer writes Oskar's response like this:

> I kicked over my chair, threw his papers across the floor, and
> hollered, "No! Of course not, you fucking asshole!"
>   That was what I wanted to do. Instead I just shrugged my
> shoulders.

The doctor cannot cure the boy, but he can add to his terrors, as
we see in the follow-up scene, where Oskar overhears portions of
Mom's conversation with the physician, as the shrink delivers (via
Foer's truncated, overheard-through-the-door rendition) his verdict: home is not a safe environment for this child; maybe he's suicidal, he should be hospitalized. We can scarcely avoid seeing that
the manic and ludic elements of the book can be coded patholog-
ically, that this child is a candidate for being institutionalized, for
going under permanently. But he doesn't. At book's end, when the
quest gives out, Oskar seems to have reached a plateau, to have
made progress in his grieving, so that he can now cry in Mom's
arms, admit to her that he's terrified of being hospitalized, and
even gesture toward a possible future: "It's OK if you fall in love
again."

Yet I think the book will be most remembered for its sound and fury, not its closing hints at mellowness. Arguably the most blood-curdling moment of the text is when Oskar, playing Yorick in the school version of *Hamlet,* goes over the edge and explodes: tired of being dead, Yorick strikes back by taking Jimmy Snyder's (Hamlet's) face into his hand and unloading. We read:

> *[I pull the skull off my head. Even though it's made of papier-mâché it's really hard. I smash it against JIMMY SNYDER's head, and I smash it again. He falls to the ground, because he is unconscious, and I can't believe how strong I am. I smash his head again with all my force and blood starts to come out of his nose and ears. But I still don't feel any sympathy for him. I want him to bleed, because he deserves it. And nothing else makes any sense. DAD doesn't make sense. MOM doesn't make sense. THE AUDIENCE doesn't make sense. . . . Shakespeare doesn't make sense. . . . The only thing that makes any sense right then is my smashing JIMMY SNYDER's face. His blood. I knock a bunch of teeth against his skull, which is also RON's skull (for letting MOM get on with life) and MOM's skull (for getting on with life) and DAD's skull (for dying) and GRANDMA's skull (for embarrassing me so much) and DR. FEIN's skull (for asking if any good could come out of DAD's death) and the skulls of everyone else I know. THE AUDIENCE is applauding, all of them, because I am making so much sense. They are giving me a standing ovation as I hit him again and again. I hear them call.]*

Here is the child's revenge against the obscenely dirty tricks that life has played on him: violence at long last. Of course—of course—the postmodern Foer "virtualizes" this (Jacobean) explosion by informing us afterward, "It would have been great." *It would have been great.* This is the very plaint of injury as it makes its dark way toward healing: to purge our violence via imaginative release. Aristotle defined catharsis pretty much this way some twenty-four centuries ago.

The death of a parent sits inside this child like a malignant tumor that must be removed so that he can live. Perhaps that is what grieving means: gradually extricating the materials of death from within us so that life can regain the field. But there's the rub: we cannot bear to let go of our dead. With this insight, we are able to see how Foer's larger story ultimately coheres. Each death we suffer is a double death: Dad dies initially on 9/11, but he is further dying, more slowly and insidiously and unforgivably, inside his son every day that son lives. And it can't be stopped. What is true for 9/11 is true for Dresden. Grandma—as war-ravaged as any, a survivor of Dresden—loves Oskar with an almost maniacal intensity because *he is there*. But the others are not: "I can't remember what the front door of the house I grew up in looked like. Or who stopped kissing first, me or Anna. Or the view from any window but my own. Some nights I lay awake for hours trying to remember my mother's face." Here is the routine theft, sacking, disappearing act that time performs on the living. We can be ravaged without bombs or falling towers. Survival cannibalizes us, eats away our past, maroons us in the present.

Hence one understands *Extremely Loud and Incredibly Close* to be a dirge against entropy, an effort to keep one's most precious memories extremely loud and incredibly close. Foer has constructed the Schell family in such a way that this challenge is especially daunting and unmeetable: they have lost everything, not only via the devastation of Dresden and 9/11 but thanks to the corrosions of both time and the human heart. The firebombing of Dresden separated what they had: Anna (Grandmother's sister) died, Great-grandfather survived but committed suicide, Thomas (Oskar's grandfather) was permanently unhinged, even though he made his way to New York and found Grandma. They are the walking wounded: one cannot speak, the other cannot remember. Thomas retreats to Dresden and writes a series of letters to his unborn son (also Thomas, Oskar's father), trying to explain his absence, letters to a man who died in the Twin Towers. Everywhere you look there are people orphaned and shipwrecked by disaster.

Coming at the very end of this corrosive serial chain is the child, Oskar, the inheritor of an entire history of separation and abandonment. The depredations of politics and time constitute the impossible hand he's been dealt. But he bears the load nonetheless, and none of it, as Oskar-Yorick insisted at the *Hamlet* performance, makes any sense. Dad died the most horrible death imaginable; but the inhabitants of Hiroshima and Dresden fared badly too. Against this backdrop it makes perfect sense that the book closes with a magisterial effort to undo the damages wrought by time. This cannot be done in reality, but it can perhaps be done in fiction. Grandma can dream of collapsed ceilings reforming, fire going back into bombs, bombs rising into the bellies of planes whose propellers turn backward, away from Dresden. Her dream goes all the way back to Adam and Eve: the apple is put back on the branch, the tree goes into the ground, the sapling becomes a seed, light itself yields to the primal darkness. A new beginning.

But of course the light cannot be put out and the apple is always/forever eaten. Knowledge cannot be undone. Hurt is real and unerasable. Oskar Schell lost something irreplaceable, and Foer enables us, in the few sweet pages devoted to the tender relationship between father and son, to measure just what it was that was lost. Thomas Schell, at once lost son and lost father, comes to us, victim of 9/11 though he is, as the freest man of the story. His whimsy, his habit of shrugging his shoulders rather than giving specific answers, his gentle and wise intimacy with his gifted son, make up some of this novel's warmest and finest pages. Nothing surpasses, in this respect, his story of New York's Sixth Borough, the borough of imagination and freedom, place of magic and possibility. The Sixth Borough used to be accessible to every New Yorker, but it began to recede, and soon enough special long jumpers were needed to make the miraculous leap all the way to this promised land, and when the long jumper was airborne, "every New Yorker felt capable of flight." Yet the Sixth Borough is destined, like so much else in this book, for disappearance, leaving as its only legacy Central Park, transplanted into Manhattan as the residual site of wonder, a place where "the children were pulled, one millimeter and one second at a time, into Manhattan and into adulthood."

That passage into adulthood is what Foer wanted to chronicle. For Oskar, such a journey forward is forever linked to a memory backward, of a man who embodied freedom most perfectly in the stories he told to his son. For that is what Central Park means: a place where you must feel that you are "experiencing some tense in addition to the present." Literature itself is made of just this: a script that brings to us time-bound people the opportunity to live elsewhere and "elsewhen." That is the father's legacy: imagination as balm, as a resource, as a tool for getting through horror, a way of remaking the world.

Oskar Schell's story may include Dresden and Hiroshima, but it is first and foremost a story about what happened to *us* on September 11, 2001: how to imagine those deaths, how to get past those deaths. All mourners know that the beast they are wrestling with is not merely loss but also time. Hence Foer's novel closes by reversing time: not merely Grandma's dream of a return to Eden but a suite of photographs displaying a body positioned next to a tall building in which each page portrays the impossible: the body is rising. There is no religious message here, only a desperate and beautiful hope of undoing the damage, repairing the injury, honoring life. This too is promised by Dad's fable of the Sixth Borough: "experiencing some tense in addition to the present." Despite all the maneuvering room made available to us in grammar—present, past, future, conditional, subjunctive—we have no known tense for such a reversal of time, of fate. As Oskar imagines this luminous fable of freedom, he narrates his dad back from the roof of the burning building to the street to the subway to the apartment (always walking backward) to the coffee going from his mouth to his mug and then to his bed to the night before and finally to Oskar's bed, leading to the story of the Sixth Borough, the final umbilical cord between father and son. The last words—logical, heartbreaking—are "We would have been safe."

A child's dream? Or the yearning that lives in every American since 9/11?

The Wild Child

Up to now we have seen a great number of children for whom growing up means learning to cope with adversity. Some are victims of their environment, some adapt to coercive and deforming circumstances, some persevere and achieve a measure of selfhood, some opt out entirely, some go under, some flourish and flower. Each seems locked in a dance with culture and society. This, we tell ourselves, is the education that life inevitably metes out to the young. How could it be otherwise?

But deep inside many of us, lurking in our dreams perhaps as the residue of Romanticism, is the notion of childhood as autonomous, childhood as a time prior to socialization. We might want to term such a state innocence, but we have seen, with the help of William Blake, the extent to which innocence is always a dialectical notion, in some covert form of collusion with experience, indeed with social and ideological norms. Yet anyone who has watched children closely, seen them at play (individually and in groups), questioned them about their experiences and wants, listened to their sometimes strange responses, knows that children often seem a different species altogether, anthropologically different. There is the eighteenth-century story of the "wild child of Aveyron," who was found in the woods and became the subject/object of Enlightenment pedagogy, yielding the meagerest of results: the child's feral natural instincts were curbed, but the acquisition of language and all the baggage that goes with it could not be fully brought off, despite the best intentions. Or the nineteenth-century German example of Kaspar Hauser, who simply appeared out of nowhere at the age of thirteen, unable to write, afflicted with catalepsy and epilepsy, known to have been locked up since infancy, destined for a short, tragic, and unsuccessful stint as an adult. Yet I'd prefer not to medicalize these matters but to focus on what seems most alien about the "wild child": namely, our own intuition that such creatures might have their own strange integrity and that they thereby willy-nilly expose the artifice and constructedness of our adult schemes. They do not play by our rules.

My first example is the enigmatic child Mignon, who appears in Goethe's magisterial Bildungsroman of the late eighteenth century, *Wilhelm Meister's Apprenticeship;* Mignon mesmerizes Wilhelm, and she has mesmerized countless readers ever since. Everything about her is a riddle, including her sex (she appears in boy's clothes and has a more androgynous than female identity), her name (Mignon is merely a sobriquet: "They call me Mignon"), and her speech (she cannot master the language spoken by the adults; it is as if she had her own code). Music and dance are her modes of expression. We know that she worships Wilhelm, but this is no ordinary infatuation, nor does it have any possible future. Above all, she is the novel's apostle of desire, and her beautiful tribute to longing itself is what educated nineteenth-century readers throughout Europe retained from this book, as a kind of haunting refrain, as unanswerable question: *"Kennst du das Land wo die Zitronen blühen?"* "Do you know the land where the lemon trees blossom?" The land where the blood oranges glow in dark groves? *"Dahin!"* is the untranslatable imperative that governs the song: *There!* To there! To that place! That place is more than some tropical grove of lemon trees and blood oranges; it is akin to the place of desire celebrated by Baudelaire in his lovely poem "Invitation au Voyage": *"Mon enfant, ma*

soeur / Songe à la douceur d'aller là-bas / Vivre ensemble!" "My
child, my sister, think of the bliss of going there and living together." A place of ease and beauty: here is the other world:
Mignon is its (doomed) emissary. The wild child, even when orphaned and languishing, has an Edenic quality, a reminiscence of
Paradise, that shimmers in contrast with the workaday world of
grown-up pursuits. Mind you: this is neither ignorance nor innocence: *"Kennst du das Land?"* she asks, "Do you know the land,"
the place? She knows it; do you?

Such places, such ambassadors, sometimes disturb. One of the
most striking examples of a wild child so emancipated that she
unsettles her environment is Nathaniel Hawthorne's Pearl, the illegitimate daughter of Hester Prynne in *The Scarlet Letter*. As the
title suggests, this novel is something of a semiotic treasure trove,
and Hawthorne lavishly wraps his plot and characters in diverse
symbolic discourses, of which the most notable, from our perspective, is that Pearl herself is often depicted as the living embodiment of her mother's sexual transgression. In a number of
well-known scenes Pearl also acts as her mother's figurative jailer,
most particularly in the powerful and haunting sequence in the
forest where Hester meets her former lover, Arthur Dimmesdale,
the sun comes out, and for just a brief moment there is the possibility of real freedom beyond the confines (physical and conceptual) of the Puritan community: the man, the woman, and the
child could flee their prison. Alas, this is not to be: not only is
Dimmesdale demonstrably not up to the challenge, but Pearl herself explodes, insisting that Hester reclaim the embroidered *A*
that she has momentarily cast away and that she reenter its symbolic domain, rebecome its prisoner.

Now, this is passing odd, because Pearl most stands out in our
minds—and in the mind of her troubled mother—as a creature
entirely resistant to such symbol systems, a creature whose character has "a hard metallic luster," as of one sprung clear of the
whole moral trap, along with its moral trappings. Hester often
wonders if Pearl is entirely human, and Pearl delights in torturing her mother at such moments, telling her at one such juncture
that she (Pearl) has no Heavenly Father at all. In the heavily laden
religious scheme of this novel, having no Heavenly Father means

that your father then must be the Devil instead, and more than
once Hester looks into her daughter's eyes and espies some strange
dark figure lurking there. One of the book's feistiest moments
comes when Pearl, interrogated by the worthies of the community
as to who made her, "finally announced that she had not been
made at all, but had been plucked by her mother off the bush of
wild roses, that grew by the prison-door." It is a splendid answer,
firmly on nature's side of the divide, and Hawthorne's tales of Pu-
. ritan life make it unmistakably clear that nature is home to the
Devil, sometimes also known as the Black Man. Yet we, who today
may find Hawthorne awfully ponderous in his investment in such
symbolic arrangements and obsessive typologies, admire such
childlike verve. It is the same verve that leads Huck Finn to realize that Tom Sawyer's magic tricks smack of Sunday school. It is
the same verve that leads Harriet Beecher Stowe's elfish character
Topsy (in *Uncle Tom's Cabin*) to proclaim, in answer to the same
question of who made her, "Nobody . . . I spect I grow'd." In short,
the wild child exposes, as little else can, the papier-mâché artifice
of adult constructs, regarding both God and man.

I want also to mention some of the obvious children's-
literature figures who opt out altogether, who remain eternally
young: one thinks of Peter Pan (whose spirit presides over high
school and college reunions, I have to believe) or the even more
beguiling Pippi Longstocking of Astrid Lindgren's wonderful stories. Pippi operates a bit like an alien come to a new world (ours):
she has the two chief attributes that no child actually possesses:
physical strength and endless money. Yet even though Lindgren
writes her as someone who always carries the day in each of her
little adventures—she routinely bests the faintly bad guys Lindgren provides her with, and she is the recipient of Tommy's and
Annika's undying admiration—we cannot escape the feeling that
she does not know how to live within culture. How to behave in
school, what to say or do when adults are having a social event,
what kinds of manners one is supposed to have and display: these
are all (charmingly) outside her ken, beyond her capacities. It's no
surprise that the Swedish public of the 1940s responded with in-
dignation when she first came into print. She is what the French
call *sauvage*, and one cannot imagine her as an eventual adult.

Huck lights out for the Territory ahead of the others; he does not want to be "sivilized" by the Widow or the other right-thinking folks he knows. Topsy is destined by her moralizing author to become a moral creature residing in Vermont. And Pearl exits *The Scarlet Letter* with her mother en route to London, where she becomes a wealthy heiress and where, it seems, her heart also gradually develops a capacity for feeling. Pippi remains an enchanting child, a young "Supergirl" ready to right wrongs as she sees them, but she never truly challenges or threatens the adult world she is placed in. But what would happen if the wild child were placed in an adult setting but remained "incorrigible" right to the end? If the wild child obeyed Ivan Karamazov's injunction and refused the ticket? If the wild child saw its wildness as a program, as a veto of the world as we know it? How would you tell such a story?

William Faulkner's Light in August

After creating the doomed Benjy and Quentin in *The Sound and the Fury*, Faulkner must have realized that public morality and racial hatred are as virulent and instrumental as lost love is, in determining whether the young survive or not. *Light in August* (1932) can be seen as a virtual laboratory experiment along these lines, for it is outfitted with two key characters who are each, in radically different ways, countercultural, marked by taboo: Lena Grove is the pagan figure of the novel, obeying nature's injunctions without regard to "moral law," nine months pregnant without a wedding ring or a scrap of guilt; and Joe Christmas, the violent man with parchment-colored skin ("written on"), thinking he has "a little nigger blood," troubled by all social rituals, including food and sex. Each is a stranger. One is headed for marriage and social incorporation, the other for crucifixion. We are a far cry from Mignon, Pearl, and company, it may seem, yet Lena and Christmas represent Faulkner's most extreme effort to imagine young people alien to culture's prescriptions, impervious to the social contract. The novel seems to be asking: is this possible?

Let us begin with Christmas, Faulkner's version of Oedipus,

the child cursed by unknown parentage. Christmas is given a glimpse of the epistemological calvary in store for him by the black yardman at the orphanage. Little Joe has asked why the black man is a "nigger," and the response/indictment goes like this: "And the nigger said, 'Who told you I am a nigger, you little white trash bastard?' and he says 'I aint a nigger' and the nigger says, 'You worse than that. You don't know what you are. And more than that, you wont never know. You'll live and you'll die and you wont never know.' " With Christmas there appears to be a double whammy: a birth shrouded in (racial) mystery yet followed by an upbringing at the hands of his Calvinist foster father, McEachern, that is all too clear in its deforming power. It is as if Faulkner wanted to massively overdetermine Joe Christmas's fate—first ungrounded, then ground down—to explore degrees of separation from the human and social order and the violence that results.

For Christmas is headed for the pit every bit as much as Quentin was, and that pit is repeatedly imaged in this book along racial, gender, and libidinal lines as "Womanshenegro," a swamp where the male goes under. In Christmas Faulkner has fashioned his fullest portrait of a misfit—a mix of fury and fear regarding the creatural side of life, especially when it comes to women's fluids but extending all the way toward food and sex in general, yet visible also in the out-of-sync nature of his neural equipment, his delayed responses, his frequent capsizing, his rages—and then taken the rather enormous step of naming this child after Jesus. (Was Jesus the first wild child?) Perhaps the Christ appellation is apt in one sense: his life is a calvary, he will be dismembered at death. Perhaps it is right in another sense as well: this man may have no redemptive spiritual vision (he has none at all), but he does come across as an exemplary victim, held hostage by his ambiguous skin color, his firing and misfiring neurons and synapses, his horror of all that is soft, his formative "othering" stint in the orphanage, his further (mis)shaping via McEachern's loveless iron discipline, his being maniacally scapegoated by his frenzied grandfather Old Doc, his ultimate cold-blooded execution/castration by Percy Grimm in the name of an entire racist culture: not to put too fine a point on it, a systemwide hounding Faulkner himself calls "an emotional Roman barbecue."

In this light, Christmas's story is an ongoing reversal of the Bildungsroman ethos, it is a tale of how not to: how to fail every social test, how to refuse all adaptation, how to turn your life into a calvary. Joe Christmas seems like a nightmarish creation, embodying everything Faulkner has to have thought of as diseased and dsyfunctional in modern life. "You little nigger bastard!" the orphanage dietitian screams at him after he has unwittingly eavesdropped on her frantic lovemaking. And he fares only nominally better with his foster parents the McEacherns, where he is routinely beaten for not learning his catechism, where he learns to live under cover, where his sexual initiation triggers the kind of somatic cyclone of violence we will see more of, leading eventually to the murder of his lover, Joanna Burden, by beheading. By story's end he is the novel's *thing:* tracked, ceasing to distinguish between night and day, asleep and awake, being weaned from life, awaiting final dispatch through the good offices of Percy Grimm. He is the man to whom things are done, and among the things done to him are his own uncontrollable mind and body, in addition to a Mississippi culture that is ready to kill.

One is stunned by Faulkner's packaging of all this venom as a story of failed rites of passage. We are meant to take the full measure of the making of Joe Christmas. The novel begins in medias res, with the murder of Joanna, but then works ever more profoundly backward as well as forward, giving us the lineaments of Christmas's birth, infancy, childhood, adolescence, and final full flowering. He is not a monster. Alfred Kazin rightly called him "the loneliest figure in American literature," and Faulkner seems obsessed with tracking him, showing us how early and definitively he was weaned from humane care. He is the Thanatos figure of the book, the death instinct.

It is for that reason that Faulkner matches him against the nine-months-pregnant, vegetable-like, pagan figure of Lena Grove, his opposite number in every respect. If Christmas is sapped by his past, (mindless) Lena is at one with her future, which means finding a father for this soon-to-be-born child. A figurative one will do as well as the biological one, so that Byron Bunch becomes the book's Joseph, exiting the community at story's end with Lena and baby to re-create some form of the family, at once comic and holy.

Teaching this novel today can be hard, since none of my female students is eager to fill the Lena Grove slot, yet there is something magnificent and profound in Faulkner's story of life's rhythms, his tribute to natural forces as triumphant over cultural ones. She carries in her womb nature's sovereign answer to culture's rules, and her baby is arriving on schedule, following the oldest and most reliable plot known to our kind. The unswerving and integral Lena breaks as many social rules as Christmas does, but the outrage of the community—does the unmarried pregnant woman really think she'll find her husband waiting for her?—comes across as weightless, whimsical, given the authority of her species' mission and the success with which it is crowned.

Lena's ascent is unstoppable, but so, too, is Christmas's descent. Faulkner strains mightily to invest this man's failed life and spectacular death with meaning, so that his castration is written as (also) a moment of miraculous salvation, as if death and love, murder and generation might be fused into one: "And from out the slashed garments about his hips and loins the pent black blood seemed to rush like a released breath. It seemed to rush out of his pale body like the rush of sparks from a rising rocket; upon that black blast the man seemed to rise soaring into their memories forever and ever." The following sentence uses words such as "serene," "steadfast," and "triumphant" to characterize its victim, but we cannot fail to see that these are Lena's terms, that he is strangely wedded to her by the beauty and figurative logic of Faulkner's writing. The two pariahs of the community, the ones beyond the pale—one giving birth, one being castrated—seem to leave our Earth altogether, to come together, as the orgasmic language boldly approximates that of the Holy Spirit, as if Christmas were actually seeding Lena and sowing a possible future; Christmas, the dead outsider, is said now to inhabit the minds and dreams of the very community that slew him.

Light in August is an unflinching account of community violence, prejudice, and hatred—all the forces that militate against growing up—but its very violence is transformed by Faulkner's genius into a parable about family, union, children, and the round of life. At that poetic level—and only there—the story of carnage, misfit, and even pariah status undergoes a sea change, yielding a vision in which the wild child finds a home. One way to follow Faulkner's lead in imagining the fate of the wild child would be to use a pairing strategy—one "wild," one "straight"—in the manner of a control study, to gauge what it might mean to opt out of culture altogether. The costs and gains will be on show. On show too will be the price of admission that each of us has long ago been asked to pay.

Tarjei Vesaas's The Ice Palace

Two of the most remarkable accounts of children in twentieth-century literature illuminate just these matters: the exquisite and largely unknown Norwegian novel of 1963 *The Ice Palace,* and Toni Morrison's brazen, sometimes surreal story of two girls, *Sula,* of 1973. What most astonishes me about both these books is their purity and rigor: they refuse to compromise or to pull their punches, and they therefore go right off the tracks of all prescribed behavior. *The Ice Palace* and *Sula* are at once fresh and unhinging, for they dare to imagine otherwise, to sketch out a vision of childhood and growth on the far side of all adaptation and socialization. Each of these books is about the majesty and terror of real freedom, about freedom itself as a compulsion that is virtually terrorist in its sirenlike ferocity.

I have been waging a one-person war for some time now to garner recognition for Tarjei Vesaas's *The Ice Palace,* largely by finding a way to include it in virtually every course that I teach, as well as writing about it in my recent book on Scandinavian literature; I was gratified to learn that the famous Parisian bookstore for books in English, Shakespeare and Company, shares my conviction about this book and its author and touts the novel as one of its "finds." This account of two eleven-year-old girls is a tale of life versus death, of the reaches of childhood, and of the extraordinary good luck that enables the young to grow up rather than to die. We all know today that childhood is a time of risk: never, in my view, have parents been more aware of the threats lurking out there in the form of predators and bad guys and drugs and so much else that can wreck children's lives and turn them into nightmares. We read daily about such matters. But Vesaas has no interest in illuminating the risks we know about; on the contrary, he is after larger game, because he positions the menace of death and annihilation on the inside, as the signature openness, vulnerability, hunger, and beauty of the young.

Vesaas writes about the simplest subject of all: the passional life of two eleven-year-olds. Here is something all parents have seen, but from afar: the mercurial, giddy, sometimes raging feelings of the young, their capacity for infatuation, the (lovely) ignorance of limits, their (no less lovely) lack of experience. Today such matters are often pathologized, and hence we are, as a culture, leery and even frightened of affective outbursts in the young; indeed, we are equipped with the drugs to tamp them down, so as to ease things. But no one reading these pages can have entirely forgotten the tumultuous emotional life that we had when young, especially regarding our peers. Every day in school had its riotous and explosive moments: conflagration, tragedy, bliss, upheaval, cataclysm. And every day Mom or Dad asks the returning child, "How was school?" and receives the standard answer: "Okay." An entire internal operatic life of desire and frustration and excitement and hunger burns in the young but rarely makes it over the threshold into language for parental benefit.

And one generally gets through it, over it. Life sees to it that such unchecked emotions are gradually—by dint of experience, by dint of being burned, by dint of the graying of life that sets in so early—reined in. We become wiser, not through any volitional effort but rather as a curbing of hunger and checking of desire that our organism seems to learn all on its own. Or, worse still, as the implacable entropy that time itself imposes on desire, as if we possessed at birth only a specific amount of it, and we spend it wildly and gloriously when young, to find that it is in ever-shorter supply as we age, like grains of sand slipping through an hourglass, like the incessant minor hemorrhaging that goes by the name of living.

That is not the case with *The Ice Palace*. I call it "simple," but I have in mind the kind of "simplicity" that Tom Lehrer expressed decades ago in his song about the new math: "It's so simple that only a child can do it." We are challenged by this book because it obliges us to go very far backward, to remember a time and a self that were open, flowing, and porous. Vesaas's novel is a love story. Siss, the putative heroine of the narrative, is more or less smitten by Unn, the death-haunted one. Siss is anchored: decent parents, school leader, most popular, self-aware, at once reasonable and open to feelings. Unn is the newcomer to the school—the setting is rural Norway—and she has proven to be unreceptive to the few overtures of friendship that have come her way, as if she chose to be the loner she is.

But the moment she and Siss set eyes on each other, things change. This happens where so much childhood sound and fury takes place: at school. Yes, school is the great formative experience of our lives, even though it may have precious little to do with teachers or books or subjects taught; rather, it is the cauldron where we encounter human heat in all its diverse forms. These forms can look calm, staid, and cool, as in small sheets of paper being passed from child to child with messages scribbled on them; but such language sizzles, and in this instance, the note saying "Must meet you, Siss," signed "Unn," has an imperious power that few poems ever possess. From initial body tingling to formal rendezvous, destiny is gathering. Their meeting that day after school will alter both their lives forever.

In Unn's bedroom (where Auntie is prominently not welcome), Siss will discover just how wild Unn is: shy, reclusive, yet filled with forbidden things that seem to seep out of her, such as the news that her (dead) mother wasn't married, such as the intuition that she might not go to Heaven, such as the disturbing question she puts to Siss when they both disrobe and compare bodies: "Did you see anything on me just now?" What might there be to see on a naked eleven-year-old body? (My students have been trying to answer this question for decades now, coming up with theories of bad conscience, hidden injury, concealed sexual abuse, pregnancy, and much else.) All we will ever know for sure is that Unn feels marked. But what the book thrusts at us even more powerfully is how Siss is going to be marked by this bedroom encounter, an encounter that achieves its most magic and troubling form when the two naked girls look into the mirror. What, Vesaas asks, did they see?

Four eyes full of gleams and radiance beneath their lashes,
filling the looking-glass. Questions shooting out and then hiding again. I don't know: Gleams and radiance, gleaming from
you to me, from me to you, and from me to you alone—into
the mirror and out again, and never an answer about what this
is, never an explanation. Those pouting red lips of yours, no
they're mine, how alike! Hair done in the same way, and
gleams and radiance. It's ourselves! We can do nothing about
it, it's as if it comes from another world. The picture begins to
waver, flows out to the edges, collects itself, no it doesn't. It's a
mouth smiling. A mouth from another world. No, it isn't a
mouth, it isn't a smile, nobody knows what it is—it's only eye-
lashes open wide above gleams and radiance.

I'm not sure that prose gets better than this. (The Norwegian
original is no stronger than the translation.) We see here an elemental fusion of beings—the kind of thing adults strive to
achieve, fitfully, in their adult fashion later in life—and it is at
once beautiful and terrifying, for it spells out the erasure of who
one is, the collapse of boundaries and contours that delineate us.
Instead, there is the hole, the abyss, that draws us in like a vortex;
call it eyes, call it a mouth, but you cannot name its owner, for that
figure is now multiple, twinned, and moreover the mirror asserts
its own irresistible tug, its pull into elsewhere. There are no good
terms for this. *Love* or *desire* will take us only so far, for we can also
sense the capsizing and shipwreck adumbrated here, the dissolution of "I": so many signs of the fluid hungry promiscuous self
that can no longer maintain its borders.

Can we be surprised that one of these children will die? Of
course it will be the unanchored one, the one with the least ballast
to offset the tug of desire that has made its way into their lives.
But whereas Mignon and Pearl exit discreetly from their books,
because they are closer to the margins of the stories being told,
Unn's departure from the living is among the most haunting
things I know in literature. She will be initiated into the Ice
Palace. My phrase may suggest a fairy-tale dispensation, but
Vesaas stays true to the world we know—the world we think we
know—by having Unn gradually, increasingly, tragically leave the

path of safety to heed the call she experiences. She will not go to school after the bedroom rendezvous with Siss, she cannot face those eyes again, she will instead (!) make her way toward the much-bruited palace of ice that has formed at the end of the lake as it overflows into the river. By page fifty-six Unn is dead; one is shocked in the same way that Mrs. Ramsay's death in Virginia Woolf's *To the Lighthouse* shocks: we feel that rules have been breached, that central characters are "supposed" to make it to the end alive. This is especially true of child characters, and Unn's dying advertises the steely truth that fuels Vesaas's book: desire can kill, openness to love and life can kill.

But it doesn't happen at once. As I said, she is initiated. Burdened by her own never-specified ghosts—"Did you see anything on me?"—Unn thinks incessantly of both Siss and the Other as she traverses the woods, remembering an early episode when she almost drowned, lying on the icy surface of the lake and seeing its denizens dart toward her, sensing deep underneath the steady roar and current of the river: "flowing through her and lifting her up and saying something to her which was just what she needed." Growing up is the concept of this book, but Vesaas gives us to understand that children are most capacious, most dimensional, most alive *as children*, that what we call maturation is likely to be a time of setting limits and closing doors, not of growth. The wild child is coextensive with the vast structure of ice—"an enchanted world of small pinnacles, gables, frosted domes, soft curves and confused tracery"—that she finally enters, exploring it room by room, finding that passages open for her for one reason only: her desire to enter. One room is a forest, another is the home of the cold, another is a room of tears. She has flitting images of her dead mother, of Auntie, of Siss. She is being writ large. She is exploring her domains.

At first reading, one keeps hoping she will snap out of it, find her way back, her way out, but of course it all flows in the other direction: she must enter, even when it requires removing her thick coat so she can slip through the next fissure; and we know, now, that death will claim her. But how grand it is. A great eye of ice, full of light, sees her, sees through her. Her final thoughts are "Here I am. I've been here all the time. I haven't done anything."

The winter solar god reclaims his palace, along with the child caught within it. Unn has lost ties with everything but light. The fiery eye drowns the room in flames, causes it to dance as the child—"languid and limp and ready"—merges with the elements. I find no spiritual payoff here, no moment of personal revelation, but rather an initiation of the child into nature's endless pageant. Whatever Unn may be concealing is dwarfed by the transformation she is undergoing. Vesaas has charted a trajectory that is commensurate with all the fierceness and wonder and desire on the far side of our rules of decorum and preservation, and it leads ultimately to the dissolution of the human subject. I see a kind of purity and valor here that are at once beautiful and heartbreaking. "Here I am," Unn says to propitiate the solar god, who will kill her, but the book's truth is other: "I" is not here, "I" is undone. The prophecy in the mirror—"I" is a fiction, fusion is everything—has come true.

The rest of the novel is devoted to Siss, and it probes, with great tenderness and wisdom, how it feels to survive and what it means to mature. You may recall the pairing strategy I ascribed to Vesaas—juxtapose the "raw" and the "cooked," if you wish to take their joint measure—and it is time now for Siss to make sense of her friend's death and of that single spellbinding moment they shared, a moment that the entire community believes to hold the secret of Unn's fate. Hence Siss is hounded to tell what she knows about Unn, but what she knows—in her marrow—has to do with the four-eyed figure in the mirror and is essentially untellable. But that is not all: her response to Unn's disappearance—no one quite wants to acknowledge that she must be dead—plays out along the lines of Freud's thesis in "Mourning and Melancholia": crucial wires seem to get crossed, and instead of systematically cutting ties with the dead one, Siss seems to blend ever further into her, en route not only to assuming Unn's antisocial, outsider status—do not forget, Siss was the class leader, the solid one—but ultimately moving toward a second death, so that she too will leave the living. Mercifully, wisely, that does not quite happen; instead, we follow Siss's painful recovery from trauma and grieving, as she is increasingly weaned from her lost comrade, indeed weaned from the tug of death itself.

Siss gets through her ordeal; she heals. Her parents, her friends, and the reader watch this child slowly wend her way back into the social fabric of the community, to align herself finally and solidly with the living. But the route to that secure and benign end station requires virtually reliving Unn's own dissolution. Nothing is volitional here. We seem to be watching the primitive moves of the organism itself that must sever its bonds with the dead, must say no to the sirenlike tug of love if it is to survive. Vesaas writes the story of survival as finely and movingly as he does the story of dissolving (for that is what Unn does: she dissolves among the elements). Siss has her own calvary, and it is arguably far more painful than anything that the doomed Unn ever went through, for Siss has lost love and must somehow be healed. It is little short of amazing that Vesaas can make us believe in the depth and dignity of what was, crassly speaking, a one-night stand, a brief encounter between two little girls in a bedroom. Yet at some spiritual level it works, and I think it does so because we are perhaps freer, more available, more flowing, less bounded at eleven than we ever are later. Hence Siss must go through her ordeal. Her parents, friends, and community understand to perfection that this child has been touched by death, that she too may succumb. That she does not is cued to a clear seasonal logic that moves through winter into spring, through frozen ice into flowing sap. At the novel's close, Siss is threaded back into the community and life prevails.

But death has had its mesmerizing run, and no one—neither Siss nor the reader—is likely to forget it. And that, I think, is what Vesaas most wanted to depict: how life sorts out who lives and who dies. Not through weakness or strength, but through something more complex and unjudgeable: the ability, or the inability, to resist going all the way, to resist nature's magnetic call or love's unraveling force. Here, it seems to me, is what the trajectory of the wild child can make visible to us: how much luck and grace are needed for the most beautiful among us to get through childhood intact, for Unn remains in our mind the exquisitely damned one, the one without defenses or cover, the one incapable of compromise or adaptation, the one doomed to go under. You cannot read this book without feeling that hers is at once the keenest and fullest life of the novel, brief though it is: keen in the way knife blades are keen and full in the sense of taking her place in that larger scheme that knows nothing of human doing. This feeling is perhaps tantamount to an intuition that Vesaas has graphed child-hood itself in his lyrical novel: childhood as our time of maximum reach and promise, a time prior to the hardening of skin that ac-companies growing up, while it quietly goes about closing the doors of experience.

Toni Morrison's Sula

Toni Morrison's Sula, in the 1973 novel of that name, is the enfant terrible of my study. The mysterious Unn, albeit fatally open to the call of desire, remains a closed figure for the reader, who can make no more of her psychology or actual secrets than Siss can. Sula Peace, however, is a different piece of work, and by book's end we have an unforgettable sense of just how wild—how free and terrifying and doomed—the wild child can be, because we have seen up close a genuine philosophic program of untram-meled, indeed unstoppable, self-emancipation that has no truck whatsoever with community values or any other kind of ethical constraints. I cannot help thinking that Morrison was trying to get something out of her system when she wrote this Rimbaud-like story of a young girl who went right over the edge and kept on going. Like Vesaas, Morrison has enlisted a binary scheme for get-ting Sula across: she is paired with the sensitive but "straight" Nel Wright, and the contrapuntal fireworks of this arrangement pay real dividends.

Vesaas's Unn is significantly without parents (even though she lives with Auntie), and much of her mystery comes from the rid-dles and anxiety of her past. About Sula's origins, however, we know a great deal, and we realize that the wild child can have a wild pedigree, can in fact be a chip off the old block. The Peace women are unforgettable: the mother, Hannah, is easygoing, free-loving, and destined to die in spectacular fiery fashion. But the grandmother, Eva Peace, ranks high on the list of astonishing Morrison creations: one-legged (and rich because of it, they say; something to do with insurance), the murderess of her drug-addicted son, Plum (whom she saved as a baby by inserting lard into his anus and whom she sets ablaze in a sequence that deserves to be anthologized: Eva descending the stairs on crutches, "swinging and swooping like a giant heron," then dousing her sleeping boy with kerosene and throwing lit newspaper on him). Poetic justice sets in when Hannah is subsequently in flames—you can be incandescent in Morrison's world—and Eva hoists herself to the window, aims her body at her burning daughter, and misses by twelve feet, as Hannah "her senses lost, went flying out of the yard gesturing and bobbing like a sprung jack-in-the-box." This is Sula's lineage.

The first signs of what Sula is made of appear when she (and Nel) encounter older white bullies aching to humiliate the black girls: Sula pulls out a paring knife, puts down her lunch pail, books, and slate, puts her left forefinger on the slate, and slashes off the tip of her finger. Then she informs the boys, "If I can do that to myself, what you suppose I'll do to you?" The next installment occurs when Sula helps the little boy Chicken Little climb a tall beech by the river: she helps him up, she helps him partway down, but before getting to the bottom, she swings him around and around. Here is how Morrison writes what happens next: "His knickers ballooned and his shrieks of frightened joy startled the birds and the fat grasshoppers. When he slipped from her hands and sailed away out over the water they could still hear his bubbly laughter." And that's it, at least until his swollen body is found by a bargeman later that afternoon. Giant herons, a sprung jack-in-the-box, ballooning knickers, startled birds, fat grasshoppers: Morrison has positioned her children in a landscape and a language every bit as animistic and roiling as that of Tarjei Vesaas.

Unlike Unn, who exits early, Sula has a lot of work to do before dying. She goes off to college and returns home ten years later, ready to make good on the apprenticeship with chaos that began with the tip of a finger and a drowned child. She walks into Eva's house and puts the old matriarch on notice that all the old contracts are breached. Told that she should make some babies and settle down, she replies that she intends to make herself. Called "pus mouth" and told that God is going to strike her, she replies, "Which God? The one watched you burn Plum." Called a "crazy roach" and told that hellfire is burning inside her, she replies,

"Whatever's burning in me is mine!" This is rough stuff: Promethean, rebellious, out to corral the elements themselves in her quest for self-enactment, self-deification. Can we be surprised that her favorite area of actualization is sex? Here is self-assertion: "particles of strength gathered in her like steel shavings drawn to a spacious magnetic center, forming a tight cluster that nothing, it seemed, could break." Lying under a man, she felt not submission but "her own abiding strength and limitless power." This power is on show when her dear friend Nel opens a door to find Sula and Jude, Nel's husband, down on all fours, naked, nibbling, barely even touching. Sula is her own creation, indeed her own experiment: "As willing to feel pain as to give pain, to feel pleasure as to give pleasure, hers was an experimental life." Nel is burned, ruined by Sula's play.

Like so many experiments, it must eventually fail. At story's end Sula grows ill and is dying, and Nel visits her for some final home truths. Sula repents nothing, claims she has lived her own life, only for herself, and has no regrets. Shocked, Nel reminds her that she is now sick and alone, to which Sula replies, "Yes. But my lonely is *mine*." Finally the big question comes: "How come you did it, Sula?" The answer: there was a space, and Jude filled it up. That's all. Nel won't let go: didn't I count? I never hurt you. "I was good to you, Sula. Why don't that matter?" Again a brazen reply: "It matters, Nel, but only to you." A venerable Judeo-Christian ethos is biting the dust here. *An experimental life:* Who has the courage to go right through existence with this ticket? Iago did; Sula does. And anyone in her path, much less someone who thinks herself her friend, is in for trouble. But what a bonfire it is. The flames of Plum and Hannah's joint death by fire seem pale in comparison to the incandescence that Sula radiates. Such people strew wreckage in their wake. The soft verities are no more. Volition, desire, curiosity, and a weird outright aesthetic imperative for self-making, self-sculpting, rule the day, rule the night, rule the book.

It is worth remembering the series of "wild children" we've seen: Goethe's Mignon, Hawthorne's Pearl, Faulkner's Joe Christmas and Lena Grove, Vesaas's Unn. Each of them is unchartable. Each goes off the map. Each exposes the artifice of rules and moral precepts. It is as if Morrison wanted to sketch out just where such wildness might go, what a truly unbounded self might do, in its quest for freedom and play. Sula stops us in our tracks. She is the *enfant sauvage,* the free, the freed spirit of this study, beholden to no one, sprung clear of the ethical gravity that most of us take to be natural. In Sula we see a new species. I don't think it will do simply to pronounce moral judgment, because that is precisely what is at issue: the weightlessness of judgment, of moral categories. If we want to invoke our central motif of growing up, we have to say that Sula grows right out of the human community. No less than Kafka's Gregor Samsa, she simply exits the human.

Like Vesaas, Morrison has paired her wild child with a civilized girl. Nel Wright has her own painful story, her own sensitive psychological responses to the injuries of race and sex. Her formative experience would seem to be the train trip to New Orleans to meet her grandmother, encountering en route white men's contempt, no toilets, urine running down her leg, the fear that her mother was all custard underneath her clothes. Back home, her only recourse is to save what can be saved: " 'I'm me,' she whispered. 'Me.' " By which she means "I'm me. I'm not their daughter. I'm not Nel. I'm me. Me." One senses easily enough that this novel was meant to be evenly balanced between these two black girls: one sensitive and insecure, one independent and virtually demonic. But Sula's magnetic pull is so stupendous that Nel fades into the background. Yes, she is there for the duration, but what we remember is Sula.

And indeed that is what Nel also remembers at book's end. In an almost Proustian passage, Nel realizes that Sula is inseparable from her childhood, from herself: " 'We was girls together,' she said as though explaining something. 'O Lord, Sula,' she cried, 'girl, girl, girlgirlgirl.' " We are to understand that the wild, destructive freedom that Sula lived and died is somehow a core truth of growing up itself, of perilous human promise, of a passionate self that precedes all rules and codes. "Girlgirlgirl" tells us something about essences. "We was girls together." Perhaps the most enduring feature of Morrison's novel is the hint that Sula and Nel are indivisible. At the deathbed scene, Nel preened about her own moral goodness, only to hear Sula ask, "How you know?" Nel is confused. "Know what?" Sula answers, "About who was good. How you know it was you? . . . I mean maybe it wasn't you. Maybe it was me." This secret sharing, this blurring of lines—reminiscent of Vesaas's double face in the mirror—is beautifully reflected toward the novel's close when Nel visits the old, senile Eva Peace, who insists that she, Nel, was the one who killed that little boy. Nel remonstrates, but Eva perseveres: "You. Sula. What's the difference? You was there. You watched, didn't you?" And later, as Nel is leaving: "Just alike. Both of you. Never was no difference between you. Want some oranges? It's better for you than chop suey. Sula? I got oranges."

What is one to make of this haunting sequence? Sula's spirit seems to inhabit Nel, just as the dead Unn can never be forgotten by the living Siss. Maybe it goes further still: the wild child stands for a secret truth in all of us, a free spirit that cannot be acculturated, cannot grow up, yet cannot quite be forgotten or discarded or fully destroyed. Literature is home to such creatures, and we recover in them, through reading, something primordial about ourselves, a kind of primitive self hidden deep inside, influencing nothing (thank God) yet free. Eva's parting words about oranges also signal the sweet, if unhinging, freedom of this book, its willingness to mock logic, its love affair with herons and ballooning knickers and fat grasshoppers, its serene certainty that the story of childhood takes you off the map, brings you closer to that faraway place where lemon trees blossom and blood oranges glow that Mignon sang of. The wild child is the emancipated, doubtless doomed creature that all of us who live choose not to be, and we can do so only by letting this creature perish so that we do not. Such stories show us that this unreformable, unsurvivable creature still lives. Literature charts places to go and places to avoid going as it maps out possible life trajectories that sometimes become anthems about death. One reads such tales with a special gratitude that they were imagined and told with such purity and force and with equal gratitude that one—or one's children—did not end up there.

Growing All the Way Up

Lazarillo finishes as town crier, Pablos lands in America, Des Grieux returns to France, Jane Eyre marries Rochester, Huck lights out for the Territory, Lena Grove exits with baby and "father," Marjane leaves Tehran, Artie writes his father's story, Oskar Schell lives through his father's death. Perhaps all of them, the living, speak, as Ellison's Invisible Man said, on the lower frequencies *for us*. Even when damaged, most young people grow up. Sometimes the mere feat of not dying, as in the case of Vladek in *Maus*, is a heroic victory. But one wants, deserves to see more than this. What would a success story look like? Given the amount of dark material that has been under discussion, what are the credible criteria for successful growing up?

To answer this question, I want to close this portion of my book by looking at two remarkable narratives: Faulkner's *Go Down, Moses* and Walker's *The Color Purple*. In my view neither of them is dewy-eyed, for both record struggle and enduring injury on all levels: personal, regional, national, international. Each of these books moves through virtually all of the rubrics we have seen up to now: the voyage from innocence to experience, the significance of love and of abuse, the threats of familial and cultural sacrifice. Each depicts, as well, the systemic forces of racial and gender prejudice, not to say warfare. Yet these two narratives also portray growth, and they are both profoundly inscribed in a project of education. It is that education that most engages me at this juncture: what have these tested young people learned? It will be seen that language and history loom surprisingly large in both of these accounts. Language appears, albeit in radically different ways, as the key enabling resource for maturation and agency, as the indispensable tool for seeing and making one's way. And history is the inevitable mesh in which the young—of every culture and every age—are caught; history—one's own and one's society's—is what must be understood if change and emancipation are to be possible. These principles may sound self-evident when posited as abstract notions, but in real life they are murky, difficult, and often bloody.

William Faulkner's Ike McCaslin

Go Down, Moses is late Faulkner (1942), autumnal in many ways: as a grand pronouncement about the South, about its tragic history as God's curse, this rich and ambitious mix of black-and-white stories often has a prophetic, oracular ring to it, bearing witness to the depredations of race and also those of property, yielding a gathering indictment of ownership (of people, of land) as the moral failing of an entire culture. Two central figures dominate this collection of stories: the white Ike McCaslin, whose coming of age as hunter and spiritual citizen of the South is narrated with great pathos, and his counterpart, the wily, humorous black sharecropper Lucas Beauchamp, who stems from the same McCaslin blood as Ike but via the old patriarch Carothers McCaslin's fornications with his black women slaves. Each of these figures has a story. Ike will be nobly initiated into the rituals and sins of the South; Lucas will go through his splendid but comic antics revolving around hidden stills, moonshine, and buried treasure. Lucas has some searing memories about the racial

"curse" besetting his family, but in Faulkner's South he funda-
mentally has no future to grow into. But Ike does have a future; he
grows into his legacy, and that is the trajectory I want to sketch in
this final salute to Faulkner.

With great delicacy and miraculously limpid prose, Faulkner
limns the portrait of the child Ike learning from his Native American mentor, Sam Fathers, both the skills and the ethos of hunting. Every year a group of Mississippi men (women have no place
here) gather for a ritual weeklong immersion in the Wilderness,
in pursuit of the great totemic animal, Old Ben the bear. Carrying
ancient echoes of hunter-gatherer tribes, these male rites, lubricated by much swapping of tales and considerable whiskey, adum-
brate an old code of honor and reverence for life, for the hunter
must both love and be worthy of "the life he spills." Ike's entire
life is cued to the eventual moment when he will be initated into
this group as a hunter himself, worthy to take his part and play his
role. We see the boy go through his paces, from the killing of one
buck to the sighting of another, larger and mythic in character, on
to the supreme gambit: the hunt for Old Ben. The old rites live:
the child is marked by Sam with the blood of the buck, and the
ancient words "Oleh, Grandfather" are spoken by the side of the
slain beast, signifying at once the boy's increasing prowess and humility, his gradual entry into the great family.

This apprenticeship is brought to its conclusion in some of the
most spellbinding pages Faulkner ever wrote, depicting Ike's initiation into the Wilderness as a spiritual pilgrimage of sorts, entailing a severe self-baring—exposure to the point of erasure—an
entry of the soul, unprotected, into nature's heart. Ike has to divest
himself of all the accoutrements of civilization, all the tools of
mastery and orientation—gun, watch, compass—if he is to take
his place as an equal in this spiritual arena, if he is to earn his vision and encounter with the bear. With a rare mix of naturalness
and cunning, Faulkner writes this as an exercise in decipherment,
in reading tracks. Able, even at a distance, to discern Ben's special
markings from those of other beasts, Ike, having discarded the implements of culture, now enters that other world—sylvan, not
human—following a very pure, primitive logic of crossing the

threshold to adulthood. The light rain is falling, and thus the prints are at the very edge of visibility, legibility:

> seeing as he sat down on the log the crooked print, the warped indentation in the wet ground which while he looked at it continued to fill with water until it was level full and the water began to overflow and the sides of the print began to dissolve away. Even as he looked up he saw the next one, and, moving, the one beyond it; moving, not hurrying, running, but merely keeping pace with them as they appeared before him as though they were being shaped out of thin air just one constant pace short of where he would lose them forever and be lost forever himself, tireless, eager, without doubt or dread, panting a little above the strong rapid little hammer of his heart, emerging suddenly into a little glade and the wilderness coalesced. It rushed, soundless, and solidified—the tree, the bush, the compass and the watch glinting where a ray of sunlight touched them. Then he saw the bear.

There is something mesmerizing in this sequence of tracks moving into and out of visibility, holding the key, it would seem, not only to the hunt but also to the very positioning of the human subject finding or losing his way, going through his rites of passage. Please note: the end stage of this process of maturation is not so much power as vision. Ike does not kill the bear, he *sees* the bear. We have here a virtual allegory of growing up. The goal of education is at once conceptual and visionary: it is an affair of deciphering prints, so as to arrive at what the prints signify. We begin now to realize that this is also an allegory of reading, now seen as the basic modus operandi of growing up. And I think we are meant to ponder the paradox in play here: the flesh-and-blood bear produces tracks in real life, yet the hunter's skill and devotion reverse this procedure, depending on the tracks to produce the bear. *The tracks produce the bear.* Is that not what reading is about? We are exiled into a world of markers, of traces, and it is for us to transform them into presence. In this luminous passage, the tracks give birth to the reality behind them; reading is commensurate with meaning. To use Derrida's famous term, *différance—*

the fateful gap between sign and meaning, representation and reality—is overcome.

Perhaps all this sounds abstruse. Faulkner is a novelist, not a linguist or a philosopher. Yet *Go Down, Moses* is his richest meditation on reading as the index of growing up. Benjy, Quentin, and Joe Christmas had no such options. They translated nothing, turned nothing into lesson, found no salvation through awareness. Reading is culture's most beautiful luxury item. We are meant to realize just how pervasive and profound the motif of tracking is in this text; and once we see this, we are ready to take the next step: tracking means reading. Hence the hunt for Old Ben is sandwiched in among other hunts in this rich collection of stories: hunts for escaped slaves, runaway wives, or even dead loved ones. Faulkner has imbued the motif of tracking with powerful, indeed epochal, echoes, evoking the racial sins and the gender injustices of the South. We have the makings here of a "thick" ideological discourse, in which one narrative strain turns out to be linked and keyed to another, figuring it also for us at some level, yielding a prismatic fiction. Thus it is that Ike McCaslin's growing up, his education as a hunter, is inseparable from his education as a reader. He must learn to read the South.

And he does. The most astonishing—and easily overlooked—sequence in the novel takes place in the commissary when Ike—age sixteen, coming of age—discusses with his cousin Cass the old yellowed ledgers that they are reading together. Indented and italicized within Faulkner's text, words abbreviated and misspelled, these ledgers contain the written history of the McCaslin family, especially the doings of the patriarch Carothers McCaslin, as registered in the exchanges between Buck and Buddy, children of the patriarch, Ike's father and uncle. I called this sequence "easily overlooked" because it seems so utterly cryptic, just a series of italicized coinages and compressed notations relating to a faraway time and virtually indecipherable to the reader. Let me reproduce the salient parts of this material, and you can see for yourself how impenetrable it looks:

Eunice Bought by Father in New Orleans 1807 $650. dolars.
Marrid to Thucydus 1809 Drownd in Crick Cristmas Day 1832

Then, a page later in the text, the two brothers' queries:

June 21th 1833 Drownd herself

Followed by

23 Jun 1833 Who in hell ever heard of a niger drownding him self

And then a final return-entry, incomprehensible as ever:

Aug 13 1833 Drownd herself

Ike had read these entries earlier, many times, always thinking they were the harmless, docile, tedious record of his forebears, but at the age of sixteen he reads them again, sensing their terrible import, and he now pursues the story of a drowned slave woman, finding that it is inextricably tied to birth and death:

Tomasina called Tomy Daughter of Thucydus @ Eunice Born 1810 dide in Child bed June 1833 and Burd. Yr stars fell

leading to the notation

Turl Son of Thucydus @ Eunice Tomy born June 1833 yr stars fell Fathers will

This is what history looks like. Via their inscriptions in the yel-lowed ledgers Buck and Buddy are telling a story, and it has to do with Carothers McCaslin's treatment of his slaves, focusing espe-cially on the acquisition of Eunice back in 1807 and her mysteri-ous death in 1832, drowned in the creek. *Who in hell ever heard of a niger drownding him self* write, incredulously, the brothers. To answer that question—and I'd want to say that all the moral power of Faulkner's book is invested in answering that question—we need to piece together the horribly coherent story being sketched out. Carothers goes to New Orleans and purchases Eu-nice. Two years later, Eunice is married to his man-slave Thucydidus and gives birth immediately thereafter to Tomasina. Seventeen years later Eunice drowns herself in the creek. Six months later, Tomasina gives birth to Turl. Yet my account leaves out all the crucial unstated information, information that Ike has understood, namely, that Eunice is impregnated by Carothers (her first lover, Ike reasons) and then married off to Thucydidus; and then Carothers impregnates his own daughter. Upon realizing this, Eunice kills herself. The baby is born six months later. *Who in hell ever heard of a niger drownding him self.* This death makes terrible sense, for it is a response to the racial transgressions that were business as usual in the antebellum South. It makes terrible sense, yet the reader of Faulkner's text is—initially—unable to make sense of it. Why? Because it is in cryptic form, misspelled, enigmatic, unreadable. It is as illegible, as indecipherable as a bear print would be for you and me, even though it stares at us in the text. Bear print. *Print.*

Print resembles animal tracks; print consists of markers on a page, such as an old ledger entry, that are transformed into meaning by the act of reading. Think, for a minute, of alphabets you do not know, such as Chinese or Japanese or Hebrew or Arabic, and then visualize them on a page: they look like bear prints. Think back further still if you can—and you can't, for it is impossible—back to your unschooled initial apprehension of English, when it has to have looked like scratchings on a page, markers without meaning, again on the order of bear prints. Ike McCaslin is performing one of the oldest coming-of-age rituals we know—call it Confirmation, call it Bar Mitzvah—which consists of reading the Holy Books to an audience of adults as a sign that oneself is now an adult by dint of being able to read just these books. These ledgers with their terrible story are the South's Scripture. Ike's task of maturation is to understand what this story of human violation means, to understand that there is a dreadful answer to the question *Who in hell ever heard of a niger drownding him self.* He does understand, and he acts accordingly. Innocence, experience, love, abuse, sacrifice: all are there. He renounces his heritage. He abdicates. He says no to the McCaslin legacy, in particular the plantation with all the land. He refuses the ticket.

We are a far cry from Faulkner's earlier doomed young men

who went under. Ike McCaslin's model is Christ the carpenter, not Jesus the crucified. Ike McCaslin refuses, forfeits all material goods and benefits, rents a cabin from his cousin who thus inherits the land, becomes Uncle Ike to the entire region but father to none. This may look remarkably clear, but it is morally as opaque as ever, since it is by no means self-evident that refusing one's patrimony is a step toward changing things. Nor is it clear that one can ultimately refuse one's patrimony, as Ike himself demonstrates in later stories by dint of his residual racial ambivalence, his inability to see black people as entirely human and entitled to the same rights and respect as whites. This is painfully clear in the penultimate story, where Ike hands an envelope filled with money to a black woman who has come looking for her lover, Ike's own relative; it is a horrible moment, for this man and this woman are McCaslins all, black and white even if distantly related, and their union, if sanctioned, might—might—signal some form of wisdom and generosity, some healing of the wounds of the past. Instead, Ike is horrified, tries to buy time, tells the woman to wait, perhaps another thousand years. Her answer to him is the strongest thing in the novel: "Old man, have you lived so long and forgotten so much that you dont even remember anything you ever knew or felt or even heard about love?"

It is as if the novel had the wisdom to pirouette its central people, to oblige us to rethink their moves. As if the novel had the courage to attack its hero, who seems to have learned so much. And one has therefore to wonder what kind of a solution celibacy itself is, not to mention abdication, for responding to the crimes committed against blacks and women. Ike is haunted by his own gesture, knows he is, in the eyes of the community, a figure of ridicule as well as probity, seems to sense the sterility, the escapism, of his choice. Yes, he did choose. But what choice do you make when you realize that your own hereditary culture is cursed, shot through with moral transgressions? Ike said no. But what is there to say yes to? And is saying no actually doable? Growing up: you're damned if you do, damned if you don't. Faulkner has not simplified things.

Yet, in the final reckoning, we must say that "reading the books of one's culture" is a prodigious step in the right direction, given the earlier fates of Benjy, Quentin, and Joe Christmas. Ike McCaslin proves that education is possible, that maturation entails an ever-increasing understanding of one's own culture, of one's place in it, even if it leads to opting out as the only option. Ike at least lives; he does not drown in the Charles River, as Quentin did in his exit from culture. And maybe there is a kind of light, hedged but real, in this autumnal text, a light, a hope for *us*. He encounters cryptic markers—bear tracks, ledgers—and he converts them into significance, indeed into ethical significance. What does education mean, if not this? What is it that every culture hopes to instill in its young—if not a capacity for understanding where they are, for reading the land they inhabit. It begins with learning one's letters, and it ends only at death. Books—perhaps especially books of literature, because they do not parade as facts, but rather demand our interpretation—are the sites of this precious commerce. This may be as good a shot as civilization is likely to have in proffering a paradigm of growing up that gives us some hope.

The conversion of signs into meaning is the school lesson that is never over and never easy. There are no "master readers" who can go on automatic pilot, certain that they will get it right. But most arduous of all is the challenge of belief, of actually feeling that words on a page—or figures in an equation or data on a screen or people on the street—require our active moral intervention if we are to understand them. Here is perhaps school's greatest failure: its failure to convince the young that what they read has an ethical import beyond the dictionary meanings of the terms involved; not just an ethical import but an imaginative life.

I look back at my own education and want to weep: I absorbed, as all students do, my share of data, of names and dates and formulas, but I was never prodded to take the next step, to ponder what they might really mean (beyond the test that was coming), how they might impact my own life, on the lives of others. Literature gratifies me because it is my second chance at schooling, my later opportunity to plumb the dimensions of words, to gauge their extended reach and bite. None of this is to be found in primers or how-to books. There exists no method for this. And there are no shortcuts, including quick visits to Wikipedia or other websites; if anything, we are awash in data today, filled to the very brim with facts, only a click away from still greater volumes of information. Yet we are short on wisdom, short on interpretation, all too illiterate when it comes to converting signs on a page into the rich—sometimes unbearably rich—human meanings they contain. It is the challenge we face every day: in our texts, in all our relations, in our world. It is not so much a question of taking books seriously as of taking life and oneself seriously. Growing up means learning to read.

Alice Walker's Celie

Alice Walker's Pulitzer Prize–winning novel of 1982, *The Color Purple,* is not much read today, I suspect. It may seem too sentimental, too much of a fairy tale; Steven Spielberg's film with Whoopi Goldberg and Danny Glover, despite the fine intentions of all involved, pushes it still further into mawkish territory. Yet Walker's novel is the right book for capping this study, because it is a much tougher, shrewder, and more ambitious work than has been acknowledged. And because the evolution of Celie, a classic study of growing up in the school of hard knocks and overcoming abuse, is indeed something to behold. So many of my young protagonists are damaged goods—Blake's chimney sweep, Pablos, Heathcliff, Jane, Benjy, Quentin, Antoinette—but their injuries pale before the brutality of Celie's childhood.

It would be hard to improve on the opening line: "You better not never tell nobody but God. It'd kill your mammy." We soon realize that these are a father's words to his daughter as he forces her to have sex with him. Celie is still almost a child, and her account of what is done to her has an unbearable eloquence, largely because of her own innocence. Blake brilliantly exploited the lens of innocence, but Walker brings it to bear on the most elemental forms of abuse and injury: "First he put his thing up gainst my hip and sort of wiggle it around. Then he grab hold my titties. Then he push his thing inside my pussy." That there might be consequences is beyond her understanding: "When I start to hurt and then my stomach start moving and then that little baby come out my pussy chewing on it fist you could have knock me over with a feather." This is what innocence looks like.

I have my reasons for referencing Blake. The God who sends angels into the dreams of chimney sweeps, to tell them to be good boys, is eventually reconceived by Walker as a white male phantom who sits on black people's eyeballs; and although Celie writes letters to God, using him essentially as a sewage system (since the dirt done to her has to be evacuated somewhere), Walker is mounting her attack even in the opening paragraphs, as in Celie's assertion to her mother that the baby is God's child and that God has taken it. The venerable old construct depicting God as the source of children comes in for some damage here, since we can scarcely avoid the inference that God is also a rapist, a child stealer, a pretty vicious force. The book makes good on this characterization, even though it takes some time for Celie to move consciously into such an indictment. Male privilege, stemming from either God or other males who do his bidding, looms large in this book, and it is against this brutally coercive system that the story of Celie's maturation takes place. Even Faulkner, who wrote about black women as the ultimate tragic victims of southern hierarchical arrangements, did not—could not—write their story from the inside. They remain silent in his books. Alice Walker can "speak" them, and she tells us what it must have felt like to be on the receiving end of sexually abusive male culture.

We've already noted Celie's sexual initiation (by "Pa"). Let's now consider her courtship (by Mr. ——). Mr., later called Albert, who wanted to marry her sister Nettie, reluctantly settles for Celie and comes over to get another look. She goes to the door. "He's still up on his horse. He look me up and down." Celie is a bit frightened by the horse. The new baby, Lucious, comes out and asks what's going on. "Pa say, Your sister thinking bout marriage." Pa goes on to add, for Mr.'s benefit: "She good with children." Mr.'s only response is "That cow still coming?" Pa seals the deal: "Her cow." Literary and sociological texts from every era have taught us that marriage is as much an economic event, a market proposition, as it is anything else, but I'm not sure I've ever seen it placed quite this squarely in the barnyard. The horse, the cow, the looking

Celie up and down: we are not far from the infamous slave mar-
kets of the antebellum South, where one purchased by the pound,
as it were, weighing the goods in terms of its potential service
along a variety of lines: manual labor, sexual productivity, capacity to take punishment. "Your sister thinking bout marriage," Pa
tells Lucious. What this entire passage tells us is: Celie's own
thinking is off limits, of no interest, since she is simply an item on
the block, being traded, ratcheted up in value by having her own
cow.

   "Reification" is the fine abstraction that is used to designate
treating a person like a thing. What might "thinghood" feel like?
Mr. beats her routinely: "He say, Celie, git the belt. The children
be outside the room peeking through the cracks. It all I can do not
to cry. I make myself wood. I say to myself, Celie, you a tree."
Making yourself into wood leads, if you are successful, to the desired result that you soon feel nothing at all. Your body decides
that feeling is unacceptable: "Then after a while every time I got
mad, or start to feel mad, I got sick. Felt like throwing up. Terrible
feeling. Then I start to feel nothing at all." There's nothing volitional or even conscious here; the body has learned its lesson. In
today's culture, stamped by hyperawareness of feelings and sensations, it is useful to realize how sentience can be put out of business if one is subjected to adequate abuse.

   What is gripping about *The Color Purple* is Celie's exit out of
thinghood and her entry into the human. Not that she is unaware
at the beginning but that she is utterly "done unto," utterly without resources. But her growing up is about to become a story of
agency. It starts with the sexual awakening triggered by the book's
femme fatale and love apostle, Shug Avery, adored by Mr. and now
adored by Celie as well. Shug asks Celie to describe her sex life:
"He [Mr.] get up on you, heist your nightgown round your waist,
plunge in. Most times I pretend I ain't there. He never know the
difference. Never ast me how I feel, nothing. Just do his business,
get off, go to sleep." Shug's reply—"Do his business. Why, Miss
Celie. You make it sound like he going to the toilet on you"—is in
line with the reification and functionalism of Celie's existence.
Time to educate this woman, Shug decides.

Listen, she say, right down there in your pussy is a little button
that gits real hot when you do you know what with somebody.
It git hotter and hotter and then it melt. That the good part.
But other parts good too, she say. Lot of sucking go on, here
and there, she say. Lot of finger and tongue work.

Critics have observed that male-driven sex has not paid much
attention to these buttons. I'd want to call Shug's intervention that
of a teacher as well as a lover: she's helping Celie toward a grasp
of not only her own body but her own estate, her own capacity for
pleasure and feeling. One senses an inventory in process here, a
moving into one's domains. As the novel registers the long passing
of time, Celie's worship of Shug remains constant, even as it mel-
lows in older age, even as Shug proves to be unownable, a free
spirit committed to loving, destined to make all her partners hungry and jealous. But Shug's greatest contribution is to empower
Celie, to gift her with a sense of her indwelling resources. I'm
talking about more than buttons; I mean that Celie is discovering
something like a bill of rights, like a creatural entitlement of the
good life.

This project of ownership marks what is most hopeful and in-
spiriting about Walker's book. Some of the most poignant scenes
between Celie and Shug are almost Proustian or Faulknerian in
character, as Celie revisits her past life of abjection and abuse and
makes it hers at last. She remembers the first time she was taken
sexually, how she "never even thought bout men having nothing
down there so big," how Pa did it to her during "intermission"
while she was trimming his hair, "how it stung while I finish
trimming his hair. How the blood drip down my leg and mess up
my stocking." Like a hemorrhage, indeed, this memory triggers a
still-deeper sense of the injuries she's received, of her entire life as
injury: "My mama die, I tell Shug. My sister Nettie run away. Mr.
—— come git me to take care his rotten children. He never ast me
nothing bout myself. He clam on top of me and fuck and fuck,
even when my head bandaged. Nobody ever love me, I say." For
me, these passages have a vitality and healing dimension beyond
the horrors they detail, for they signal that Celie is at last process-

ing what has been done to her and that she realizes she is entitled
to being loved. The warmth of Shug's affection catalyzes this
growth, this newfound sense of worth, against which the treatment meted out to her must be measured. For that is the beauty of
Walker's retrospective manner: measures are being taken, the voyage into adulthood requires "owning" your earlier self, even if—
especially if—it was abused.

Up to now, I've said little about the Nettie plot. She has disappeared out of Celie's life but, lo and behold, has found her way not
only to Africa but even to Celie's own lost children. She writes regularly to Celie, we later learn, but Mr. hides the letters. This material has a mix of fairy tale, anthropology, and crash course on
African history, and it is written in a way that does not quite
match the pathos, sass, and brilliance of Walker's rendition of
Celie. But the Africa story fulfills another role: it makes the entire
narrative stereophonic, two-eyed, and hence vital to the project of
growing up and seeing clear. Africa rewrites America. Uncle
Remus is seen to have African origins. Jesus is now seen from an
Ethiopian perspective as wooly-haired and darker-skinned. All
this is akin to Celie's own growing awareness, abetted by Shug,
that the old white God who has dictated so much of what folks can
think or see needs to be unseated, cast aside. Ike McCaslin learned
to decode the history of the South. Celie's exposure to Africa—as
a control case for the culture that has trapped her—leads, indirectly but crucially, to her slowly growing sense of agency.

I'd link this African plot material to something equally dramatic: namely, Nettie's piecing together of the family mystery and
realizing that Samuel's two children are in fact Celie's lost babies.
Of course this is incredible, from any realist perspective, but it fits
into a larger "might-be" perspective that opens up closed facts and
constraining principles into something partaking of desire and
fable. And it is no less fitting that Nettie informs Celie that the
man who impregnated her—"Pa"—is not her real father; hence
there has been no incest. Here too we see the miraculous transformation at work: hard facts, facts you can barely live with, yield to
new fictions that set you free. What you thought imprisoning suddenly opens up and is seen in the light of a new prism. The dread-

ful connections turn out to be illusory, the severed connections turn out to be retrievable.

Walker is reversing the fateful logic we saw in the story of Oedipus. He thought himself free and found out how heinously abused his vision was. Celie is not the victim of some illusion—she was indeed abused systematically, denied any form of recognition as a person—but there is a building project here, an artisanal drive of self-making. And it doesn't hurt to find out that at least some of the worst injuries done to you were not quite what you thought. *Oedipus the King* closes with a dreadful family reunion: the Shepherd and the Messenger arrive on scene in order to tighten the noose entirely, to bring the parricide/incest plot to full visibility. Walker too closes with a family reunion, but it is life-affirming, not condemning. Growing up so often entails cutting the cord, leaving the nest, vanquishing (even if symbolically) the parents. Not so here. From faraway and long ago, the lost and the exiled come together. At life's late stage, Celie will come into the larger family. Can a writer get away with this?

As acknowledged, *The Color Purple* evinces a triumphalism that sticks in some readers' throats. It closes with Celie and Nettie, both old and young at the same time, hugging each other, happy to be united, happy to be alive. And the big family comes together, wedding Africa to America, retrieving the lost or stolen ones, yielding a vision of harmony, showing that the fullness of time might bring a true harvest. But some finish better than others. Sofia has been permanently damaged by her fight with the system, and her rage will not easily disappear; she remains in our minds as what Celie too might have become, as what outright resistance might lead to. Harpo and Squeak have taken their hits too. Injury is real, it doesn't simply go away. And one needs to ask: does getting your lost children back when they're almost adults really constitute a happy ending?

For all these reasons, I'd like to close my remarks on this powerful novel by focusing on what I take to be the single strongest force that it hallows as resource, as weapon: *voice*. By voice I mean many things. First of all there is the splendid, inventive, lively, sometimes breathtaking idiom that Walker has fashioned in order to "write" Celie: a black English that has chutzpah, poetry, piz-zazz, and wit. This is what most embarrasses the "Nettie material" and the African saga, because the social science discourse in that part of the novel is limp, virtually academic, in comparison. Be-yond that, however, I want to emphasize Celie's language as a trump of a different sort altogether. Underlying this entire argu-ment are questions going all the way back to Quevedo's *Swindler:* Can language itself be a tool, a weapon, a resource for making your way? Can words play a determining role in growing up? Faulkner's Ike McCaslin traced a history of subjugation from scribbled entries in a ledger. Celie's use of language is outright lifesaving.

Celie is, as noted, among the most victimized figures in narra-tive literature. Yet Walker wants to show us that people who have nothing still have words. Initially Celie writes to God, but the richer conceit of the book is that she writes to us. And what she writes displays a marvelous dialectic, a redressing of wrongs achievable by the elemental magic of words and thought. Let me explain. At one point, Celie is visited by Mr.'s two sisters; they are predictably condescending to Celie but try to compliment her nonetheless, observing that Celie is a "good housekeeper, good with children, good cook. Brother couldn't have done better if he tried." These are forms of banality we've all seen, heard, and ut-tered. But note what Celie then says to herself: "I think about how he tried." In my view, this is how you fight back. You cannot change the givens, but you can season them, you can ironize them, you can replay in your head, and all this gives you a kind of agency you don't have in any other way.

Here's another instance. Celie is scrutinizing Albert: "I look at his face. It tired and sad and I notice his chin weak. Not much chin there at all. I have more chin, I think." Again small beer, you might say, yet these are the materials of rebuttal, of assertion. Celie's gaze stalks her husband's face, sizes it up, finds it lacking, finds herself more imposing. Nothing is uttered out loud, but then it needn't be. Celie hears it well enough. That homely little pas-sage starts in observation and closes in affirmation. These are the tiny closet dramas that parse every life, consisting of moments—not years—of ascendancy, scattered moments when you right

your vessel, take the lead, come out ahead. No declaration of war
is required; this minute guerrilla warfare goes on, on the inside,
and nobody is the wiser except for the silent resister. I'd argue that
the true balance of power in human relations might well lie in
this hard-to-measure direction. Certainly whatever balm we find
for our wounds, whatever stand we make against circumstances, is
likely to be situated, at least in part, in such virtual precincts. Perhaps literature is our best entry into this strategic field, our best
glimpse of how we fare, since it rarely gets into the public record.

But eventually in this novel, these small skirmishes are indeed
going to go public, and when they do, we see a veritable explosion
of rage, energy, and agency. Celie is about to come of age. It happens at the dinner table, when Shug coolly announces to Albert
that Celie is going to go back to Memphis with her. He is stunned
and says (and believes what he says): "I thought you was finally
happy, he say. What wrong now?"

Don't forget: Albert has not only brutalized her, he has also
hidden all of Nettie's letters from Africa. Time to let loose:

> You a lowdown dog is what's wrong, I say. It's time to leave you
> and enter into the Creation. And your dead body just the wel-
> come mat I need.
>
> Say what? he ast. Shock.
>
> All round the table folkses mouths be dropping open.
>
> You took my sister Nettie away from me, I say. And she was
> the only person love me in the world.
>
> Mr. —— start to sputter. ButButButButBut. Sound like
> some kind of motor.
>
> But Nettie and my children coming home soon, I say. And
> when she do, all us together gon whup your ass.
>
> Nettie and your children! say Mr. ——. You talking crazy.
>
> I got children, I say. Being brought up in Africa. Good
> schools, lots of fresh air and exercise. Turning out a heap bet-
> ter than the fools you didn't even try to raise.

What strikes us most is the sheer vehemence and unstoppable
force of Celie's outburst. Mr.'s sputtering is rightly compared to a
motor, but we see Celie's attack as a volcano. My simile is not cho-

sen lightly. Walker wants us to grasp the elemental power of Celie's responses, as if earth, wind, fire, and water were all brought into play as carriers of human volition. A few pages later, when Albert refuses to tell Celie if further letters from Nettie have arrived, language now begins to take on the character of fate itself, as if Celie had the power of the Delphic oracle:

> I curse you, I say.
>
>   What that mean? he say.
>
>   I say, Until you do right by me, everything you touch will crumble.
>
>   He laugh. Who you think you is? he say. You can't curse nobody. Look at you. You black, you pore, you ugly, you a woman. Goddam, he say, you nothing at all.
>
>   Until you do right by me, I say, everything you even dream about will fail. I give it to him straight, just like it come to me. And it seem to come to me from the trees.
>
>   Whoever heard of such a thing, say Mr. ——. I probably didn't whup your ass enough.
>
>   Every lick you hit me you will suffer twice, I say. Then I say, You better stop talking because all I'm telling you ain't coming just from me. Look like when I open my mouth the air rush in and shape words.

I cannot think of a purer example of an empowered woman in all of literature. Albert is, after all, no fool: he recites Celie's weaknesses, indeed her stigmata (as he sees it): black, poor, ugly, woman. With this against you, what is going for you? The answer is: the universe; the trees, the wind, and the air are in collusion with Celie's declaration of independence, have given them a fierce authority on the far side of any social logic. She is a chthonic force. I referred to the Oracle, because the utterances from Delphi were thought to have the character of fate itself, to be the language of the gods. And that is what is put forth here. Not only is Celie invincible, but her power has a frightening boomerang dimension to it, so that it reverses all efforts at resistance. Whatever Albert *does*—hit, dream, speak—will be *done to* him, will be part of Celie's own arsenal. And this will happen: Albert will suffer, will be unable to sleep, will stay up listening to his heart, listening to it go crazy, "beating so loud it shook the room. Sound like drums." Africa again. There is a stunning economy at work here, and perhaps we are meant to see this as a parable about justice and revenge.

But given the abased and abused life Celie has led in this book, I want to insist on the verbal as the key to the spectacle. Language is Celie's greatest strength: we see it move from early unvoiced reflections all the way to oracular indictment, and Walker wants us to recognize that it is vehicular, galvanizing, capable of changing the order of things. One might cavil that such a view confirms our suspicion that we are reading a fairy tale, but I'd want to argue the opposite: such a view confirms the unsuspected indwelling potency of language and thought, a shape-shifting energy that operates on the world. Celie's progression from thing to person centers on the power of language as tool, as means of self-enactment, as currency. Here is a resource that even the most deprived possess. It might be said that virtually all of the growing-up stories we've studied are reprised and transfigured in the humble Celie's rise to power.

That is why this book satisfies. Gloria Steinem remarked that it resembles the great nineteenth-century Russian novels with their intricate plots and far-flung relationships far more than it does the minimalist fare being written at the time of its publication. This story of a fissured family and a fissured globe moves toward healing and oneness. To see that as a fairy tale, as something beyond the logic of human doing, is to sell the book short, because Celie's empowerment is no tinsel fable borrowed from children's literature, no Cinderella parable requiring a magic prince. On the contrary, Walker's novel is rooted in the stubborn potentials of human feeling and human development, in the belief that adversity—terrible adversity—may, yes, destroy you but may also leaven your character, catalyze what is strongest and most vital in you, bring you to (and into) life. Especially if love enters the frame. Shug Avery—the splendid bitch-goddess of the text who is all heat and much tenderness—midwifes Celie, helps her birth herself, catapults her onto her own road of selfhood. Growing up is an organic concept. Celie's marvelous rise to power and adulthood testifies to the marvel of our species: we grow in time. Yes, time can be ferocious, and Walker does not dodge this: flesh changes, desire withers, beauty goes; Celie, Shug, and Albert learn this lesson. But at novel's end, they are more—not less—than they were at the beginning.

Walker's closing image of two old ladies, two separated sisters, hugging each other—one came all the way from Africa to do so, bringing the other's biological children with her—offers a beneficent model of what we harvest, what we grow. And we can scarcely avoid seeing what is most triumphant in this affirmative fiction: *family*. From beginning to end, Walker positions the individual subject within a larger framework, and Celie's trajectory displays how that cocoon changes from prison house to enabling construct. *Construct.* Walker moves right past blood bonds to show us that the family is built, is a made thing. As if to carry further the symbolic logic of *Père Goriot* and *Great Expectations*—each driven by a family-making impetus, even in a corrosive setting, as the father-son gestalt takes shape: Rastignac and Goriot, Pip and Magwitch—*The Color Purple* breaks clear of fathers and redefines family altogether by casting its light on what women of generosity and heart can do: hence Squeak fills in for Sofia when she is imprisoned, takes on the mother role for a sister, and we see this throughout the book: strong, capable women banding together, nurturing children, reconceiving family beyond the lines of blood.

Thus it is right to close on a family reunion: two old ladies feeling younger than they ever have before and some grown-up children, outfitted with scarification markings, looking bravely at the new world they have come to, knowing they are in it together. Is this not the richest outcome of growing up? To realize that one is always part of the human family, that one's maturation is never just an individual performance but rather a growing recognition of one's fit within the larger community? The old rites-of-passage paradigm dear to anthropologists finishes on just this note: the final stage of maturation is reincorporation. To say this is to acknowledge how rarely we find such an outcome in the books we read. The modern focus is inevitably, perhaps tragically, on the individual's fate, the individual's dance with fate, the individual's final tally. It is what I find in the young people I teach: a hunger to achieve their private form, a sense that their (expensive) education is intended to outfit them, to credentialize them, for the Darwinian struggle ahead. Out of the nest and into the world. Alice Walker dares to close her novel on a different note altogether. Growing up, in this novel, is not a single runner's marathon through life; at its wisest, it codes misery as solitude and understands happiness as the miracle of human relation, of the ties that sustain, nourish, and fulfill.

But it is worth remembering how this novel started: with the young girl Celie being sexually abused by the man she believed to be her father. Given this diseased picture of family—on the surface as incestuous and damning as in Sophocles' play—we are in a position to measure how much ground, both conceptual and existential, has been traversed. That is the point I wish to emphasize: that our capacity to overcome horrors is real. Alice Walker has tapped into a kind of native resilience that does honor to our species. Over and over in this study I have remarked that we are not equipped to look inside people's hearts, to read their story. And often enough, my meaning has been that we cannot see the scars that show what life has done to them. But scars themselves testify to healing, to the stubborn affirmative drive of life. You are cut, perhaps cut badly, but your skin knits, your skin toughens, you go on. The triumphs of the human spirit are also genuine.

Time's Paths, Literature's Paths

Picture this: two old ladies embracing, saying they'd never been so young before. Is Eden behind us or ahead? Is it reachable? Staying safe by reversing time: many of the hurt figures of this book could have wished for just that. Sophocles' chorus says it is best not to be born; Heathcliff is wrecked by his Edenic bond with Catherine; Jane Eyre never fully escapes the Red Room; Joe Christmas's grandmother wished for her grandson the reprieve of just one free day; Oskar Schell reverses in his mind the falling Twin Towers, so as to retrieve a father telling his son a story. But it is not to be.

The unfurling of time not only puts an end to innocence but positions us on the treadmill that leads to all the crossroads that must come: the old man in the wagon bearing down on you in anger, the blind man who smashes your head against the stone, the Capulet masked ball where your life changes altogether, the Parisian boardinghouse with its exploited old man and its cynical seer, the mysterious inheritance that takes you to London with great expectations, the runaway slave who joins you in your escape on a raft, the Mississippi commissary with the yellowed pages you must decipher, the trip from Tuskegee to Harlem as your racial education takes form, the glittering ice palace from which you do not return, the ferry crossing near Saigon where the Chinese man watches you, the streets of New York after your father's death on 9/11. These are some of the fates that attend growing up. They are not to be reversed. The sun goes from morning to noon.

But as literature, each of these trajectories can be made again and again. The virtuality of art turns it into a precious tool for expanding human experience and growth, for repeated use, without expiration date. Readers are the most privileged folks on the planet: fellow travelers, frequent flyers, but with special benefits. Even as you near your own path's end, you are free to start over with books, to live other, to immerse yourself, as the case may be, in stories of growing up and coming of age. One, then another, perhaps a third, even dozens or hundreds, and as many rereads as you wish. As many trips from morning to noon as you can manage. Plots end stories, but reading knows no end. Tracking characters, pondering their fates, trying them on, is a renewable activity, can even be thought of as a renewable energy source that fuels our craft, even if along vicarious, imaginative lines. No one has ever taken the measure of this kind of traffic, for it is immeasurable in every sense: not subject to any statistical tool we might devise but also endless, curbed only by our own appetite. Such psychic voyages furnish our minds, for—fictive though they are—they help us to espy the figure in our own carpet. One is enriched and lessoned by the shifting shapes and evolving selves of the young in literature. Our own affairs are enlarged when echoed and shadowed and nourished by stories of the past. Art grows us.

GROWING
OLD

Itinerary:
Noon to Night

I now come to the part of my book that has a decidedly existential flavor for me, as well as constituting a subject—indeed, a field, an arena, sometimes a pit—that I explore more fully, more wonderingly, and often more painfully every day I live: growing old. There is no way these essays will not appear biased in that regard. Innocence and experience apply as much to me as they do to the growing-up and growing-old stories I analyze, because all authors occupy the experience position. That is what I write out of: the experience of working a lifetime with these books, but also the experience of growing old. I believe that my personal angle of vision has its place in this book, for there can be no panoptic view of growing old, and hence there will be many moments when personal asides accompany analysis.

Again I will draw on a wide historical sweep of materials, from Shakespeare to our time. As always, I choose the books I love, since they are the ones about which I may have something of value to say. And I cluster them in order to delineate the phases of a gathering, unfolding, larger critical narrative about the trip from noon to night: how growing old has been recorded and interpreted by the great writers. It comes as no surprise that many of the categories in play in the discussion of growing up will again be referenced, but this time from a different perspective. Our familiar major themes—the dialectic of innocence and experience, the joys and trials of love, the acquisition of knowledge and power—are no less central in the journey from noon to night, even though they will be accented in radically different fashion, seen now from "the far side."

Growing old entails many things that have been viewed differently at different historical and cultural moments: becoming wise (is this fully credible today?), losing one's powers (physical and sexual, but also professional, social, familial), exiting from the center of the stage, suffering the onset of illnesses, becoming acquainted with death (one's friends' and loved ones', eventually one's own), looking at a horizon that must bring loss yet might bring gain. Old, we ponder our "estate," in every sense of the term: what our life has been worth, what worth it still has, what value we will leave. Let us recall the respect accorded to the old in all traditional societies: they were the repository of knowledge, they were revered, they were at the center of the story. Maturity, gravitas, experience, wisdom: these were the virtues and rewards that time brought to those who lived into old age. Is this still true?

Even the rites-of-passage paradigm—as articulated by anthropologists who have studied traditional (as opposed to modern) cultures—so evident in the first half of this book is inseparable from this maturation scheme that venerates age: the young make their way into the adult world in order eventually to take their place, indeed to become old in their own right. Nonetheless, the privileging of childhood in European Romanticism and the arrival of the Bildungsroman in the late eighteenth century signal to us, as literature and intellectual history, epochal transformations, for they place the young at the center of things, and they affirm for us that the story of the young has become the key story within culture. That story—the subject of the first half of this book—is, as we've seen, one of either adaptation or critique, inevitably shedding light on the adult values, recognized or not, that inform society and bear on all young entrants taking (or abandoning) their place. Where does that position the story of the old?

Yet if one widens one's angle of vision and looks back far enough, one finds a very different kind of ranking. Homer would not have dreamed of giving as much weight to the plight of Telemachus as he does to the adventures and trajectory of Odysseus. And I cannot help feeling that Shakespeare is more deeply and creatively alive to the issues of age than those of youth: to be sure, we have the wonderful romances, the saga of Romeo and Juliet, and we have a fascinating variant of the youth/age relationship in the dyad Prince Hal/Falstaff in the *Henry IV* plays, not to speak of the immortal saga of Hamlet's revenge, but the tragedies by and large have a different hue, seem inevitably death-haunted, age-haunted, as seen in Othello's sexual anxieties, Macbeth's late remorse, Prospero's islanded powers, and most spectacularly, of course, the unforgettable fates of Lear and Gloucester.

The old, whatever their station or centrality in society, have never been impregnable, have always been subject to aging and loss of power, have always been potentially tragic figures. The Oedipus story writes this large for us: Laius is slain by Oedipus, and Oedipus himself later suffers the erosions of time. In short, even if contemporary society glorifies the culture and positioning of the young, it is merely accentuating the oldest story of all: out with the old, in with the new. That tale of exit and entry was told in skeletal form by Sophocles; it has been told throughout the centuries, and each time it is told, it teaches us something vital about our own affairs. To "make friends with the necessity of dying," as Freud characterized the plot of *King Lear*, is the most arduous friendship any of us is to encounter. But the only way to escape it is to die young. Even the most reactionary patriarchal culture cannot keep its old from perishing, from knowing they will perish. Nor can it keep the young at bay. That is the larger prey I am after: to see how the experience of aging has been understood and told throughout the centuries—and how such understanding might enrich our own personal trajectory from noon to night.

The story of aging is a coat of many colors. It can be comic or tragic, it can betoken recognition or ignominy, it can inspire or repulse, it can be fueled by adaptation or revolt, it can be riddled with both somatic and mental infirmity or it can conjure up a final grandeur, it can depict love's triumph or failure, it can gesture toward wisdom or catastrophe. But no matter what its coloration may be, it is always about power: holding on to it, ceding it, refiguring it. In approaching this broad canvas of literary depictions of old age, I want to spell out some of its major articulations, its chapters, so to speak, with a view toward bringing into ever-greater focus the scale and weight of my topic, the building blocks of an edifice we can call the narrative of old age, the voyage from noon to night.

The Crisis of (Male) Power

As we saw in Part I, all growing-up stories are cued to the workings of power, inasmuch as they depict the efforts of the young to make their way in and understand the culture they inhabit. If the forward drive of the young is keyed to this educational project, the story of the old is caught between two crucial directionalities: a future that must betoken eventual death and a past that still (and only) lives in memory. Whichever way you look, authority is in trouble, especially in regimes we think of as patriarchal, where male power has exercised its so-called rights: the creation and imposition of law; the governing and policing roles that accompany the law, including the power to deny or oppress; the control of women and children, derived from sexual function and titular authority; ownership of property; even control of language.

What happens when this traditional construct of power is subjected to the ravages of time? What happens when men age? One might answer: theoretically, nothing changes. Old men still are (notionally) in control. Eventually power will pass from old man to young man (or first son). But everything we have seen about the coming of age of the young suggests that these matters are more vexed and precarious, more conflicted and subject to change, than would appear. For starters, as the parricidal act of Oedipus implies, the young are active, impatient; they want to take over, to move the old from the stage or destroy them altogether. The old are slated to lose their physical powers and are hence seen as increasingly vulnerable, but their authority in other areas as well—intellectual, moral, political—is liable to waver and shrink. As their prowess diminishes, they experience the generic drama of decline, of entropic fate. This can be very hard medicine.

The Undoing of Fathers

Just how hard it can be is what we stand to gain by examining some of the major Western texts that address this crisis. And crisis it is, in the most famous of all literary works devoted to the undoing of a father: Shakespeare's *King Lear.* Lear, and his counterpart Gloucester, will be made to drain the cup of suffering and indignities meted out to them as fathers. To be sure, Lear is also a king, and hence his travails have a profound political character as well, but it would seem that the most virulent punishment each receives—one going mad, the other being blinded—is, above all, familial, thrust upon them by their own children, coming as a kind of savage, internecine war that is virtually cannibalistic in its operation.

Balzac's *Père Goriot* consciously replays Shakespeare's tragedy in nineteenth-century Paris, locating it in the fate of an old man being bled dry by his two rapacious daughters, and hence displaying in his very calvary the inhuman workings of the new capitalist order, which reveres the cash nexus at every turn, thereby wrecking all traditional codes of family loyalty. Goriot, deranged and delusional though he is, nonetheless takes the measure of his fate: the collapse of fathers, the repudiation of the old law. My final instance of troubled fathering is Arthur Miller's classic *Death of a Salesman.* Willy Loman completes the parade of progenitors facing obsolescence, and it is hard going, but much of the play's heartbreak lies in the collapse of yet another American dream: the success of our children as the reward awaited in the fullness of time. Each of these texts is at once luminous and heartbreaking in its account of parenting as eventual time bomb and of power and authority under siege.

Exiting the Stage

One remembers the old man in the wagon bearing down on Oedipus, trying to force him out of the road. But he fails. The young are destined, by both nature and culture, to take over the stage, and the old must learn when and how to exit. *King Lear* exemplifies this injunction, and we will follow its legacy in two remarkable plays, Ibsen's *The Master Builder* and Ionesco's *Exit the King*. Ibsen's protagonist, the architect Solness, does all in his power to resist the inexorable rise of the young, but the burden of the plot is to escort him from the stage. Rarely has the male climacteric been written with such poetry. If Lear speaks of moving "unburdened" toward death, Ionesco succeeds in finding a magnificent theatrical language for showing us what those burdens are, and we realize that they are the injuries and scars written onto and into us by life itself but that dying might be our moment of healing, of freedom, indeed of retrieved majesty.

The Old in Love

Falling in love was deemed a central, indeed defining experience of growing up. And of course love confers pleasure and pain, pith, complexity, and meaning to our life at any temporal stage. Moreover, I will later close my discussion of growing old by focusing on mature love—enduring love—as its highest and richest quarry. But I want now, in this segment of my book, to examine the problems of "old love," ranging from dysfunction to inappropriate lust, for the issues of sexuality can loom very large in the affairs of the aging. Literature shines its beam here, sometimes offering a mirror in which we may be surprised to recognize ourselves.

Old Age as Postsexual?

It might be thought that old age is (at last) a time when one is free of sexual passion. Arguments for this view may have a somatic or philosophical cast to them. (One's views on these matters may well vary according to age.) Yet just as the old often do not "go gentle into that night," so too is sexual need often enough a stubborn thing, all the more stubborn when at odds with culture's prescriptions. Gender is also frequently at issue here, given that male sexual desire is often accommodated by social mores, whereas (older) women's libidinal needs can be subject to very different, very severe judgments of value and decorum.

Arguably the hero of the postsexual (male) life is Washington Irving's Rip Van Winkle, who slept twenty years, right through his marriage, and woke up to reap the benefits. August Strindberg's overheated play *The Father* turns ostensibly on the issue of unknowable paternity, but it also speculates on what a world of "bearded women" and impotent men might be like. We close with a discussion of William Faulkner's Joanna Burden, the New England spinster of *Light in August*, who moves fatefully from frenzied desire to menopause, her "Indian summer" of passion, and pays for it with her life. Is there a male vendetta here?

Sexual Anxiety

And then there is the issue of sexual anxiety and performance. These matters are rarely trumpeted, either in literature or in life, but some of our great literary works hinge intriguingly on them. Shakespeare's Othello can be fruitfully understood along just those lines, for we must ask ourselves what goes into the making of a man who murders his wife because of suspected infidelity; and once we pose that question, issues such as Othello's age and unfamiliarity with Venetian mores acquire a surprising pertinence. Tennessee Williams's heroine of *A Streetcar Named Desire*, Blanche DuBois, a creature of romantic dreams and fading charms, finds herself libidinally underequipped in an overheated New Orleans setting, replete with her stud brother-in-law, Stanley Kowalski.

Unsanctioned Lust

From time immemorial, however, the still-hungry or oversexed old have received their comeuppance in literature, regardless of how they may have fared in reality. Molière's plays often deal with old (rich) men obsessed with possessing young nubile females, and even though this scheme invariably finishes poorly, the tone can be more complicated than you'd think, as in the fate of Arnolphe of *L'école des femmes*. Dostoevsky builds his patricidal plot in *The Brothers Karamazov* around old Fyodor, lecher of the first rank and sexual competitor of his son, slated to be murdered but getting off some wonderful lines in the process. These renditions make for broad comedy, but there can be pathos, cruelty, and violence there as well—and a standard that may be rather different for men than for women, as we discover in revisiting Hamlet's mother, Gertrude, enmeshed in a full-blooded sexual relationship with Claudius and therefore subject to an almost hysterical diatribe about deviance, delivered to her by her anxious and indicting son. Early literature's richest instance of an older woman's sexual yearning is found in Racine's *Phèdre*, in which the force of desire reaches mythic proportions, no matter how censured it may be otherwise. Racine is unequaled when it comes to the depiction of human longing, especially forbidden longing. This segment closes with a discussion of Thomas Mann's Gustav von Aschenbach, the writer-champion of discipline who is destined to be inflamed with desire at the sight of the Polish boy Tadzio while vacationing in Venice. Aschenbach's feelings are out of bounds both morally and temporally. In each of these texts about desire and hunger, whether comic or tragic, we may detect the sound of a ticking clock, adjudicating the rights of eros.

The Final Harvest

Metaphors matter. "Growing up" and "growing old" may seem to be innocuous phrases, but they invoke growth, organic process, as their modality. As for growing up, all of us can agree that there is a dosage of literal truth in the expression that infants grow into children who grow into adults. They actually get bigger. But what about growing old? What kind of growth is this? Nature is eloquent here: an apple or a bottle of wine moves from new (young) to mature (ready to eat or drink) to dead (rotten, vinegary). Harvest matters in another sense as well: it figures a tantalizingly seductive picture of our last chapter: finally we possess the fruits and plenitude of our days and works.

Or do we? The story of growing old is often cued to this brutal dialectic: harvest, yes or no? It is, if you like, a replay of the innocence/experience paradigm so central to growing up but now seen in a more complex, sometimes corrosive fashion, since experience itself evolves, can even move from certainty to mirage.

The Final Harvest as Mirage

We now investigate a number of dark but fascinating texts that explore major trouble: old age as a time of disastrous discovery. What might one discover, beyond the obvious slights of time? In Ibsen's final play, we get the proposition that we learn we have in fact never lived. This is tough medicine. In Henry James's "The Beast in the Jungle," this vexing issue is presented as a perceptual trap: the protagonist learns that he has walked right past possible happiness, unable to see it right (and thus seize it). In Kafka's "Before the Law," it turns even more sibylline as we see that the long wait for truth and illumination has functioned as paralysis, as a spending of days and years with no payoff. These issues become most heartbreaking of all in the beautiful yet remorseless film of Ingmar Bergman *Wild Strawberries,* in which the eminent old doctor is obliged to learn that he has been a cold, unloving fraud all his life. Each of these works pulls the rug out from under us, wrecks our fond notions of happy harvest, but they disturb most of all because they point to our own blind spots and faulty vision, to our capacity to go amok and only realize it at the end.

This is harsh material—but valuable. Texts about missing your life, about discovering its fraudulence at the end, are texts we need to read for the simple reason that life is too important to miss, that the fraudulent might be followed by the genuine, and that skewed vision may be more rightly aligned to the truth. *Art enables us to imagine things we cannot afford to experience.*

The Good Fight

Many religions promise an afterlife. Hard-bitten fellow that I am, I cannot escape the feeling that such a beautiful and inspiring belief is meant as a radiant alternative to the entropic spectacle of decay that time imposes on flesh. Could we end up victorious on this side of the grave? We will examine two unflinching, yet satisfying, accounts of this last chapter of life, to see what literature offers us, in the way of staying the course, with honor and pride. Hemingway's *The Old Man and the Sea* deserves to be read as a tale about finalities, about what is left when age sets in—a great deal, as we shall see. In this spare account of an old man and a fish, Hemingway amplifies our understanding of the resources that remain. Philip Roth's *Everyman* is a beast of a different stripe altogether: Roth's protagonist takes the often bitter measure of a life ruled by fleshly wants and finally condemned by fleshly frailties. A good life? A bad life? That's for you to decide. I see no transcendence in either of these books, no grand visionary moments, yet they are satisfying in their rendition of life as contest. In both of these books there is fight, even glorious fight, left in the old, and that struggle does honor to our species.

Life's Plenitude

Even with my boundless optimism about literature's gifts, I am hard put to find works that convert dying itself into joy. But if dying marks our finish line, there might be much to say about our efforts, performance, and satisfaction en route to the end. Is this not the ultimate truth, at once empirical and imaginative, of growing old: that you do it for a long, long time, that your challenge is to see it right, to see it as a time for living rather than dying? This would be the wisdom of a species that, at its best, never loses sight of life's goodness. Could old age be the time for coming into this estate?

"Staying the course" emerges as the ultimate wisdom in Daniel Defoe's eighteenth-century classic *Moll Flanders*. Defoe fascinates most because his characters go through an unending number of disguises, avatars, and roles in their trip through time. Hence this novel whispers to us that—more basic than any moral code—breathing and coping are the crucial activities of the species that moves from morning to noon to night. If Moll's sights are largely on her own fortunes, the case is more complicated with Bertolt Brecht's *Mother Courage*, for this low-to-the-ground heroine faces huge odds in her struggle not only to stay alive but to keep her children alive during the tumult of the Thirty Years'

War. She comes to us, as does Hemingway's Santiago, as a figure of endurance, of never quitting; but unlike Santiago and his marlin, Courage's loyalty, pluck, resilience, and salty wisdom are tested by the crushing, impersonal forces of history.

This discussion closes with an account of the most richly embodied (and "em-minded") figure in modern literature, James Joyce's Leopold Bloom. Bloom faces entropy and losses galore, but the marvel of *Ulysses* consists in his manner of facing these generic slights of growing old by seeing life as a fount of endless stimuli, by nonstop reflection and reaction to the everyday. Bloom's plebeian (brilliant) humor and Odyssean resilence, his capacity to duck the bad and to savor the good, are never served up to us as doctrinal fare. Still, I see in the antics of this man coping with trouble an excellent formula for the wisdom of old age.

Life's Lessons

One of the major purposes of this book is to consult the literature of growing up and growing old, in order to see what it teaches us. Why else would one read? Yet the lessons of art have little to do with religious sermons or bottom-line thinking, and frequently enough we are obliged to sort these matters out ourselves, to glean, for example, from the travails of Lear or Goriot or Phèdre or Mother Courage something of value for us personally. How characters manage their lives always tells us something about managing our own. Whether the texts are cautionary or triumphant, we will find ourselves in their reflecting mirror. The works discussed in this chapter are meant to have a valedictory cast to them: exit works that richly illustrate the larger argument about the light literature sheds on growing old.

Keeping the Heart Alive

Cardiologists play their little role in the life of the aging, for we know that the heart is a muscle and blood-supply system increasingly subject to wear and tear. Is this not the case morally and psychologically as well? Can the old maintain their emotional vibrancy and élan right to the end? In some sense, all the prior discussions of growing old revolve around these basic questions, whether we emphasize the sexual, the somatic, or the spiritual side of things. Perhaps the most frightening fate that could await us is to die while still living, to cease to feel or to care about the lives around us. Gabriel García Márquez has left us an unforgettable portrait of such a condition in his portrayal of Aureliano in *One Hundred Years of Solitude;* a famous general waging war throughout most of his lifetime, Aureliano elects to immure himself affectively, literally to enact Christ's *"Noli me tangere"* injunction. Is this the "cost of living"? Against this calcification of the heart, I propose the counterexample of Helena, the beautiful old matriarch of Ingmar Bergman's final film, *Fanny and Alexander,* who offers us a deeply theatrical model for keeping the heart alive: role playing, with the caveat that you must *become* the role you play, so that you enact an entire repertoire over the course of a life in time.

The (Longitudinal) Eyes of Love

Remember the eyes of desire: Romeo gazing at Juliet on the balcony, Des Grieux entranced by Manon, the Chinese man smitten by the French girl on the ferry, Phèdre inflamed by the sight of her stepson Hippolyte, Aschenbach mesmerized by the Polish boy Tadzio. The French call this vision the *coup de foudre,* the thunderbolt, for it is electrifying in its power and immediacy. But there are other kinds of love and other kinds of eyes, and they reverence the ongoing, unfurling reality of time. Unlike the hunger of desire, this love incorporates memory, transcends the retinal, makes room even for death. It is stamped by generosity, and we will see much of it in the culminating chapters of this study.

Perhaps the most exquisite text we have about old loving is Shakespeare's Sonnet 73, which begins by depicting a body beset by its final winter, knowing it will not flower again, headed for a permanent sleep. What is sublime is the response to this spectacle of decay: the deepening and intensifying of love, so that death and life feed each other, so that my dying grows your love. At long last our phrase growing old finds its lovely coherence. The poet Baudelaire has none of Shakespeare's idealism, but his poem "The Little Old Ladies" has a comparable form of generosity, for it obliges us to see the old "in time," to perceive their dimensionality and fullness. Proust is our great master on this theme, inaugurating a kind of "fourth-dimensional" vision of loved ones, hallowing the actual scope of their lives and our bond with them; yet there is nothing easy in such perception, and Proust even suggests that our own love militates fiercely against factoring death and oblivion into our grasp of others. But if we can do this, we can finally approach an ethos of old age, a way of looking and feeling that is nourished—rather than sapped—by the passing of time.

Enduring Love

With this burgeoning view of love as death's opposite, we will complete our discussion of old age by examining three powerful narratives that are unflinching in their awareness of time's entropic work but that honor the reach and dimensions of human love. None of these books is triumphant. Each can break your heart. I begin with the astonishing and largely unknown *Out of Mind*, written by the Dutch novelist J. Bernlef and dealing with the grisly reality of Alzheimer's disease. Here is the ultimate failed harvest, you might think, for the protagonist, Maarten, is indeed going to be systematically "erased" by his neurological disorder, thereby losing his entire grip on "reality." But things are not this simple, and we see the stubborn, undying hold of the past, even as this man can no longer recognize his wife or his setting. Love itself endures as a primitive pulsation, even at the cost of sanity; it is the last thing to go, even though it too must eventually cease.

The next entry is Virginia Woolf's magnificent *To the Lighthouse*, it too under the shadow of death and oblivion yet remaining in our minds as a moving tribute to the continuing life of those who love and nurture and die. Woolf displays a rare kind of generosity in re-creating, from the inside, the story of her own parents, and in the figure of Mrs. Ramsay, the novel's "earth mother," we have literature's richest portrait of a mature woman's love, as deep as Phèdre's but cued to the fates of others. Can this die? Woolf weaves together many strands of my argument: the life of the heart, the reign of mortality, the legacy of love, the virtues of art.

We close our discussion of enduring love with a book that picks up every issue studied up to now: fathers undone, exiting the stage, unsanctioned lust, postsexual life, final harvest, and the eyes of love: J. M. Coetzee's masterpiece *Disgrace*. Not unlike *King Lear*, Coetzee's novel is about learning to accept aging/dying and learning to see clear. The protagonist, David Lurie, does not go mad, there is no heath, and his child does not harm him, yet he must come to understand that many overdue bills have now come due, some of his own making, others the work of racial history, still others concerning the very elemental rights he has thought his. Lurie is to be altered entirely by the events that befall him. Eros must yield to *caritas*. Professor that he is, he learns that life does teach right up to the end—especially, perhaps, at the end.

Fathers Undone

William Shakespeare's King Lear

King Lear digs into the pit. To gauge how deep it goes, how dev-astating its news is, a contrast with Sophocles is useful. Recall the equally devastating Oedipal plays, especially the earlier play about a man who slew his father and fornicated with his mother. Only with the help of Freud and so many others can we see this text as a blueprint of our deepest programming, implanted so deeply that it is able to govern behavior while eluding all consciousness. Yes, much debris is strewn as pieties hit the dust: peaceful coexistence between young and old, made up of love and instruction and mu-tual respect—our fond dream of these matters—has no place in this scheme; war is its ultimate truth. But the Greek playwright never tells us why the choice must be either infanticide or parri-cide. One wants to know more about the prerogatives of youth and age. Reverence for one's elders was a deep-seated Greek virtue, firmly established, essentially unassailable; yet the play assails it, annihilates it. Sophocles writes about this crisis from the angle of prophecy, knowledge, and ignorance, but he says very little about what it feels like to be on either side of this parent/child divide: what it feels like to be rising son or falling father.

For just these reasons one turns to the richest text in Western literature concerning these matters: Shakespeare's *King Lear.* Just as all philosophy has been construed as a footnote to Plato, it seems fair to say that much of our literature about the fate of growing old seems to be a footnote to *Lear.* The story of the king who was cannibalized by his daughters, who was required, in Freud's words, to "renounce love, choose death, and make friends with the necessity of dying," shows up everywhere: in Balzac's *Père Goriot,* Ibsen's *The Master Builder,* Miller's *Death of a Salesman,* Ionesco's *Exit the King,* Bergman's *Wild Strawberries,* Roth's *Everyman,* Coetzee's *Disgrace.* Shakespeare illuminates every issue that matters; it is harsh stuff.

Lear's very first words announce the trajectory he will take, even though he has no inkling of its horrors. He will divest himself of his kingdom so that he can prepare for the final phase of his life: "'tis our fast intent / To shake all cares and business from our age, / Conferring them on younger strengths while we / Unburdened crawl toward death." Seems rational enough: time to retire, let the children take over, withdraw from the stage, approach one's end. It's a sensible plan, still very much in evidence today, ratcheted up to levels Shakespeare could not have imagined as estate planners work out their models with the old with means. But the plan goes amok, opens onto an abyss. For five acts it piles on, needles in, hollows out, unstoppably. At play's end, Edgar's commentary on this old man's long ordeal suggests that its dosage of pain and terror is unimaginable for the young: "The oldest hath borne most; we that are young / Shall never see so much, nor live so long." There is an outright generic feeling in these lines: The old bear the most; one does not, as Lear fondly assumed, "shake" away cares. Far from ever being "unburdened," one is laden with pain of a new kind; crawling toward death is okay notionally but unbearable experientially. Good-bye, death with dignity.

King Lear strips us of all illusions and fantasies we might entertain about the last chapter of our life. For starters, we see that the old men of this play—for Gloucester is unmistakably Lear's double, his counterpart in suffering to come—have achieved precious little wisdom via their long years, are in fact prey to grotesquely rash and precipitous decisions, tragic ones. They are due for some lessons, and they are going to get them. Lear seems monstrous to us as he demands to know how much each of his daughters loves him—as if their feelings were as quantifiable as the lands he is divvying up—and he seems more monstrous still when he cuts off Cordelia from her inheritance in one fell swoop. "Nothing will come of nothing, speak again." Mind you, Cordelia is something of a chip off the old block, so stubborn is she about not fawning and prettifying her devotion to her father; after all, she might have found some temperate words to assure him of her loyalty. But no. She can be as headstrong as he is. She will not bend, not flatter. And so he undoes an entire life—his as much as hers—in a few sharp words: "Let it be so, thy truth then be thy dower. . . . Here I disclaim all my paternal care, / Propinquity and property of blood, / And as a stranger to my heart and me / Hold thee from this forever." She is now his "sometime daughter."

All are shocked. Kent courts (and finds) banishment by repeatedly urging Lear to "check this hideous rashness." Neither Burgundy nor France can believe his eyes and ears. Goneril and Regan see in this behavior not only their own private gain but a very palpable proof that Father is not right in his head. Errors are dear in this play, dear in their price, dear to the one who commits them; Lear disinherits his daughter with lightning speed and then explodes with fury when Kent begs him to reconsider: "Come not between the dragon and his wrath." No doubt some of this vehemence and anger is ascribable to kingship, to the absolute power Lear is accustomed to, but it is hard to be on his side at the play's beginning, so intemperate and out of control and violent are his actions. How not to agree with the diagnosis put forth by Goneril: "You see how full of changes his age is; the observation we have made of it hath not been little. He always loved our sister most, and with what poor judgement he hath now cast her off appears too grossly." Regan's rejoinder is both famous and true: "'Tis the infirmity of his age; yet he hath ever but slenderly known himself." Shakespeare is about to rectify this last problem: Lear is headed for a good bit of new self-knowledge.

He is not alone in being rash and intemperate. Gloucester falls into Edmund's trap with such consummate ease that we have to wonder about his wits as well. Yes, Edmund is a clever boy, silver-

tongued, and knows how to fake letters and put on a show to in-
criminate his brother, but how quickly it all goes, how absolute the
father's indictment of the older son is after just a few cunning
tricks: "Abhorred villain, unnatural, detested, brutish villain—
worse than brutish! Go, sirrah, seek him: I'll apprehend him.
Abominable villain, where is he?" Here we are, midway in scene 2
of the first act, and two fathers have made disastrous mistakes
about their children, have misread the signs, have started the terrible machinery of internecine familial slaughter that is beginning to hum and go into action. One is shocked by the speed of it
all—that truth should be extinguished so easily; that old men
might go tragically wrong and off course, with so little prodding,
in so short a compass. Of course we readers know that Shakespeare has much in store for these two fellows, but we are
nonetheless lessoned about the gullibility and foibles of the old,
what fools they can be, how easily they are taken in. "Ripeness is
all" will eventually be the key to this dark play's wisdom, but we
can already see that achieving ripeness can take considerable time,
that getting old has little to do with getting wise, that much suffering is going to be brought in for the pedagogy.

The old should command respect. Lear's and Gloucester's double station—as king and earl, as fathers—figures a seemingly natural hierarchical ranking. We see this perhaps most profoundly in
the symbolic acts of defiance and subversion required by the plot,
namely the mishandling of Kent (the king's man) by putting him
into the stocks and indeed the blinding of Gloucester by Albany
and Regan, a vicious and sadistic act all the more terrible because
the old man is their host, entitled to their homage. We are not far
from the sacrilegious in these scenes of violence and disrespect,
putting us on notice that the old contracts no longer bind. Shakespeare wants us to see that a systemic undoing of cosmic proportions takes place when the old are savaged. Gloucester waxes
oracular on just this topic:

These late eclipses in the sun and moon portend no good to us.
Though the wisdom of nature can reason it thus and thus, yet
nature finds itself scourged by the sequent effects. Love cools,

friendship falls off, brothers divide. In cities, mutinies; in countries, discord; in palaces, treason; and the bond cracked 'twixt son and father. This villain of mine comes under the prediction: there's son against father. The King falls from bias of nature, there's father against child. We have seen the best of our time. Machinations, hollowness, treachery, and all ruinous disorders follow us disquietly to our graves.

As we know, this indictment of the world order is immediately followed by Edmund's brilliant mockery of such schemas, as if to say that the old take refuge in referencing the grand design, thereby freeing themselves from all responsibility:

This is the excellent foppery of the world, that when we are sick in fortune, often the result of our own behaviour, we make guilty of our disasters the sun, the moon, and stars; as if we were villains on necessity, fools by heavenly compulsion, knaves, thieves, and treachers by spherical predominance, drunkards, liars, and adulterers by an enforc'd obedience of planetary influence; and all that we are evil in, by a divine thrusting on. An admirable evasion of whoremaster man, to lay his goatish disposition to the charge of a star!

As so often in the great tragedies, one sees the clashing of two worlds here: the traditional order is being rent asunder, but the interpretations are as different as night and day. The old man sees in such upheaval a fissuring of the divine plan and refers the anarchic violence of the moment to an older paradigm of order. Discord between parents and children is but another face of cosmic disarray, to be found in eclipses, espied most particularly in social and political unrest, in the joint failures of love of and respect toward one's fellows, family, and masters. Yet the son seems to announce a new regime altogether, a regime of biological and libidinal currents that knows nothing of morality or hierarchy. Edmund sounds the modern note as he blasts the old order, terming it a haven for blind cowards who cannot accept the consequences of their own natures, who cloak themselves in symbolic robes, cling to alibis, point their fingers always outward, never inward. One feels that an old world—not merely a moral order but also an interpretive order—is going under and that a brazen, naked, unechoing new universe is coming into view, closer to Machiavelli and Hobbes than to the ancients. (Iago philosophizes along these same fierce lines in *Othello*, gleefully casting the old verities of honor and loyalty and friendship and virtue as just so much idiocy, indeed as a "fig.")

The old way of seeing things is in trouble. The old people themselves see things awry: Lear misreads all three daughters, taking counterfeit coins for real, discrediting the real as nothing; Gloucester raises Edmund and expels Edgar, for he is taken in by the show of the one and cannot perceive the truth of the other. Vision and interpretation are having a bad day. The Fool spells this out for his master: "Thou canst tell why one's nose stands i' th' middle on 's face?" The answer is "Why, to keep one's eyes on either side 's nose, that what a man cannot smell out, he may spy into." But Lear and Gloucester smelled nothing, saw nothing that needed spying into. The Fool's conclusion is not long in coming: "Thou shouldst not have been old till thou hadst been wise." There you have it: old age makes you old, but it is no guarantee of wisdom. *Till thou hadst been wise.* What does it take to become wise? What are you if, old, you are not wise?

Goneril put it clearly: "Idle old man, / That still would manage those authorities / That he hath given away!—Now, by my life / Old fools are babes again." But the Fool puts more zest into it as he intones the same message to his master, alleging that the father has reversed nature's order, "e'er since thou mad'st thy daughters thy mothers." The family is turned inside out, and the once-all-powerful father is now helpless, infantilized, literally spankable:

> *for when thou gav'st them the rod, and put'st down thine own*
> > *breeches,*
> [sings] *Then they for sudden joy did weep,*
> > *And I for sorrow sung,*
> *That such a king should play bo-peep,*
> > *And go the fools among.*

How did this happen? Why, we see it from the beginning: the old man gave away his power. Lear asks, "Dost thou call me fool, boy?" and the reply is "All thy other titles thou hast given away; that thou was born with." An old man turned babe: there is a geriatric note here that gets our attention even today, with or without the Fool.

Behind all this banter about wits and loss of wits lies a simple but profound practical, material issue: do not give away your estate. This is the play's payload: your authority as king, as father, lies in your continued possession of your estate, your kingdom, your money, and your goods. Once they are gone, good-bye, allegiance and respect. Listen again to the Fool: "Fathers that wear rags / Do make their children blind, / But fathers that bear bags / Shall see their children kind." Sweetly cued to the trope of vision, recalling nature's plan in placing eyes on each side of our nose, this passage nonetheless advertises the promiscuity and fallibility of seeing—indeed, the charade of seeing, the theater of appearances. Give away your money and dress in rags, and lo and behold, your children are blind; i.e., blind to you as a worthy parent; hold on to your goodies, and you will note the respect and loyalty of your children. It could not be put more simply: hunger and greed set the stage—for it is only a stage set—and the comedy of filial devotion lasts only as long as the old hold on to their power. (And do not forget: Lear held on pretty long; "I gave you all," he tells Regan, and she replies, "And in good time you gave it," telling us something about the different clocks of age and youth, shedding light on the waiting of youth.) Is this not the "naturalist" code that Edmund subscribes to? Obedience, reverence: only appearances, only theater. Appetite rules. The young want their due.

(The young want their due. Imagine, for a moment, Edmund or Goneril or Regan as the major protagonist of this story, and you'd not be far from the literary fare of Part I. Lazarillo, Des Grieux, Rastignac, Jane Eyre, Heathcliff, the Invisible Man, Celie, even little Marjane: they wanted their due. But how different it looks from the other side, from the angle of those holding on.)

The Fool offers, in keeping with the language of optics, the play's corrective lens. In his inimitable fashion, he becomes the philosopher of the piece. The Fool's wisdom would seem to be that it could have been avoided. You should have recognized the true daughter, sniffed out the false ones, kept your titles, and things might have been okay. Yet the greatness of Shakespeare's play is that it wreaks havoc on all forms of advance knowledge, that it blows sky-high any corrective vision, even any retrospective fix on things. In short, the unfurling spectacle of Lear writes large for us the irremediable law of time: we do go backward, we do regress, we become children in our dotage. No amount of seeing or smelling trouble helps: we are fated to be undone. Dividing your kingdom is redundant and unnecessary; you lose your power no matter what. That is the play's bad news.

How does an old man become a child? Lear does not lower his breeches, but he weeps, and he is shamed by his weakness: "I am ashamed / That thou [Goneril] hast power to shake my manhood thus, / That these hot tears, which break from me perforce, / Should make thee worth them." Later, he collapses yet again into tears and again registers this onslaught as ignoble, as an undoing of stature, power, and manhood. At this juncture, we realize that old age and tears are locked in a dance, that tears themselves—of rage, suffering, impotence—announce the coming of something new and frightening, bidding to cancel out all that we were, against which we have no resources:

> *You see me here, you gods, a poor old man,*
> *As full of grief as age, wretched in both!*
> *If it be you that stir these daughters' hearts*
> *Against their father, fool me not so much*
> *To bear it tamely. Touch me with noble anger,*
> *And let not women's weapons, water drops,*
> *Stain my man's cheeks. No, you unnatural hags,*
> *I will have such revenges on you both*
> *That all the world shall—I will do such things—*
> *What they are, yet I know not, but they shall be*
> *The terrors of the earth! You think I'll weep;*
> *No, I'll not weep;*
> *I have full cause of weeping, but this heart*
> *Shall break into a hundred thousand flaws*
> *Or ere I'll weep. O fool, I shall go mad.*

In a play larded with suffering, this speech has for me a special pathos. Lear seems to recognize a tyranny in grief—the tears he cannot quash—that matches any so-called power he exercised as king. He calls upon the gods to free him from this servitude, but the gods have little to do with the punishment he is suffering. Shakespeare gives us the very language of impotence as Lear gestures toward revenge—I will do such things, though what they are I know not yet—and comes up empty, can only posture, look for all the world like a hollow charade. Power, station, control, dignity: so many empty postures, destined for undoing. Hence tears close the passage they opened. The old man thinks tears are women's weapons, but the play tells us otherwise: tears are the natural language of our species when it collides with reality: "When we are born, we cry that we are come / To this great stage of fools."

The reality I speak of is the core issue of the play, the reality of parents and children, of growing old and growing up. Here is the lesson Lear never stops learning. Here is why the drama of ungrateful children usurps everything else in the play, serving as the hideous compass of Lear's new life, the madness that would be the alternative to tears. Seeing Edgar (as poor Tom), Lear predictably asks, "What, have his daughters brought him to this pass? / Could'st thou save nothing? Wouldst thou give 'em all?" There is but one Ur-betrayal, coercing Lear's vision, as echoing as the Crucifixion, and it is lodged in the bond between parents and children. This is why Lear transposes a wild heath into a decorous court of law, so that he can serially enlist poor Tom as noble philosopher, as learned Theban, as good Athenian, to get himself justice at last, to indict once and for all these monstrous offspring. If there is any law, if the old standards have any validity, these two daughters must be found guilty; but the actual law coming into visibility has a grisly truth of a different cast. For here is the pit he has indeed fallen into, even though he never saw or smelled it in advance: that your children kill you. One cannot overstate this: your children kill you, and it has precious little to do, I think, with whether they're evil or not. Lear has encountered Shakespeare's ground zero: nature's plan is warfare between child and parent, nature's plan is homicidal.

And Edmund is its spokesman, its vessel: "Thou, Nature, art my goddess; to thy law / My services are bound." That law cares nothing for custom or legitimacy or the station of fathers or kings. "I grow; I prosper; / Now, gods, stand up for bastards!" But the play does not require the gods to stand up; the children themselves will do that, must do that. They stand up, they grow, they prosper, and it is no more nor less ethical than photosynthesis. Hence, Edmund has no compunction about telling Cornwall of Gloucester's efforts to aid Lear, even while knowing that it will spell doom for his father: "This seems a fair deserving, and must draw me / That which my father loses: no less than all. / The younger rises when the old doth fall." Loss/gain, falling/rising: these roles, apportioned to the old and the young, would seem implanted in us, scheduled to happen, virtually genetic in character. Even the beautiful, hallucinatory scene in which Edgar, disguised as poor Tom, escorts his blind father to "Dover" so that the old man can end his life is, when seen right, a parable of the child leading the father to his death; Edgar fabulates to Gloucester that it was a fiend who thus led him, and we are meant to ponder the relevance of the term; at play's end, Edgar discloses his true identity to his father, which leads straightaway to his death.

Shakespeare digs ever deeper into this morass as the plot moves into ever-escalating forms of warfare. The very first exchange of the play delves into child making and presents it as cavalier, as the prerogative of lusty fathers: Kent, confused as to Edmund's station, tells Gloucester, "I cannot conceive you," only to hear the riposte "Sir, this young fellow's mother could." And the men have their little joke. But the joke is on them, for these are no laughing matters. Cordelia and Edgar know something firsthand about parental injury, and Edgar—witnessing Lear's madness and pain—expresses in one compact phrase the awful symmetry of the play: "He childed as I fathered." This is not bad luck or even evil, it is the bedrock of things as they are. "Childed" and "fathered" are the names Shakespeare gives to human destiny, for they limn and bound individual life, constitute its unfurling, time-fueled contours, contain at once its limits, horizons, blessings, and horrors.

Nietzsche said of Oedipus that he had invaded nature's secrets via his twin transgressions of incest and parricide: "*ein Verbrechen an der Natur.*" Shakespeare's Edgar penetrates no less deeply, late in the play, when he avows his identity to Edmund at the onset of their duel: "The gods are just, and of our pleasant vices / Make instruments to plague us. / The dark and vicious place where thee he got / Cost him his eyes." It is a remarkable utterance, and it covers much ground in the great distance between titillating "pleasant vices," on the one hand—siring illegitimate children may bring you trouble, old sinner—and that more forbidding other "dark and vicious place," now seen as a double site: woman's genitals but also, somehow, where one's eyes are put out, where one pays nature's "cost." No one is laughing about manufacturing children anymore. You are seeding your own death, you are courting blindness. Death marks copulation: the sexual itch that draws both Goneril and Regan to Edmund finds its rightful conclusion in the man's death: "I was contracted to them both; all three / Now marry in an instant."

We increase the species via fornication, but the balance is kept when our children cannibalize us. Growing up and growing old are not two distinct life phases in *King Lear:* they are a lethal dialectic, for the one flourishes by vanquishing the other. Sex is central here. Sex is the creature's entry into the game, the entry into the creation, the triggering of one's own eventual demise, since one seeds one's end. That is why the play may seem so violently, insanely misogynistic in its assault on female sexuality. Consider Lear's crazed diatribe against Goneril:

> *Hear, Nature, hear, dear goddess, hear:*
> *Suspend thy purpose, if thou didst intend*
> *To make this creature fruitful.*
> *Into her womb convey sterility,*
> *Dry up in her the organs of increase,*
> *And from her derogate body never spring*
> *A babe to honour her. If she must teem,*
> *Create her a child of spleen, that it may live*
> *And be a thwart disnatured torment to her.*
> *Let it stamp wrinkles in her brow of youth,*
> *With cadent tears fret channels in her checks,*

Turn all her mother's pains and benefits
To laughter and contempt, that she may feel
How sharper than a serpent's tooth it is
To have a thankless child.

The last two lines about filial ingratitude are known the world over, but one needs to link them to the manic indictment that precedes them, an indictment of reproduction itself, a feverish effort to hit this woman where it hurts: in her genitals, in her capacity to give birth and make life. "He childed as I fathered," said Edgar; Lear wants to lay just this curse on his daughter, let her know what it feels like. A bit later, he returns to the charge: "You nimble lightnings, dart your blinding flames / Into her scornful eyes! Infect her beauty, / You fen-sucked fogs, drawn by the powerful sun / To fall and blister." Starting with her eyes, he then moves to her face, seeking to deform her altogether. Sexed, constituted for conception, she and her sister are the very embodiments of libido in its many guises: not only do they both lust after Edmund, but they outdo each other in cruelties, never more visible than in Regan's treatment of both Kent and Gloucester: she lengthens, for sheer pleasure, Kent's time in the stocks, and she does still worse to Gloucester: first plucking his beard, then urging that his second eye be gouged out as well. I see sexual warfare writ large here, as the women torture or symbolically castrate the old men, as they act out their lusts. And it is against this backdrop that we see the nasty but clear logic of Lear's wildest ravings, as in this outburst on the heath:

Behold yon simp'ring dame,
Whose face between her forks presages snow,
That minces virtue, and does shake the head
To hear of pleasure's name.
The fitchew nor the soilèd horse goes to 't
With a more riotous appetite.
Down from the waist they're centaurs,
Though women all above.
But to the girdle do the gods inherit;
Beneath is all the fiend's.

There's hell, there's darkness, there is the sulphurous pit, burning,
scalding, stench, consumption.

Let me repeat: this is more than an attack on false *pudeur* and
hypocrisy, more even than an indictment of female desire: it is a
delirious assault on that very "dark place" where the work of appetite and insemination is carried out, where nature's laboratory
for making children is located. This is what cannot be borne, what
must belong to the fiend, what catapults Lear into a frenzy of somatic disgust and terror.

As we all know, that mad speech takes place on the storm-
buffeted heath, the time and the place where Lear's initiation into
truth and madness is enacted in all its horror. "Madness" is a term
I tend to shy away from, inasmuch as it frequently closes the door
on analysis and understanding, but one cannot get free of it in this
play, since Lear himself is so prescient and insistent about these
matters, recognizes early on that madness is threatening, that it
may take over entirely. Madness alters you from yourself. Lear's
education in self-altering began when Goneril sets about reducing
the scale of his retinue: "Does any here know me? This is not
Lear: / Does Lear walk thus? speak thus? Where are his eyes? /
... Who is it that can tell me who I am?" On the heath, however,
the stakes are considerably higher. Now the elements themselves
have come to full voice and full pitch: cataracts, hurricanes, fires,
thunderbolts, all "singe [Lear's] white head," demonstrating once
and for all the mirage of kingship. Yet this brutal warfare is
anonymous—"I tax you not, you elements, with unkindness. / I
never gave you kingdom, called you children"—whereas the betrayal of flesh and blood cuts to our very core. Kingdom, children:
so many things one thought one's own, the very props and uprights of identity and power; they mutiny, and you are undone.

Madness opens the door to vision, and what we will see un-
veiled is the hubris and blindness that characterized his earlier life
and beliefs, now smashed to nothing, now heralding a chastened,
rawer view of our common condition, shown in Lear's recognition
that poor Tom figures us all: "Unaccommodated man is no more
but such a poor, bare, forked animal as thou art." No one has prerogatives or rights. In such a scheme, any view of station or privi-

lege would be a fantasy. The man who began this play claiming he would crawl unburdened toward death has learned a good deal about crawling, but the trip toward death is itself a weighty affair, a burden we cannot shrug off or divide among our heirs, for it is the price we pay for our very flesh, our white hair and fragile wits that are no match for either the tempest's unabating fury, always ready to strike, or our children's muscular hatred, coiled in them since inception. Lear has come to understand the dynamics of power: the young rise, the old fall, the elements press, death is at the door. He wages a futile war against sexuality, for it is the engendering principle that dooms him, that fuels the systemic warfare of the play, that decrees the waxing of the young and the waning of the old. He is slated to lose everything, including the one true daughter whose murder Edmund arranges as a final testimony to natural unkindness.

Yet he does win vision. The price paid for it is madness—he becomes unreturnably other unto himself—but at the peak of his suffering, he *sees*. Maybe this is what Shakespeare is telling us: that old people are scheduled for undoing, for draining the cup, but they may make wisdom out of their calvary. Lear's wisdom is perforce about the nature of power, about what he has so drastically misconstrued during his life. The fury on the heath carries echoes of the Last Judgment, that moment when posturing is over and truth shows: "undivulged crimes" are on show, the seemingly pious are seen through as incestuous, "pent-up guilts" break through concealment. Theatrically speaking, the curtain is going up. Lear, become horribly knowing about his own mortality, his private agony, now opens his register, begins to realize that his kingdom is filled with "unaccommodated" subjects, all of them "more sinned against than sinning":

> *Poor naked wretches, wheresoe'er you are*
> *That bide the pelting of this pitiless storm,*
> *How shall your houseless heads and unfed sides,*
> *Your looped and windowed raggedness defend you*
> *From seasons such as these? O I have ta'en*
> *Too little care of this. Take physic, pomp,*

Expose thyself to feel what wretches feel,
That thou mayst shake the superflux to them
And show the heavens more just.

Take physic, pomp: that is indeed one take on this play. Your privileges are illusory, your power a fantasy, but physic is required to learn this hard lesson, and when you do learn it, you are initiated into a broader community of sufferers. The larger family— a constellation beyond daughters and sons-in-law—is coming into view. And Lear now sees the vile but ubiquitous logic that is customarily hidden from our eyes: the strong victimize the weak, the wolf devours the lamb. What is happening at home goes on throughout the kingdom. I am undone; all are undone. Many lessons for an old man: the old are programmed for impotence, "bare, forked animals" are the norm, but nonetheless vice and cruelty and all our so-called order have their corrupt card to play, so that the kaleidoscopic world goes through its prancing and abusive power antics wherever you look. In his hallucinatory courtroom on the heath, Lear pronounces judgment on the whole charade: the beggar runs from the farmer's dog, the (lusting) beadle lashes the whore, the usurer hangs the cozener. The Fool told him that parents' rags make children blind but parents' bags make them kind; this lesson is now transmuted into a searing panoptic vision of culture: "Through tattered clothes great vices do appear: / Robes and furred gowns hide all. Plate sin with gold, / And the strong lance of justice hurtless breaks; / Arm it in rags, a pygmy's straw does pierce it. / None does offend, none, I say none."

The stately arrangements at the beginning—a powerful king dividing his kingdom among his children—have yielded to something close to a horror show. Abuse and victimization—propped up and thus hidden by pretense—are culture's master plan, the mirage of order that is exposed as systemic abuse. Lear's fate is Gloucester's fate is business as usual in every corner of the realm. Must one be a betrayed father and abused king to learn this lesson? Must one grow old? Perhaps. It is hard to imagine the young moving into such a dark wisdom, no matter how acute their vision is. Old, you inhabit the very position of authority—you have spent your life acquiring and asserting it—only to find that it is a charade, a prop, and you find this out by being turned inside out: from father to fool, from old king to forked animal. A tragic lesson plan.

As always in Shakespeare, the visionary and the theatrical are inseparable. Lear was blind, Gloucester is blinded, so now the age-old game of hypocritical crime and punishment is trotted out for us all to see. It is all tinsel, all spectacle, and morality is the toy of cunning appearances: corrupt, rigged, a play within a play. Robes and gowns are the arbiter of truth. Only a man who has lost all robes and gowns comes to such knowledge. To get that far, he has been "bound / Upon a wheel of fire," suggesting that we must burn through to truth. Such incandescence illuminates for us in unforgettable fashion what growing old might entail. There is something vital, tonic, and beautiful about the widening nature of Lear's chastened vision, as it becomes systemwide in its purview and depth. He learns to see. "Nothing will come of nothing," he angrily told Cordelia at play's beginning. But he now knows what it feels like to become nothing, to be treated as nothing, to be expelled from the game altogether, to experience for five acts a banishment worse than anything he could inflict: nature's exit command. He was old when the curtain rose. He has come far since then. This is not nothing.

How to say something upbeat about this merciless play? No one has ever felt that much order was restored at its close, and the death of Cordelia seems grotesquely unnecessary. Yet I feel that both Lear and Gloucester suffer into wisdom. In Lear's case it entails an unbearable lifting of the curtain, so that he sees the endless machinations of the strong devouring the weak all across his kingdom, all in the name of custom and propriety, parading as virtue, stinking to Heaven. Gloucester's range is less, but his blinding and subsequent pilgrimage to "Dover" with poor Tom have a pathos that we are not likely to forget. There is no reward in sight for either of these old men, but I persist in believing they have become sighted at the end of their lives, sighted into awareness of how the universe works. Blindness is an obvious motif in the play, just as it was for Sophocles, but at the close of *Lear* we are talking about the blindness that comes from looking directly at the sun or looking directly at the white blast of nuclear holocaust:

you will be consumed by what you see. The ferocity of this play cashiers the polite terms of my argument: growing old sounds like an avuncular pastime when contrasted with the apocalyptic force of these events. Yet, survivable or not, theirs is a trajectory toward truth. That is something.

Honoré de Balzac's **Père Goriot**

I have already discussed *Père Goriot* as the story of Rastignac's education in learning how to get ahead without losing his soul. But we know that Balzac had *King Lear* in mind. How would you imagine in Paris in 1835 the story of a king who gave away his fortune to two ungrateful daughters, failed to appreciate the one true child, and never stopped paying for his errors? Well, if you can't make him a king, you might nonetheless transform him into an echoing symbolic figure of this newer moment, so we can hardly be surprised—even if we're a little embarrassed—when old Goriot is called *"le Christ de la Paternité."* Nothing if not direct, Balzac signals that this story of an old man's passion is to be understood as a variant of the Passion itself, that (blind, obsessive) love for one's daughters can be a formula for crucifixion in modern times. It is a sobering view. As if nineteenth-century Paris were not sufficiently inhospitable to fathers with poor judgment, you also remove Cordelia from the scene. Then you go on to evoke a new, emerging world order in which blood ties have little traction, can and will be stamped upon when worldly pressures demand it. Because that very same order, into which Goriot has managed to marry both of his daughters, is ravenously hungry for money, your modern Lear is going to be bled dry—blood ties do count for something, one sees—over the course of several hundred pages, for his two daughters function very like vampires, returning for their required ration of blood, their regular infusions of cash.

How does one get to this pass? Balzac is bent on conveying Goriot's evolution as a cautionary fable that is rich in information. The novel goes into considerable detail in describing how Goriot made his fortune during Revolutionary times by dint of shrewdness, cutting corners, wrangling and finagling and outright muscling himself into property and francs. This "success story" from the first years of the nineteenth century is recognizably modern, for it suggests that volition and smarts are adequate resources for making one's way. This would not have been possible in Shakespeare's class culture, but we can already imagine Gatsby here. A man with sufficient appetite could do this. But that is the easy part, we understand. Goriot's troubles come via his children, the two beautiful little girls whom he cannot spoil enough—his wife is dead—who become increasingly his lifeline, his reason for living. One reads this tale today and sees at once that this man has done his two daughters no service whatsoever by agreeing to all their whims, by understanding his role in life as absolute provider for his children. Bad parenting, we may murmur, may produce problems for the girls.

But himself? What happens to parents who live through their children, not entirely unlike the dreadfully sick who are hooked up to respirators and can breathe in no other way? Goriot doesn't have a life; he has no other interests, no other views, than the welfare of his daughters. True enough, the old fellow still understands how money is made—he is rightly suspicious of all the various men (husbands, lovers, sharpers) who want to get their hands on his daughters' dowries and knows to perfection how many sharks are out there—but no reader can avoid the feeling that this old father, Christlike though he be, is also deranged, a cretin of sorts, is offered to us as a kind of pathological specimen, a case study. An overinvested parent, a doting father, an old man whose life takes the shape of his daughters: well, now, in the new Parisian culture Balzac is chronicling, this kind of fellow is going to be a doomed species, a ticking time bomb.

All of Balzac's intended fireworks—Goriot as Lear, Goriot as Christ, Goriot as worthy tragic victim—cannot succeed in veiling for us the author's mixed feelings about such a creature. He is one of Balzac's supreme monsters, a crazed figure of staggering passion that has but one libidinal outlet: his daughters. Balzac never flirts with incest as such, and indeed the daughters display no physical affection whatsoever for their progenitor, but his involvement in their lives and fortunes has a distinct erotic tinge to it, never more visible than when he and Delphine arrange to buy in secret an apartment for Rastignac, where he may meet the (married) daughter Delphine at his ease. Goriot is well-nigh ecstatic in this episode, almost pimplike in his role as go-between, thanking the young student profusely for making his daughter happy, behaving like a child: kissing his daughter's feet, gazing into her eyes, rubbing his head against her dress. Balzac informs us that the young couple is not fully at ease here, and Rastignac confesses to himself that he feels twinges of jealousy. It is a little kinky. And what the boy cannot quite say is: I can never love her, perhaps even never desire her, as her father does. Is that the fate of fathers? To love their daughters too deeply, in too fleshly a fashion? Goriot emerges as the most (and only) sensual figure of the book, the man who genuinely palpitates with desire, whose affect is red hot and volcanic. One senses that his death will be ghastly, for he will die like a spurned lover, in addition to being a tortured, played-out, doomed body.

Monomania is a narrow thing, a narrowing thing. Its deep vein of sentience seems to require closed passages elsewhere and everywhere. At a key moment late in this melodramatic tale, a moment when stupendous things have happened in the boardinghouse—Vautrin has been exposed and arrested as a criminal, Michonneau and Poiret have been expelled from the premises, young Taillefer has been murdered in a duel, Victorine (now rich) has exited for better things—Rastignac seeks to apprise Goriot of the happenings, only to learn that the old man is utterly indifferent, couldn't care less. Why? He's going to dine with his daughters. The world could go up in smoke (as it seems to be doing), and he cares not a fig. One feels that Balzac has an intuitive sense of weights and measures, that the depths of a man's passion cancel out its breadth and scope. If you live intensely enough "here," you are dead "there." It is an intriguing arithmetic: one would like to know how Lear or Christ would show on a scale of this sort. Old age, too, seems on the line, even pathologized. We tend to think that the impassioned ones are the young, but this novel tells us otherwise: in Balzac, the old are the crazed ones, the old are those who burn and lust and rage, the ones who smolder in their narrow way.

This is queasy-making because it comes to us as intensely somatic. Goriot has no decorum at all. He is not easily manageable;

even old and dying, he has heft, can be violent. He is a lit fuse on the subject of his daughters and a vegetable on other subjects. To have this kind of love, this kind of absolute passion, is a form of sickness, indicates either crossed wires or staggering deficits in your equipment. It's little wonder that Goriot is the object of the medical gaze in so many passages or that Bianchon the medical student regards this suffering, soon-to-die old man with a mix of compassion and scientific curiosity. The entire novel has a laboratory aura.

All of this reaches predictably operatic proportions in the late segment of the novel devoted to Goriot's dying, to what the French call *l'agonie*. Here is where the medical and moral discourses come fully and unforgettably together. We have so sanitized dying today, by relegating it to hospices at best and impersonal hospital rooms at worst, that Balzac's pages have a rare power to shock and move us. Ugly, unpleasant, indecorous, in our face: this fully rendered death—apoplexy, cerebral edema, leaking exudate, groans, hot and hard belly, incessant pain, exploding head, all taking place in a squalid, unheated garret—squats heavily and immovably at the center of things and dares us to duck it. This death seems to announce: I am important. My dying matters. My exit is not merely personal but downright allegorical. Measures are being given here, and measures must be taken.

Lear died horribly, but he was reunited with Cordelia and managed to slay her murderer before his final exit. Goriot dies utterly abandoned by his two daughters (after they have competed in raids on his last remaining francs). Anastasie is kept at home by her furious husband, Delphine has a major ball to attend, namely the one where Mme. de Beauséant will be revealed as betrayed. Rastignac initially begged Delphine to comfort her dying father but then intuited that nothing would come of this: "she was quite capable of treading on her father's body in order to go to the ball." Note the systemwide failure: Delphine's, Rastignac's, and even Mme. de Beauséant's lover. Human relations, even blood relations, are shown to be fair-weather friends, fickle and disposable, unbinding. Both the young and the old experience love's failure. But whereas the young make knowledge of it—this will be Rastignac's great lesson—the old are crushed entirely. Yes, Goriot too is learning something, but he cannot bear it, for it announces the end of his world, as well as the end of his life: when children cease to love their parents, apocalypse is nigh.

The vermicelli trader who made his fortune by sharp dealing now understands that more than pasta is in play, that sharp dealing, no less than serpent's teeth, wrecks the human family. Like Lear, Goriot perceives that one seeds one's death by having children: "You give them life, they give you death. You bring them into the world, they drive you out of it." Unlike Lear, he held on to some of his money, dribbling it out in installments, recognizing that the finally emptied purse spawns a hardening of heart: "Money buys everything, even daughters. Oh! where is my money? If I still had wealth to leave, they would be tending me, looking after me." It is a businessman's truth. But at the height of his agony, this mercantile truth triggers an awareness that is more cosmic in nature, more frenzied in tone: "My daughters, my daughters, Anastasie, Delphine! I want to see them! Send the police after them, force them to come! Justice is on my side, everything is on my side, nature, civil law. I protest. The country will perish if fathers are trampled down. That's obvious. Society, the world, turns on fatherhood, everything breaks up if children don't love their fathers." Here is the Shakespearean moment: the *agonie* in question, the death rattle one hears, is not solely that of this old man but of his universe, which is imploding, shedding its skin, becoming monstrous. Fatherhood is the oldest contract of all, and it is being breached. What is fascinating is the secular brilliance of these outbursts: police, justice, civil law, and society are undone when fathers are undone. There is no help anywhere. Even the logic of the marketplace is defiled: "I want my daughters! I made them! They are mine!"

I made them! They are mine! Children are—or should be—the last possessions of the old. They are the one property that one has bought with one's flesh, that one has paid for with one's love, that one relies on for one's waning; the law of nature should ensure that they remain ours. That is what is annihilated here. Old age dispossesses us entirely. Money, health, children: nothing can be retained, however great the purchase price was, whatever role we had in the production. Balzac's mix of economic insight and scientific curiosity lays bare a brutal scheme that has parallels with Lear's chastened vision of "unaccommodated man," of "bare, forked animals." At our end, we have nothing, not even a clean sheet to die on, not even enough francs for the funeral. For a very long time, money and goods shield us from this stern truth. But not forever. The young law student alone attends the old man's funeral—there are no daughters in sight, just empty coaches sent by their husbands—and sheds "the last tears of his youth" as he watches the body being lowered into the grave. Much is being buried here. Rastignac has completed his own little course on growing up and growing old.

What about us? What have we learned, we who were not in that garret ministering to the dying, abandoned old man? And please note that the other two mentors finish badly also: Mme. de Beauséant exits Paris to bury herself alive in the country, and Vautrin is en route to prison. The old vacate the scene altogether. Maybe that is what we are meant to grasp: Goriot is presented by Balzac as something of a freak because the conditions of modern life (as seen in 1835) spell disaster for fathering. There is no comfortable way to exit this novel, inasmuch as advice to "hold on to the money" seems altogether too cynical to be called wisdom. No less disturbing is Goriot's outright mania for his children, warning us that obsession of this stripe is a recipe for disaster. I think Balzac knew all this, knew that his version of *Lear* offered little in the way of rules for living. And perhaps that is the French writer's ultimate strength: to link the Father with Christ is to say that parental love, when absolute (and blind and quasi-bestial, as it is for Goriot), leads to crucifixion.

The Aging of a Salesman: Willy Loman

Goriot had no idea he had become obsolete. Willy Loman knows it all too well, for it stamps both his life and his work. The doomed father-protagonist of Arthur Miller's *Death of a Salesman*, Willy may seem, in the light of the twenty-first century with its Internet shopping and telemarketing, a sepia figure of yesteryear, a time when salesmen got into their cars and crisscrossed the country with their satchels full of wares, constituting a breed that is bordering on extinction. There is a distinctly elegiac feeling to this play: we see in it an America of the 1950s that bought everything on the installment plan, only to find out that the products are cunningly programmed to fall apart just when they're finally paid for: the car, the refrigerator, even the house (Linda has made the last payment in the play's last lines, but it will be an empty place). Worse still, the man paying the installments is also caught in this time trap, also subject to wear and tear, threatened with obsolescence and death.

Time is the great cheat, and much of the pathos of the Loman family derives from the sweet poetry (fantasy?) of their earlier days: the boys endlessly simonizing the Chevrolet, Biff accomplishing his mythic exploits on the gridiron, Willy himself treated as the prince of the road, the man who "knocked 'em cold in Providence, slaughtered 'em in Boston." Willy boasts to his boys of the warm reception he receives everywhere he goes, and we get a glimpse of an America that has largely disappeared: "America is full of beautiful towns and fine, upstanding people. And they know me, boys, they know me up and down New England. The finest people."

There are no riots, no depressed economy, no complaining about taxes or public services or failing schools or social unrest or crumbling infrastructure. Yet the double vision that we readers bring to Willy's arcadian view of New England cities is not merely our hindsight but is hardwired in the play itself: Willy himself knows that he is a dinosaur, a creature of the past; he knows that the figure of the salesman no longer commands the respect it once did. We hear of the legendary salesman Dave Singleman, who was still going strong at eighty-four, "remembered and loved and helped by so many different people," whose funeral was attended by hundreds of salesmen and buyers. Not so anymore. Not so with Willy Loman. This aging salesman is dying, and there's nothing ceremonial in sight.

Miller's play is about the clockwork of human affairs: it runs down, must run down. No one tells you, when you start a job or enter a profession, that you're slated for obsolescence, that your effectiveness and productivity are likely to die before you do. In short, Willy Loman is learning the hard lesson that aging often brings to those who work right into their late years: they become outmoded, their labor is undervalued, they cannot keep up, they are going under. Part of this is his own personal decline: he tells Linda that he talks too much, he's getting fat, no one respects him anymore, he can no longer concentrate, he's distracted while driving, he almost hit a kid in Yonkers. He is used up. It makes good if grisly economic sense for Howard to lay him off. This is market logic. We also see it as tragic. Linda puts it succinctly: "He works for a company thirty-six years this March, opens up unheard-of territories to their trademark, and now in his old age they take his salary away." Willy himself puts it with more pith as he begs Howard to let him stay on: "You can't eat the orange and throw the peel away—a man is not a piece of fruit!"

But being discarded from the workplace is only part of it. Despite their obvious differences, *Death of a Salesman* registers the same murderous view of fathering and childing that we saw in *King Lear*. It is not simply that Willy Loman can no longer cut the mustard. (Though he can't.) The damage is greater than that: he has lived long enough to see that his deepest investments have gone wrong, have come to nought. I'm not thinking of refrigerators or cars or houses, but of the essential human investment of Willy's life: his two boys, Biff and Happy. To be sure, they are a far cry from Edmund or Goneril or Regan (or the Goriot daughters), but time itself seems possessed of serpents' teeth and ingratitude. The Loman brothers—the Loman brothers! so talented and promising in their youth, so gratifying for their father—haven't amounted to much: Biff's athletic prowess has led nowhere, whereas his character flaws and academic failures (stealing, flunking math) have proven to be massive impediments; and Happy has become a sharp, hustling womanizer, unfocused, no plan, breezy, low wattage. And Willy is no longer what he was. This is a grim picture of time's incursions: Willy can no longer drive properly, deliver his spiel, or sell his wares, and his two sons have more or less gone amok.

Arthur Miller was well aware that pathos came too easily to him as a writer, yet the pathos here is unbearably central to modern secular life: what are we living for? Or, as the mythic Uncle Ben asks, "What are you building?" This play lays it out with great clarity: all you've got is your work and your family, and it turns out that both of them are in the process of going kaput. That is the dirty secret: we do not build, we (and our projects) fall apart. There won't be an idyllic retirement in the country. There won't be a garden to putter around in. There won't be aging with dignity. There won't be a continuing paycheck. And the one glory that seemed utterly guaranteed, given how rich and fail-safe it seemed when one was younger—the beautiful promise of one's children—that too is not to be. Nothing is going to bear fruit.

I called this the tragedy of modern secular life because it targets much more than salesmanship. Miller has (perhaps unnecessarily) put a drama of sexual betrayal into the mix, thereby motivating the adored Biff's failure still more profoundly: the boy has discovered his father's infidelity while on the road, and it has sapped his belief in him. But we are to understand that Willy was an imperfect father in other ways too, that he should have counseled his boys more wisely, insisted that they do their homework, that they eschew chutzpah and glamour but commit themselves to hard work and decent grades. But he couldn't see them in such a steely-eyed way, because their glamour and charm were visible to the naked eye, advertising an immediate, all-powerful force that nothing—certainly not a grade point average—could rival. Fond familial love, fond to the point of blindness, is on the docket here. We are, all of us, romantics, inasmuch as we believe—or want to believe—in our children's magic promise; they are our future, our genetic carriers, our afterlife. "Because you got a greatness in you, Biff, remember that. You got all kinds a greatness," Willy, exhausted, tells his disillusioned son, who walks out, having heard it all before, knowing it for a sweet cheat, sensing that it is toxic, has been toxic all along. And we realize that this is Willy's lifeline even more than Biff's, Willy's sustaining fantasy, Willy's religious faith.

An entire American belief system is in its death throes here. It has to do with the cult of personality, the notion of charisma, the seductive beauty of human promise and dreams. Not just Dale Carnegie but Jay Gatsby and today's photogenic politicians and captains of industry are on the line: aura, authority, grace, magnetism, popularity, president of your class, prom queen, voted most likely to succeed, all this is in trouble. Of course we realize, in moments of lucidity and sober judgment, that Willy should have understood that charm and the smile on your face are not enough to guarantee success in life. But how could he have known? He was a salesman. His own career was fueled by just those virtues. And he did just fine. For a while. There's the rub: *for a while.* Time exacts its price. Growing up and growing old: Miller illuminates how interlocked they are, how the generations both sustain and poison each other, how parental dreams are built on shifting sand (if not minefields), how all families incubate reciprocal fantasies that can rarely be actualized, how severe the final reckoning is likely to be when the curtain goes up late in the game: you are old, they are not magic. No villains are needed in this modern story of disillusionment: it is life that betrays you, because time undoes dreams.

Your children won't carry you through, nor will your job. "You can't eat the orange and throw the peel away," Willy cried. Reportedly, at the end of one early performance of the play, a business magnate came to the stage to announce that henceforth he would increase the pensions for all his old employees going into retirement. But can the problem be fixed? We know that retirement, even decently paid retirement, has its own casualties as people try to readjust, recalibrate their energies, reconceive who they are, face the dilemma that they may be nobody (in their own eyes) if they're not working and using that old skill set. The car's steering goes, you still owe on the washing machine, the vacuum cleaner, and the fridge, one fine day you can't concentrate on the road, another fine day Linda's hair turns gray, and at the end the man who has worked thirty-six years at the same job is put out to pasture. Could it have been otherwise?

These matters are admittedly cultural, not universal. I have French and Swedish friends who move effortlessly and rewardingly into retirement, who have long regarded their work as a time-bound activity, to be followed by a still more gratifiying chapter in life. But Willy Loman? But those of us whose work and success hinge on day-to-day personal exchange, personal powers of persuasion? It's odd, isn't it, that we never know for sure what Willy was selling, what his actual line was. But maybe we do. His only currency, his real merchandise, was himself. That was what he was peddling all along. And at some point in time either the well dries up or there are no buyers left. He was a creature of belief, convincing others that they needed what he had to offer. At play's end, Charley spells it out: "And for a salesman, there is no rock bottom to the life. . . . He's a man way out there in the blue, riding on a smile and a shoeshine. And when they start not smiling back—that's an earthquake. . . . A salesman is got to dream, boy. It comes with the territory."

How long is the dream good for? Smiles, like Chevrolets and Studebakers, are time-bound vehicles, and your ride on/in them will only last so long. What are you building? "Breathing," Faulkner once wrote, "is a sight-draft dated yesterday." But a chunk of you can die while you're still drawing breath. You can live long enough to become obsolete and to learn that your deepest hopes and desires—the ones that fueled you, kept you going, were your article of faith—were fool's gold, illusory, undone by the passing of time. For Willy Loman, there will be no children around the hearth, no harvest to reap, no golden age of retirement and tranquillity. The most valuable property he still possesses at this late juncture in his life is his insurance policy: secular culture's supreme response to mortality, the final paycheck in the sky that comes at your exit.

Let me close by asking: would one want Willy Loman any different? Like Goriot, he loved his children too much, but how much of a failing is that? It is true that Goriot played the *papa gâteau*, bringing up his girls to see him as an endless source of financial support, but I have to wonder how many modern parents are not guilty of such excess. Yet Willy Loman's tragedy breaks your heart, because his belief in Biff and Happy is something beautiful as well as dangerous. If you spend your days selling . . . shoes, refrigerators, cars, real estate, insurance, stocks and bonds, whatever, well, then, it might make some sense for you to see your flesh-and-blood children as your ultimate compass: a nobler, more permanent, more spiritual form of belief. To then find that the entropic law of obsolescence that dooms you in your work is no less corrosive when it comes to your kids, that is dark indeed. Growing old makes for such unwelcome discoveries.

Exiting the Stage

Henrik Ibsen's The Master Builder

In Part I, Ibsen's *The Master Builder* was discussed as one more instance of child sacrifice. But I believe the play most stands out in our minds—and sticks in our craws—as a bold and fierce meditation on old age, as seen in the end-game antics of Solness the master builder, a privileged strong male now faced with the inevitable injunction to exit the stage, to make way for the young. *"Gi plads!"* is the phrase Ibsen repeatedly uses—"Give place, give way"—but it may also be understood, against the grain, in a more creative and generative (and architectural) sense: *"make* room, *make* space."* That ambiguity is at the core of the play: how to offset the story of entropy and approaching death—the fate of the old—by its counterpart: creativity, engendering, outright making. Can the old "make"? What do they make? It strikes me as a wonderful question, so different from the humbling solemnities of *Oedipus, King Lear,* and *Père Goriot,* as if potency itself were a stranger gift than is realized, were perhaps extendible beyond flesh. One feels that Ibsen is mightily taken up with these matters in his late plays, as he himself increasingly feels the weight of age; yet even the renditions of Borkman and Rubek do not have quite the reach or poetry of Solness's final gambit. Rarely has the drama of the male climacteric been written with such pathos.

The old crowd this play. The first figure we meet is the exhausted, wheezing, palpably dying old Brovik, Solness's older but now junior partner from whom he more or less wrested the architectural firm; the stakes for Brovik are stark: he will soon die, but he is begging Solness to give his son Ragnar, an apprentice in the firm, a chance to show his stuff, to make way for the next generation. And that is Solness's nightmare: the next generation. They are, as Ibsen's rather portentous imagery has it, poised to knock on the door, knock down the door. Brovik seeks, in accordance with the logic of the species, to find a future for his seed, but sowing is in trouble here. Ragnar may never get his chance. What, Ibsen is asking, is required for the old to make room? Do they want to dominate forever?

More significant still: having a living child at all is more than the protagonist Solness and his wife, Aline, have managed. This is a play of empty nurseries, of child cadavers: Aline gave birth to fine, plump twin boys, but the great ancestral house caught fire, Aline became sick, and her mother's milk poisoned the two little babies. A dark allegory, this. Ibsen makes astonishing poetry of dead babies, for these deaths become richly and horribly motivated. We learn that Solness halfway wanted the house to burn down, sensing obscurely that his own career as master builder could not be properly launched until Aline's inherited house came down; and so, come down it does, but it brings the little twins with it. Solness sees this as at once intolerable and logical: they too had to die for him fully to live. There will be a price to pay. He says he is chained to corpses, that his success has blood on it, that he has taken on the characteristics of the troll, made use of infernal helpers: all in the service of relentless self-assertion, of never yielding an inch. Children down: so be it. It is as brutal as the infanticidal/parricidal arrangements in Sophocles, Shakespeare, and Balzac, but Ibsen recognizes the special monstrousness of the old killing the young, and his play is about the ineluctable revenge of the young, the threat they pose. Solness's life is cued to stopping the clock, to keeping the door shut. Ibsen's question is: Might that threat also be a harbinger of promise for the old? Do the old also yearn to exit? Where to?

If Solness feels guilt at the death of his twins, what is one to say of Aline? In a moment of shocking candor, she confides to Hilda that the loss of the babies, terrible though it was, hurt less than the loss of her dolls: "Because, you see, in a way there was life in them too. I used to carry them under my heart. Just like little unborn children." In lines such as this, Ibsen reveals himself as the unrivaled poet of displacement, for he seems intuitively to know that our libidinal wires get crossed, that symbols and fetishes carry as much weight as so-called flesh and blood, that they inhabit your womb as well as your mind. But what happens when you trade flesh for symbol? Aline goes through the play with her litany of "duty, duty," as if her blood had indeed been sucked out of her, turning her into a kind of righteous marionette, postfeeling, on the far side of passion. You look at this group of old folks—Brovik, Solness, Aline—and you feel the geriatric character of the play, even though Solness is hanging on to life and power as hard as he possibly can. He is good at this: unlike so many of Ibsen's wimpy males, the architect Solness is sexually charismatic—I cannot read this play without thinking of Frank Lloyd Wright, also a visionary, sultanlike architect—able to mesmerize women, hence bent on using this natural resource to keep both Kaia and young Brovik under his control, thereby using the energies of the young while retaining his position as top dog. It is not pretty. And he is in for some surprises.

They come in the form of Hilda Wangel, a young girl with a surprising history and dirty underwear who indeed knocks on his door, makes her entry into his life, and rearranges everything she touches. It is here that the decorous Ibsen injects a huge dose of libido, kinkiness, and displaced desire into the script we saw in *King Lear*: Ibsen's Cordelia lives, but she lives as a vibrant, hungry young girl who fills the empty nurseries in this house of death and who suavely explains to Solness that she has come to make good on his proposals of ten years ago. What proposals? Solness remembers nothing. "I want my kingdom. Time's up," she says. He is bewildered. She repeats: "Give us the kingdom, come on. . . . One kingdom, on the line!" One doesn't know whether to laugh or cry at this reworking of Goneril and Regan, transformed into a demanding virgin who will not be put down.

What is it that the old man doesn't remember? (Is he amnesiac? He could be.) Well, there is this matter of promising to carry off the princess to the Kingdom of Orangia, and then there is the matter of solidifying this pledge: "You held me in both your arms and bent me back and kissed me—many times." I don't think theater gets more delicious than this: Solness, generally quite poised and in command, is befuddled, remembers nothing about kissing this girl—who must have been thirteen then, just at puberty—and can't quite make sense of her story. Yet we've already noted the hypnotic power he has over women—exerted even silently, even without gesture—so he decides that yes, he must simply emanate rays of some sort, Hilda is probably not entirely wrong, he did not quite bend her over and kiss her, but he doubtless wanted to, and that was enough. *Desire is enough.* Here is the fertile terrain of *The Master Builder;* might this be the potency of old age?

Hilda is growing up, Solness is growing old. The play stages their pas de deux. So often Ibsen is misconstrued as "was drama," as the master who pulled skeletons out of closets and cast his light backward, pastward. But his great plays go just the other way: they are "is drama," and nowhere is this more spectacularly on show than here. All this twaddle about what happened ten years ago is essentially foreplay, since the real gambit is the strange music that Solness and Hilda make *now.* Hence, Hilda's fable of a dashing architect who excited her to frenzy by climbing higher and higher, right up to the top of the church tower—critics have noted the erotic fervor of much of this—and then had his fiery dispute with God, all this evokes a man in his full prime, yet, like all men, a man primed for unraveling, undoing. Such is the force of gravity: we may climb, we may rise for a while, but inevitably we fall, inevitably the very weight of flesh carries us down. But old Solness climbs again; he does so by dint of the love aria he shares with Hilda as they go through their dreamlike romp. Hilda's youth is intoxicating. With her help, he will build again:

HILDA: ... We two, we'll work together. And that way we'll build the loveliest—the most beautiful thing anywhere in the world.

SOLNESS (*caught up*): Hilda—tell me, what's that?

HILDA (*looks smilingly at him, shakes her head a little, purses her lips, and speaks as if to a child*): Master builders, they are very—very stupid people.

SOLNESS: Of course they're stupid. But tell me what it is! What's the world's most beautiful thing that we're going to build together?

HILDA (*silent a moment, then says, with an enigmatic look in her eyes*): Castles in the air.

It is customary to smile or yawn at Ibsen's long-winded stage directions, but he sweetly captures this play's mystery in those lines of Hilda's, where she initiates the older man into a kind of erotic, imaginative trance, which it might not be wrong to term intercourse. Whatever may or may not have happened ten years ago, this is happening now. He is climbing, rising again. Forgive me if I say there is tumescence here. What might they make together? A castle in the air? A child? A shared ecstatic dream? We cannot know the answer, but we see the growing fusion of these two figures, their increasingly fluid and trancelike entry into each other's wishes and dreams. This play is haunted by the specter of empty forms—Ibsen referred to himself as an architect, and Solness worries that he has wasted his years building soulless structures, devoid of life—but this scene posits human desire as the creative force that does not die, that resists the work of time. To be sure, we all know that it cannot be done. Yet it is done: Solness once again mounts the church tower (this time of his own house), led, lifted, indeed fueled by Hilda's desire. No, this is not quite phallic, but it is splendid in its way. He goes to the top; he once again quarrels with God. And then he falls. Gravity has the last word.

But not quite. "My—my Master Builder!": those are Hilda's (and the play's) final words. It remains a paean to human wanting, even human design. Yet as we draw back from the gruesome ending—Solness has plummeted straight down from the top, gone smash—we are stunned by the poetic logic Ibsen has conferred on these events. Hilda has come to initiate Solness into death. The door must be opened to the young. (Ragnar will be given his chance.) Herself a child, she is on a species mission to honor life's forward drive, with its inevitable bias toward the young. Some have called her a Valkyrie. Yet—and perhaps this is the old Ibsen's fondest fantasy—her intervention is erotic, signaling that she is sexually drawn to this father figure who must die. But die he must, and all of us can see in her "ensnaring" of Solness a radical reworking of the child/parent death struggle so evident in Sophocles, Shakespeare, and Balzac. She is the bright, irresistible face of life, and her tidings are: I shall escort you lovingly to the other side, I shall transform the journey of dying into an ecstatic duet of longing and shared hunger, I shall awaken all your forces for this final building project: to make your own exit. (Just how patriarchal, insane, and fantasy-ridden all this might be is another question.)

I think of Rilke's poem "Herbsttag," which begins with the injunction *"Herr, es ist Zeit"* and includes in its autumnal sketch a warning that could have come directly from Ibsen's play, given its architectural figure: *"Wer jetzt kein Haus hat bildet sich keines mehr"* ("Who now has no house will not build one"). Rilke revered Ibsen but perhaps got this last part wrong, perhaps failed to see that the seasonal fate might nonetheless be overcome. Maybe it *is* given to us to build, right to the end. Maybe Ibsen came to understand his entire enterprise along just those lines: a dramaturgy that appears utterly cued to the hard facts and heavy data of the past is actually something far airier, far freer, far more invested in freedom than in bondage. Yes, one is coerced by one's past—who doesn't have cadavers somewhere?—and one cannot keep the door forever shut against the young, who are ready to step in and cancel out one's future: this double lesson sinks in ever more acutely as we grow old. So: how does one spring clear?

To move this aging man from the center stage he cannot bear to quit, more than Hilda is required. Another time and place are needed, some actualizable realm outside the day-to-day world we all negotiate, the dreary material realm where, indeed, Ibsen's plays are thought to take place. Far from being only a chronicler of the stifling and stifled European middle class, as is often thought, Ibsen is surprisingly dimensional. He has fashioned a place for desire—*Gi plads!* He has turned desire itself into a room, a place, a stage we know as the theater, an unfurling and happening that we can actually witness taking place in the arias between the older man and the young girl in *The Master Builder*—and offered it as the shimmering final station in a man's trajectory. As is said of the Thane of Cawdor in *Macbeth*, "Nothing in his life became him like the leaving it." *Castles in the air.* It is all too easy to interpret Hilda's phrase for what she and Solness are to make as an empty illusion, baseless phantasm. But we would do well to turn it the other way: to realize that our most inhabitable castles are doubtless to be located in the air, in our dreams and desires, for they are the place where finally we perform our deepest negotiations with life and death. Would that every climacteric possessed this kind of beauty.

Eugène Ionesco's Exit the King

Ionesco's remarkable play about dying, *Exit the King,* far from being "theater of the absurd," deserves to be read as a bravura modern response to *King Lear.* The story seems grim—King Bérenger is obliged to accept the fact that he's dying, king though he is—but it is leavened by the playwright's tonic and irreverent humor. This Bérenger has had quite a run: building Rome, New York, Moscow, and Geneva, founding Paris, inventing gunpowder, airplanes, automobiles. Yet his most miraculous achievements are the pedestrian ones of sleeping and waking up, breathing, and having a body that works; and those are the "gifts" that are now going to be called. The systems we take for granted play out, and this might well seem a freighted, heavy subject; but Ionesco puts us on notice that death is not only the oldest of all topics but arguably one of the funniest and most idiotic, inasmuch as we foolishly and futilely wage war against it all our lives. That battle is what I want to focus on, for it suggests that life—not death—is our stubborn, insidious, ceaseless assailant, wounding us from the day we draw breath, scarring and warping us in ways we cannot see. Dying, in this play, makes those injuries visible. Bérenger, like

Lear, like Solness, must be readied for his exit. Ionesco makes beautiful use of the theater here, for he sovereignly puts names to things we could not otherwise see:

MARGUERITE: There are still some ties that bind you which I haven't yet untied. Or which I haven't cut. There are still some hands that cling to you and hold you back. (*Moving around the King, Marguerite cuts the space, as though she had a pair of invisible scissors in her hand.*)

KING: Me. Me. Me.

MARGUERITE: This is not the real you. It's an odd collection of bits and pieces, horrid things that live on you like parasites. The mistletoe that grows on the bough is not the bough, the ivy that climbs the wall is not the wall. You're sagging under the load, your shoulders are bent, that's what makes you feel so old. And it's that ball and chain dragging at your feet which make it so difficult to walk. (*Marguerite leans down and removes an invisible ball and chain from the King's feet, then as she gets up she looks as though she were making a great deal of effort to lift the weight.*) A ton weight, they must weigh at least a ton. (*She pretends to be throwing them in the direction of the audience; then, freed of the weight, she straightens up.*) That's better! How did you manage to trail them around all your life! (*The King tries to straighten up.*) And I used to wonder why you were so round-shouldered! It's because of that sack! (*Marguerite pretends to be taking a sack from the King's shoulders and throws it away.*) And that heavy pack. (*Marguerite goes through the same motions for the pack.*) And that spare pair of army boots.

KING (*with a grunt of sorts*): No.

MARGUERITE: Don't get so excited! You won't need an extra pair of boots any more. Or that rifle, or that machine-gun. (*The same procedure as for the pack.*) Or that tool-box. (*Same procedure: protestations from the King.*) He seems quite attached to it! A nasty rusty old saber. (*She takes it off him, although the King tries grumpily to stop her.*) Leave it all to me and be a good boy. (*She taps on the King's hand.*)

You don't need self-defense any more. No-one wants to
hurt you now.

This stunning evocation of the corrosion that a life in time exacts upon the living—the inner wounds, the twisted and warped
postures, the gruesome responses (rifle, machine gun, saber)—
comes to us as the privileged vision that dying inaugurates: at last
you see clear, at last you can measure and gauge the shocking extent of your injuries, the ugly price you've paid for getting by. This
is certainly at odds with Saint Paul's religious view of seeing clear
at the end, "face to face," but as a visionary discovery of what
one's life (on this side) has produced, what one has become, it is
unsurpassable. The writer finds images—horribly pedestrian ones
of warfare, anxiety, fear, aggressivity: all now written into our
bodies, all on show in the physiological spectacle that a life of
stress makes of us—that are at once familiar yet never before
seen, since we have no lights about the routine deformations of
spirit that have been meted out to us. CAT scans and MRIs are not
likely to get a sighting on the damage shown in this play.

But I'd go on to claim that we are not obliged to place this at
death's door, as a kind of exit gift from living. Remember Lear's
initial confidence that he was unburdening himself by dividing up
his kingdom, and remember how dreadfully wrong he was, how
besieged and assailed he was slated to become, in body, mind, and
heart. Ionesco seems to have reversed gravity itself by imagining
our exit from the stage as both liberation and self-possession, as an
ascent into true majesty. Could we not see this as a form of "spring
cleaning" that old age—the calm after the storm—might confer?
Could there be a mellower, leaner, less encumbered, freer self waiting for us? Could our last chapter take place in airier fashion?

The Old in Love

If love is a central formative experience for the young—as we've seen in so many of the growing-up stories, ranging from *Romeo and Juliet* on to writers as diverse as Prévost, the Brontë sisters, Rhys, Duras, Walker, and others—what is its place in the lives and values of the old? These issues are immense and of immense importance; they will even return to constitute the final rubric of my book. But I want to begin dealing with them—and narrowing them down—by emphasizing sexuality and desire, which add a very particular element to the discussion. Again recall the tumultuous love stories of the young, and then ask yourself: to what extent do those stories hinge on sexual desire? The anthropologists tell us that puberty is a key marker in all rites-of-passage scenarios, and even though great literature is rarely bound by raw somatic data, who can fail to see that the tempestuous feelings and sensations of the young are keyed to a biological clock?

This clock is still ticking when it comes to the "affairs" of the old, and that is crucial for the issues we now turn to. If puberty seems like a natural miracle in the lives of the young, thrusting them into a new somatic career, it has a very different resonance for the aging. To exit the stage can also mean to exit sexual passion, to stop being a candidate for it, to stop being "authorized" for it, to stop being (physically) capable of it. These issues can be comic or tragic, depending on circumstances. How does society judge older sexuality or indeed lust? Are the rules different for men and women? How graciously do the old accept "quittin' time"? How worried are the old about their sexual aura or chances or performance? (Modern Western culture and media seem fanatically invested in a view of libidinal sufficiency—armed with the right cosmetics or medications—that knows no end other than the grave.) Yet even if we know that life itself is longer than romance, what does the postsexual life look like?

Postsexual

Ever since Plato, the philosophers have claimed old age as the happy reprieve from the pressing wants of desire: "For certainly old age has a great sense of calm and freedom; when the passions relax their hold, then, as Socrates says, we are freed from the grasp not of one mad master only, but of many." We see here a view of the passions as taskmasters, as despots that rob us of agency and dignity. From this perspective, aging moves us finally into peace and thence into wisdom, for at last we are free to judge according to our inborn reason, unhampered by the sting of flesh. As I have implied, modern life seems distinctly at war with this view of old age as sanctuary, as liberation from flesh and desire. In part this has to do with the valence accorded to peace and calm: Are they indices of wisdom or of death? Do we regard roiling feelings and libidinal hunger as curses or blessings? One's own age also has a great deal to do with judgments in this area. The young may find it not only unseemly but downright unthinkable that old folks continue to be sexually active. The old, I venture to say, find that their views on these matters are murky, evolving, and difficult.

Rip Van Winkle

In early-nineteenth-century America, Washington Irving created an emblematic figure for these issues. Rip Van Winkle may stand in our imagination as the fellow who slept for twenty years and then woke up and returned home. But if you look closely at Irving's classic story, you note that Rip was a distinctly ineffective husband even in his salad days and particularly so in the conjugal sex department: "but as to doing his family duty . . . he found it impossible." Dame Van Winkle, we gather, was a demanding, indeed shrewish, figure, whom Irving describes in a rather menacing fashion: "a sharp tongue is the only edged tool that grows keener with constant use." Is there a hint of castration anxiety here? One thing is certain: our man Rip, out for a walk, comes upon the gods at play in their splendor and games and falls into a twenty-year slumber thanks to the liquid in their flagon. Waking up to a changed world—Irving is especially interested in contrasting the pre- and post-Revolutionary Americas that this plot allows him to sketch—Rip is discomfited by what he sees, but there is one piece of good news: his wife is at last dead. A long sleep has some benefits: no more "petticoat government"; "he had got his neck out of the yoke of matrimony."

And that is how we leave the old fellow: reunited with his daughter, idle, sitting with the elders, telling stories. Free at last. The story closes with Irving's generalization: "it is a common wish of all henpecked husbands in the neighborhood, when life hangs heavy on their hands, that they might have a quieting draft of Rip Van Winkle's flagon." Rip's flagon is a potion for aging: but how many of today's drug companies would buy into that? There is much concern today with the riddance of wrinkles and the arrival of erections, but not much interest in getting past the sexual altogether.

Charles Dickens

Is getting past sex such a good thing? Consider, in this regard, Miss Havisham in Dickens's *Great Expectations*. Her life seems to have stopped at the moment of sexual betrayal at the hands of Compeyson, so everything remains frozen in the most ghastly way: clocks stopped, wedding cake still on the table, inhabited by spiders, beetles, and rats. Yet this panorama of arrested time is deceiving, since the old lady not only continues to live but exercises her will and her revenge on the two young people who come into her orbit: Estella, who is systematically deformed by her mentor into a cold, heartless beauty, a beautiful puppet/bloodsucker, and Pip, who thinks she is bankrolling him, who is convinced that she has arranged for him to marry Estella, who insists on seeing her as a fairy godmother. In my account of Pip's education, I drew attention to the grisly scene where she catches on fire and Pip leaps upon her, wrestling with her on the floor, and I suggested that there were overtones of rape in the language Dickens used; I'd go on to say that that sequence constitutes a peculiar climax for Miss Havisham, that it images precisely the sexual act that has been monstrously held in abeyance, prevented from happening.

August Strindberg

In his play about male sexual anxieties, *The Father*, the Swedish playwright Strindberg is obsessed with the issue of time-bound potency (male and female), and although the overt concern of the text is patrimony—can a father be sure he's sired his child?—the strongest passages evoke the crisis of male sexuality as a primal force in the universe. What happens when engendering stops? Consider, for example, the following crazed speech as a hallucinatory figuring of what a postsexual regime might look like:

> When women grow old and stop being women, they get beards on their chins. I wonder what men get when they grow old and stop being men. And so, the dawn was sounded not by roosters but capons, and the hens that answered didn't know the difference. When the sun should have been rising, we found ourselves in full moonlight, among the ruins, just like in the good old days.

In these compressed lines we discern the lineaments of a truly postsexual geriatric world, one where the spawning and fertility principles have gone out of business, and Strindberg is nothing if not democratic, for he locates this condition among the animals too, while finally linking it to the engendering work of Genesis itself: let there be light. But in this new dispensation, conception, photosynthesis, and growth are all gone. Bearded women, impotent men, capons, dysfunctional hens inhabit the scene: no roosters in sight to signal the beginning of the day, no sun left to irradiate the earth and its living creatures with heat and warmth and the life principle; just moonlight and ruins. It is a surreal evocation of what time does to life, of the end of "siring" of any stripe, and it is no accident that Strindberg's male title figure is entirely cashiered by such arrangements and ends up in swaddling clothes, having been systematically regressed by the machinations of his shrewd wife and his own paranoia. Growing up, growing old: Strindberg's Father makes the trip in reverse, and ends up *infans*.

I include the Strindberg piece because it turns its man into both child and woman; maybe that is what we are to learn from it: that time alters the forms we took to be stable, so that old parents rebecome babies and are ministered to by their children. But it also posits a notion of what the Creation might look like, if impotency and menopause were the new dispensation of things. (What would Strindberg think of our modern sperm banks, substitute wombs, and test-tube babies?) Once the play's male is sufficiently undone, the misogynist author has no choice but to declare the young wife the winner. Laura triumphs entirely, becomes the "man of the house" by play's end. Her husband has been reduced to silence; patriarchal power has been dealt a severe blow. She wins; she may have lovers to come. But what future is there for the bearded women? Even Strindberg couldn't imagine that scenario.

These matters achieve a surreal, indeed sublime form in his late play *The Ghost Sonata*, an unforgettable account of the living dead, of desexed ghouls who cannot die but live behind elegant walls and continue to feast on one another's entrails with lies and deceptions, capping an entire existence of betrayals and poisoned relationships. The crown jewel in this viper's nest is Polly, a woman turned literally into a mummy, living in her closet-cage, staring intently at a beautiful statue of her in her youth, measuring incessantly the dismantling life has done. When her now-old former lover stumbles upon her in her lair and cannot believe his eyes, she sets him straight: "Yes, this is how I look!—And (*pointing to the statue*) that's how I *used* to look! Life teaches us so much."

Strindberg's surrealism frees him to give material form to time's lessons. Our eyes have trouble registering the progress of aging, for the human face and body evolve so very slowly, but look what a playwright can do: a lady now transformed into a mummy lives in a cage with her eyes fixed on a statue of a nubile girl. Live long enough, Strindberg tells us, and you are the grotesque twisted living dead, permanently on the far side of libido, but there is a catch: you never quite forget the beauty you long ago had, a beauty whose every feature you remember with bitterness, which is there in sculptural form permanently to haunt you. Stone does not age; mummies cannot die; put them together, and, voilà, the story of growing old—the generic heinous two-way traffic between statue and mummy—is told once again.

William Faulkner

In other writers these matters can be more virulent. Faulkner's *Light in August* seems entirely cued to the war between conception and entropy, as illustrated in the thematic tug-of-war between the fertile, unmarried, about-to-deliver Lena Grove and the neurotic, death-oriented Joe Christmas (who thinks he has "a little nigger blood" in him). Their joint stories occupy center stage in this violently overheated fiction, but the figure whose fate is inseparable from these matters is Joanna Burden, the older woman, the white New England spinster who becomes Christmas's lover ("nigger lover" according to her neighbors, once they find out about Joe) and whose tempestuous awakening to late sexual frenzy occasions some of Faulkner's most remarkable writing. One feels that the Mississippi writer is pulling out all the regional and libidinal stops in fashioning a nymphomaniac New England spinster who explodes into mad lust, profanity, and excess in her trysts with Christmas. (It is in these sequences that breathy coinages such as "womanshenegro" enter the text, displaying Faulkner's sense of crossed wires, of racial taboo as fierce aphrodisiac on the woman's side, whereas the male sees himself entering "the pit," drowning in the female genital morass. *Light in August* is Faulkner's most unzipped novel.)

Joanna perhaps comes most fully into our argument at the

point when she tells Christmas she thinks she is pregnant, but this assertion is followed by increasing evidence that her pregnancy is either mendacious or illusory. It is not to be, and Faulkner graphs her entry into menopause by insistently representing her passage through erotic fury on to quiescence in the charged imagery of Indian summer, "that final upflare of stubborn and dying summer upon which autumn, the dawning of half-death, had come unawares." There is a clear seasonal logic to this novel, and it is grisly in its ramifications: " 'You haven't got any baby,' he [Christmas] said. 'You never had one. There is not anything the matter with you except being old. You just got old and it happened to you and now you are not any good anymore.' " This exchange reaches its conclusion in homicidal violence: Christmas cuts off her head.

Granted, Joanna has designs on him that he cannot abide—such as acknowledging his black blood, going to a Negro college—but her primary offense seems to be that she is "not any good anymore," and that suffices as a death sentence. The severity of this indictment testifies to a crazed but stubborn prizing of potency and fertility as the gauge of one's human viability. Faulkner's older women often come across as a postsexual, embittered, even smoldering lot. Caroline Compson (in *The Sound and the Fury*) stands indicted for coldness of heart, Addie Bundren (in *As I Lay Dying*) exercises steely and vengeful control over her husband and progeny even beyond the grave, Joanna Burden's false pregnancy and affair with Joe Christmas leads to decapitation, more minor figures such as Mrs. Armstid and other decent farmers' wives come to us as pinched and bruised and pickled, as victims of a system that has been busily coercing them for some time now, drying them out, taking their juices, leaving them only with a fine residual rage at what life brings them. Rosa Coldfield (in *Absalom, Absalom!*) is imaged as both enraged shrew and living mummy, as if she were sealed (while at full boil) in formaldehyde after the insult Sutpen meted out to her more than forty-three years earlier. Her fateful journey out to Sutpen's Hundred at the novel's close is written by Faulkner in orgasmic language, as an affair of moaning and panting and outright somatic release: her life too is climaxing at last.

Is that how male writers see it? Wait long enough, old bearded

women, and some violently displaced form of sexual deed comes
to finish you off: your head gets cut off by your younger lover, you
burn alive with a boy writhing on you to put out the flames, you
whimper and pant and moan en route to the encounter of your life
(with a wasted ghost whom you finally see in the decaying flesh
after all these years) so that you can at last die. It's a severe script.
Are there no accommodations with time's injuries? Might appetite
and libido be more sinuous and creative than these scenarios suggest?

Sexual Anxiety

It must be the case that the young also experience sexual anxiety,
but time is on their side, their equipment is new, and they are on
the front side of a glorious chapter in our species' affairs. In my
discussion of *Manon Lescaut* I did point to some passages that
evoke a kind of figurative sexual doubt, but the general tone of
the growing-up stories is one of confidence. But the drama of
aging can scarcely be understood if we refuse to factor in doubts in
this key department of our emotional and libidinal careers, doubts
brought on by the passing of time or even by the outsize amorous
expectations cultivated by our media culture. Life, as we know,
can be devilishly complicated when it comes to the bedroom, and
I have no interest in studying outright dysfunction or sexual failure. Great literature is neither pornographic nor clinical, yet it
sometimes speaks powerfully to these very issues of power at risk.

Othello

We will never understand *Othello* unless we consider the significance of age as an element of Othello's undoing. Iago understands
to perfection that this paragon of power, this martial African who
descends from chieftains, has a special Achilles' heel: not only is he
an outsider to Venetian culture—read: Venetian women, women
he is unequipped to decipher—but he can be made to feel sexually
anxious. Iago is of course the play's "naturalist," the man who
tells Rodrigo that Desdemona "must change for youth," that "her
delicate tenderness will find itself abused, begin to heave the

gorge, disrelish and abhor the Moor," and not only does Iago believe it, but he goes a long way toward persuading Othello himself
to believe it, telling him straight out that there is something rank
and foul and unnatural in Desdemona's decisions and affections.
He manages also to infer Cassio's sexual superiority: "Although 'tis
fit that Cassio have his place, / For sure he fills it up with great
ability."

All this is washing through Othello's mind—to the Senate, he
has already acknowledged "the young affects in me defunct"—as
he measures his own possible limitations in this department:
"Haply, for I am black / And have not those soft parts of conversation / That chamberers have; or for I am declined / Into the vale
of years—yet that's not much— / She's gone: I am abused, and my
relief / Must be to loathe her. O, curse of marriage! / That we can
call these delicate creatures ours / And not their appetites!" Much
is in play here: wrong culture, wrong age, along with a recognition
that bodies—one's own, that of one's own wife—are not actually
ownable at all. But it is also the plaint of a man on the far side of
youth, a man who perhaps met on his wedding night (if indeed the
marriage was consummated then, something much debated by
scholars) those very "appetites," possessing a kind of energy and
violence unlike what he'd seen on the battlefield.

And perhaps there is a significant dose of misogyny in all this.
After all, Shakespeare is utterly reversing the clichés of his own
moment: rather than giving us a testosterone-larded African with
genital power (which his audience would have expected), he limns
an unforgettable portrait of an older man in trouble, prey to the
brilliant if diabolic innuendo of his ensign, recognizing that
prowess in one area does not mean confidence in another. This is a
formula for disaster, and Othello will explode. But female sexuality has its card to play: it has been pointed out that the infamous
handkerchief—the domestic implement given to Othello by his
mother, then gifted to Desdemona, then thought to have been offered to Cassio, retrieved by Emilia, ending up in Iago's hands, to
serve as a specious "proof" of infidelity—with the embroidered
strawberries connoted to the Elizabethan audience the very
iconography of Desdemona's sexual parts: nipples, clitoris. Ah,
those "appetites" the male cannot control.

For Desdemona, innocent and pure though she is, has the courage of her own wants and feelings, loves Othello with enough strength and guts to challenge all male authority, notably that of her own father; after all, she has eloped with him. At first Othello is touched by her feistiness—yes, she is feisty; just listen to her claiming her "domestic rights" to the Venetian Senate, as well as speaking hard truth to her stunned father about priorities and duties—but soon enough her very boldness works against her (just as her "moist" hands do), testifies to her increasingly paranoid husband that she is wanton, is thrall to sexual hunger and excess, is a monster of deceit and appetite. Misogyny, yes; but also the uncontrollable fears of an older man confronting and imagining his own inadequacy, his helplessness and victimization. Revenge will be his response. Hamlet, beset by the same generalized anxiety about female desire, told Ophelia to get herself to a nunnery; Othello, a military man hit in his very vitals, will murder his woman.

The critical reception of *Othello* has been an up-and-down affair: it was long considered inferior to *Hamlet, Macbeth,* and *Lear* because its emphasis on domestic rather than dynastic crises was thought to be a lesser subject. Needless to say, its explosive mix of racial prejudice and sexual violence gives it an immediate interest for modern readers, and any American who remembers the O. J. Simpson trial will concur that Shakespeare touches on deep-seated social anxieties. To add age as motivational factor to this mix is not to diminish the play but to understand more fully what Othello is up against and why he goes down. "Jealousy" is our all-encompassing term for his plight, but the ticking male clock (and the vulnerabilities it opens onto) also parse these bloody events.

Tennessee Williams's Blanche DuBois

The portrait of Blanche DuBois in Williams's *A Streetcar Named Desire*—fragile, affected, desperate, neurotic, slated for sexual execution—is among the most arresting things in American theater. It would seem as though all of Williams's wounds and fears were packed into this doomed woman: her young first husband was gay, and her denunciation of him caused his suicide; her profound need for civility, gentility, and tenderness was quashed by reality, so it went "inside" to become the generative source of ever-greater evasions and disguises and manic acts. Blanche is death-haunted: by the blood on her hands, by the fantasyland of decorous conventions she holds on to, by a past that cannot be hidden or faced.

And by the clock. Blanche lives by a code of southern gallantry and female charms, and she is destined to die by it. She cannot bear too much light. As she tells Stella, "And so the soft people have got to—shimmer and glow—put a—paper lantern over the light. . . . But I'm scared now—awf'ly scared. I don't know how much longer I can turn the trick. . . . I'm fading now!" *I don't know how much longer I can turn the trick.* Here is sexual anxiety writ large, and it speaks volumes about the brutally eroticized setting in which women may find themselves obliged to perform and give their measure. In her desperate last play for a man, her doomed tryst with Mitch, she acknowledges that her "youth was suddenly gone up the water-spout" and that she needs peace and kindness. Perhaps her most sublime moment comes when she faces Stanley head-on at play's end—minutes before being taken sexually (raped?), though she cannot know this—and speaks her truth/ fiction about womanhood:

A cultivated woman, a woman of intelligence and breeding, can enrich a man's life—immeasurably! I have those things to offer, and this doesn't take them away. Physical beauty is passing. A transitory possession. But beauty of the mind and richness of the spirit and tenderness of the heart—and I have all of those things—aren't taken away, but grow! Increase with the years! How strange that I should be called a destitute woman! When I have all of these treasures locked in my heart. [*A choked sob comes from her.*] I think of myself as a very, very rich woman!

These lines may seem crazed and exaggerated—after all, Blanche comes to us (as well as to Stanley) as a lush who has been drummed out of town for her more-than-loose behavior with all manner of men, both young and old—but it represents the idealist code that Tennessee Williams wants more than anything to be-

lieve in: a kind of love that outlives entropy, that recognizes a
beauty that is of the mind rather than the body. Aging as increase,
not loss, as a different kind of beauty: how to make this stick?

I have especially wanted to bring Blanche into the argument
because she is *not old.* Yes, she is fading (as so many of us are). But
even Stanley finds her plenty appetizing: "maybe you wouldn't be
bad to—interfere with." Not old, but too old nonetheless. Gender
is the key here. Blanche DuBois lies about her age, says she is
Stella's younger sister, claims she is twenty-six, even though all
parties know it to be a sham. Her great tragedy is that she is no
longer in her prime, that she still must compete in the sexual
game even though her charms are not what they were, will not
sustain direct light. Williams's play positively crackles with libidinal energy, as we see in both the hungry, panting, pawing, moaning couples onstage: Eunice and Steve, as well as Stella and
Stanley. His New Orleans is a place first and foremost of fornication, of fornication's rights and power. And by that standard
Blanche DuBois fails the test. Yes, she is sexually hungry—the
film version of her final encounter with Stanley shows arousal—
but her plaint is about the passing of beauty, about the tragedy of
seeming old when you can no longer pretend to be twenty-six. I
said "gender," because this is all too often woman's fate. Men get
away with murder on this front, it seems to me: Adonis or not, pot-
bellied or not, even toothless, lame, and bald to boot, the (American) male seems forever green, unindicted, still able to pass the
test, still a candidate for the bed. Mitch, inarticulate, ungainly,
overweight, and sweating, is still a catch.

But Blanche hides from the light. Blanche's elaborate yesteryear fantasies of courtesy and valor and refinement seem like a retreat into medieval courtly love, given how utterly alien the New
Orleans scene is to such niceties. I believe that entire genteel code
that Blanche subscribes to—defined by her urging Stella:
"Don't—don't hang back with the brutes"—is cued to the passing
of time and its despotic power against women. "Without your
love, it's a honky-tonk parade," she sings in the bathtub, and the
play suggests she's right: the kind of love she posits is one that includes but transcends the body itself, whereas the raw lust of the
play is one of coupling bodies, of smashing lightbulbs as part of

the copulating fun, of honky-tonk parade. Belle Reve was doubt-less never the haven of beauty and manners that Blanche says, but it does function as a beautiful dream, *un beau rêve* as the French has it, and Williams understands that life wrecks these dreams.

The play ends with Blanche being institutionalized as Stanley and Stella resume their passional life. What is being carted away is more than Blanche DuBois: it is the entire dream of beauty and sensitivity and refinement that she clung to. The animal regime of the play will not countenance it. She begins by fading, and she ends by being incarcerated. I want again to say: this is a woman's fate. It is a fate that can be seen everywhere as women fight against the clock, as they are bombarded by media and songs and advertising about ways to trick time, ways to seem twenty-six for-ever, ways to stay in the game. How much of life is taken up by our war with time? By our fateful and coercive contract with beauty? With beauty as the indispensable ticket for love? At what point does growing old begin for women versus for men? Strindberg lo-cated it in menopause, but Blanche DuBois's nightmarish fate suggests that it begins much, much earlier.

Unsanctioned Lust

If growing old can sometimes entail sexual anxiety or the advent of a postsexual life phase, it is by no means the case that the old routinely hang fire. Life and literature are filled with instances of active oldsters, and that is fine. But let there be a great difference in age between partners, and these matters are apt to receive a dif-ferent coloration. We know that traditional patriarchal societies confer substantial sexual rights to males even into old age, whether in Western or other cultures. Older women's sexual rights seem a more vexed issue, often subject to (male) censure. One feels that nature itself is of the party here, seems to want the young to mate with the young, so as to produce the fittest offspring. All the in-gredients of a plot are in place here: how to curb the lust of the old, so as to keep procreation on track and coerce the old into with-drawal. Once again we see the injunction to exit the stage, and once again we see that these matters are rarely simple or easy to take for the old.

Molière

The story of lusting old men has been told forever, and almost always for laughs, not tears. It is the staple item of comedy in Molière, where invariably an old male trying to hold on to power has designs on the damsel of the play, only to be predictably, often hilariously, sometimes movingly, undone by nature's own plot of proper mating: the young belong together; the old should have the decorum, if not the wisdom, to bow out of this game. One sees this most vividly in his *L'école des femmes*, where Arnolphe's lust for the young girl he has brought up and maintained in utter ignorance, covetously saving her for marriage with him, runs afoul of reality: Agnès, devoid of learning though she is, is instructed by her own senses about the sexual attraction of the young and its natural corollary, the dearth of appeal of the old. She blossoms and, by play's end, displays considerable pluck as she asserts the "rightness" of her feelings. But Arnolphe follows a different trajectory, one of increasing desperation as his control project runs into ever more trouble. It is as if Arnolphe were progressively blinded, Agnès progressively sighted. This is love's egalitarian work.

It is also literature's work. The old in Molière are *not* wise, fall ever further into mania and obsession, become increasingly pathological and disturbing figures. And the young grow in self-awareness and self-possession, becoming ever more aware of the stakes of the game, of biological and social seriousness underneath the plot of errors and deceptions and self-deceptions leading finally to seeing clear. *L'école des femmes* can be seen or read in the course of a few hours, but those few hours trace a remarkable evolution in each of the principal figures: the maniacal old man and the naive maiden each undergoing a transformation in front of our eyes.

All this would simply be funny—which is how Molière must have initially seen it—but it moves into something darker as Arnolphe genuinely suffers from his desire. There is one late moment where he is begging the girl to consent to his needs, and he simply explodes with hunger: *"Sans cesse, nuit et jour, je te caresserai, / Je te bouchonnerai, baiserai, mangerai"* ("Constantly, night and day, I will caress you, fondle you, kiss you, devour you").

This irruption of *tu* into the man's otherwise formal speech, this unstoppable display of unseemly, eruptive appetite, is harsh medicine for the man speaking it, and his next lines have an almost tragic ring to them, for they could have been written by Racine: *"Jusqu'où la passion peut-elle faire aller?"* ("How far can passion move us?") And, not unlike Racine, Molière understands to perfection how desire reveals us to ourselves. This was true for Romeo and Juliet, for Des Grieux, for Catherine Earnshaw and Jane Eyre, for Duras's girl protagonist. But whereas love opened a door for them and propelled them through, it is destined to close one for Molière's older man, to educate him into sentience and then to dispose of him, so the young can mate.

This play disturbed Molière's contemporaries, for they sensed that he was muddying the genres, that an old lecher who actually hurt was at once laughable and not entirely laughable. We know enough about Molière's own marital and erotic problems—not only did he marry a very young actress, but he himself invariably acted the role of the cuckold onstage—to feel that this drama had a personal tinge and a special bite. He cuts, I think, an interesting and appealing figure: in play after play, year after year, he mocks the foibles of the old and unloved, the elders who try to resist nature's plan, the stubborn ones who don't have the smarts to let go—finally—of the money or the girl. But one wonders if this theme eventually got under his skin. We are aware that he died shortly after performing the role of Argan, his great hypochondriac in *Le malade imaginaire,* but I can't help feeling that illness and sexual disfavor merged in his mind as the cardinal indignity of staying alive too long.

But I want to close on the comic, not the tragic, side of things. What is fascinating in these comedies is the deep knowledge they display of mania and obsession and the still-deeper conviction that nature's sweet laws must in the end be obeyed. Descartes had proclaimed that *le bon sens* is egalitarian, to be found everywhere among thinking humans; Molière, the connoisseur of libido and creator of utterly delusional characters, reorients this confidence in sanity by ascribing it to the ways of the universe and the turns of his plot. The old will be brought into line. Their feverish longings will not be honored forever. They will be coerced into deco-

rum. And we laugh, even if the older among us have trouble forgetting the amount of pain and heartbreak that may go into "natural selection."

Hamlet Accusing Gertrude

As we saw in the discussion of *King Lear*, there is at times an outright horror of female sexuality, of generation itself, in Shakespeare, most notably seen in Lear's crazed vision of the prudish
old lady who, below the waist, is given over to the centaurs and
the fiends, possessing a vagina characterized by burning, scalding,
stench, and consumption. Such a phobic vision seems present to
me in *Hamlet* as well, as we see in the young prince's savage indictment of his mother's unseemly behavior. Gertrude scarcely
qualifies as old in our eyes, but her son does not see it that way, and
he wastes no words in spelling out to her how obscene it is for a
lady of her years to indulge her sexual appetites. "You cannot call
it love, for at your age / The heyday in the blood is tame, it's humble," he suavely explains to Mom. In case she doesn't get the
point—but she does, she begs him to cease, she is looking inward
at the "black and grainèd spots" on her soul—he turns up the heat
and proffers this account of her activities with Claudius: "Nay but
to live / In the rank sweat of an enseamèd bed, / Stewed in corruption, honeying and making love / Over the nasty sty." He will
speak daggers to her, he told us; and he has. We are not far from
torture.

Not only is this sadistic, but it seems more than a little
voyeuristic as well, as if Mother's sexual behavior were mesmerizing, had a steaminess and carnal rankness that could be neither
brooked nor gotten past by her son. His words have a breathy heat
that gets our attention as well as hers. But is it fair? We are made
to see Gertrude's "betrayal," and so much else, from Hamlet's own
perspective of nausea and disgust, but one would like to know
more about the queen's fuller predicament, fuller response. It has
been pointed out that both she and Claudius have their deeply
human side, have deep feelings for each other, even if Hamlet
himself is venomous and unforgiving on their score. So the young
man perseveres, shames her into submission. To what end? To be

sure, she is repentant and promises to change, but change what? To give up Claudius? Or to give up sex altogether? Perhaps she too should get herself to a nunnery? Lady, your time is up.

A contrast with Molière may be illuminating. Arnolphe must be removed so that Agnès can marry someone "proper," someone her age. One might claim that Hamlet's rage also has to do with nature being contravened, since presumably the sex between Gertrude and Claudius will not yield an heir, but I feel that her real offense is different: what is unacceptable (to her son!) is a mother's libido, an older woman's libido. The familiar argument that Hamlet has an Oedipal complex makes no sense to me, since he is filled with sexual revulsion for both women, Gertrude and Ophelia, as if female sexuality itself were the serpent in the kingdom.

Jean Racine's Phèdre

Arguably the most famous figure of older female lust in classical literature is Phaedra. It is instructive to contrast Euripides' version of the woman who desired her stepson with that of Racine, who dealt with these same matters more than twenty-one centuries later. In the Greek play *Hippolytus* Phaedra herself is a virtuous woman who is utterly altered by Aphrodite in her ongoing warfare with Artemis; the goddesses are duking it out, hence the goddess of love smites a decent woman (in order to punish someone else altogether) and transforms her into someone aflame for Theseus's son Hippolytus, her own stepson. One sees absolutely no volition or collusion here on Phaedra's part, no psychic or libidinal truth, as it were: it is the dirty trick of the gods. But Racine significantly keeps the gods and goddesses offstage, and even though his Phèdre wails to the gods and indicts Venus for her burning desire—"*C'est Vénus toute entière à sa proie attachée*" she shrieks in a famous line that evokes the goddess of love as predator battening onto prey—one cannot avoid the realization that this play is taking place at ground zero, at the base level of human flesh, and that the gods are essentially just the names we give to the elemental feelings that course through us and sometimes destroy us. Phèdre too is not old, but Racine has taken the step of adding a nubile *young* girl—Aricie—to his cast of characters, as if to underscore the impropriety—indeed, the obscenity—of this older woman wanting this younger man. One of the strongest things in the play is how both Phèdre and Hippolyte feel dirtied by the lady's desire. Let the young mate with the young.

But what we remember this play for is its magnificent depiction of a mature woman's physical desire for a beautiful young man who is also her stepson. There is in Toni Morrison's *Beloved* an almost throwaway line about Paul D's innate grasp of female sentiment, including late lust: "Strong women and wise saw him and told him things they only told each other: that way past the Change of Life, desire in them had suddenly become enormous, greedy, more savage than when they were fifteen, and that it embarrassed them and made them sad; that secretly they longed to die—and to be quit of it." Racine wrote in the 1670s what that enormous, greedy, savage feeling was like, and the woman who feels it speaks it openly to her confidante Oenone and covertly to Hippolyte himself. This is what it felt like when she saw the proud, virile young male (so much more desirable than his famous, famously womanizing, but much older father, Theseus): *"Je le vis, je rougis, je pâlis à sa vue; / Un trouble s'éleva dans mon âme éperdue; / Mes yeux ne voyaient plus, je ne pouvais parler; / Je sentis tout mon corps et transir et brûler."* This language hisses. The economy of French classical verse, with its Alexandrine metrics and rhyme scheme, is in the service of a physiological, almost clinical vision. I saw him, I reddened, I turned pale, darkness rose in my lost soul, my eyes could not see, I could not speak, I felt my body freeze and burn. Note how this reverses the venerable truism that men gaze at women's bodies; here the desiring woman is almost transmogrified with lust by looking at the young male.

To the boy himself she is, in her remarks, initially, understandably under cover. When they meet, he sees she is moved, aroused, but she claims her longings are for Theseus. Yet it is not any Theseus we know but rather someone *"fier,"* *"même un peu farouche,"* *"charmant,"* *"jeune"* (!): proud, even ferocious, charming, young. Thus begins one of the most sinuous and haunting love evocations in Western literature. (Euripides avoids this scene altogether by having the confidante tell Hippolytus of his stepmother's feelings.) Phèdre reinvents the myth of Theseus and the Labyrinth, and the result is a shimmering spectacle of substitutions and displacements. At first she invokes Hippolyte as the replacement for his famous father: Hippolyte is now imagined to be the monster slayer, the man who made his way into the maze, armed only with Ariadne's thread. But this feverish desire is followed by its still more feverish counterpart, the crucial second substitution that now puts Phèdre herself into the Labyrinth, paired with her young lover, teaching him how to explore its sinuous reaches and depths: *"C'est moi, prince, c'est moi, dont l'utile secours / Vous eût du Labyrinthe enseigné les detours."* (Twice the first person bursts forth—me! me!—"I would have taught you about the twists and turns of the maze to be penetrated.") And even this vaginal discourse does not say it all, for the final desire is for darkness itself, for an ecstatic lostness together: the older woman and the young man, descended into the pit, forever united, never to return: *"Et Phèdre au Labyrinthe avec vous descendue / Se serait avec vous retrouvée, ou perdue."* This bold yet exquisite mythic venture into the dark realm rewrites a woman's longing as a dream of coupling, of going further and further into the bowels of the universe, penetrating—being penetrated?—ever more deeply. *Jouissance* and orgasmic pleasure are not only the goal, they may be said to be scripting the entire delirious speech itself as the older woman lets fly.

Even the obtuse Hippolyte senses that this is not kosher. One need not be an expert on Greek mythology to see in Phèdre's crazed yearnings not only a reformulation of the myth via substitutions but a transformation of the burning woman into the monster itself, the Minotaur who famously lodges in the heart of the maze. Racine's play does full justice to this motif, and Phèdre is insistently imaged as a monster to be slain. (After her declaration, she points to her breast—bares her breast in some stagings—and orders Hippolyte to strike, to slay that monster; she even takes his sword, a gesture that Freudians have not failed to comment on.) At play's end, Hippolyte himself will both kill and be destroyed by the actual sea monster, who materializes as if to show that sexual desire is the beast that cannot be conquered or kept in the dark. And Phèdre herself finally commits suicide, reclaiming a kind of lost purity as the poison enters her veins, indicting sexual hunger as the flaw in the Creation, the pollution that must be found and purged, so that her death might cleanse the heavens, *"rendre au ciel toute sa pureté."*

It has been argued by critics that Racine is the supreme analyst of female love, the man who found language for a kind of brutal, affective realism that is new to literature, certainly new to French classical tragedy. Yet there is something horribly punitive about this play. As the author himself wrote in his preface, desire itself—as opposed to acting on desire—is coded as evil and rebuked by everything Racine can throw at it. After all, Phèdre herself wants only to die at the play's beginning, anything other than to reveal her feelings. We can ascribe some of this severity to the playwright's leanings toward Jansenism—a virulent Catholic religious sect (in which he was brought up) that damned the flesh and its desires—but we cannot avoid seeing here an indictment of woman, of an older woman in the throes of passion. The soma is shockingly present in this play, despite the elegance of the verse and the decorum of the dramaturgy. The body speaks its imperious needs: through blushing, panting, burning. Of course language matters too. Once spoken, passion acquires an unstoppable, unorientable life of its own, catalyzing feelings, engendering actions that none could have premeditated or even considered possible when the curtain first lifts. Once spoken, words can never be recalled. Theseus will learn this hard lesson. The animal will out, labryinth or not. And in its romp there will be much destruction.

Yet readers of *Phèdre* will not easily forget the sheer moral scope and dimensionality of its heroine, whom love chose. In contrast to her ever-growing lucidity, the other figures of the play seem both blind and puppetlike, going through their motions but unattuned to the world they inhabit or that inhabits them. Yes, the virtuous Hippolyte is initiated into the pangs of love, but he never has a clue to the conflagration that is his stepmother. The great Theseus seems to yearn, even at the play's bloody close, for more darkness, for some escape from truth and light. Lear understood, at story's end, the savage and lethal histrionics of power, causing him to discover and inhabit a subject position he could never have imagined: bare, forked animal. Phèdre's pilgrimage seems no less momentous, even if her knowledge is of a different kind.

Phèdre has not only drained the cup, she has gone the route, has moved through the very landscape of desire via her reenactment of the myth, right to the calamitous moment of its brutal undoing, its collision course with reality. And even that is not all. Urged by her confidante to slander Hippolyte before he slanders her, she initially moves in that direction. She had thought this disciple of Artemis impervious to women altogether, but now she learns that he loves Aricie, and this is intolerable. *"Hippolyte est sensible, et ne sent rien pour moi!"* He has feelings, but feels nothing for me! With this discovery, her voyage continues, and masochism takes over entirely: not only does the fierce young man have sexual urgings, but he's probably an easy catch, probably loves many other women, probably loves all women *except* Phèdre. Here is the generative algebra of sexual paranoia, the kind of thing that led Othello to muse that Desdemona's "sweet body" might perhaps be known to the entire army. Rage ensues: for *this* crime he must die. She must dirty him before he does it to her. It is not pretty.

But she imagines, as well, an Edenic love for this young couple—so different from how Racine has depicted them, for Hippolyte is anything but proud of his appetite, feels almost defiled by it—as if Eden had come into being as the lost, utterly fantasized homeland of those exiled to Hell. *"Tous les jours se levaient clairs et sereins pour eux."* Each of their days is clear and serene. Told that the young lovers will not get away with it, that they will be caught and punished and even killed, Phèdre sublimely counters, *"Ils s'aimeront toujours."* They will love forever. Not unlike the ecstatic descent into the Labyrinth, we see here a dream of innocent lovemaking, of desire sanctioned, of desire gratified forever. The borders of the play are being expanded almost beyond recognition, as Racine charts the landscape of the soul: not what it gets but what it wants yet cannot have. Is age significant here? Yes. This is an older person's plaint about craving more from life than she has received. There is wistfulness, perhaps even nostalgia, as well as bitterness and outright mania in Phèdre's imagined Eden, an Eden for the young. It's not that Racine bears a grudge against the old but that Phèdre is on the wrong side of the divide, that her yearnings are unnatural in more ways than one.

That is why I insist on this woman's lucidity as one of her claims to greatness: she sees it all, sees the entire dark machinery of lust and revenge that is driving her, sees her own actions as taking place on a larger stage, one that includes the gods, her ancestors. Thus, in midimprecation against the offending couple, she stops, looks up, takes measure, realizes to the full just what she is doing, just what she has become. *"Je respire à la fois l'inceste et l'imposture. / Mes homicides mains, promptes à me venger, / Dans le sang innocent brûlent de se plonger. / Misérable! Et je vis? Et je soutiens la vue / De ce sacré soleil dont je suis descendue?"* It is one of the great recognition moments in literature. It has none of the self-servingness that one detects even in Oedipus and Othello as they confront their actions at play's end. Instead, this woman sees herself as the miasma, the living proof of a wrecked world: she breathes incest and deceit; her hands want to plunge into human flesh, burn to do so, reminding us of ancient sacrifice, primitive rites. How can it be? she asks. A granddaughter of the sun itself, mythically, she is a blot against the light, even as she creates more and more light, unbearable light, illuminating every nook and cranny of her libidinal wants, beyond anything that, say, Ibsen will do in his light-obsessed theater. Her crime? Sexual desire.

I quite realize that a seventeenth-century tragedy about an older woman's forbidden desire for her stepson may well seem out of step with today's cultural assumptions and views about sexuality. And I am the first to admit, even to emphasize, the extreme severity of Racine's vision. Yet I feel this play has no rivals when it comes to depicting the landscape of desire and the mechanics of both jealousy and injury. Phèdre's reenactment of the descent into the Labyrinth with her young lover—an erotic journey possible only as ecstatic dream scenario, a scenario slated to be smashed to pieces by the male's horrified rejection—stands as one of the great formulations in our literature about the dimensionality, the cartography, of feeling, the yearned-for, even if censored, fusion that is not to be. Is this not the terrain of art: to chart a territory that is true to the magnitude of our longings even if it is never to be actualized?

Likewise, I find her anguished certainty that Hippolyte and Aricie loved innocently, were free to love forever, even beyond death, no less stirring and unforgettable as testimony about the workings of human longing and its sibling, jealousy: when we cannot have what we desire, we all too easily imagine others, especially hated rivals, having it all. As readers of the play, we know how erroneous Phèdre's fantasies are: the young lovers are as ill fated as she is, and Hippolyte is almost as guilt-ridden as she is. So what? She projects onto them exactly the pleasure and ease that will never be her portion. Jealousy is horribly creative. It may be that rebuffed desire knows no age, but I sense in Phèdre's grand twisted emotions, in her dashed hopes and self-flagellation, in her being inflamed by a beautiful young man, something particularly cued to her moment in time, akin to a dawning awareness that she is on the far side of things. She has exceeded her rights. To burn, as she has burned, as she still burns, is pollution, is a crime against nature and cosmos. At play's end, she, dying, and Theseus, haunted by his murderous oath, both know that the world is darkening, the story of love has come to an end.

A final word on this ravaged woman. She is admittedly no matriarch, and she certainly botches her son's chances for the throne, so I can scarcely claim political clout for her. But she is a queen. And even if she suffers horribly, she has a kind of sheer authority that dwarfs all the other characters, including her legendary husband, Theseus. I have noted both her lucidity and the magnitude of her desire, but I want also to say that she simply radiates power, even when it is in the form of agony: she cannot choose not to love, but otherwise hers are the supreme acts of the play, hers the governance of events, including her own self-removal. She is the mesmerizing figure of the drama, and her affairs turn out to be those of the cosmos. Her grand mythic aria about descending into the Labyrinth with her youthful lover is a testament to the greatness of her soul.

Fyodor Dostoevsky's The Brothers Karamazov

The Greeks followed their tragedies with a satyr play, and I will do likewise. Racine's Phèdre is a tragic character of immense dignity, but the desires of the old are often enough the subject of ridicule. Doubtless the prizewinning old satyr in literature is Fyodor Karamazov. He is also a doomed father. Dostoevsky reprises the Oedipal drama but in grotesque fashion. If Oedipus unknowingly killed his father, Fyodor's son Dmitri expresses, from the outset, an unbearable loathing for his progenitor, whom the author describes in meticulous detail: bags under his little, leering eyes; huge, fleshy Adam's apple; at once sensual and repulsive. Repeatedly, Dmitri warns us that he just might kill the old man. Of course, all readers come to understand that Dmitri is innocent of the parricide, that Smerdyakov is the actual murderer, and that Dmitri's brother Ivan will be posited as the "secret sharer" in the slaying: technically innocent, psychically guilty. It seems amazing, given how much he's hated, that the old guy lives as long as he does.

But Dostoevsky needs the sexual rivalry between father and son if his plot is to hold water. And we must confess that Fyodor does hold up his end as womanizing lecher right on through. "Even in the whole of my life there's never been an ugly woman for me," he proudly tells his sons and then goes on to flesh out the theory by expatiating on his manner of taking (sexually) his late wife "by surprise"; this little strategy is spelled out as a mix of crawling, cringing, and commanding—guaranteed to set the woman off into shrieking spells; she's called the "shrieker"—closing with juicier forms of warfare, such as spitting on the lady's crucifix, causing her to collapse straight out. All this is offered as conversation with his children.

To be sure, Dmitri cannot stomach him as a rival for Grushenka's favors, but we readers of the book find ourselves sometimes savoring this old man's incorrigible prurience. Only he would cite Scripture to the Elder Zosima in the following fashion: " 'Blessed is the womb that bare thee and the paps which thou hast sucked'—the paps especially!" Keep your eye on the ball, or the paps, seems to be his motto. Karamazov sensuality is cited over and over as a signature family trait, to be found (in different guises) in all of the old man's sons. Yes, the novel tackles the great metaphysical debates of the nineteenth century, but the rendition of Fyodor—his egalitarian lust for women, his unflagging sexual energies, his bid for Grushenka, his malicious view of all the book's pieties (as shown in his delicious account of the "hooks" of

Hell, which are supposed to drag him down to perdition; Which hooks? he asks; Where do they make them? Is there a hook factory down there?)—remains in our minds as a zaftig portrait of impudent, old, unbending testosterone slated, yes, for execution, but getting a number of laughs on the way.

What can it mean to enjoy, as a reader, a character who fully deserves to be taken down? I think old Karamazov appeals to the lawbreaker in us, for he is the man who mocks all pieties, including the existential ones that his author takes seriously. Given the stupendous amount of metaphysical jousting in this novel, given the hyperspirituality of Father Zosima and company, we groundlings are perhaps a bit grateful for the dependable maliciousness of Fyodor, the guy with the salty tongue and riotous appetites, the fellow who incorporates id into the Dostoevskian scheme. He is the novel's chthonic figure, a sensualist of a different stripe from his son Dmitri, an older man who seems redolent of brandy, earth, flesh, semen, and feces. But die he must. So it is that his murder becomes the grand nineteenth-century showpiece of detective fiction, the whodunnit that fuels the entire novel, the emblematic removal of the father. Who knows, he might have been happy to know what an ambitious fate was in store for him.

Thomas Mann's Death in Venice

Lusty Fyodor Karamazov's death is predictable: joker, buffoon, lecher, failed father, despised target of most of his sons; there are plenty of reasons for him to exit the stage. Thomas Mann's elderly male hero, undone by a fateful trip to Venice, my final instance of unsanctioned lust, represents a very different kind of sexual overreaching. This famous tale from 1911 seems, when read in the twenty-first century, curiously dated by its marmoreal style and its many overwritten passages yet remarkably prescient as well, for it not only speaks openly of homosexual passion but is susceptible to a "pedophiliac" reading (as was noted in part I of this study). An aging man—widower, father of a married daughter, national icon of German literature whose work epitomizes the virtues of clarity, discipline, and reason—falls in love with a Polish boy while on vacation in Venice: Is this a story of growing old? Or is it a view of aging as a grisly form of truth telling, of truth "outing," about one's most basic intincts and arrangements? Do we lie to ourselves all the way till the end and only then confront who we are? Do all our efforts and dodges and feints and attempts at mastery simply evaporate or unravel when we age? What remains then? Mann's story asks these questions.

William Burroughs once quipped that a well-run police state would need no police, because we do it to ourselves. Hence Gustav von Aschenbach is a culture hero (of severe morality, of contempt for the "bohemian") who has proudly and publicly and influentially said no to the abyss. It has never occurred to him that he might one day be headed there. And not by accident or by bad luck or by some evil call of fate but as the grisly but logical consequence of his own deepest artistic and philosophical beliefs. It all began on a spring day in Munich when the famous writer, tired, goes to the North Cemetery on his walk and sees a strange man who stares at him with unconcealed boldness, exposing "long, white, glistening teeth." This encounter then triggers a hallucinatory vision of a "primeval wilderness-world of islands, morasses, and alluvial channels," a tropical setting rife with monstrous growth, causing Aschenbach to feel both fear and longing. This is all a bit heavy-handed, I suppose, but it functions nonetheless as handwriting on the wall: cemetery, male hunger, raw and rank and fertile nature, yielding a composite message to our man: you are to choose between death and life, but the life you choose (the life that is about to choose you) is going to be anarchic, primitive, and utterly contrary to the denials and repudiations you've glorified so long. Aschenbach's response to all this? Time for a vacation, time to go to Venice.

The ominous signposts and markers start to pile up, and they signal especially the portentous drama of age. On the boat he sees a party of riotous young people, all absorbed in drinking and carousing, but the closer he looks, the more certain he is that the loudest of the group is no youth at all: he is an old man, with rouge on his cheeks, dyed mustache, and false teeth. Later, still more darkly, he notes that the pretender cannot hold his alcohol, that he stutters and giggles and leers, that he is more than a little obscene. What Aschenbach cannot know, of course, is that this figure in disguise is exactly what he himself will become. It will all come to pass. Late in the story, when Aschenbach has doubtless already contracted the cholera that will technically kill him, he nonetheless signs on for whatever cosmetic aids he can get in his hopeless effort to woo the Polish boy Tadzio: he has his hair dyed black, his skin "freshened up," his "dry, anemic lips" turned the color of "ripe strawberries," the lines around his eyes are treated with facial cream. It is thus, trumped up in garish colors, a clown pretending to roll back the clock and retrieve the accents of youth and vigor, that he will die on the beach, still hoping to capture Tadzio's gaze, waging his final war against time, succumbing.

What makes this story so rich and provocative is that Aschenbach's trajectory from hero of discipline to pining old man is larded with echoes, has a reach beyond its apparent bounds. One sees in it a reworking of Nietzsche's famous theory of the Apollonian and the Dionysian (as argued in *The Birth of Tragedy*), so that Aschenbach's late-life encounter with bestiality and frenzy are to be understood as an overdue corrective to his severely classicizing view of art (and life). His cult of form as containment—which is how Nietzsche saw Greek tragedy: as a formal frame with chaos inside—is reconceived. Still another perspective has to do with Venice itself—a lush, romantic site of dark lagoons and throbbing desire, a place where the frail structures of order and decorum might easily come undone—suggesting that this vacation is also a rebuke to the austere earlier ethos of the writer. And then there is the issue of plague itself, an imperious onslaught of disease and rot and decay and sickness that visits Venice at exactly this juncture and thereby functions as the precise analog to Aschenbach's own rotten erotic secret of lust for a young boy. All these threads are woven into Mann's text. Now, one might demur and claim that these different versions of Aschenbach's "fall" are awfully literary, awfully symbolic; but I'd want to claim just the opposite: Mann has sketched this older man's climacteric in a stunningly rich fashion, and thereby shown us that the assault of sexual desire upon the old is a multilayered event, reaching further than just some kind of libidinal itch or lecherous want or delayed coming out of the closet.

On the contrary, Aschenbach may well be a professional stu-

dent of beauty, finding in the exquisite Tadzio a perfect embodiment of the harmony and grace he has worshipped all his life, but
I'd claim he stands thereby for all of us older people, all of us on
the far side of physical perfection, on the downward slope of our
own somatic careers. That's not all: this man's reverence for form
is quite simply exploding on him, for he is now realizing that the
human body displays beauty and order in a way that dwarfs the
creations of art itself. And even that's not all: the most lovely poem
or statue or sonata invites our admiration, but lovely bodies invite
something more: our desire. Aschenbach is indeed hoisted by his
own petard, inasmuch as his cult of beauty is completely, even if
unhingingly, actualized in this fetching young boy outfitted with
so many charms. Is it not utterly logical for the old to desire the
young, for those who are on the wane to lust after those who are
rising? This is not the warfare that shines through so many of our
plots but something rather different: desire.

Forget, for a moment, moral scruples, and you see life itself
shining in this story: life as physical grace, as a corporeal form of
perfection that our species attains only early, only briefly, and then
is condemned to distance itself ever further from. And consider
how shrewd, ingenious, and tactical civilization has been in dealing with this war against entropy: we speak of maturity, of wisdom, of intellectual and professional and material attainments
that somehow right the balance, keep us in the "plus" camp, even
as our bodies age and wither. Mann is calling the bluff on all this.
His story says: our trade-offs, our denials, our sublimations, our
projections, our substitutions, they all fail at some point. They fail
to make us happy, they fail to shield us from the mesmerizing, in-
cendiary spectacle of physical beauty, they fail to extinguish desire, to banish appetite.

Gustav von Aschenbach is paying the bills that accrue from inhabiting a body. He is held hostage to a magnetic force that is as
natural as sunlight. In his particular instance, the issue of same-
sex desire is also in play, and, astonishingly enough, it seems to
make little difference, for the generic issues themselves are so
despotic and naked. Many have seen in this story a tragic outcome:
a humiliation for the great artist, a mockery of his earlier achievements, a sinister and ultimately fatal apprenticeship with secrecy

and rot and disease. But one can also argue it the other way: in Venice, on the last stage he is to inhabit, Aschenbach moves from denial to assent, from asceticism to pleasure, from dying to living. He finds himself large with desire, even (until the very end) with energy and interest and human vitality. Yes, he dies, but he feasts upon the spectacle of carnal beauty right up to the end, and even though it may indeed wreck his moral and ideological schemes, even though it rebukes all he thought he stood for, it is nonetheless testament to a final reverence for the vibrancy and irresistible appeal and goodness of the flesh. What moral lessons, what lessons for living, we are to derive from such a view is a thorny issue I'll leave to my readers to decide.

Arnolphe, Gertrude, Phèdre, Fyodor, Aschenbach: they do not go gently into the night, they do not willingly renounce desire, they do not hallow either culture's or nature's injunctions about sexual propriety. Their stories all finish badly—each is punished, burned—yet it is not all that easy to fault them for wanting to remain at life's feast. Blake proclaimed that the poet is always of the Devil's party, and I'd like to reorient this by saying that desire has rights. I choose exactly this phrase because we shall see it reappear at the end of this study as the cardinal belief of J. M. Coetzee's protagonist David Lurie, and it will be blown sky-high. Then we will have occasion to explore what kind of values and aspirations for the old might lie on the far side of desire.

The Final Harvest

We reap what we sow, says the Good Book. I have always read those words as a kind of threat: the evil you do will come back to haunt you. Obviously, one can also read this truism in a more angelic fashion: the good we do returns to us. In this light all our deeds, perhaps even our desires, are possessed of a kind of longevity that surprises, that is destined to remain alive, that may become destiny itself. (Oedipus certainly thought that his slaying of a violent old man at a crossroads was a mere detail in his life, an event that would have no shadows or repercussions.) One might well be frightened by the sowing/reaping scheme—there is something to be said for things being forgotten, for things dying, for thoughts and deeds being short-lived or ephemeral—but on the whole it seems to me a deeply affirmative view of life. Indeed, the phrase itself bespeaks an organic regime, cued to sowing and harvesting, and it tells us that existence keeps its books, that a human trajectory through time is a gathering proposition, larded with seeds and promise and futurity, consisting of gestures and sentiments that bear fruit, that are there for the long term.

I call this affirmative, because it seems especially seductive as a way of seeing old age. That is why I title this part of my book "The Final Harvest." Old age ought to be a time of harvest. After all, we have spent our lives becoming who we are, and this late phase should be a chapter of self-possession. I want this to be understood broadly: if you've spent your life learning to be a carpenter or a farmer or a lawyer or a doctor or a professor or a scientist or a businessman, well, then, you have earned your laurels and should be positioned more or less at your peak. If you've committed decades to being a loving spouse or parent or child, you are entitled to believe those achievements solid, not whimsical. Seems logical. And it is scarcely fanciful to extend this further still: you're now a grandparent or a respected elder, you've traversed many of life's central experiences, you now encounter many people younger than you, you are properly expected to know things; so shouldn't you possess some kind of existential authority? You've put in your time. Surely any serene or happy view of growing old must buy into this quasi-organic model. Yes, our body may well go, but the compensation is that we have acquired experience, perhaps even wisdom.

Experience. Remember Blake's famous dyad of innocence and experience. Growing-up stories are almost inevitably cued to this dialectic, as the careers of Pablos, Simplicius, Rastignac, Jane Eyre, Pip, Huck, Celie, and so many others demonstrate. But the experience of the young is a briefer proposition than the experience of the old. In fact, one could say that we go through our entire lives adding to our ever-growing stock of experience, and toward journey's end, shouldn't we have an impressive tool kit for assessing life, for pronouncing judgment? And wouldn't old age be exactly the time for mature reflection? The final gathering? In this chapter we will examine a spectrum of works that all ask, directly or indirectly, sweetly or savagely, What do life's experiences add up to?

The Final Harvest as Mirage

What if there is no harvest in old age? What if you don't recognize it as such? You may have no clue as to what you sowed. All too often, the only way we ever realize what we've prepared for ourselves is when disaster comes: lung cancer follows smoking, cirrhosis of the liver follows drinking, angry children follow . . . well, that's trickier, but some kind of logic must be there. All too often, you understand the causes only after you encounter the effects. Sowing is perhaps the most invisible activity of our species. But still other gnawing questions arise: in today's technologically oriented world, time works against you, not for you. You become less knowledgeable, less informed, less able to keep up. Solness was done building; Willy Loman became obsolete. This can be legion at the university, my place of work: the old (me included) are still holding forth about issues and notions that they absorbed early on in their studies or careers but that may have become outmoded or dismissed decades ago. Paradigms do shift, even if people often stay rigid.

But all these scenarios are downright rosy in contrast to other horrors that may foul the desired harvest. Here are some outcomes to consider. Old age teaches you that you've never lived at all. Old age exposes the nullity of your life, the wrongness of your choices, the hollowness of your convictions, the obliteration of your self-image. Old age exposes you as a ghost. And there is another variant of this nightmarish view: old age exposes your life as trompe l'oeil, as tinsel facade, as shadow play, as charade. Now, this is grisly, yet it happens all the time, in both literature and life, but the catch is: it comes only in the last chapters. Didn't Lear experience this? Didn't Goriot? Didn't Aschenbach? (All of them were doing just fine, thank you, up to the moment we meet them and watch them implode.) At the end the curtain goes up, and what it reveals is unbearable. It is as if life made a terrible bargain at the time of our birth: we will go our merry way, do the best we can, feel that we are managing, perhaps even thriving, only to have the rug pulled out from us at the end, learn that it has all been shadow play, delusion.

Sadistic as these matters seem—and I have tried to accentuate their melodrama—they contain their own special *son et lumière*. The forking path of a life in time that we encounter in literature is not without lessons for us who are making our way. Thus we have much to learn from the subversive texts that make up this chapter: Ibsen's late play *When We Dead Awaken,* Henry James's novella *The Beast in the Jungle,* Kafka's echoing parable "Before the Law," Bergman's heartbreaking film *Wild Strawberries,* all of these are about the sometimes corrosive discoveries of old age, including the view that maturity and accomplishment may be, in the last analysis, a mirage. These literary texts belong here because they shed a bold and shattering light on our own habits and assumptions. Once again, art enables us to imagine futures we cannot afford to experience. There are lessons here.

Discovering That You've Never Lived: Henrik Ibsen

As said, the most seductive view about growing old is that it is a time of harvest, of possessing your life and experience, of seeing it in the round, of acquiring wisdom. Living into your seventies and eighties only to learn that you got it all wrong is a ghastly idea. As Bogart says in *Casablanca,* regarding the absence of the sea, "I was misinformed." Are we misinformed? The question is unanswerable, since today's certainties can be tomorrow's exposed fantasies, since we may not yet have received the bad news.

Henrik Ibsen's last play offers a rather grimmer assessment of these matters. The plot of *When We Dead Awaken* hinges on the recovery of the past, in particular, the return of the sculptor Arnold Rubek's former love/model, who was, in all ways, key to his great artistic success. She left, we learn, because Rubek had "used" her for his art while denying her in her humanity; i.e., she had posed naked for him over and over, and he had responded via his sculpture but never touched her in the flesh. Since her departure, Rubek has gained fame but somehow lost his way, become ever more the cynic, but now—years and years later—her return into his life betokens the possibility of future creative work, for she alone has the key to his genius. And we sense already how this play is going to end: Rubek and Irene will have their final chapter together, yet it will be not on this earth of ours but rather in the ether, that spiritualized realm beyond the mountaintop to which they are headed at play's end.

But it seems to me that Ibsen cuts deeper and more darkly than this spiritual happy ending suggests, and I am particularly struck by an exchange between Irene and Rubek late in the play where the search for freedom and retrieval takes on its starkest hues:

IRENE: We'll see what we've lost only when— *(Breaking off.)*
RUBEK *(with an inquiring look)*: When—?
IRENE: When we dead awaken.
RUBEK *(shakes his head sorrowfully)*: Yes, and what, really, do we see then?
IRENE: We see that we've never lived.

With this remark the curtain lifts, and it lifts onto a vista that is bleaker than any drama of choosing well or choosing badly in one's own life; instead Ibsen shines his beam on life's fundamental cheat, its transformation of experience into nothing, its fierce alchemy that erases us as we go. On this head, aging is especially tragic, for its finest trump card—at last we come into full possession of our lives—is shown to be fraudulent, a joker. Of course, one is free to interpret Ibsen's line mystically, and to claim that the spiritual gaze exposes our material strivings as null, illusory, *maya*. But the full force of this awful perception has, I think, little to do with some higher truth and everything to do with the ongoing theft that life perpetrates on the living, if they live long enough: you look back, and there is nothing there. Wisdom has no purchase here. You discover that you've been a ghost throughout; that all those busy, "full" terms about the arc of time—maturity, understanding, significance, pattern, even legacy—are bogus. You have missed the show, your show.

Yes, we go through our paces, our motions, but when all is said and done, the vault is empty, the purse contains only ashes. What is theatrical is our deep-seated belief that we are heading toward illumination or possession of some sort, that the last act will be a conclusion, a bottom line that will spell out what we have wrought. Here is arguably the species' oldest strategy for offsetting the entropic fate meted out to the body: in mind and in soul, we might recoup what we are destined to lose somatically. No such luck, Ibsen seems to be saying. Theatrical, too, is the very belief in revelation, in a curtain going up, making it miraculously possible to transmute the murk of a lived life into the beautiful cogency of truth, our truth, whether it be emotional or moral or spiritual. That these matters have every bit as much to do with time and growing old as they do with classic religious or philosophical issues is what I now want to argue.

You Missed Your Life: Henry James

To do so, let me reference what I take to be Henry James's most haunting novella, *The Beast in the Jungle*. The story concerns the relationship between John Marcher and May Bartram, a relationship based on a very remarkable covenant that they have established. Marcher confided to Bartram, when first they met in their youth, that he has forever had a secret but overpowering conviction that he was destined for something special in his life, that, as Bartram put it, "something rare and strange, possibly prodigious and terrible," was to befall him. What it might be seemed to matter less than the necessity to be prepared for it, to be on the ready so as not to miss it. And that is to be the solemn, virtually sacred nature of their bond: she pledges to watch with him, an entire lifetime if need be, as partner in his strange "passion play," as faithful friend, indeed as co-sleuth, eyes forever fixed on what time brings, so as to espy the Event when it comes, the Beast whose rendezvous has been ordained.

Time passes. Years pass. They are the fondest of companions, they meet regularly, at the opera, in the city, at her lodgings for meals together; they are ever finely aware of the gap between their private, invisible, unshowable, yet shared intimate conviction and the great wide dense world that knows nothing of it. As the years go by, however, he begins to worry that he may be mistaken or that he may fail to perceive the miracle, so he relies ever more fully on her perspicuity and loyalty, while also sensing that she somehow knows more than he does, something potentially deadly about his aspirations and destiny, but that—out of compassion—she won't tell him.

Then, late in the story, she becomes ill, then worsens, grows ever more feeble, is demonstrably stamped by impending death. James has written their habitual routines in such a manner that we actually feel the texture of their shared life, such as it was, and thus we understand all too well Marcher's anxiety at losing his "coworker" too early, before her labors pay off: "What if she should have to die before knowing, before seeing——?" James offers us several beautifully drawn farewell scenes—she suddenly seems older to him, making him realize that he too is older, that time is pressing on him, making him ever more desperate to get his Vision before it's too late. The final parting is something that gathers, that seems at once brutal and exquisite. He accuses her of being done, of having had her experience, of leaving him to his fate, and he feels dreadfully cheated, for now the door will be shut in his face. She, almost too ill to speak, tells him that the door's still open, looks at him with all her soul, asks the ultimate question: "Don't you know—now?" "I know nothing," he answers. Her maid then assists her out of the room, en route out of his life, yet words are again exchanged, solemn, foreboding words. He: "What has then happened?" She: "What *was* to." James reserves one more encounter, where she repeats that it *has* happened, even though he did not know it, telling him at the end, "I would live for you still—if I could," then adding, as final postscript, "But I can't!" And she doesn't.

At her death, at her funeral, Marcher is full of sorrow, but it is a sorrow that cannot be explained or shared or even made sense of, just as their secret could have no public dimensions, and thus he is treated as a stranger; and he feels himself indissolubly bound to her while being regarded as the merest acquaintance, with no claim to grief. Another year passes, during which he travels to Asia, but he is untouched, beyond reaching, as if already dead, locked out of the secret of his own life. Returned to London, his only place of solace is her grave site, to which he makes regular visits, and it is there that the final Event transpires. It is occasioned by the sight of a younger man—Marcher is quite old now—in the grip of unmasterable grief, wrecked by his loss, ravaged, and this encounter triggers the long-overdue, awful truth: this other man has lived and loved and lost; he, Marcher, has not. The great event he was to have in his life, the event that he missed, was her. "It was the truth, vivid and monstrous, that all the while he had waited the wait was itself his portion." As he then remembers her, "pale, ill, wasted, but all beautiful, and perhaps even then recoverable," at that moment when she had said her fateful and defining truth, her Sphinxlike riddle, "Don't you know?" light at last comes, and the story moves inexorably to its close as the Beast finally leaps upon the man whom it haunted, and he flings himself down, dying, onto her tomb.

Is this a fable about truth or blindness or time or growing old? Doubtless all of the above. "The wait was itself his portion." One doesn't ordinarily think of Beckett when one thinks of Henry James, but I'd argue that *Waiting for Godot*'s depiction of two tramps suspended forever, waiting for the mysterious Godot to appear, is cued to the same chilling, corrosive truth that James is uncovering: that our life, our portion, is waiting. Our apparatus—both perceptual and conceptual—seems to be such that we focus on what we're waiting for and hence neither see nor measure the waiting itself. The doctor's medical report, the lover's response, the employer's reply: these get our attention. James's story whispers to us that we have it wrong, that waiting is weighty in itself, that not only are we blind to the huge significance of waiting, but waiting may itself blind us. Each moment, each week, each year we wait, we move that much closer to death. Waiting suspends life, yes, by postponing decisions, by holding off action, by locking our eyes on a specific target while concealing its own price tag, its own cancerous role in silently consuming our existence. "I have measured out my life in coffee spoons," T. S. Eliot wrote in "The Love-song of J. Alfred Prufrock"; so have we all: coffee spoons and all those other rituals that parse our trip through time. As readers, we are in a tight place, interrogated: Did we see it coming? Did we realize that Marcher had his treasure right there all the time but was blind to it?

The mind itself is targeted here, charged with faulty vision, rebuked for its accounting methods, its hideous capacity to "hold its breath" through long stretches, its propensity for outright error: looking left instead of looking right, checking out minutiae and missing the Main Event. I used to fantasize, in my younger days, that Grace (or some stupendous happiness) would come one fine day (or night) to my life but that I'd be, at just that moment, looking in the other direction and miss its arrival. (You didn't hear the telephone because the water was running. You looked left, but the Promised Land was on the right.) James's story suggests that we could look right at Grace and never see it, because of the tragic misprision that addles our vision, that sees our (potential) loved ones as familiar decor, part of our personal entourage, rather than as vibrant living creatures with whom life might be——might have been——shared. All that is what it means when we discover that we have never lived. It's a late discovery, and it casts a terrible light on the long voyage we have completed prior to seeing. One's past life scarcely disappears in this equation: on the contrary, it is out there in all its monstrous vacuous plenitude, yet fallow, empty, never made "real."

Waiting for the Light: Franz Kafka's "Before the Law"

I claimed that the mind is targeted, even though one might prefer to indict Marcher's heart as the faulty organ, the blind instrument. But are we in fact equipped to give time's passing its proper due? Are we capable of converting waiting into life? One of the nastiest wake-up calls I know on this topic is Kafka's sibylline little parable "Before the Law." In this haunting piece a man from the country arrives at the "Law" but is prevented entry by the doorkeeper on guard, who explains that he cannot be admitted "at the moment." The man proceeds to wait. "There he sits waiting for days and years." Small talk passes between the man and the doorkeeper concerning the doorkeepers farther down the line; bribes are proposed and accepted, "only to keep you from feeling that you have left something undone." The man grows old, grows childish, starts to fade, approaches death, yet glimpses in the darkness a "radiance that streams immortally from the door of the Law." Before dying, he poses one last question to the doorkeeper: How is it that no one during all these years has sought admittance here but me? The answer: "No one but you could gain admittance through this door, since this door was intended only for you. I am now going to shut it."

At which point Kafka begins a kind of extended midrashic analysis of the parable, coming at it from all possible angles, trying to interrogate it for its hidden meaning about life, truth, and salvation. There is much talk about the doorkeeper; much talk about the man; much talk about who is deceived, who is not. But not a word about waiting. Remember the doorkeeper's words when he accepts the bribes: "only to keep you from feeling that you have left something undone." I want to suggest that something monstrous was left undone: the man stopped living; his life became only a wait for truth. Utterly unaccented in this story is the tragic notion that the (maniacal) quest for meaning and truth and salvation blinds us to the passing of time. I see John Marcher in Kafka's story.

Unmasked at the End: Ingmar Bergman's Wild Strawberries

Everyone has heard the adage that no one on his deathbed bemoans not having made enough money or clinched enough deals; instead, one feels regret and remorse and perhaps horror at having shortchanged one's human relationships, at having given all to ambition and not enough to love. It is a pass to which no one growing older can wish to come. But how to avoid it? Can you love enough? Can you see the wastage of your life? What does it take to get this right? When is it too late? Ingmar Bergman's film *Wild Strawberries* seems to me entirely cued to these matters. In this haunting film, the old and venerable physician Isak Borg is scheduled to receive an honorary doctorate at Lund in recognition of a lifetime of selfless achievement. Bergman's plot consists of Isak driving from Stockholm to Lund, with his daughter-in-law, Marianne, as passenger; it's going to be a roller coaster for the old man, who is slated to make some awful discoveries about his life. Enlisting an unforgettable film arsenal of hallucinatory scenes that indict the doctor from every angle, we are made to measure the huge gap between this man's surface manner and appearance (including his appearance to himself) and the nasty psychic reality that is unfurling shot after shot, coming into indicting focus.

Having seen and taught this film literally dozens of times, I find myself invariably on the old doctor's side, as indeed are others in the film: in one key scene a gas station attendant (played by a young Max von Sydow) refuses to take money for filling up the doctor's tank, and we realize that he is indeed a hero for many

many people, making us wonder if Bergman is not being outright punitive in unmasking this kind old man. (It also matters that the old man is played by Victor Sjöström, a famous silent film director, in his own final years; we know that Sjöström was depressed, suffered through this film, repeatedly begged Bergman to let him off.) Finally, I cannot bear to see this old man discover that he "has never lived" or that his seemingly successful life has actually been the fraudulent thing Bergman seems intent on portraying it as. But alas, the film is unflinching on just this front. I look at the screen and find this man irresistibly winning and charming, but then Marianne informs us (the old man and me) that it's just a facade: "You are an old egotist, Father. You are completely inconsiderate, and you have never listened to anyone but yourself. All this is well hidden behind your mask of old-fashioned charm and your friendliness. But you are hard as nails, even though everyone depicts you as a great humanitarian. We who have seen you at close range, we know what you really are. You can't fool us."

Ouch. What hurts most is that Borg himself is utterly stunned by her remark. It has never occurred to him that he might be a hypocrite. Of all those conceivably fooled by his act, he himself takes honors. But Bergman has a lesson plan prepared for the old doctor. It begins with the surreal opening sequences, where we see a nightmarish scene of a horse-drawn wagon with a coffin heading toward the old man, banging into a lamppost, causing the coffin to slide off, followed by the top coming off and a hand slowly rising out of the coffin: this is major rendezvous. As the doctor fearfully looks in, he sees the dread contents: himself as dead— not quite dead, however, since the hand tries to pull him down into the casket. The message is clear: death has come calling, your days are numbered, time to think about your final exit. Or grislier: you are dead; you've always been dead; now you can see it. With those happy tidings in place, the trip to Lund can begin, so as to deliver the next installments. With beautiful economy, the spatial trip through Sweden inaugurates a temporal trip through the old man's past life.

You discover you've never lived. Borg recaptures his past, but with a number of twists. Instead of the Proustian rebirth whereby all of Combray magically emerges out of a cup of tea and a dunked madeleine, the old doctor revisits family haunts, experiences the past coming back to life, but he is weirdly part of the action: an old guy looking in. First off, he sees his lovely cousin Sara (played by Bibi Andersson) betraying him (despite her best intentions) with his raffish older brother, Sigfrid, and we begin to hear the motif that will gather into an indictment: Isak is too otherworldly, too pure, too aloof. This initial scene has as much comedy as pathos in it, but when Sara is teased for kissing Sigfrid, still more data on Isak come in: he is refined, moral, sensitive, kisses only in the dark, talks about sinfulness, seems strangely like a child. Bergman has stacked his deck by inserting a "real" Sara into his road trip: a young girl (also played by Bibi Andersson) with her two boyfriends, who are hitchhiking south and join Borg and Marianne; this creates a lovely counterpoint, for we see the gentle flirtation between the old man and the young girl with the same name and face of his first love, as a kind of coda for the lost past. (We know that Bibi Andersson flirted continously with Sjöström during the filming, partly in response to Bergman's urging, for she was able to get the old actor's tired blood flowing again for the camera, and it shows.)

The next piece of the past comes in the form of a near automobile accident, involving Mr. and Mrs. Alman, who then join the group. They are soon expelled because of their vicious marital fighting, but their work has been done: we see a Strindbergian marriage as snake pit, and we will soon realize that it doubles for Borg's own almost unmentioned marital past, a past that is about to come out of the casket where it's been lodged all these years.

The next installment takes us to Borg's aged mother, living alone with memorabilia of her (largely dead) children, cold as the grave, striking a kind of terror into Marianne, who now sees her husband, Evald, Borg's son, as a lineal descendant of these living-dead people, as she informs Borg in her account of her pregnancy and her battle with Evald, who refuses to be pulled into life, who is waiting for the right moment for suicide. The pieces of the puzzle are falling into place: Bergman's film is about death in life, about the failure to love. This is the obscene secret that makes a mockery of Borg's honorary degree: he is the corpse of the nightmare, a guilty corpse, a corpse with, as it were, cadavers. He has denied love all his life. It's a secret he's not known about. The film sets out to change all that. The next dream/memory sequence has the old man talking again to the Sara of the past, who forces him to look into the mirror—that is what the entire film is about—and gives him the news: "You are a worried old man who will die soon. . . . I'm about to marry your brother, Sigfrid. He and I love each other. . . . Look at your face now. Try to smile!" This scene is almost unbearable to watch, for it consists of a young girl from the past telling an old man what happened in his life, how he either lost or failed love. He tells her, "It hurts." She responds, "You, a professor emeritus, ought to know why it hurts. But you don't. Because in spite of all your knowledge you don't really know anything."

All our advanced degrees, along with our material accomplishments, don't mean zip when it comes to the essentials: Have you lived? Have you loved? If not, why? Why indeed? Isak Borg, en route to an honorary degree, is put through his paces, and the coup de grâce goes right to the vitals, as if the initial gentle, bittersweet prodding and exploration of his weaknesses had been just prep work, leading now to a full-scale assault. Famous doctor? Ha! Just another of the old man's mirages. So Borg is to be examined as a medical student—old man though he is—and he is going to fail spectacularly. Put into the very lecture hall where he formerly taught and gave exams, the doctor is first asked to identify the bacteriological specimen in the microscope; he peers in, adjusts it, but finds nothing except his own eye staring back at him. Next he's asked to read a text on the blackboard, but he can make nothing of it; the examiner (Mr. Alman, reappearing) explains that this text states the first duty of a doctor and inquires if Borg knows what that is. Borg thinks, thinks harder, and confesses that he's forgotten. Alman obliges: "A doctor's first duty is to ask for forgiveness." He is then notified that he is "guilty of guilt." What guilt? What forgiveness? We'll soon see. But first he must pass the clinical test: to diagnose the woman wrapped in a hospital robe (Mrs. Alman, reappearing). Borg does so and pronounces her dead. She then stands up and laughs wildly. The exam is over; the grade is "incompetent." Alman then adds that there are some further offenses, further accusations—made by Borg's wife.

Wife? She's been dead for years, the old man says. At which point the examiner leads him outside for his final trial. A long, slow seduction scene is now played out: the woman is Borg's wife, the man is large and sensual, it is a mating ritual: each is panting, he closes in, she puts up a charade of denial, he brings her with increasing brutality to surrender, it closes with her collapsing, rolling over, as he holds her by the hair, makes her look at him, straddles her, and enters her. The examiner tells Borg (and us) that this is a scene from Tuesday, May 1, 1917, and that Borg witnessed exactly what has now transpired and that he can still recall it at any time. The postcoital part is the hardest to take. Now we see where Sara's remarks about high-mindedness and purity were headed: the wife says she'll confess to Isak, that he will say he pities her, that he forgives her, but that those words mean nothing "because he's completely cold." He'll then be tender, even aroused, adding that he understands everything, that he's to blame, "But he doesn't care about anything because he's completely cold."

Borg asks what the punishment is. Alman answers: "Loneliness." Failure everywhere: as doctor, as person. It would be hard to imagine a more severe rebuke to any view of old age as golden, old age as wisdom, old age as harvest. Instead Bergman is peeling away at the facade of Isak Borg, exposing him as a charlatan, an actor who's heretofore won people over but whose exposure as a fraud is now out in the open. Again, what is most painful in these sequences is Borg's stunned reaction. He has not known. He has not thought himself cold. In the midst of his humiliating trial, he begs Alman to spare him, saying "I have a bad heart. I'm an old man, Mr. Alman, and I must be treated with consideration." Alman responds, "There's nothing concerning your heart in my papers." Much of the film's richness is caught in this exchange. Bergman has succeeded in convincing us of two contradictory things at once: Borg is cold and alienated; Borg does have a heart and is suffering. Every viewer of the film is caught here as well. This man is more sinned against than sinning. And of course Bergman elects to ascend from this horrid moment of truth, to move toward warmth and love, so that the final part of the film exits the pit and shows us Isak Borg receiving his honorary degree and perhaps wiser than he was before. Marianne kisses him good night, and we feel that peace has been made: with her, with his son, with himself.

One reason I love this film is because of its lifelike ambivalence. All of us are susceptible to the scathing indictment inflicted on Isak Borg. All of us are, at some level, disguised, puffed up, and fraudulent. None of us has loved enough. But do we deserve crucifixion? The film closes in quasi-sentimental fashion, and one is entitled to feel that the warmth is merited. Isak Borg has had his trip into the mirror. He has confronted his ghosts, even to the tune of realizing that he himself is something of a living ghost. He has been spared nothing when it comes to the evasions and failures of his life. But he does not go under. There is uplift. Maybe it is not impossible to learn, to mend one's ways, even when one is very, very old.

But the most disturbing feature of this film is its masochism, and I'd like to say a word about that in relation to its view of growing old. We watch old Isak being hurtled into times and places where he meets awful humiliation and pain. We watch him being turned inside out: famous, dignified, generous man of medicine exposed as a selfish, cold, love-denying corpse. Who would order such an exposé? My answer: oneself. I am not proposing that this film is actually an autocritique on Borg's part. But I am saying that Bergman understands to perfection the radical doubt that, given time, plagues all striving and achieving. Bergman seems to me a connoisseur of the 3 A.M. wake-up moment when you are covered in sweat and *know* that you're a fraud, that you've fooled everyone except the fellow on the inside who is letting you know that he's not been taken in. Here, perhaps, is the film's truest dirty secret: none of us is "ague-proof"; none of us is free of the corrosions that set in with time; none of us can shut out the little voice that whispers, "I know you." And nothing good is ever meant. Can an outsider ever possess the dirt on us that we ourselves know or imagine? *Corrosion:* time dismantles, time fouls, time takes apart. We spend our early lives building, building, but the later chapters are apt to recast what we think we've done by hollowing it out, exposing it as theater, bathing all in doubt. In this view each of us is slated, if we live long enough, to "ghost" our own lives.

Return, for a moment, to Isak Borg's calvary: he is forced to drain the cup of miseries about his terrible marriage, but now seen as *his* failing much more than hers, a failing that stems from a disguised egoism that parades as understanding and acceptance while actually being coldness of heart. For this he watches—repeatedly, we are told, since his memory can produce this scene whenever it chooses—his wife copulate with her lover. Yes, it was a bad marriage, but it indicts him, not her: he was the toxin. But do not forget that this pièce de résistance was preceded by the gory spectacle of the honored doctor failing his medical test. Bergman has lined up two massive humiliations for his old man, and for years I found the professional boomerang rather quaint and lightweight when contrasted to the vicious marital/sexual exposé. Seeing one's wife fornicate with a lover (and then to blame it, persuasively, on oneself) ranks at the very top of my list of imagined punishments. Yet, in some gruesome sense, failing the medical test is worse than failing the marriage. I'm hardly saying that professional expertise trumps personal life; no, I'm arguing that the deep corrosive logic of old age is more perfectly displayed in the medical debacle. After all, Borg is not getting an honorary degree for having been a husband; it's for having been a world-class doctor. And that is what Bergman has wanted to target. Hit the man in his professional competency rather than in the genitals, if you really want to hurt him.

One reason the assault on Bergman's old doctor moves me is that my own experience confirms it. For years I believed that the repeated humiliations meted out in the dream sequences were over the top, but I have come to see them as all too accurate, indeed as a forbiddingly cogent assault on the very notion of "harvest" or "achievement." At this juncture, the story I need to tell is my own. I am not the recipient of honorary degrees, but I hold a chaired professorship and I lecture routinely to large numbers of students who see me as authoritative and intact (in my field). But my dreams tell me otherwise, just as Borg's dreams do. In those nighttime visits, the same humiliation awaits me over and over. I cannot find the lecture room. I arrive too late. Or I arrive there but cannot find my lecture notes. Or I open my lecture notes, but they are the wrong notes. Or I look at my lecture notes, and I cannot read them. In each of these scenarios, what I seem to do best is being systematically erased, undone, exposed as either fraud or mirage. Who could be sending these awful tidings to me except myself? Initially, I construed this as a form of masochism, but I now see it as the emerging truth of time and age: I spent my life acquiring and honing this skill, and it is precisely this skill that must now be dismantled, cashiered, taken away from me. Bergman points to the fiction of owning anything, including your own talents and expertise.

At the risk of seeming overindulgent, I want to include the latest installment of these dream wake-up calls of old age. In the dream I am somehow—more on this later—in a temple, where I am the speaker of honor, and it is very likely located in Memphis, where I grew up. My text, as I mull this over in the dream, is an ambitious account of Jesus's parables and especially the figurative and metamorphic activity in them, giving us a powerful imaginative experience. But somehow I am missing the biblical references themselves, and I spot someone in the congregation—a young adult with his children—and ask for his assistance in locating my references. He is evasive, suggesting that they may not actually exist. Worse is yet to come. Gradually, it dawns on me that this talk on Jesus is perhaps not the ideal topic for a Jewish congregation— how could I not have thought of this earlier?—and I begin to worry, realizing I'm going to have to do some fancy footwork as I deliver the talk, making some crucial shifts and substitutions from Christian to Jewish motifs. I am increasingly nervous and anxious about this, but then I experience a ray of hope: my text itself is sufficiently polished and broad that it just might get past the suspicions and scrutiny of my audience anyway, especially if I deliver it with pizzazz. With this small sense of uptick, I open my briefcase—you can now see the trouble coming—to pull out the speech, but I find only other papers: an e-mail from my twin brother, notes from earlier lectures I've given on different topics, but nothing whatsoever on *this* talk. I am now in real distress, because I'm on the verge of being exposed as a fraud.

I wake up.

And I ponder: why am I dreaming of this awful exposé in a temple in Memphis? I know the answer. The prodigal son returns to Memphis so he can bomb. Admittedly, this is not exactly the fate of Isak Borg, but it is not all that far from it either. What do I learn from this? That you get away with nothing. Once again, time is the great unraveler, and it will take the complex figure on the loom that you've spent your life weaving—those threads are your life—and undo it, take it apart, destroy the pattern. You will be dismantled. "Dust to dust," goes the old saying. But that is a mild punishment, somehow happening after consciousness is finished, after we're in the earth, in comparison to the real-time psychic leveling and piecing apart that seem to be in store for us as we move into our later phase. The higher you build or climb, the further you fall. You are the architect of your debasement.

Since I am being anecdotal, I'll go a little further, in a different direction. The nightmare of professional undoing shares the stage with the real-life threat of somatic undoing. I could have a stroke in midsentence. As is, I find myself coughing, clearing my throat, and doubtless displaying a host of other bodily ailments each time I stand up and hold forth to my students. Sometimes my voice goes. When it does, or when the students actually think it is not going to return, I cannot fail to notice a look of malaise and even slight panic on their faces, as if they sensed calamity in the wings and had no clue as to how they were supposed to respond to it. My throat has always cleared, my voice has always returned, but a day will perhaps come when it does not.

And when I personally confront similar distress, I too am at a loss. I saw a great actor whom I know and admire giving a speech and trying to overcome his Parkinson's symptoms as he did so, and I found that I was covered in sweat and trembling. I saw a close colleague "lose it" when introducing a speaker, so that he stood there, groping for words, unable to make sense or to stop, and I found it unbearable. Doubtless the worst I've seen took place at Harvard in the mid-1960s when I was a graduate student taking a course from the famous American literature scholar Perry Miller: in the middle of a lecture, Miller had what must have been some kind of aphasic attack or stroke, so that his words became jumbled, scrambled, incoherent, as if they were borrowed tools now in mutiny, no longer domesticatable, and he could not complete his sentences, so finally he simply stumbled away from the lectern.

And he did not return. Ever. (A junior colleague took over his course.)

As I write this book, I interpret Miller's story in ways I could not do more than four decades ago, when I was young and fit. I see its awful cogency. I see the outright mugging—robbery of one's most precious assets: oneself, one's mind, thoughts, words, all that one has spent a lifetime acquiring—that time sometimes metes out to those who live long. The sheer economy of this undoing makes me marvel. "Finders keepers, losers weepers." We are doomed to be losers and weepers, but what we lose is not some shiny coin or jewel but rather ourselves, the self we have worked artisanally to craft over the years; but now, in old age, like a fabric that one pulls apart, returning it to separate, disparate threads, annihilating its pattern, one ravels out. "If you could just ravel out in time," Faulkner's Darl Bundren muses in *As I Lay Dying,* a book Faulkner wrote when he was all of thirty-two years old, and I wonder how on earth he could have known, back then, in his jaunty salad days, that raveling out in time is our common fate.

Experience as Fraud: Montaigne, Sartre, Burroughs, Calvino

Already in the sixteenth century Michel de Montaigne recognized the temptation to believe that one matures and improves over time when he commented on the revisions of his work, acknowledging that the later versions might not be one whit superior to the earlier ones, "I do not trust my thoughts more because they are second or third or first. Often we correct ourselves as stupidly as we correct others. . . . After a long stretch of time, I have become older, but certainly not an inch wiser. Me now and me then are two, but which is better I could not say at all. It would be great to be old if we always progressed toward improvement. It is like a drunken movement, tottering, vertiginous, shapeless, like reeds moved fortuitously by the wind." Mind you, this is the same philosopher who wrote so richly about the nature of "experience," yet his signature note is expressed, I think, in the closing line, where he characterizes his trajectory through time as halting, lurching, precarious, patternless, governed by inhuman natural forces.

I am also reminded of Sartre's malicious put-down of experience in one of the strongest passages of *Nausea*, where the venerable figure of Dr. Rogé—the hero of "experience," an older man able to convert life into label with great fluency and authority—comes in for major undoing. Sartre suggests that our entire repertoire of cognitive tags is a form not only of bad faith but of helplessness in the face of oncoming life, amorphous life that refuses to be corralled into the specious forms we enclose it in, in our hopeless bid to choke ever-unruly experience into something we might call knowledge. In Sartre's view, this corruption starts around the age of forty, at which time one "christens" everything in the name of "experience," approximating a slot machine: "put a coin in the left hand slot and you get tales wrapped in silver paper, put a coin in the slot on the right and you get precious bits of advice that stick to your teeth like caramels."

Growing old is when this hardening of the cerebral arteries takes place, not because of plaque in our passages but because we are no longer in the fray, and all we can do is dispense pithier and pithier word product of the "believe me, I've been there" stripe. Education itself gets a bad name on this head: the efforts of the old to con the young, to substitute a regime of labels and legerdemain—mind's bogus frames—for the viscous and unchartable flow of reality from which we, the aging, have been banished. What, Sartre asks, is Dr. Rogé's actual *truth*? The answer is: he is soon to die. In this scheme, tagging events and data with ever more frenzy is a pathological sign that we are nearing our end—not a happy vista for the old.

As an old professor, I feel outright queasy more and more often as I discuss literature with my young students, not merely because the age gap between us is truly immense but because I cannot get clear of the suspicion that I am peddling my goods, rehearsing my spiel, taking the life-and-death issues of my texts and warping them into pedagogy and rehearsed views. Even Kierkegaard indicted professors along these lines, claiming they routinely transformed fierce old fables into serviceable pap, removing all the "fear and trembling" from them, defanging them for academic use (and reuse). Perhaps the most vicious rendition of the gaga palming off their snake oil is to be found in William Burroughs's

Naked Lunch, where venerable old folks, one of them (resembling me, I fear) sweetly described as "some old white-haired fuck" by our author, seem to be a permanent threat, always there ready to "unlock" their "Word Hoard" and spill it onto innocent by-standers in their bid for power. I see myself, white-haired, perma-nently on the far side of life's élan and open-ended vibrancy, holding forth year after year to my youthful captive audience, spraying them with words. What kind of generational trap is this? Wisdom as spittle, as sclerosis?

In closing on this harsh topic, let me shift gears a bit and dis-cuss a remarkable sequence from the Italian writer Italo Calvino's *Invisible Cities,* which I read aloud to my students every year (never getting a rise out of them) and which moves me ever more deeply and disturbingly as I age. The story is one of the manifold portraits of imagined cities that Calvino's protagonist, Marco Polo, describes to his royal host, Kublai Khan—the city of Adelma. Each face he saw reminded him of a dead person: a sailor holding a rope resembled a soldier comrade who is dead; a fishmonger's face was that of an old, long-dead fisherman of his youth; a fever victim on the ground had the same yellow eyes and growth of beard as his father a few hours before his death. Polo no longer dares to look anyone in the face:

> I thought: "If Adelma is a city I am seeing in a dream, where you encounter only the dead, the dream frightens me. If Adelma is a real city, inhabited by living people, I need only continue looking at them and the resemblances will dissolve, alien faces will appear, bearing anguish. In either case it is best for me not to insist on staring at them.
>
> A vegetable vendor was weighing a cabbage on a scales and put it in a basket dangling on a string a girl lowered from a balcony. The girl was identical with one in my village who had gone mad for love and killed herself. The vegetable vendor raised her face: she was my grandmother.
>
> I thought: "You reach a moment in life when, among the people you have known, the dead outnumber the living. And the mind refuses to accept more faces, more expressions: on

every new face you encounter, it prints the old forms, for each one it finds the most suitable mask."

Filled with exotic color and charm—sailor, fish market, vegetable vendor, girl on a balcony—this airy account of overdetermined perception has a feeling of fate, of out-of-sync clocks that misregulate human life, so that you are still alive but your brain, unwilling to budge, locked into a kind of reverse gear, can no longer move forward, can only choose images and tags out of the past to affix to what is coming your way. Two clocks: one for body, one for mind. This formulation may sound overly mechanical, but it captures the disjunction that time brings the living, the odd mix of paralysis and motion, of frozen and fluid. Note that Calvino never even whispers the words "old age," yet he has offered us a neurological portrait of how we process life in an evolving fashion that one fine day stops. Calvino has sweetly told this as a fable about Adelma, about the place you finally come to when your mental operations lose their connection to experience and start spitting out their own stored in-house data. But one can also see this little saga as a parable about the frozen attitudes, assumptions, and values that characterize the old, that advertise their rigidity, their condition of being stuck in time, of being living dead—a parable about experience as dysfunctional, about old age as literally out of sync.

I look around me at a world that is far more exotic and mysterious (to me) than Calvino's Adelma—a regime of iPods and hedge funds and credit default swaps and blogospheres and rap music and melting ice caps and genocide and terrorism and much, much else—and I feel myself to be almost prehistoric, almost fossilized, unable to put a label on what I see, painfully aware that my stock of captions has no purchase on much coming my way. (I could use some help from Dr. Rogé.) Maybe Calvino had it right: if you live long enough, your brain starts to resemble an overloaded bookshelf where no new text can be put, but that series of old and older books is your (abiding, tyrannical) source of information and (mis)recognition. Perhaps we never leave the company of our dead father, our dead grandmother, now functioning as ghosts who arguably stamp the present with more authority than they ever possessed (for us) while living. Such transactions sometimes go by the name of "inheritance" or "tradition," but for the most part they happen invisibly and unknowingly. Is it possible that our so-called wisdom might be nothing but projections of the dead, performed by the old and dying?

Freud used the term "uncanny" (*unheimlich*) to characterize a split-level type of perception whereby we intuit that our present situation is somehow prescripted, somehow an overlay of past experience, even made up of past residues. Calvino's Adelma carries this arrested form of vision even further, unpacking its unavowed complicity with death: not the dead who now seem to populate our perceptions but our own death as thinking individual, no longer able to respond to life in the quick. Freud was drawn to the psychic layers in play when we encounter the uncanny, when we sense the bristling underside of seemingly tame, docile moments and perceptions, but I see this *décalage* or misfit as the very language of impending cognitive misprision, even bankruptcy, of what time does to our equipment, of our vain efforts to cope by substituting false currency for real, by throwing dead, past-owned words at fresh, living matter. Getting old makes you realize that your currency might be debased, that your tools—even your naming tools—might be necrotic.

Final harvest?

The Good Fight

I have attempted, up to now, to face the worst, to do justice to the countdown that literary depictions of growing old sometimes proffer. Undone fathers, old folks hauled off the stage, old people unhappy in love, fouled harvest, discovering you've never lived, in short, undoing in so many phases. Hence, I hope I will not be accused of sentimentalism if I now insist as well on the resilience, pluck, grit, and sheer zest that are no less a part of our human equipment as we move from noon to night. Andrew Marvell's witty seventeenth-century poem "To His Coy Mistress" closes with this well-known couplet: "Thus, though we cannot make our sun / Stand still, yet we will make him run." The poem is said to be about making love while you can, Horace's carpe diem or "seize the day," yet it seems wonderfully apt for our topic as well: to summon one's all in the final chapter, to display even at the end a radiant kind of human doing that rivals the sun in energy. "Death be not proud" is John Donne's well-known phrase; could there be a pride in old age?

Ernest Hemingway's The Old Man and the Sea

Hemingway's famous late story stands for many of us as a noble, if sometimes nearly mawkish, tribute to old Santiago's courage and spirit in the face of awful odds. This fable of an old man matching his skill against the hugest fish of his life and finally bringing it in, only to lose it to sharks, would seem to be a parable about human endurance, about never quitting, about what Hemingway memorably called "grace under pressure." Santiago models himself after none less than the great DiMaggio, a cult hero who comes across as the text's male god, the pantheon figure who routinely achieves epic results despite his bone spur, his Achilles' heel, his marker of mortality. Both he and DiMaggio, Santiago remembers, are sons of fishermen; both are tested, not unlike the way Kierkegaard's Abraham was tested by God: to show their true mettle, their soul. It is a satisfying and fitting picture, I think, of the challenge of old age: to give your true, your final measure. How different this is from the entropic plot of accommodation, indeed extinction, we are so accustomed to! At the end of your course, you display everything you are made of. You triumph, old though you are, over the indignities of time. Remember the decrepit Oedipus at Colonus, rising to majesty at play's end.

For we must never forget that Santiago is a man well past his prime. His great days would seem to be behind him. We learn this through his dreams: "He no longer dreamed of storms, nor of women, nor of great occurrences, nor of great fish, nor fights, nor contests of strength, nor of his wife. He only dreamed of places now and of the lions on the beach." And that is how the story will close: the lone fisherman will make it back to port, dragging only the skeleton of his enormous, once beautiful marlin, and he will drag himself home to sleep and to dream of lions. Yet he himself wonders, in midbattle with the great fish, when he is aching for sleep, whether his life is a diminished thing: "Why are the lions the main thing that is left?" Are dreams all that remain?

What is left? Is that not the resounding question that besets old age? Well, one was once young, and memories are still there; hence, it is pertinent that some of the story's most riveting pages are devoted to the memory of Santiago's epic arm-wrestling battle against the giant Negro, a battle he won, a battle that tested his very limits, it would seem. That was Santiago at his prime. But that is the past. He no longer possesses that fabulous strength. Old, he is now the owner of a hand that might cramp on him, that cannot be depended on when final efforts are due, when you either meet or fail the challenge. These handicaps—how right that word, "handicap," seems in this story of bodies, especially hands themselves, that may or may not perform—are front and center in the old man's battle with the great fish, and he knows quite well that raw force cannot be his strongest suit, that he must count on shrewdness, cunning, and the fruits of experience. As he tells the boy, "I may not be as strong as I think, but I know many tricks and I have resolution."

Many tricks and resolution. That is how the field is shaped at this juncture of Santiago's life—perhaps at every juncture of every life. In some sense, it expresses the elemental truth (or hope) of humanism: the human ultimately triumphs via brain, not muscle. Oedipus's victory in front of the Sphinx, the giant animal-god, says the same thing: thinking is our trump card. How much truer still when weighed by an old man who knows his physical resources are not what they were? What will I do, Santiago wonders in midbattle, if the great fish decides to go down? What will I do if he sounds? "I don't know. But I'll do something. There are plenty of things I can do." This little story is out to inventory the shrinking human tool kit, out to measure what you still have when age has taken its bite. Over and over, Santiago acknowledges he is too old for this kind of a contest; and over and over, he replies to himself: I will figure out something, I have plenty of tricks. There is something virtually Darwinian in this logic: to succeed as a species, you must possess survival skills that surpass those of the other denizens you share the stage with.

With Hemingway, these matters are wonderfully literal: this story is about living, embodied creatures having it out, engaged in mortal combat, and whether the two-footed one has the requisite resources to carry the day is an open and daunting question. There is no buffer and no frills here, nothing sublimated, nothing metaphorical. "Bare, forked animals" all humans are, as Lear realized, but Santiago's situation would seem more primitive still. A man, a fish, the sea, and that's it. Does the man have—does he *still* have—what it takes to prevail, what it takes to assert the dignity of his species? In this light, growing old is to be understood as a supreme challenge for our kind: are we still worthy? Even my term "worthy" seems too cerebral, and notions such as the Italian Renaissance concept of *virtù* or the French word *vaillance* seem closer to the mark: a gauging of human strength where the physical, the mental, and the moral are inseparable. Because this is Hemingway, it comes across as pure and clean, stripped of psychology, located on a small skiff riding the great sea, delivered as a ballet between man and fish, down to the bare essentials, each enacting the role nature has assigned it, leaving it for us, the readers, to assess the moral and existential stakes of what we're witnessing.

What kind of ballet does an old man do? We know his glory days are in the past and that he relies a great deal on the assistance of the young boy, who idolizes him. We know he no longer dreams of fights or women. We are told that "[f]or a long time now eating had bored him and he never carried a lunch." It would appear that he is postappetite, postpassion. Yet the novella stays in our minds as the saga of intimate contact, of an unforgettable bond between man and animal, of an encounter on the ocean that has as much bodily fervor, contact, and twinned fates as any fable of *Liebestod* you're likely to read. I have no interest in eroticizing Santiago's relation to his marlin, but I think it highly significant that he remembers a marlin romance, remembers it as something of great beauty and pathos. He had hooked the female fish—the male always let the female feed first—and the male stayed loyally with his desperate and doomed mate throughout the time she was being brought in—stayed, in fact, so close to the boat that there was a risk his tail would cut the line. He stayed by the side of the boat, playing his role in his passion play as the man gaffed and clubbed his mate and hoisted her on board the skiff. At that point, knowing she was dead, "the male fish jumped high into the air beside the boat to see where the female was and then went down deep, his lavender wings, that were his pectoral fins, spread wide and all his wide lavender stripes showing. He was beautiful, the old man remembered, and he had stayed." That is one form of ballet.

Here, then, is a spectacle of natural love and fidelity proper to fish, rich in beauty for the old man who witnesses it. I wonder if Hemingway is not remembering the beautiful story of the bird couple that Whitman sang of in "Out of the Cradle Endlessly Rocking," also a story of fidelity in the face of loss and death, of the natural world as our first lexicon for the most important lessons we are to learn. In Whitman's poem, this event acquires a seminal importance for the young poet-to-be, for he now understands death to be nature's primordial message, and he imagines the very sound of poetry as "song of the bleeding throat." In Hemingway the story is accented differently, and one is to place great emphasis on those fine last four words: "and he had stayed." One stays to the end. Santiago will do no less, himself. I'd also want to claim that the magnificent remembered display of the male fish's dazzling body—his fins figured as wings, his entire form godlike—lends a ceremonial, mythical aura to this story of a man fishing at sea, and I believe that we can best grasp the stakes of Santiago's minutely detailed, physically rending, emotionally rich encounter with the giant marlin as a kind of love/death match, as a maritime version of the *corrida* that Hemingway so often wrote about. That is what Santiago's ballet consists of: being conjoined, bound body and spirit, to the beautiful undersea creature in the fullest embrace of his life. It begins with courtship, and it ends with death. It is a worthy exit gambit for an old man.

One is struck by the decorousness of it all. Santiago virtually sings a love song to the animal in the deep. He begs the fish to eat the sardine and tuna offerings (with enclosed hook), he sings the praises of his dish: "Make another turn. Just smell them. Aren't they lovely? Eat them good now and then there is the tuna. Hard and cold and lovely. Don't be shy, fish. Eat them." The fish serves himself well—to call this "taking the bait" is to miss its sweet civility—while the host readies his reserve line and urges his guest to consume still more, so that the hook will be fully ingested: "All right. Are you ready? Have you been long enough at table?" Once eating is over, more strenuous activities begin. Now the fight is on, but never does Hemingway construe it as a battle or a conflict; of course Santiago labors mightily to contain the enormous beast, but love is the driving force. Repeatedly, he refers to the marlin as his brother, his equal, even though that in no way alters the killing plot: "Fish, I love you and respect you very much. But I will kill you dead before the day ends." Later: "I'll kill him though. In all his greatness and glory." Santiago evinces great empathy for the huge animal: he wonders how old the marlin is, how much the marlin can see at that depth; he knows that the "setting of the sun is a difficult time for all fish." He knows the huge fish must be ravenous; and he is sensitive to the animal's great pain, a pain that could possibly drive him mad. Above all, he is acutely aware of the fateful structural drama unfolding in front of our eyes: he is bound to the beast. For good. "Fish, I'll stay with you until I am dead."

As the struggle reaches epic proportions, lasting three days and draining virtually all of Santiago's strength, the old man realizes ever more fully the nature of their bond: "Fish, you are going to have to die, anyway. Do you have to kill me too?" And a moment later: "You are killing me, fish, the old man thought. But you have a right to. Never have I seen a greater, or more beautiful, or calmer or more noble thing than you, brother. Come on and kill me. I do not care who kills who." There is something deliriously egalitarian on show, and it makes perfect sense that the exhausted old man wonders whether, at the end, once the marlin is dead, he is bringing in the fish or the fish is bringing him in. They are mated, even though one has killed the other. This is not a poem of the earth but a poem of the sea, in which the creature on the surface and the creature in the depths fuse with each other in a final, consummate embrace.

Why is this? We see here the absolute severity of the Hemingway world, one with no hiding places or compromises. And perhaps *The Old Man and the Sea* is the purest of the entire lot, for Santiago articulates the elemental law at work, the elemental command given to humans: "The fish is my friend too, I have never seen or heard of such a fish. But I must kill him. I am glad we do not have to try to kill the stars." *I am glad we do not have to try to kill the stars.* I can imagine no writer other than Hemingway with an ethos of this stamp. Killing is what is expected of us; it is the supreme act that enables us to give our measure, to truly enter the Creation. Santiago muses still further: "Imagine if each day a man must try to kill the moon ... imagine if a man each day should have to try to kill the sun? We were born lucky, he thought." There is an outright cosmic feeling to these remarks, positioning the lone old fisherman in a setting of extraordinary scope, yet a setting in which he is called upon to act. One is accustomed to romantic effusions about the stars and the moon, calling us to reverie or awe or worship. But murder? I see no paean to violence here, no hint of bloodthirstiness, but rather a bizarre homage to the Creation and the fierce requirements of those who inhabit it. The softer virtues have no place: man proves his mettle by pitting his very life against the elements. Now, in the contest of his life, he must prove it once more, for it is the code he has lived by. "The thousand times he had proved it meant nothing. . . . Each time was a new time and he never thought about the past when he was doing it." DiMaggio, with his bone spur, did such things each time he came to bat; so too will old Santiago. One last time.

But DiMaggio had only to hit a speeding ball coming at him; Santiago is locked into a *danse macabre* with his great marlin, connected to it by a taut line that will snap if overpulled, a line that is becoming etched into the old man's flesh and exerting monstrous pressure on his shoulders, his hands. But it is also a kind of umbilical cord, exquisitely sensitive to each of the giant fish's moves, moves that Santiago reads as if he had X-ray vision. Their love/death relationship lives through this line, makes them a couple, takes every single bit of the old man's strength. But we are to remember: he has, on his side of the ledger, "tricks and resolution," for they are the trumps, the only trumps, of old age. Will he win by smarts, by having more savvy than the creature on the other end of the line? Will experience carry the day?

No, it will not, in itself, be enough. Strained to the utmost, no longer as powerful as he was, Santiago knows he must make that tired body of his into something stronger. Arguably the single most striking feature of this story is its depiction of eating as the primal act of living creatures. Remember the hungry child we saw as far back as Lazarillo and Pablos; customarily we assume such matters to have less urgency as one ages and grows old. But Santiago, whose appetites have waned, who finds eating boring, also finds that he must eat if he is to be the equal of this giant fish. We learn as well that he had feasted on shark liver oil and turtle eggs aplenty in the old days. Time to start again. With great simplicity and cleanness, Hemingway writes of Santiago slicing his own tuna bait into large strips and eating it raw; and when that does not suffice, when the struggle is still at its most intense, he eats the flying fish as well; and when that too is not enough, he eats raw a dolphin, a sweet-tasting fish whose flesh may well cause him to vomit when ingested like this. Each time the old man puts sliced raw fish into his mouth, he chews it with utmost care, then swallows it carefully, and we the readers can virtually *see* the chemical breakdown of raw fish flesh into human energy.

Eat or be eaten; that is how the wild ones live, and it is how Santiago must live if he is to capture the marlin. Yes, the sharks will make their evil appearance in the final act and set about devouring the beautiful great fish—and Santiago hates sharks, sees them as divested of dignity, as utterly unlike the godlike animal he has caught—but we readers are struck by the parallels on show, the absolute command to eat that tyrannizes all life. And it works. He feels the calories, the raw sustenance and oomph entering into his bloodstream and his muscles. It is hard to be more primitive than this. "I could not fail myself and die on a fish like this," Santiago says, and we can almost put a sexual stamp on this performance. Almost. It is instructive reading, in a time of athletic and sexual mania, a time of steroids and Viagra, to see that no pharmacy is required, that the ocean has what you need if you're resourceful enough to get it.

Yet the spectacle of an old man gathering every resource imaginable—knowing how to position his body, how to use his lines, how to read the winds and the currents, how to gauge the movements of his silent partner the marlin, how to wrest raw food from the sea—in order to meet his challenge is perhaps not what one most remembers in Hemingway's story. Hemingway's genius was always a talent for dialogue, for wry, playful, muscular, tight-lipped, almost elliptical dialogue that required reading between the lines. Santiago is a man who talks aloud to himself, the gift of old age. But he also listens to himself: "Aloud he said, 'I wish I had the boy,' " which is followed by this: "But you haven't got the boy, he thought. You have only yourself." From speech to thought, from thought to speech: Santiago suddenly feels fear about this huge, "calm, strong fish" who "seemed so fearless and so confident." Now the riposte: "You'd better be fearless and confident yourself, old man."

I want to call this the language of maturity; it displays a capacity to hear and to respond to one's own thoughts and words, to take possession of one's verbal being, to inventory one's resources. Its repetitions are rich as the adjectives move from fish to man, from assertion to doubt. It also displays the sinuous beauty of Hemingway's style, a style that looks taut and monosyllabic but can surprise us by its turns and forkings. We overhear Santiago in this tale. We watch him do his tally, take his findings, establish his bearings, reestablish them. Here is a form of doing that goes beyond ingesting flesh or bearing pain. Late in the story, once the sharks have begun mutilating the great fish and old Santiago knows that worse is on the way, he moves along just this verbal axis toward a kind of wisdom:

"I shouldn't have gone out so far, fish," he said. "Neither for you nor for me. I'm sorry, fish."

Now, he said to himself. Look to the lashing on the knife and see if it has been cut. Then get your hand in order because there is still more to come.

"I wish I had a stone for the knife," the old man said after he had checked the lashing on the oar butt. "I should have brought a stone." You should have brought many things, he thought. But you did not bring them, old man. Now is no time to think of what you do not have. Think of what you can do with what there is.

"You give me much good counsel," he said aloud. "I'm tired of it."

Much of this text's flavor is found in sequences of this stripe. "Going out too far" is a modest formulation for hubris, for over-reaching, and there is evidence in the text to support a kind of Greek reading of this sort, even as there are pointed Christlike echoes of sacrifice and redemption. But just as Santiago has little time to waste worrying about sin, so too is this meditation inter-rupted by the pressing material business at hand: lashing the knife to ward off the sharks. Again the mind interrupts, chastising its holder for not bringing a stone, and again we see the riposte: a stone is not the only thing he forgot to bring, but the game is about making do with what you have. One is *bricoleur* all one's life, most especially toward the end, when the bits and pieces you can use are themselves used up. All of which is capped off with the lovely notation that this kind of verbal Ping-Pong—the thing Hemingway does so very nicely—is just so much twaddle, and it's tiring to boot. One feels in the hands of a stylistic master here, a laconic rhetorician, someone out to measure the respective pur-chases of brainpower, muscle power, fish power, food power, and word power. Again I want to call this the discourse of maturity, the final weighing of resources, gauging what our final assets are when we are stripped to the essentials. What's left?

What's left is exactly the arsenal that one sees being marshaled on that small skiff—a body that is no longer what it was, a mind that often threatens to go, a heart that is unfaltering, and a tongue that gets its licks in. Santiago has been tested and comes through it. Some critics have lambasted the old man for not burying his fish at sea, but I think there is a reverence in this book for remains, for what's left. Hemingway closes the text by returning Santiago to his dreams of lions on the beach. He has earned his vision. The great marlin may be devoured by sharks, but this old man's doggedness—the climactic embrace of a lifetime with the great fish; the nonstop ingenuity and moral fiber enlisted to hold up his end, not to fail; the bittersweet return home—is nonetheless a beacon in my study, offering a view of aging that is shot through with grace. He did not falter. He stayed. He returned. He was wor-thy of DiMaggio.

Some reviewers who admired the taut, unvarnished reporting of violence and pain in the early Hemingway works choked a bit on the "softness" of this late text. One cannot quite imagine Nick Adams or Jake Barnes regarding the animals or the stars as "brothers"; theirs is a darker, more hostile world. But the hero is now an old man past his prime. And his great bout with the marlin acquires, in my view, a kind of poetry and vibrancy that are beyond the charge of sentimentalism. As I've tried to show, there is nothing easy in this late work, but there is a luminous sense of purpose and fit, of utilizing the resources you've gained by a lifetime of experience (so that the long years are additive, not merely corrosive), of actualizing one's self to the uttermost via courage and art against a disaster you cannot prevent, that confers on *The Old Man and the Sea* a place of pride in this study of growing old. I see greatness of soul here. Many believe that the old man lying in bed dreaming of lions at the book's close is a man who is dying, who will not wake up. If that is true, and I tend to think it is, he has exited well. He has given his measure.

Philip Roth's Everyman

Philip Roth is our most Rabelaisian writer. Whether it be the antics of the frustrated Alexander Portnoy growing up or Mickey Sabbath performing his sovereign and exalted erotic rites, Roth understands flesh, knows it to be imbued with needs and rewards and sheer autonomy that go a long way toward defining who we are as a species: not always pretty, but always vital, always pumping. If chemical help is needed in the form of Viagra, as we see in the aging Coleman Silk's acrobatics in *The Human Stain*, so be it. Animal appetite has authority. The show must go on.

Not that Roth has not written about death. But *Everyman* seems to be in a category by itself. From beginning to end, it is stamped by an almost Greek awareness of the body's fragility, its absolutely guaranteed role as time bomb. Hence the narrative not only begins with the protagonist's funeral but goes on to register an astonishing number of other funerals and breakdowns: the deaths of both parents; the strokes suffered by Gerald, the husband of his art student, and by his second wife, Phoebe; the intolerable migraines experienced by Phoebe; the unsurvivable pain meted out to Millicent (Gerald's wife), so severe that she commits suicide; the triple somatic undoing of his friend Brad (suicidal depression), colleague Ezra (terminal cancer), and boss Clarence (death of old age, after lunch).

All this funereal material flaunts the story's obsession with mortality, yet Roth wants us to realize that these incursions do not wait until old age to make their appearance: nowhere is this more evident than in the protagonist's vivid, often recalled memory of his childhood stint in the hospital to treat his hernia, a visit reeking of terror and leaving a lifelong scar. The child's surgery receives full honors: maniacal attention to the doctor, eerie exposure to another hospitalized child who very possibly dies during the night before our boy's procedure, memory of a drowned seaman's body that washed up on the Jersey shore. So there is a grim sense of coherence and continuity toward the book's end as we learn of the protagonist's continued failing health, involving catherizations, defibrillator, shunts put into his vascular system, heart disease, and two surgeries on his right carotid artery, the second of which proves fatal and closes the book.

There can be no victory against such odds, even though some, like his older brother, Howie, blessed with brains and brawn, seem to have been given a free pass, much to our man's envy and resentment; and those angry and petty emotions shame him, given the generosity and kindness shown him by Howie all his life. You live with (and die from) the hand you've been dealt, but only in the fullness of time does the full nature of that hand become clearer, for that is when the bills start coming in. The haunting episode of the childhood hernia announces with great clarity that we live under a sword from the moment we draw breath, even if the bulk of our sufferings is likely to take place in later years. That late reckoning is rendered in almost majestic tones toward the book's close as the protagonist reflects on the multiple deaths and deprivations faced by his friends and loved ones at life's end: stories of "regret and loss and stoicism, of fear and panic and isolation and dread," of being parted "from that that had once been vitally theirs," leading to an inescapable judgment: "Old age isn't a battle; old age is a massacre." We watch this once-vigorous man going down: his sexual fire is dimmed, his nerves are shot, his nightmares are on the rise, his awareness of looming disaster seems almost palpable; he knows he is approaching extinction.

But because this is Roth, he does not go out without a fight. In a fetching, moving late sequence, he approaches a young, shapely female jogger he's been studying for days and tries to come on to her; not unresponsive, she is quite willing to hear him out, and for a moment the reader feels that maybe, just maybe, one more escapade may be in the cards. He asks her the operative question: "How game are you?" A good bit of Roth shows in that line: how *game* are you? For our sexual life is a game, a great game, and Roth's players will stay at it right up to the moment they are removed from the field. She takes his address; she never calls. The game really is over.

But the reader understands that it was played with intensity, ranging from the young secretary who daily knelt on the floor in his office and raised her rear for him to the fateful, marriage-wrecking affair with the Dane Merete, whose regal body and little hole provided both of them such delight. Yet he comes ruefully to understand (after he's married Merete) that a little hole is truly incommensurate with a whole life and that he has traded one for the other by wounding the one woman who was right for him, Phoebe his second wife, so deeply that their marriage dissolved on the spot. And he understands more still as the darker and more menacing chips start to land on the table: that his two sons from the first marriage, the ones who seemed to revel in hatred of him for ruining their childhood by divorcing their mother, those two sons may not have been wrong after all. (Up to now, he has been stubbornly persuaded that they are deranged in their spite.)

Seeing the end come—around you and building inside you—triggers something we'd have to call remorse, a kind of late recognition that he has truly fucked up his life in the places that matter and that now he's on the verge of exiting it altogether, it can't be fixed:

He saw himself racing in every direction at once through downtown Elizabeth's main intersection—the unsuccessful father, the envious brother, the duplicitous husband, the helpless son—and only blocks from his family jewelry store crying out for the cast of kin on whom he could not gain no matter how hard he pursued them. "Momma, Poppa, Howie, Nancy, Randy, Lonny—if only I'd known how to do it! Can't you hear me? I'm leaving! It's over and I'm leaving you all behind!" And those vanishing as fast from him as he from them turned just their heads to cry out in turn, all too meaningfully, "Too late!"

It is an astonishing athletic image: at the end, you are racing as fast as you can toward those whom you have not loved enough, but you can't reach them. Worse still, you now realize you flunked the one lesson that mattered: *if only I'd known how to do it!* This is as close to self-knowledge and grace as he will come. It is not all that far. Yet it does betoken a widening of his most afflicted organ—his heart—in ways that no shunts or medications could possibly achieve. You die alone. The loved ones are destined to vanish, and it is always too late.

Roth closes his text in pitch-perfect fashion, I believe. This writer, who is so good at depicting flesh and carnal reality, who is the master of a zaftig tone and style, brings his doomed hero to the place where the book began: the cemetery. And in that place, in a prose that is reminiscent of the early Hemingway, as dry as ash, we are instructed about the life of bones. The bones of the dead—his dead, all the dead—lie there as the final community he is to join, and their cult is one of dignified and careful labor, as we learn through the words of the black grave digger, who explains in full the nature and tricks and turns of his craft. Roth is remembering *Hamlet,* to be sure, but there is no Yorick, no puns, no metaphysics in sight, just the artisanal discourse of earth and stones and shovels and readying the soil to receive its inevitable next guest to take up a final residence. Our man was prepared to leave his retirement community by the shore, hoping to move in with his beloved daughter, Nancy, but that was not to be: not only because the mother, Phoebe, was felled by a stroke and got there first but because our man is headed for another place, one of bones and cleanly cut soil.

He goes under the knife one more time and does not come

back. But all the book's beauty is caught in Roth's account of his final thoughts:

> Nothing could extinguish the vitality of that boy [himself as child, still remembered] whose slender little torpedo of an unscathed body once rode the big Atlantic waves from a hundred yards out in the wild ocean all the way in to shore. Oh, the abandon of it, and the smell of the salt water and the scorching sun! Daylight, he thought, penetrating everywhere, day after summer day of that daylight blazing off a living sea, an optical treasure so vast and valuable that he could have been peering through the jeweler's loupe engraved with his father's initials at the perfect, priceless planet itself—at his home, the billion-, the trillion-, the quadrillion-carat planet Earth. He went under feeling far from felled, anything but doomed, eager yet again to be fulfilled, but nonetheless, he never woke up.

Shakespeare and Rabelais join in this final tribute to the miracle of both the planet and our lives—wonderfully cast in the language of the jeweler and his loupe and his precious stones, the very profession of the protagonist's dead father—yielding a tone that is anything but morbid. Even at the very end, actually under the knife, one is "eager yet again to be fulfilled." The "good fight" must finally be lost, but appetite, zest, and verve are the creatural endowments we are born with, and if we are lucky, they never die. Roth does add two final sentences claiming that the trip to nowhere has begun and mentioning fear, but those last words seem weightless in contrast to the grandeur of the image of the child riding the wild ocean back to the shore and seeing the glory of the Creation displayed on a summer day in New Jersey.

Life's Plenitude

Plenitude may have a Latinate sound to it, but I invoke it in the hope that it will convey weight, pith, reach, and dimensionality. These terms all point to the sheer scale of a life, its spatiotemporal scope, its large tally sheet of works and days, its inevitable variety and gravity. I do not think anyone easily "possesses" who he or she is and has been, given the amplitude of the self's journey through time. I have repeatedly urged literature itself as a precious resource along those lines, a script that helps us both widen and possess our own existences by dint of experiencing vicariously those of others.

These issues do not, I think, loom large when we are young. As we grow up, our forward propulsion is so great, our appetites so real, our enmeshment so thorough, our past itself so relatively short, that little time or energy is often spent on either retrieval or review. It is as if we were not yet attentive to either our own shadow or our own larger estate. But these matters go well beyond the narrative lines of one's own life, for they extend into the world itself, the manifold variegated pulsing strange world that contains us and warrants our attention. Perhaps one reason the old often seem so engaged in travel and tourism has to do with a heightened later sense of all that one has missed, of the teeming spectacle that one never attended to, for one was so busy making one's own way. Pondering such matters—one's own plenitude and that of the stage one has been on—is a project of old age, when a good bit of one's doing has been done, when measures ask to be taken.

Daniel Defoe's *Moll Flanders*

It is dumbfounding to realize how often literature seems to have been hijacked by romance, by the story of love quests and social struggle; i.e., the affairs of the young. One longs to find more stories that do justice to the temporal span of an existence, that track a character from birth to death while offering some sense of life's sheer zest and vibrancy, beyond all moralizing, located in the endless material particulars that flood all of us every day. Defoe's novel of 1722, *Moll Flanders*, is a raucous and episodic picaresque fiction devoted to the wit and survival tactics of one shrewd woman (without fortune or papers, equipped only with good looks and smarts) trying to make it in London. Defoe has given us a rare account of staying power in his portrait, and I want to claim that staying power, the sheer fact of having managed for a lifetime, deserves recognition as one of the rewards of growing old. Yes, this sounds a bit like a marathon view of old age, with the disturbing corollary that its greatest (and only?) significance is simply that you make it to the end. But there is more than that.

We call Defoe's book *Moll Flanders,* but this is how he titled it: *The Fortunes and Misfortunes of the Famous Moll Flanders, &c. Who was Born in Newgate, and during a Life of continu'd Variety for Threescore Years, besides her Childhood, was Twelve Year a* Whore, *five times a* Wife *(whereof once to her own Brother), Twelve Year a* Thief, *Eight Year a Transported* Felon *in* Virginia, *at last grew* Rich, *liv'd* Honest, *and died a* Penitent. This is quite a mouthful. There can be no doubt that Defoe was counting on the shock value of Moll's crazy quilt of a life—and much of the book's richness inheres in how Moll continues to be Moll, even though she changes course with such prodigious frequency—but I want to insist on something else that shines in this title: the chameleon-like nature and sheer longevity of a life. In reading Defoe, one grasps a shocking truth: that all lives, looked at longitudinally, are picaresque. (This dirty secret is fiercely elided from all résumés.)

Here, then, is a story that transcends romance, even though Defoe is much exercised to depict Moll's erotic escapades and liaisons; but he also limns her second career as thief, and he goes on to chart her stay in America, replete with reversals of every sort, including incest, continuing all the way to her return, late in years, to London with ample funds. The book has the heft of a long and varied life, full of turns and surprises, chugging on. This medium-length novel gratifies us by its gargantuan but egalitarian gift of a life's ongoing density: Moll as child, as young woman, as seasoned manhunter, as infamous thief, as mother, as Newgate prisoner, as exile to Virginia, as returnee to England—gargantuan and gratifying because most of us cannot easily summon up our own longitudinal story. It is not by accident that Moll informs us that she was judged "the greatest artist of her time," and although she is referring to her prowess as thief and impersonator, we should assess her real artistry more along existential lines: she has constructed a life.

Because living is an artisanal proposition. And old age is the moment when the amplitude of existence most fully shows. One of the most pungent notations of Defoe's novel comes when Moll meets up again with Mother Midnight, the woman who ran the Lying-in, who helped her years earlier when she was down and out and ready to give birth, the lady who got her back on her feet and nursed her spirits. What has time wrought for Mother Midnight? Moll discovers that

> she was not in such flourishing Circumstances as before; for she had been Sued by a certain Gentleman who had had his Daughter stolen away from him, and who it seems she had helped to convey away; and it was very narrowly that she escap'd the Gallows; the Expence also had ravag'd her, and she was become very poor; her House was but meanly Furnish'd, and she was not in such repute for her Practice as before; however, she stood upon her Legs, as they say, and as she was a stirring bustling Woman, and had some Stock left, she was turn'd *Pawn Broker,* and *liv'd pretty well.*

I am humbled by this passage. It is supremely politically incorrect—Mother Midnight indulges in major-league vice, stealing children—yet it is a testament to grit and fortitude. Proust wrote that bodies are the material that makes time visible, but I'd want to revise his (true) statement by claiming that time is required to demonstrate character, to display mettle. One might quarrel with me by saying that morality is absent from Defoe's view of character, that lasting to the end is perhaps not all that praiseworthy in itself. What did you do (worthwhile) during your life? would be the tough question. It's a test Mother Midnight would have trouble passing, on ethical grounds. Yet there is a kind of quiet pride expressed in that portrait of this stirring, bustling woman, for it suggests that qualities such as resilience, pluck, and initiative deserve our serious consideration as virtues.

Raw capitalism is what Defoe is said to be giving, according to some, raw survivalism, Darwinism before Darwin; but what most appeals to me here is the glimpse of a pact we make with life: we are dealt a hand, and our honor consists in making the best of it we possibly can for as long as we can. Mother Midnight is a *bricoleur,* someone who bounces from role to role, using whatever small trumps she has, intent only on staying in the game. Roth's

Everyman was fueled by the same drive. There is a pleasure in staying in the game: it is the pleasure of using one's indwelling resources, including the wit to harness circumstances, bric-a-brac, and "realia" and to transform them into resources. Then, in old age, you can look back at the journey—and Defoe is a chronicler in just this sense: he makes us see the journey—and see that it dwarfs any one of its single episodes, that it is a long road and it is, cumulatively, you. Getting this far matters. To be sure, no one beats mortality; we know we must die. But we know almost nothing about why we live. Mother Midnight's dance through time whispers to us: life is good. Defoe's writing breathes on every page a paean to living, living a long time; it is about the rightness of staying the course(s), about the savor—not the value—of experience after experience, as the reward of existence.

Bertolt Brecht's *Mother Courage*

Moll and Mother Midnight make it successfully into old age. They have the survival skills that our young protagonists Lazarillo and Pablos, not to mention Rastignac and the Invisible Man, were bent on learning, and they exercised those talents from decade to decade, over the long haul. But please note: each of those figures carries no baggage, is ultimately a loner. But life does not always afford us the luxury of needing only to save our own skin. Lovers know this. Families know this. "Life's plenitude" has a very different value when the life you're talking about is that of a loved one. Sickness and war can cut plenitude short, thereby conferring on it an unbearably poignant value. The story of private want and private need yields, in terrible times when the sky falls in, to a larger and graver narrative of responsibility and linkage. On this front, little surpasses the account of a mother's pluck, travails, and losses during the Thirty Years' War as depicted in Bertolt Brecht's magisterial drama of 1938, *Mother Courage*.

Brecht is arguably the trickiest writer of modern times. A committed Marxist, he devised a model of dramatic writing stamped by what he termed the *Verfremdungseffekt*, or the "alienation effect," by which he meant that the audience forms a critical judgment of the events depicted onstage that is at radical odds with the attitudes of the stage players themselves. These matters can become rather abstruse, but Brecht's basic target was the famous notion of identification with art, which, in his view, was virtually a narcotic for the audience rather than the badly needed comprehension or critique, which might show how the play's actions were either wrong or blind or self-defeating. (Mind you, this is an uphill fight, since audience involvement has been a central element of theater ever since Aristotle defined catharsis.)

I called Brecht tricky because his great plays seem inevitably to work against his theoretical program, inasmuch as they not only depict humans caught up in powerful ideological forces, but the audience all too often bonds/identifies with these trapped players, sees them as noble and moving victims but not as dupes who should have behaved differently, not as creatures of a system that needs utter overhauling, indeed overturning. Nowhere is this truer than in the reception history of *Mother Courage and Her Children*—Brecht's epic account of a feisty, strong-willed woman (based on a seventeenth-century Grimmelshausen work) plying her (capitalist) trade as canteen woman with cart from 1624 to 1636 and losing her three children in the process—where the public invariably identified with Anna Fierling (Mother Courage), and saw her as an irresistible tragic victim whose stubborn energy and loyalty to her kids mattered far more than her presumable political blinders. After the play was launched and lauded, Brecht wrote tirelessly about the mistakes made by actors and theaters, who repeatedly failed to foreground the writer's key point: that Mother Courage loses everything but learns nothing. We should leave the theater in anger, Brecht claimed, but instead we leave it in tears.

And we do so, I believe, because Brecht's elemental grasp of human nature—a concept he would surely dispute, deeming it constructed—is incomparably richer and more affecting than his politics will ever be. Anna Fierling's twelve-year struggle to get through the endless war without losing her children, while also making a profit, deserves a place of pride in this study of growing old. Brecht never accentuates Mother Courage's aging as such, but he shines his light on what it takes to keep your (grown-up) kids out of harm's way, and he makes us realize that it's impossible.

Perhaps the fallacy inherent in our notion of growing old is that we see it as an individual fate handed to us by time, whereas often enough the truth is a more plural proposition: we are meshed with loved ones, and we cannot protect them or prevent them from dying. Further, in war, the logic of mortality that usually ensures the death of parents before the death of children is often smashed to bits, as the voracious war devours half of Germany and demands its due. Mother Courage never had the eminence of Oedipus or Lear or Gertrude or Phèdre; she is common stock, low profile, scraping by, yet somehow indomitable and filled with folk wisdom. As the play opens, we see her and the cart, pulled by all three children: Eilif the daring, Swiss Cheese the honest, and Kattrin the mute. When the play closes, all three children are dead and gone, but the old lady and the cart are left, so the old lady puts herself in harness to continue plying her trade. Life goes on.

"Like the war to nourish you? / Have to feed it something too" is what the recruiter says to Mother Courage after he has successfully lured her son Eilif into signing up for the army. Brecht put all his political anger into those two lines, showing us that the woman with the cart who traipses across Germany selling her wares and making a living via her bargain with systemwide destruction is logically, fatefully caught up in a wager that will use her children for fodder and kill them. Moreover, at each critical juncture when a child is either lost or killed, Courage is inevitably in midbargain with someone else, trying to cut costs and boost gains, seeking to eke out a living in very hard times. The most heartbreaking instance of such behavior happens with Swiss Cheese, who has had the bad luck and bad judgment to be taking care of the regimental cash box for the Second Finnish Regiment just as the Catholics gain the upper hand. Immediately they are on his tail, sending out a one-eyed spy to trick and trap him, and we watch the mute Kattrin try desperately and futilely to warn him, via hoarse but incomprehensible noises, as he takes the money out of hiding and slips it under his tunic. Moments later he is led back by two men, put face-to-face with his mother; it is a tight corner: he claims he doesn't know her, a claim she goes along with. At this juncture he is again taken away, and Courage learns that he can be ransomed via a bribe of 200 florins; her only way of getting this money is to trade the cart for it to Yvette Pottier, the friendly whore, whose decrepit Catholic colonel lover will be good for it. Courage is in a tight spot and tries to bargain, offering 120 florins, thinking it may be enough. At the last minute, she springs for the full 200, hoping it will save the day.

It doesn't. We hear the drums roll, and we know that Swiss Cheese has been executed. Then comes one of the most awful moments in theater, and it is lodged entirely in the stage directions:

> *Yvette fetches Kattrin, who goes to her mother and stands beside her. Mother Courage takes her hand. Two lansequenets come carrying a stretcher with something lying on it covered by a sheet. The sergeant marches beside them. They set down the stretcher.*

SERGEANT: Here's somebody we dunno the name of. It's got to be listed, though, so everything's shipshape. He had a meal here. Have a look, see if you know him. *He removes the sheet.* Know him? *Mother Courage shakes her head.* What, never see him before he had that meal here? *Mother Courage shakes her head.* Pick him up. Chuck him in the pit. He's got nobody knows him. *They carry him away.*

Not a word is spoken by the mother, who disavows her executed son. What could words do here? All the eloquence in the world pales in front of this horror. All we see is a woman twice shaking her head to signal "No." It is unbearable to watch, even if brief to read. In my view, this sequence has the harrowing quality we associate with Mary attending the crucified body of her son, except that this mother has no saintly or divine aura, is just a hustling canteen lady losing her most precious goods. And having to look hard, hard—twice—at what she's lost.

I have pointed out that Brecht was ever irked by the tendency to sentimentalize Mother Courage, rather than to indict her for being a party to her ruin, for never understanding that her "business" puts her on the side of the warmongers. This grim lesson will be taught again at play's end, when Courage is away while Kattrin goes to her own heroic death. Catholic troops have come to a peasant's farm where Courage and Kattrin have been staying, and we see the peasants beaten into submission, into silence, as the troops steathily make their way toward the sleeping Protestant village, where they will slaughter everyone, children included. Kattrin—who mutely seeks love throughout the play, caressing animals, tending the wounded, drawn to babies, hungry for tenderness, all this despite having been disfigured early on, hence destined for solitude, for no husband—takes hold of a ladder, climbs onto the roof, hoists the ladder up with her, and begins to play the drums for all she is worth, to emit a sound that might wake (and save) the village (and the children). Once again it is pure, almost wordless theater: the Catholic soldiers and ensign are desperate to silence her, but of course she cannot even hear their screams and commands and pleas, so at the end they have no choice but to shoot her, yet her last drumbeats (as she dies) are heard in the village, doubtless saving it from destruction.

The next and final scene of the play has Courage squatting by her (dead) daughter, singing a lullaby, covering the body with a tarpaulin, giving some coins to the peasants to arrange a burial, harnessing herself to the cart, hearing the fife and drums of a marching regiment, and crying "Take me along!" And the play ends with a song expressing belief in life:

> Tomorrow is another day!
> The new year's come. The watchmen shout.
> The thaw sets in. The dead remain.
> Wherever life has not died out
> It staggers to its feet again.

What to say? Brecht's play stays with us as a tribute to the life urge, not to ideological brainwashing. I saw this play as a college student in 1960 at Brecht's own theater in East Berlin; Mother Courage was played by the famous Helene Weigel, who made the role immortal. I was mesmerized by the spectacle of raw will to live shown in the face and body of a still-living woman who cannot save her children, again shown at play's end as she takes on the Sisyphean labor of getting in the harness herself to move on. Capitalist fool? I felt then, and feel now, some five decades later, that this woman has borne every possible blow that can be meted out to her but is still standing, still moving.

Old age? Not a word in the play speaks directly to our issue. Yet this play stands in my mind as the pendant to Hemingway's *The Old Man and the Sea.* The American novelist offers us the thoughts as well as sinewy actions of a man past his prime, doing battle with both the elements and his own aging body. It is an old man's final performance, and its DiMaggio references perfectly convey its impact as final sporting event, final tally of what pluck and muscle and will can achieve against bad odds. I wrote that this novella does beautiful justice to our longing for a final chapter with grace in it. The sharks prevail, the contest is unwinnable, but human dignity wins nonetheless.

Against this spectacle I put Brecht's play. This woman catches no great fish, nor does she soliloquize or ruminate about the stars. Her task is to get by. She rightly says, "You don't ask tradespeople their faith but their prices." She is leery of heroism, believing instead that in a decent country no heroes are needed. DiMaggio would mean nothing to her. It is all far more basic: Germany is ravaged by war as Protestants and Catholics take turns (for thirty years, all told) destroying one another, the land, and the people who live on the land. We are witness to a twelve-year endurance test—not quite a three-day marathon such as Santiago's—in which the supreme gambit is to feed and clothe and maintain alive both yourself and your children.

And we see that it is a wager that cannot be won. Eilif, Swiss Cheese, and Kattrin all die; they cannot be protected. All Mother Courage's cunning and prudence and wit are invested in keeping them alive: she tries to outsmart the recruiter, she hands the children black cards to mark their status as death-threatened; she counts on Eilif's dash and agility, Swiss Cheese's sweetness and thickness, and Kattrin's scarred face and mute tongue to keep them on the living side of the ledger. All fail. Each loss appears, almost wordlessly, onstage like an amputation. But the old lady goes on. The children are dead, the mother is not. The author wanted our judgment; he wanted Courage's blind stubbornness to be exposed as collusion with the war, and his ultimate sights were on stopping wars. In some grim way, he was saying, she got what she deserved, she reaped what she'd sowed. Ideologically speaking, there may be some final truth here. Yet I cannot help seeing this woman's nonstop mix of struggle and stratagems—undeniably, unstoppably, hypnotically ruling the play, in your face—as the supreme resistance that our species puts up in its final chapters, even in the midst of carnage and death. Her elemental resilience defies, indeed dwarfs, all our fine categories of heroism and moral beauty. She does not die. She trudges on.

James Joyce's Leopold Bloom

Brecht is well known for his interest in the "little people," the common man and woman who do not always make it into our literature. James Joyce, on the other hand, thought of as esoteric and "high culture," gives us in his hero Leopold Bloom as shrewd and instructive a case of everyday survival skills as we saw in Moll Flanders and Mother Courage. And he knows something about the problems of aging. In fact, Joyce reprises old Rip Van Winkle, who slept through his marriage, as a figuration of Bloom's issues of belatedness. We first encounter Rip in the "Nausicaa" chapter of *Ulysses*, where a prodigious amount of erotic information has been coming our way. Bloom sits alone on the beach, busily ogling the young Gerty McDowell (who no less busily fantasizes about the "dark stranger" so intently watching her, so demonstrably worked up by what he's seeing), who is rocking back and forth, showing her silent admirer ever more leg and thigh and higher up still. Joyce maliciously cuts this mutual arousal scene with a prayer retreat devoted to the Virgin Mary, so that we are obliged to consider all these rapturous ventures—Bloom masturbating, Gerty moving ever further into romantic reverie, the men at the church moving no less deeply into their own passionate adoration of a woman's body—as a lesson in hydraulics, in what it takes to move the human machine into some kind of altered state and release. What, you may ask, does this tell us about growing old? Bloom is not old—only thirty-eight—but we see him as distinctly past his prime, because that is how he sees himself. While his wife, Molly, is fornicating with her lover—that is what she is doing—he is masturbating on a beach; onanism has replaced copulation. He has arrived at the period of substitutions; in fact, he is something of a genius at substitutions. That would be the lesson of time.

Spent sexually, Bloom muses about his current lot: "he [Boylan, the lover] gets the plums, and I the plumstones," sensing that youthful passion is now gone, "Only once it comes." He now recalls a game of charades in which he played Rip Van Winkle, with Molly looking on, and he muses about how he now fits the part: "Twenty years asleep in Sleepy Hollow. All changed. Forgotten. The young are old. His gun rusty from the dew." *His gun rusty from the dew.* Irving's character was grateful for being out of the action, but Bloom is a wryer figure, unable to change things and to turn back the clock but heartbreakingly unable also to forget the sexual entente he and Molly once shared: "Wildly I lay on her, kissed her: eyes, her lips, her stretched neck beating, woman's breasts full in her blouse of nun's veiling, fat nipples upright. I tongued her. She kissed me. I was kissed. All yielding she tossed my hair. Kissed, she kissed me." Growing old means realizing you'll never have this again. "Me. And me now," as Joyce's text has it. Time deals you out; you make the best of it.

But *Ulysses* is out to insert Rip Van Winkle into a stormier, murkier scenario. The long convulsive, metamorphosing chapter called "Circe" is set in a brothel, and Bloom has been subject to considerable bullying—his putative wishes and daydreams are trotted out as if they had been actualized, and he is repeatedly put on trial for them—which reaches its apex in a morphological fantasia: he changes sex; he becomes female, and the brothel madam, Bella Cohen, now becomes Bello. One is free to interpret this psychologically: maybe Bloom has always wanted to be a woman? Maybe he has. But—and this is a real question, not a rhetorical one—has he wanted the kind of upbraiding and sadistic treatment that he's going to receive at the hands of Bello? Bello threatens the female Bloom with whipping, sits on him, rides him, plunges his arm "elbowdeep in Bloom's vulva." With unerring logic, the humiliation game moves to Bloom's most anxious area, his genitals, as Bello ridicules his limp organ, contrasting it with the rather more robust business going on between Molly and the hugely endowed Blazes Boylan: "Well for you, you muff, if you had that weapon with knobs and lumps and warts all over it. He shot his bolt, I can tell you! Foot to foot, knee to knee, belly to belly, bubs to breast! He's no eunuch. A shock of red hair he has sticking out of him behind like a furzebush!" Here is a growing-old male nightmare of serious proportions.

Bloom is driven mad by the taunting, claims he "forgot"—forgot what? to maintain sexual relations with his wife? to stay young?—but Bello informs him that all is changed in his marriage since he's been sleeping "horizontal in Sleepy Hollow [his] night of twenty years." And on cue, Bloom is now shown "in tattered moccasins with a rusty fowling piece," looking into the past for Molly, seeing a girl in a green dress and golden hair, only to learn from Bello that it is his daughter, not his wife. Milly Bloom speaks (for the only time in the novel) and informs her father of the central home truth of his life: "My! It's Papli! But, O Papli, how old you've grown!" Out of the mouths of babes the truth is spoken.

We know that Bloom and Molly have not had sex since their infant son Rudy died at the age of eleven days. We also know that Bloom is not, *pace* Milly, old, but the days of sexual heat are behind him. Yet his case is illuminating for us, precisely because he is so wise and inventive when it comes to ersatz solutions to the problems and crises life presents. That his wife is cheating on him is problem number one, but scarcely the only problem: he also reflects on other unchangeable facts, such as the mentioned death of his son and the death (by suicide) of his father. This is a heavy burden, but it has its unarguable generic truth: the older you get, the more hard-to-deal-with cadavers there are in your story. (Dodging bullets is an increasingly urgent and frenetic pastime after one reaches a certain age.) I believe that Bloom evinces, in the face of these hard facts, virtues worthy of Homer, for he has learned that life still engages and charms even when deaths press and youth and passion are past.

One should in fact regard all the Bloom chapters in the novel as prima facie evidence of how one copes with trouble, how one gets back into the game (conceptually) after being cast out of it (factually, even biologically). There is true wisdom here, even if it has nothing to do with grand pronouncements or moral truths. *Ulysses* most fully rewards us by transforming Ulysses into an ordinary man coping with a boatload of troubles—troubles that mount as you grow older, as you find yourself on the far side of things. To borrow a term from Dickens, Bloom is the "artful dodger," the man who has a peerless talent for slithering through. Slithering through may seem unheroic, but going under is still less palatable. Yet to call Bloom evasive or cowardly is to give him the short end of the stick, for the genius of Joyce's novel has to do with Bloom's activism, not his escapism: his capacity for day-dreaming, for musing, for pondering, for changing the subject, for getting out of the way, for savoring what there is to savor while maneuvering around what is coming at him.

What is there to savor? A fried kidney for breakfast. A walk to the butcher shop, where he can admire the haunches of the girl in front of him. A curiosity about the way Dublin itself works: its businesses, its cemetery, its taverns, its waterworks, its politics, its stories. A renewed sense of life's pulse even in the cemetery at the funeral of a friend, where the processes of dissolution and creation—a cemetery is also a picnic ground, Bloom opines— merge in their crazy dance, whetting his appetite for more life. A capacity to "let fly" on the beach when young female limbs are being paraded for him. (Why not? He and she both get something out of it.) An equal capacity to tend to the brilliant but drunken young poet whom he helps out of the brothel and invites to his home. An unequaled capacity to put time's injuries into perspec-tive, so that he still returns to his marriage bed at the day's close, and what he finds on the bed—his wife's body (plus the imprint of her lover's body)—is still "home," is still the "ample bedwarmed flesh" that is his anchor.

Many of culture's traditional pieties are overturned here—no moralizing, no revenge, no heart-to-heart with the wife, no the-atrics, no higher vision—as Joyce's hero pays his homage to life's plenitude. Here is the wisdom of the comic vision: life itself trumps any and all truisms or judgments that might be said about it. Leopold Bloom remains a man in his thirties, a richly carnal figure, and I have to wonder what he would be had Joyce tapped into him two or three decades later, when he would be more des-iccated, more ailing, closer to death. But he stands even now as a wise man, one who understands that what life overtly robs you

of—youth, passion—it nonetheless covertly gifts you in the form
of endless opportunities for thinking, reflecting, musing, even remembering: all ways of taking your craft right on through.

A final word on Bloom and on *Ulysses:* the calculus I have tried
to outline in discussing Bloom's strategies for getting through
life—a calculus that interweaves facts and fictions, loss and substitution, deprivation and fantasy, past and present—seems to me at
once radiant in wisdom and altogether invisible to the naked eye.
Joyce's character is a fabulous piece of work, because he never
stops responding to the incessant blows and stimuli life presents,
and he thereby fashions, just like an artist, his own special song
and dance. It is not for nothing that he is Joyce's candidate for a
modern-day Ulysses—a survivor, an artful dodger. Are his skills
not the right ones for aging? Even the happiest, healthiest, and
most serene among us know that losses, renunciations, and exits
are in the wings, that life's bills are coming due. It's time for wit
and cunning—not only for strategic purposes, for warding off
hurt, for being able to stay in the game, but also for positive and
invigorating reasons: the sheer vitality of managing, the almost
muscular pleasure of avoiding, some of those Scyllas and Charyb-
dises that aging inevitably sets in our path. Is there no Ulysses in
each of us?

Love's Legacy

Growth is how we want to see our final phase, but shrinkage and dispossession are all too often the hallmarks of aging. From King Lear to Willy Loman and Isak Borg, the apprenticeship with death commands the stage. Passion recedes, entropy is real. Even the good fight must eventually be lost. Even the keenest sense of life's plenitude and artful dodging are temporary reprieves. Literature's players perform a service for us here. I am nourished each time I reread *Ulysses*, because Bloom shows me how mercurial and prancing the human mind is, how many bargains and stand-offs remain to be made with trouble and even catastrophe. Even tragic outcomes, such as that of Lear or Phèdre, can be luminous with knowledge about the theatrics of power and the landscape of passion. Sometimes the book is cautionary, and we hope to avoid the failed life of a John Marcher, who could not see the love offered him.

Marcher's experience warrants further reflection. His maniacal focus on the Great Event he felt coming testifies, tragically, to defective vision. If aging is to be a time of growth, not diminution, it seems clear, from the cumulative testimony seen throughout this study, that one key human resource is at the core of things: love. Love is both perspectival and vehicular, for it enables us either to see aright or to transform, indeed transcend, the empirical circumstances of our lives. As far back as Ibsen's Solness, we saw that love could be a generative force, capable of creating a space for living that is not located on any map. But love gone wrong looms large in this study—democratically poisoning the existences of both the young and the old, operating like Robert Frost's rendition of fire and ice, quite capable of wrecking human life through heat or cold, abuse or indifference, dooming a Heathcliff or a Goriot—and we realize that love, to be redemptive for old age, must be reoriented, reconceived, made into something generous, something that can outlive flesh itself. This is not easy, and it is especially not easy as one ages.

Keeping the Heart Alive

So much of this study has been about the inroads of time, especially in connection with loss of power and the law of mortality. These matters are often shockingly tangible: think Lear on the heath. But time can be deadly in still other ways, drying us up over time, cooling our affections, atrophying our capacity to love. Heart disease is known to be a killer for the old, and medical science rightly pays attention; but we have neither statistics nor remedies for the numbers of people whose hearts die while they continue to go through their paces.

Gabriel García Márquez's Aureliano

The undisputed masterpiece of magic realism, *One Hundred Years of Solitude,* is remembered as an explosion of folklore, color, fantasy, desire, and freedom. Larded with scenes that sweetly annihilate Western logic—the dead return, rooms explode with yellow butterflies, Rebeca has a voracious hunger for dirt, Remedios the beautiful simply ascends into the air—this book nonetheless recognizes solitude as the inevitable carceral condition of the human subject, no matter how vibrant the spectacle may be. Many of its characters end up being walled off from the world: Rebeca, Fernanda, Amaranta. But the towering figure in this regard is Aureliano, the son who became a colonel and devoted his entire life to unending war, with the result that he increasingly lived out Edgar Allan Poe's favorite plot of immurement, of being buried alive.

The first sign of this withdrawal is to be found in his radical decision "that no human being, not even Úrsula, could come closer to him than ten feet." We watch the spate of realpolitik military decisions, entailing the death of feeling and trust, the drying up of the heart. And we recall the novel's haunting first line—"Many years later, as he faced the firing squad, Colonel Aureliano Buendía was to remember that distant afternoon when his father took him to discover ice." It is a cunning opener, inasmuch as Aureliano does *not* die by firing squad but ice will indeed stand as his permanent element, his fate. No passage conveys the frigidity and solipsism of his life better than the heartbreaking moment when he looks at his aged mother and actually sees the wreckage time has made of her:

> Her skin was leathery, her teeth decayed, her hair faded and colorless, and her look frightened. He compared her with the oldest memory that he had of her, the afternoon when he had the premonition that a pot of boiling water was going to fall off the table, and he found her broken to pieces. In an instant he discovered the scratches, the welts, the sores, the ulcers, and the scars that had been left on her by more than a half century of daily life, and he saw that those damages did not even arouse a feeling of pity in him. Then he made one last effort to search in his heart for the place where his affection had rotted away and he could not find it.

This is unflinching. Every reader anticipates that the sequence will end on an uptick, that the final, searching effort to retrieve his love for his mother will succeed, will bear fruit. But it doesn't. And we are awed, I think, by the physiological and perceptual detail here: he is taking her measure, he is missing nothing of her decrepitude, her nearness to death, what time has done to her. One wants to think that such a clinical, unsparing eye—for we rarely see our loved ones in this naked fashion—will trigger feelings, will be followed by compassion. But García Márquez will not cater to our fond wants. Two deaths seem announced here: hers in the body and his in the soul. Should Aureliano's hollowing out be ascribed to ice? to continuous war? to the erosions of time? The book leaves it open, but its presentation of characters whispers to us that we are victims of many histories: not merely the depredations of colonialism and Western imperialism but, no less insidiously, the eating up of the heart by time itself, as if that key muscle were not constituted to respond to, even to withstand, the presence of other people over the long haul.

Mortuary vision: Aureliano sizing up his old, old mother; seeing, in virtually clinical fashion, every single incursion inflicted by time and feeling nothing. To forbid anyone to come within ten feet of you is to make yourself into a mausoleum, as well as to construe all other living beings—including those who love you—as death threats. But the sought-after protection comes too late; the invader has already entered and struck his blow. What we cannot fail to see is that Aureliano himself is the dead one, that he has at last fully succumbed to ice, that his apparent use of limbs and brain is illusory because rigor mortis has taken over. García Márquez suggests that a life of waging war is responsible for calcifying the heart, and maybe that is so; but at the end of his legendary career he stands in our minds as entombed alive, as exiled from the pulse of life, as the corpse he will become. How not to see this also as allegory of aging?

Ingmar Bergman's Helena

Aureliano loses all mobility of feeling. He becomes a mummy, dead to all stimuli. Against this cautionary fate of rigor mortis, I want to present what I take to be its opposite number: someone who remains supple and capable of love right to the end. Helena, the grandmother in Bergman's final film, *Fanny and Alexander*, exhibits a kind of warmth, power, resilience, and maturity that we find all too rarely in art, even if it must indeed exist in life. One of my favorite scenes comes early as Helena (well into her sixties) and her friend/lover Isak (the old Jew, the man of magic) await the arrival of all the sons and grandchildren for the sumptuous

Christmas feast, the *Julbord.* In a very sweet shot, we see the old couple peer out in all directions, making sure that nobody is watching them, and then sneak a nice kiss. A kiss, not a peck. A further installment in this vein occurs late at night, after the grand feast, as the old couple awaits the dawn. Helena then talks of the infirmities of aging, of crying fits, of the problems (financial and emotional and moral) encountered by her grown children, noting that both Gustav and Carl are oversexed, just as their father (her dead husband) was: "He was insatiable. At times I thought it was too much of a good thing, but I never refused."

Although one might cavil at "I never refused" and see in it a form of patriarchal bullying, I'd rather put the emphasis on "too much of a good thing." Yes, he wanted it too often, but then this is one of the good things one wants. This leads naturally to reminiscences involving their own long-term love affair, including a memory of the husband surprising them in a moment of intimacy: she with an unbuttoned blouse, he with unbuttoned trousers, and the paterfamilias initially wanting to get his pistol but finally becoming friends for life with old Isak. Helena then turns weepy, fearing that the good life is over—Isak has already concurred, bad times are upon them, upon their world—but the scene does not finish in tears. On the contrary, Helena gets past her cry and begins to ready herself for the Christmas Day activities. Her words speak Bergman's late wisdom: "No, my dear sir, this won't do at all. I shall wash, repaint my face, do my hair, and put on my stays and silk dress. A weepy, lovesick woman turns into a self-possessed grandmother. We play our parts. Some play them negligently; others play them with great care. I am one of the latter."

Perhaps this is what a life in the theater teaches a filmmaker (Bergman's career spanned both); or perhaps it is what Bergman learned from Shakespeare's own baroque vision of life as a stage, of life as stages. Later in the story, Helena speaks to her dead son, Oscar (who has returned as resident ghost, who died of a stroke incurred while rehearsing the role of *Hamlet*'s ghost), and she formulates what I take to be the wisest perception of the film, concerning, once again, the roles we play and the responsibilities we bear: "I enjoyed being a mother. I enjoyed being an actress too, but I preferred being a mother. I liked being pregnant and didn't care tuppence for the theater then. For that matter, everything is acting. Some parts are nice, others not so nice. I played a mother. I played Juliet, Ophelia. Suddenly I am playing the part of a widow. Or a grandmother. One part follows the other. The thing is not to scamp. Not to shirk."

When we reflect on the negative valence that role-playing has in ordinary parlance, on how we customarily associate it with inauthenticity and deception, we can grasp the power and beauty of this doctrine. We are always playing. To live in time requires this. *One part follows the other.* Shakespearean wisdom: we inhabit a theater world, and unless we die young, we are destined to occupy many positions, to respond to evolving conditions (including those of our own body, which alters over time), to try out many selves. What counts is that we treat each role as genuine while we play it—that we authenticate the roles and parts that life deals out to us by leading with the heart. And even that is too simple, as one role does not fully cancel out another. Here, then, is the plenitude of life. And of heart. Helena's response to the dance of time is offered without even a whiff of regret or wistfulness: each life phase brings its requirements, opportunities, and rewards. Helena is simultaneously the reminiscing lover of Isak and the self-possessed grandmother who rules over the family's rites. And it is within this larger spectrum of positions and selves, of a moving stage and a moving "I," that the role of love—including physical, sexual love—assumes its proper place. It has nothing to do with compartmentalizing, everything to do with a plenary sense of human doing, not all that far from Shakespeare's "readiness is all" but oriented toward life, not death.

I called Helena the matriarch of the story, and that, too, warrants a final word. We see her throughout the film presiding over the affairs and catastrophes of her family, including the emotional and erotic careers of her three sons. But do not forget: she remains not only the wise one who counsels, who has a special, tender relationship with her grandson Alexander, but she seems as well to have learned the lesson Lear never learned: she holds on to the money. She hosts the great family feast, bankrolls the theater, pays off the loans of her profligate son Carl, and closes the film in business discussions with Oscar's widow, pondering whether or not to stage Strindberg's *Dream Play*, perhaps even to return to the stage herself. In a film where men do rather badly—one son is impotent and dies, another is oversexed and a joke, a third is a failure in marriage and work, and the grand villain of the piece is the handsome bishop Edvard, who does what he can to ruin everyone's life—she is a remarkable success story. Old, yes, but ever vital: she never scamps, she never shirks. Is it too much to say that she is an empowered woman? Perhaps few cultures formally assign roles of power to women, but this old lady lives long enough to rule the roost.

The Eyes of Love

In the following pages I want to argue that there is also a richness in growing old, a wealth that has nothing to do with material assets or nest eggs but rather a human gift conferred on us by time itself—time, the capricious and brutal thief that is so adept at robbing us and diminishing our estate, erasing our gains, dismantling our achievements. Could time be generous? What can it offer?

In Virginia Woolf's *Mrs. Dalloway*, Peter Walsh philosophizes about just these matters: "the compensation of growing old, Peter Walsh thought, coming out of Regent's Park, and holding his hat in hand, was simply this; that the passions remain as strong as ever, but one has gained—at last!—the power which adds the supreme flavour to existence,—the power of taking hold of experience, of turning it round, slowly, in the light." One is gratified by this perception of late power, this grounded, anchored condition of at last being equal to experience, being even superior to it, able finally to examine it, make sense of it. On this head, age turns us into masters, turns our life into a laboratory, in which we hold experience in our hands—experience, the most mercurial, ungirdled, flowing thing of all—and squeeze it into truth, our own truth. A late clarity that orders the affairs of our life: that would be a vista worth attaining.

Taking hold of experience... in the light. I want to talk about light, about vision: how we see the old, how the old see themselves and their world, and finally how growth might be located precisely here. Could we learn to look differently upon the world? Could literature help us toward a more generous optic about the density of human lives, especially the sheer temporal richness of those we have lived with and cared for during our time? The inner vision of old age is uniquely constituted to balance the momentary retinal evidence of our eyes with the rich invisible testimony of years gone by. Old people acquire a longitudinal perspective on the people and even the places they have known and loved, and their memories are filled to the brim with things that no longer exist, children once young but now grown up, spouses once in their prime but now old, parents and grandparents once present and dear but now dead: "vanished but not gone," as Faulkner puts it in his haunting tale of mourning, "Pantaloon in Black." No, the retina cannot manage this vision, but the heart can. And so can literature.

William Shakespeare's Sonnet 73

One of Shakespeare's most haunting evocations of old age is to be found in Sonnet 73:

> That time of year thou mayst in me behold
> When yellow leaves, or none, or few, do hang
> Upon those boughs that shake against the cold,
> Bare ruined choirs, where late the sweet birds sang.
> In me thou seest the twilight of such day
> As after sunset fadeth in the west,
> Which by and by black night doth take away,
> Death's second self, that seals up all in rest.
> In me thou seest the glowing of such fire
> That on the ashes of his youth doth lie,
> As the death-bed whereon it must expire,
> Consumed with that which it was nourished by.
> > This thou perceiv'st, which makes thy love more strong,
> > To love that well, which thou must leave ere long.

Perhaps the most striking feature of Shakespeare's poem is the harsh, unavoidable klieg light beam that it insistently focuses on the spectacle of decline. What is it thou mayst behold, thou seest, thou seest, thou perceiv'st? My decrepitude. My wreckage. My descent into death. The poet avails himself of seasonal and elemental images to convey this common fate: the trees, once animated by birds, are now leafless and quivering; the sunset heralds the transformation of light into dark, into sleep, into death (the death we encounter nightly); one still possesses heat, but it is only a glow, a turning in on itself of the vital fire of youth now become ashes, a fire that is going out, en route to extinction, cold and dark. Paraphrasing Shakespeare always embarrasses, for his own images are at once sharp and mysterious, as in the indeterminacy of those leaves—yellow, none, or few—which may or may not still be on the bough, yielding a bristling picture of growing bareness, growing bereftness; likewise the conflation of sunset and sleep, common enough in Elizabethan poetic discourse, manages also to invoke a dead body being sealed up or a coffin being sealed shut; and the final sinuous account of fire and glow is simply untrackable, inasmuch as the living heat of the old person now appears to be a remnant of youth, a borrowed flame—as perhaps all our flame is, meted out to us at birth and slowly diminishing over time—yielding an image of old age as a form of suicide, a self-consumption, a supreme economy by which our organism plays out, returns to quiescence. This entire suite of metaphors dwarfs any notional account of aging by conceiving of it as a complex natural undoing pageant of sorts, a programmed end to vitality, heat, light, and life.

All this is what thou seest. And now the poem turns sublime: seeing this, one's love for the wintry, death-gripped person becomes more strong, grows. At this juncture the unidirectional, death-driven organicism of the poem turns inside out, reverses course, bequeathing a view of human love as victorious over death, as indeed strengthened and nourished by its war with entropy, as feeding on death. As a commentary on old age—on the "lovability" of the old—it is a welcome piece of news, and it beautifully inverts everything in its path, turning loss into gain, diminishment into growth, death into life. Of course our death cannot be stopped by another's love, but the poem nonetheless posits human affection for us as a clear countertug against the exit we are doomed to make. The economy is perfect: our own weak-ening is matched, degree by degree, by the intensifying feelings of our loved ones, as if they were cued to the same natural phenom-enon. One is the face of the other.

But they move in different directions, and that is what is so beautiful. It is because life is transitory that it is so unspeakably valuable. It is because the signs of old age are nature's script of an impending death that we cherish even more intensely those whom we know we must lose. Would that not be the lesson we must learn: to see all those we care for in temporal, even fatal terms? To realize that each life carries its death and is hence all the more urgent and precious? Who more than the old should take this vision to heart?

Old Cities, Old People: Sigmund Freud

There is a fine moment in *Civilization and Its Discontents* where Freud evokes the temporal/spatial history of Rome: he points out that the city of his (modern) time is a layered place, that the many Catholic edifices are built over the ruins of the earlier known pagan temples, which themselves were erected over still earlier monuments, signaling still prior cultures. The eye can see none of this: two buildings cannot occupy the same site. Only the in-formed inner eye can take in this layered space, and even then one cannot visualize it. I want to enlist Freud's Rome portrait as a par-adigm of age itself, and I want to go on to say that old cities and monuments have always exerted a fascination on viewers and vis-itors for just those reasons: they are the living residue of times and peoples seemingly long dead. The great cultural centers of the world are storied places, virtually palimpsest-like in their overlay of signs and markers. We are drawn to these dense sites in some primitive fashion akin to hunger, as if they afforded entry into (and possession of) the halls of time. Of times. We decipher and pay homage to such structures, sensing that they are big with time, that they are the still-breathing stone language of the past. Is it too much to say that they extend our own reach when we enter their precincts?

Cathedrals, castles, cities: storied structures anchored in time, vast in space. Are these not appropriate figures for our lives? I began this book by suggesting that none of us possesses our figure in the carpet, the melody that will cohere our days and works; nothing in your safe deposit box manages to give the fuller measure of your estate. How can you bring it to visibility, bring it back to life? None of your assets, nothing the doctor prescribes or the priest recommends, will propel you again into those spaces or ferry you again into those waters, so as to miraculously bring those days and years back to life. No matter how "wired" and connected you are, no matter how great your electronic and digital reach may be, your grasp of your own long itinerary—and those of others— must needs be meager. How can we recapture our dimensions?

Poetry and Memory: Charles Baudelaire

Charles Baudelaire, arguably the patron saint of modern poetry, wrote a number of astonishing urban portraits of life in Paris during the 1850s, and some of his most haunting pieces are built out of double vision, out of the sharp contrast between what the retina takes in and what the heart or brain remembers. "Le Cygne" ("The Swan") offers a magnificent picture of Paris as palimpsest, as multilayered. *"Paris change plus vite, hélas, que le coeur d'un mortel,"* observes, elegiacally, the poet as he compares the altering cityscape with the turns of the human heart. What moves me in this poem is the countermove required by reading: we are asked to perceive the invisible temporal and moral depths that undergird the cityscape: the hidden origins and precursors of its buildings and its denizens, all the while knowing that none of this is "on view." All of us contain ruins. There is an ethos here, an ethos for the old.

Ruins. Is that not what weary Oedipus at Colonus is, at least until the prophecy of redemption for Athens is actualized? Old Lear, old Goriot, old Isak Borg: are they not ruins? Consider the teeming modern cityscape, filled with decaying people and buildings, and ask yourself if you do not see entropy writ large. This is why another Baudelaire poem, "Little Old Ladies," is so remarkable. The poet begins with a merciless, clinical look at the old women who trudge the streets of Paris, creatures at once *"décrépits et charmants,"* women shrunken and twisted and buffeted by the wind, compared to puppets, to bells, to small children (for they have in common tiny caskets), women now become debris, wreckage, outright grotesques. That is what time does. Yet in the fourth segment of the poem, something miraculous occurs: they are transfigured by the vision of the poet. Once upon a time they were giddy actresses and fabled beauties in their dazzling prime, now they are seen trudging through the polis; once their names were known by all, but now no one recognizes them. Drunks insult them, children mock them. They are frightened, wizened, shameful, hovering in the shadows. But the poet restores them in his mind's eye, imagines their fiery youth, bonds with them with a kind of intimacy and empathy that borders on the obscene: he watches over them, he senses their secret pleasures, he lives their lost days, his heart is expanded by their vices, turned luminous by their virtues. *"Ruines. Ma famille."* They are ruins; they are his family.

Baudelaire and Freud are cartographers of a special sort: they are alive to the temporal density of cities and humans. What they tell us, in their own way, is that humans are also historical monuments, replete with stories, memories, scar tissue, and the living pith of days and works. Baudelaire is almost vampirish in his approach to the little old women (one can imagine a policeman arresting him if the contents of his mind were visible; but then, many of us would be in jail if that were possible): he feels the pulsing blood and the pulsing past that yet lives in these derelicts that litter Parisian streets. And he battens onto this matter, this magma, sensing that it is his nourishment, his family. This is queasy if you wish, but it is also generous, indeed sublime. And it figures the landscape and territoriality of human time in sharp, pungent, affective terms. The sheer vibrancy of the old ladies' distant past functions as a libidinal fuel for art; it finances his poem, it composes his family, it makes him larger than he was. In this we see a generosity proper to art, and it is something nourishing and elemental that we, the readers, can, cannibal-like, also partake of, by the simple act of reading and imagining. We too become fellow travelers. We resurrect monuments, cities, and people.

In Freud, it is a question of hallowing the historical density of places. In Baudelaire it is a matter of imagining the past vibrancy and beauty of those whom time assails. Age is a capacious entity, but what it contains is invisible to the eye. Remember again Aureliano's cold, diagnostic, clinical view of his own mother, Úrsula. He sees it all: mother as monument, mother as dimensional; yet he feels nothing at all. Against that calcified image, place Shakespeare's lover of Sonnet 73, equally acute and unflinching in its ocular testimony but fueled by tenderness and love. That you are to die makes me love you the more.

The Optics of Love: Marcel Proust

Proust, whom I take to be the master of "fourth-dimensional vision," the longitudinal vision of life in time, had no illusions about how arduous such a vision is. Arduous not because we are hard-hearted and refuse to think of our loved ones' mortality but precisely because love itself censors such thoughts, because the very nature of love must blind us to the reality of death. I mean "blind" quite literally. This is shown in the sequence where the young narrator speaks to his grandmother by long-distance telephone and is able to discern in her very voice that she is ailing, hearing "for the first time the sorrows that had cracked [her face] in the course of a lifetime," realizing that he urgently needs to see her. *To see her:* that is what is at stake here. Can you "see" a loved one? It is not an idle question. He rushes back to Paris and hastens to her room, opening the door on her without any warning at all and getting an eyeful; because she does not know he is there, he is, in some significant sense, not there but merely a photographer taking a photograph of "places which one will never see again":

> The process that automatically occurred in my eyes when I caught sight of my grandmother was indeed a photograph. We never see the people who are dear to us save in the animated system, the perpetual motion of our incessant love for them, which, before allowing the images that their faces present to reach us, seizes them in its vortex and flings them back upon the idea that we have always had of them, makes them adhere to it, coincide with it. How, since into the forehead and

the cheeks of my grandmother I had been accustomed to read
the most delicate, the most permanent qualities of her mind,
how, since every habitual glance is an act of necromancy, each
face that we love a mirror of the past, how could I have failed
to overlook what had become dulled and changed in her. . . .
And . . . I, for whom my grandmother was still myself, I who
had never seen her save in my own soul, always in the same
place in the past, through the transparency of contiguous and
overlapping memories, suddenly, in our drawing-room which
formed part of a new world, that of time, that which is inhabited by the strangers of whom we say "He's begun to age a
great deal," for the first time and for a moment only, since she
vanished very quickly, I saw, sitting on the sofa beneath the
lamp, red-faced, heavy and vulgar, sick, vacant, letting her
slightly crazed eyes wander over a book, a dejected old woman
whom I did not know.

This long, rich, intricate, and gruesome passage challenges
Shakespeare's injunction to look on old age, because it says that
such objective notation—measuring the damage, scouring the
landscape—is possible only via distance and indifference. We are
not constituted to be able to see our loved ones in this way, Proust
asserts. Our love freezes them in time, pickles them (as it were),
and hence blinds us to the unceasing work of time that goes about
dismantling all human creatures who live long enough.

We see easily enough what this passage tells us about love, but
what does it tell us about old age? I'd want to say that it helps to
explain how surprised many of us are to find ourselves, one fine
day, old; and then to realize that we've been old for some time now.
The surprise comes, in part, from the conspiracy of silence that
surrounds us: our friends and loved ones do not pass on the news
that we are becoming gaga because they do not truly see it themselves, given their affection for us. Resisting the testimony of time
seems almost hardwired in us: one retains an image of self from
childhood, fancies that one is still on the front side of one's trajectory, poised to enter the fray, to engage in life's battles, that one
still possesses youthful energies, still has bridges to cross and horizons to conquer. It seems fair to assume that this quixotic certainty

deserves credit for much of what is great in life, the energies we marshal, above all our sense of promise and futurity. How dreary life would be, how permanently dispirited one would be, if you knew, early on, the exact number of days you had left to live.

But intimations of mortality cannot stay hidden, no matter how stubborn and "freezing" one's love of others, or indeed of oneself, might be. Proust disposes of many registers as he deals with the shocking realization that human bodies never stop altering. He writes in the final volume of a reception where the narrator, now old, simply cannot link together the "feather-light fair girl" of his youth with the "massive white-haired lady" in front of him, and he realizes that life's slow, imperceptible projects of dismantlement and reconstruction—carrried out on human bodies—utterly dwarf the work of architecture. Some have white hair, some have none, some limp, some have had strokes, some have palsy, all display the relentless tug of gravity that is inexorably bringing them into the earth. The Sphinx told us of a creature that moves from four legs to two legs to three legs, but it ain't just the number of legs that alters over time. When I look at the photographs of myself on the suite of books I've written—in 1974, 1981, 1988, 1993, 2003, 2006—I get dizzy at the biological countdown staring at me in the smiling face of somebody I know very well but whose entropic trajectory has usually been mercifully hidden from me. I see the lines appear, the flesh sag, the bones protrude, and it makes me wonder if my sequentially smiling face is not a joke (on me): what am I smiling about? Live long enough, and you become something of a morphological carnival.

We know how such carnivals finish. Or we think we do. Arguably the most beautiful segment in all of Proust focuses on the grandmother's "double death." The old lady suffers the slights of time and illness: a stroke, bedridden, loss of hearing, then sight, then speech. At last she dies, and the child narrator is awakened by his parents to bid her farewell, but what he sees is a "beast" on the bed whom he does not recognize, who does not recognize him. Proust writes this as a version of Little Red Riding Hood: if this is not Grandmother, where is she? Rather than answer that question, the novel goes its merry way, the protagonist starts to get some lessons about sexual love, but then the boy returns to the coastal town of Balbec, where he had earlier vacationed with his (already sick) grandmother. Tired from his travels, bending down to remove his boots, the boy is violently struck by a living force that explodes into his life: it is Grandmother, Grandmother of long memory, possessed of all the little acts of goodness and kindness bestowed on him, including her tenderness right here in this coastal hotel a year earlier. What we see is that it is only now that the grandmother truly dies, for it is only now that he truly realizes what she was for him.

Was? No, still is, as the testimony of dream and memory makes clear, for he stays locked in his room, prey to a series of almost intolerably beautiful and painful visions and reminiscences and outright oneiric versions of dying/dead Grandmother, of seeking her in the hidden little room where, dead, she still lived but failing to find her, to tell her how much he loved her, to say farewell. It is a moment of loving grace, even if she is buried in the ground and he is alone in a room. Here, then, is a narrative drastically different from the spectacle of a beast on a bed. No, we cannot make the sun stand still—we cannot prevent the old from dying—but love constitutes our rival creation, our ability to create a space (*Gi plads!*) that still lives. Memory itself is the afterlife for which no religious creed is required.

Must we discover what people mean to us only after their death? Proust's narrator is in a room remembering Grandmother's sweet love, and he is tortured by the knowledge that nothing can now be done. But something can be done. We are capable of envisioning those we love with this long-angled perception and thereby seeing what they were, what they have ceased to be, even as we take in what they are and perhaps face the horror of a time when they will not be at all. To look at people with the eyes of memory is the ethical injunction, I believe, for growing old. Again I cite Proust: such a vision would endow our loved ones "with the beautiful and inimitable velvety patina of the years, just as in an old park a simple runnel of water comes with the passage of time to be enveloped in a sheath of emerald." *The beautiful and inimitable velvety patina of the years:* such is the creative work of time.

Creative, not entropic. Time as the maker of beauty and value,

not time as despoiler. Growing old is the indispensable require-
ment for such gathering, ripening perceptions. In this model, our
loved ones acquire a kind of narrative and temporal density that
we ourselves map and cherish. In this model, fidelity and marriage and family emerge, memory-fed, as the great creations of
life, the fashioning of a vision that hallows what has been while
meshing it with what is while knowing what is eventually to
come.

Of course we must die, perhaps even become a "beast on a
bed." But before we reach our ultimate undoing, we are still
sighted and sentient creatures, capable of remembering, charting,
even imagining the work of time in those we know and love. A
homage is due to this. For time does not simply dismantle us and
our projects; it also coheres and completes them, brings them to
visibility, confers on them their gathering plenary form. Time is
at once the currency and the structure of love, for it frames and
parses the life of the heart. This is the work of generosity, this is
the true architecture of our lives. Perhaps old age is our final opportunity to reach toward such cohesion, in our loved ones as well
as ourselves. Old age is when we might finally carry out our harvest.

These are the creations of love. They are the direct opposite of
mortality's decimations. And I have no illusions about what I am
up against. Old age is also, I know only too well, a dyspeptic, corrosive time, a time for measuring losses, not gains, a time for acquiring an unwanted gift for seeing ruin everywhere. I know what
the cumulative testimony of the books discussed here tells us
about the "cost of living" and the diminishments meted out by
age. *"Det var bättre förr,"* my Swedish relatives tell me, "It was
better before," and the "it" in question is capacious: the world we
live in, as well as the people we are. Of course we must exit the
world. And ourselves. Yet we remain impoverished, I think, when
it comes to vision, for the spectacle of decline all too easily erases
the memory of growth, and it is their tandem that gives the measure of who we are and how we have lived (as opposed to how we
are dying).

One needs to learn to appreciate the accretive and fulfilling work of time: constancy, fidelity, friendship, respect, tenderness, love; these virtues are drenched with temporality, become richer and fuller as we go on living. I do not proclaim that we should be antiquarian about this or blindly venerate the sheer longevity of our human connections. But that patina of which Proust wrote speaks to the beauty and beneficent changes brought about by time, and only by time. There is no shortcut to enduring love. No one but you can have the dimensional perspective of loved ones that you have, just as you alone can gauge the layers and reaches of your own existence. I sometimes wonder if the appeal of the new, when it comes to our moral and imaginative life, doesn't stem from a deep-seated fatigue with oneself, with the same old body and heart and mind that one came to this earth with and that one wearies of, wants to trade in for a new model, for new departures. Libido and desire batten on to the new. Surely, divorce and adventure and change are secret ways of starting over, of closing up shop on what was.

All of this is real, and I cannot deny it. But there is something benighted and reductive and almost vandalizing in such a stance. We are crimping our own lives by not grasping or valuing their plenitude. We diminish our kingdom. In our hunger for the new and different, we give something up, for we seem to have so little imagination for the old, for continuity and fidelity, for the gathering shape of time-drenched things and people, a shape that is for us to imagine and value—not just our own story, but our loved ones' story: we *are* our brother's keepers. Moreover, literature itself gifts us, again and again, with these dimensional portraits, helping us to widen our optic, expand our take, perceive the larger contours of individual existences. In this I am profoundly and literally conservative, because what is at stake is the discovery and conservation of one's temporal estate: sometimes private, sometimes shared, never given, always created. Old men ought to be explorers. Growing old is not an oxymoron: we grow old, and the great challenge is to transform our hearts and perceptions so as to see time's richness, our richness.

But more even than memory and reverence for the work of time, enduring love is the life force that resists Thanatos.

Enduring Love

Love resists Thanatos? Easier said than done. Death comes to all, no matter what strategies and maneuverings and triumphs of heart and spirit are put in its way. In writing this book I have wanted never to lose sight of how things must end. That truth is, if you wish, my moral compass, and it parses even the most affirmative stories I've discussed, just as it must constitute something of a baseline in the mind-set of the old, no matter how much wisdom or courage or humor one has mustered for the journey. With this rather severe principle in place to keep me honest, I have chosen three utterly remarkable works of literature to conclude my discussion of growing old. Each shimmers, I believe, with a radiance I term *enduring love*, but there is nothing saccharine or blissful about them. Each bears witness to the worst that life can—and must—deliver. Each of these books is deeply cued to death: as rupture of self, as cessation of life, as nature's elemental command. Enduring love is not a paradisiacal concept; we shall see that love emerges in these three books as an utterly primitive force, prior to the forms we assign it, anarchic in its power, yet fueling our last wants and deeds every bit as much as it does our youthful entry into things. Time-fed and death-fed, love endures and makes us endure, whether we term this memory or art or grace.

J. Bernlef's Out of Mind

J. Bernlef, despite being a celebrated Dutch author, is not a household name in the United States. His one translated book, *Out of Mind*, deals with what is arguably the single most grisly and nightmarish threat of growing old: dementia, the onset of Alzheimer's disease, the systematic erasure of who we are. Not a happy topic. Above all, a seemingly strange choice to illustrate "enduring love." As we shall see, Bernlef is deeply drawn to the question of what remains when everything, including sanity and self, goes. Yet this short novel is astonishing in its richness and vibrancy, as if the dementia spectacle of overt dissolution and diminution were miraculously offset and even transcended by the rival spectacle of the heart's emotional and temporal fullness, suggesting a dynamic of loss and gain, suggesting that we go out in horrible splendor, not tranquil submission. And it posits love as the stubborn, undying, anonymous, indeed reconfiguring force that stays to the end. Like all great art, this book humbles us, makes us realize how torpid and impoverished our habitual thinking often is when it comes to the essential experiences of living.

The novel's protagonist, Maarten Klein, is a transplanted Dutchman now living, retired, with his Dutch wife, Vera, in Gloucester, Massachusetts. The book records his rapid descent from functional old age to complete dementia. Bernlef understands the routine slings and arrows of getting old: "Year by year things happen to your body. Your feet lose their springiness. You go up and down the stairs once and you have to sit down to catch your breath. Your eyes start to water when you look at one spot for a long time. The shopping bag moves more and more often from one hand to the other and you meet fewer and fewer people's eyes." Yet these generic infirmities, unpleasant but manageable, are different in nature, Maarten senses, from what is now beginning to happen to him. He is increasingly unable to recognize, or make sense of, where he is, when he is, and what he sees. Where, when, what: these are the situational anchors of our sanity and composure, the indispensable markers that locate us in time and space, that give some shape to our existence, that frame our narrative, that undergird our identity. One takes these frames for granted, assumes they are stable and in place; it never occurs to most of us that they might be movable, might indeed be constructs that could metamorphose or evaporate.

At the beginning it all seems rather innocuous. Maarten thinks it's morning when it's evening; he wonders why the schoolchildren aren't coming home on their buses because he thinks it's a weekday when it's Sunday—a liability, yes, but more an annoyance than a catastrophe. Life could still go on in its course; Vera could still steer him. Other mistakes are more embarrassing: Maarten asks about Jack or about the dog Kiss, not remembering that they are long dead and putting his interlocutors into real discomfort. Up to now, I've listed these "errors" or infirmities as deficits, but they are also openings, for the old curbs and brakes that invisibly shape for us what is sayable or doable or possible no longer function for Maarten. Things begin to move. The dead acquaintance, the dead dog: are they dead?

Other residues of Maarten's past also come back, or perhaps they've never left. The war, especially the terrible privations of hunger and fear during the Nazi occupation of Holland, remains as a kind of permanent subscript for Maarten, ready also to pop out at any time, usurping the present time and space. Finally, not surprisingly, Maarten's memories of his family, especially his distant and authoritative father, remain as a kind of affective cluster that is still active, not fully processed or worked through. Likewise, Maarten's earliest erotic longings and experiences remain inside him as a living substratum of sensation and pulsation: his sexual initiation with the beautiful Karen, whose luscious body made him want to kneel in front of her and worship her; and earlier still, his infatuation with his piano teacher, Greta, for whom he hungered with all his might, desiring the impossible: to be able to put his head onto her lap and taste/absorb her overwhelming sensual presence. All this lives, all this moves, showing us that there seems to be a psychic law of energy conservation, decreeing that contemporary losses are matched by long-term resurrections. Or, to put it still more accurately, to reveal—now that the busy present scene of bustling reality is losing its authority, is exiting the picture, going up like a curtain—the never-ceasing affective life of the past, now returned to visibility and force, still playing.

Hence Maarten enters a Gloucester tavern, but when the barmaid turns to face him, he has to hold on to the bar: "Of course, I must have changed a great deal in fifty years. Grown fatter. Her nails are painted bright red. The nature of the work requires it. When the phone rings I hear that her voice is deeper, rawer. From smoking, of course. Even in those days she used to smoke a pack a day. Beautiful firm round buttocks." It is, momentarily, the beautiful and desirable Karen, with whom he had his first love affair. And he knows it can't be her, even though it "is" her. Or the way Greta, smelling of perfume, continues to live in his mind, so much so that when he later sees Phil (the young girl hired by Vera to help take care of him) playing the piano, all the pieces fall beautifully, tragically, and absurdly into place:

I pull a chair up and look at the strong ringless fingers as they seek their way effortlessly over the black and white keys. How beautifully she plays! And then I do what I have always wanted to do but have never dared. She briefly goes on playing, but then she lifts my head from her lap and pushes me upright. In her fright she starts talking to me in English.

"You mustn't do that again. Otherwise I shall have to leave."

All in rapid English. The lesson is clearly at an end, although I haven't played a single note to her yet. She leads me to the settee and then goes to the kitchen.

What does one say in the face of a scene like this? Neither Phil nor Vera could possibly see or grasp the larger gestalt taking form here, as Maarten thinks he is at last showing his adoration for Greta the teacher (speaking English, oddly enough, instead of Dutch). Time avails not; he is in Holland fifty years earlier. The child you were returns and takes over; growing old recedes into growing up. Of course it is an awful mishmash of time and place, and no amount of lovely crystallizing private fantasy can offset the grotesque human errors on show here. But in some deep sense, Bernlef's story is about finding as well as losing, about things coming together as well as apart. Love endures: what Maarten felt for Greta and Karen decades ago not only has not died but scripts the realia of his life, even gives him an awful second chance. The patterns that now come into focus are permanently at odds with the here-and-now real world, and the people he sees are increasingly counters for the shadows and ghosts of his past.

But none of this diminishes the reader's dread of seeing a man's very life become alien and unreadable to himself: he looks at photos of his children and does not recognize them; he sees an image of his mother and likewise draws a blank. His life has become musical chairs. Dr. Eardly appears several times, yet each time he is a mystery to Maarten, who wonders who this man is, sitting in his living room, asking him questions, arranging for a hypodermic; as said, Vera has employed a young woman helper, Phil, to look after Maarten a few hours a day, and even though he is (often) introduced to Phil, she repeatedly slips out of the frame, becomes "other," sometimes in midconversation. The mobility on show here has a roller-coaster feeling to it—that is what most unsettles about this narrative—since at any and every moment, things slip out of their recognizable skins and become anonymous, threatening. After all, Maarten is in his home, but the things and people in it are metamorphosing at great speed, becoming alien objects whose strange presence confuses and even torments Maarten. Dementia dismantles home. Throughout this entire siege—for that is what it is—Maarten never stops cogitating, never stops responding to the altered scene, and there is great pathos here. When he sees a strange man in his house, said by Vera to be a doctor, his initial reaction is: is *Vera* ill, in need of a doctor? Later, reacting again to the (always new) doctor, he thinks that Fred is sick: Fred, his now-long-grown-up child, moved far away; Fred, now present in his mind as the sick youngster he once was; Fred, filling in the interstices; Fred, enabling Maarten to make some kind of sense of the jumble coming his way.

In one almost unbearable sequence, he experiences his bedroom as a hotel room, shorn now of all its years-long familiarity (a familiarity we think of as an extension of our own skin), transformed altogether, turned alien. Bernlef shows us how much awful interpretive freedom comes into play as Maarten inventories the new space:

> I lie on my back and look around me. This is a room with a so-called personal touch in the furnishings. I'm not too keen on that. As if just before your arrival somebody had lived in it who hurriedly grabbed his belongings together. And forgot half of them in the process, I notice. Toothbrush, shaving cream. I'll collect it all together and take it down to the reception. No, give me a Holiday Inn or the Hilton any day. . . . I undress, throw my clothes—as always when staying in a hotel—on the floor, and climb into bed. I leave the light on. I always do. Should there be a fire, every second matters. Make sure you get to the emergency exit before panic breaks out and people trample each other.

This is the voice of sweet reason, yet it has utterly slipped its gears, is functioning independently, tells us that the mind never stops producing its pitter-patter, never stops attending to the scene, never stops assessing, no matter how severed its connections to reality may be. Yes, one might somehow read these lines positively—after all, they suggest that dementia is a form of vacationing, a way of getting new digs at every moment—but I read the lines and shiver, remembering the look on my senile mother's face in the nursing home, that faraway look that was uninterpretable, as well as what we had to term the non sequiturs that came out of her mouth, concerning who and where and when she was. Was she reliving some long-distant past, known only to her? Were musical chairs in play? Was her heart scripting everything anew? Was home reconceived? The strangeness in Maarten's "hotel thinking" cuts to the bone, because it displays ratiocination in a vacuum, affixing labels to the changing spectacle, nailing down a world in flux. It also displays the shocking tenuousness of our hold on things, reminding me that Galileo's audacious claim about the earth itself—*it moves*—can wreak as much havoc on human sanity as it did to the Church's view of the solar system. Sooner or later, we readers know that *everything* will be stripped of recognition, will be new. Hence we are sickened but not surprised to read the following:

> Behind me in the doorway stands a woman. Her brown hair falls in a lock towards the right across her forehead. Remarkably smooth cheeks in an otherwise old face that seems to move away ever further and comes closer again only after I have briefly looked away from the mirror to the wall beside it. She is keeping an eye on me. (Could she have been assigned to me? By whom?) Tie, where is my tie?

This is what a long marriage now comes to: you eye an old face, looking at it with considerable focus, but it is entirely unknown to you. Who is this person? Maarten wonders if she's been assigned to him, and this is absolutely logical, inasmuch as a strange person in your home must be there for some reason. Then comes the shift to the tie. The tie. Bernlef registers the brutal capriciousness of senile thinking, the breakup of clusters of meaning, the atomistic regime that is now coming into authority. So the unknown woman has about the same "weight" as the missing tie. Here is an egalitarian arrangement that threatens to cancel out all the old priorities and privileges that we fondly believe a life over time offers: that some forms—my spouse, my children, my past life—have a kind of earned resonance and density and indeed dignity that reflect the harvest of our experience, the meaningful shapes of our life. But dementia cashiers this, erodes this connective tissue, for it respects no such temporal or moral or emotional ties, vectors that subtend and bathe our world with whatever significance it is to have. We move toward the absolute erasure of this cocoon scheme, which sometimes goes by the name of love.

For love is a caretaking, memorial proposition. Love relies on time. Love is built on the accretions of our experience. The vision that love casts on the world has no truck with the egalitarian ocular take that our eyes achieve, for love inserts its own rich remembered data, its own weights and measures, parses the visual field, adds dimensionality and resonance, edits the spectacle, thereby achieving the miraculous tapestry that every full life displays. The photographs in your scrapbook or on your desk, the dolls or toys or memorabilia that you still hold on to: these have an echoing private, sometimes unbearably rich meaning for *you*, whereas they are just objects for anyone else. Maarten's love for Vera has had exactly this richness:

> Vera. She has grown thinner. And even smaller, it seems. When she was in her early forties she was almost plump. And then my left hand would run all along her sleeping back until I held one of her breasts in the cup of my hand, gently rubbing the nipple with my thumb. . . . The excitement of the unknown has given way to recognition, the recognition of Vera as she is now, as I have seen her become through the years. With most women of her age the young girl they must once have been cannot possibly be reconstructed. They look as if they have always been like that. But in Vera the features and gestures of the young girl have been preserved like a painting underneath. The reckless speed with which she sits down,

even now, the exuberant hand-wave when she sees someone she knows, the outward-pointing feet, a leftover from ballet lessons, the straight neck, despite the wrinkles, still turning as proudly and inquisitively as that of an ostrich.

We are free to interpret this passage along strictly theoretical lines: if you've lived with someone, you espy their past form in their present appearance. But I'd want to call this also the very perception of love, alive to the actual (but invisible) reaches of loved ones, constituting a plural and layered vision that dwarfs the flat, reductive snapshot that our eyes register. Even earlier in the novel, Maarten says, "I am the only person who can see in her all the women she has been. Sometimes I touch her, and then I touch all of them at once, very gently. A feeling only she can evoke in me, no one else." At the risk of sounding very sentimental, I want to insist on the beauty of this notation. Enduring love is the recognition that our loved ones alter and become "plural," but that just amplifies our love, gives it more dimensions, turns the lover into the one who takes measures, keeps tally, remembers, restores. This is the edifice we build by loving each other over time. The rich temporal awareness of shared experiences, of countless earlier days and nights, of an entire textured existence together, of a "we story": all this makes marriage into a profoundly vertical proposition, shot through with time, built out of the materials of the past, resonating in such a way that the present moment is only that: a moment. I am emphasizing these matters, because they are precisely what will be destroyed in this unflinching novel about the collapse of self, about going out of mind.

Out of Mind is a heartbreaking novel because it graphs for us what Maarten has had and what he is now systematically losing. We see him repeatedly trying to hold on in a literal sense: to the table, to stair rails, to the physical setting that seems bent on shape-shifting in front of his eyes. But Maarten is on a treadmill, and even the haunting scenes of present replaced by past take place early in his descent. He is en route to greater and greater incoherence, fuller and fuller exile. At first one senses that some things will resist erosion: his past loves, his memories of his family, his guilt at his father's death and his colleague's suicide, his psychic scars from the war. The contents of his heart, the affective record of a life. As I've said, for each thing that goes, something else comes. Vera recedes, but Karen and Greta appear. And we realize that guilt obeys the same temporal rules by keeping the heart's injuries alive—damage from long ago such as his colleague Simic's suicide, his father's dying—by maintaining them just behind the curtain, ready to re-present themselves as unfinished business, as regret.

The war takes honors here as the major unprocessed, unprocessable abrasion of the heart, even though the conscious memories of it seem relatively picturesque and innocuous; but let his current life move into danger, and out pops earlier crisis. The doctor is about to force a hypodermic into him, and he hisses, "We know that from the war." A moment later he speaks of heroes and betrayal, of the need to persevere, "no matter how hungry we are." This reasoning reaches its apogee when he is again jabbed with a needle and threatened with a straitjacket, causing him to shift gears back to the ever-waiting war backdrop: "You've got the wrong man. I wasn't on the wrong side. Maybe I was no hero, but I wasn't on the wrong side. I never hid any fugitives in my house, that is true. I wouldn't have minded, but I never came across any. Or I didn't recognize them in time. Or it was too late, all finished, and I never realized what trouble he was in. Not even afterwards." We see indices here of wounds that cannot heal concerning ethical failures—not being a hero, not taking in Jews during the war, not realizing that his friend Simic was about to kill himself—that stud his life, that no doubt stud all our lives but that we won't fully know about until the end, when they will reveal themselves as stubborn residues, undying, wanting to be resolved at last. Once again Bernlef is showing last things in more ways than one. Your heart and spirit never stop keeping score, registering deeds and misdeeds throughout your life; sanity keeps this old record under wraps, but dementia reveals its stubborn hold.

In writing about *Out of Mind*, I have tried to convey what an expansive and visionary book it is, in contrast to the grim expectations readers must have as they pick it up, knowing (from the blurb) that it depicts someone's descent into dementia. Bernlef helps us to see that our last chapter might be a grand tally of sorts, in which all the scattered pieces of our lives enter into a strange dance. The cost of this plenary spectacle, with the past gliding into and out of the present, with our current scene becoming unreadable, with everything stable going topsy-turvy, is severe, for the proprietary uprights of self, time, and space are radically loosened, are shown to be fictive constructs that will, under enough dissociative pressure, give way. This is a bracing if destabilizing portrait of old age and dementia, for it pays homage to the dimensionality of a life and reminds us that our tidy picture of present-day order—"I" am stable, the others retain their form, life behaves—can exist only at the expense of all the rest that is swept under the carpet, consigned to oblivion.

In this book, oblivion fights back. And we learn that it never was as quiescent as we had thought. The human heart is our longest-lived organ, whatever the cardiologists might say, because it stores the emotional data of a lifetime, and those data pulsate still, live still. In dementia, it retakes center stage. Bernlef has to have been powerfully influenced by Proust, even though there is no paradisiacal celebration of involuntary memory, for the two writers share a sense of the vertical monumentality of all lives and of the staggering drama that takes place when lost time enters the scene with all its shattering power.

One finishes this book with an enhanced sense of human feeling, even of human thought. "Insanity" is the term that applies least here. At no point does Maarten yield to true despair or true chaos. Things lose their names, but he never stops being the scribe, tagging and assessing what he sees and feels, factually describing the hotel room we know to be his bedroom, the old face with brown hair and smooth skin we know to be his wife's. The world jumps out of its skin, yes, but the demented one keeps tallying what he sees. Yet it would be misleading to close my discussion on this ultimately upbeat note. Bernlef is too unflinching not to render the gruesomeness of dementia's corrosive effects, and in a striking phrase Maarten defines the exit drama he is being forced to act out: "This body is pressing me out. Like a turd I am being pressed out of myself." For all the splendid mind work of this tale, there is an equivalent amount of sheer body work, carrying out its wreckage. Soma rules entirely by book's end.

Maybe it does. Maybe the body finally exits all fictions, all definitions, all significations. Those of us who have looked carefully at the very senile, the very demented, must wonder if this is not our universal end stage, a freedom on the far side of self or meaning. Yet even there, who is to say whether the heart might be conducting its final dance? Bernlef's novel will be remembered most for the rich poignancy that inheres in the story of Maarten's descent into dementia. That poignancy derives from the spellbinding mise-en-scène of an entire life in time, of a man's far-flung memories and experiences now reshaping themselves into a new constellation of striking beauty. Maarten loses his citizenship in the present and thereby loses his wife, his children, and much of his self to boot. But the extended coordinates of his life are stunningly graphed into a new, emergent form, one over which he has no control whatsoever but that writes his life wonderfully large. All the feelings that have ever animated him—desire, longing, fear, regret—take over the final act, tyrannically rescripting everything, erasing "him" in the process. There are worse ways to imagine our last chapter.

And there are better. As grand as it is to have the fuller temporal warp and weft of one's entire existence become visible and finally interwoven in the tapestry of dementia—and it is grand—there is no solace for Maarten in this. This story closes with a man burning all his bridges—actually burning them, as he tears up family photos and burns them—while feeling a particular aversion and horror for the strangest figure of all, the one who stares at him in the mirror. It is hard to imagine a more thorough form of exile, of *Geworfenheit.* That is why Maarten's memories of the distant past are so moving, for they are the possible anchor of his life, the affective structures from which he began, the structures that actually composed the person he was, and there would be a certain poetry and justice in having him return, at life's end, to their fold, to reclaim himself in his entirety. But he does not. Instead he waits endlessly for his life's winter to finally cease, for the anonymous and formless white murk that ensconces him to yield to some kind of clarity and form. Looking out at this barren landscape, close to the end of his voyage out, Maarten thinks homeward: "I must be near the sea now. Then I can follow the shoreline and cut across the beach to our cottage where Mama is sure to be getting worried. Maybe Pop has already gone out to look for me. I want to be found. I want to go home."

These heartbreaking final utterances seem those of a child permanently lost, lost in his own psyche that can no longer keep shop. The mind has not so much deteriorated as exploded, wrecked all notion of a cocoon where one might nestle, safe. Home must mean: body plus mind, housed together, "on the same page"; but that precious contract, that covenant, which almost all of us take for granted, has been breached. The oldest romance of all is the link between mind and body: here is the marriage, the union, that matters most. Dementia ruptures this bond, despoils us of this elemental home. We "open out" into time and space. The world of senility resembles nothing so much as a secular, emotional, but utterly alien form of Last Judgment: all your days and works are there, you are the sum of your parts. "You" do not endure, but your heart does.

I want to be found. I want to go home. That is, I have come to believe, the ground-zero longing, the final injunction, that most profoundly parses our experience of growing old: to go home. I say this because, once again, I recognize it as the recurrent tidings of my dreams. They are always the same: I am back in Memphis, where I was born, Memphis, which I left in 1958 but which has demonstrably never left me. That's where I lived from birth to high school graduation, at which point I left the nest. In the dream I seek a cab and give the driver the address: 3912 Walnut Grove Road. That's where I grew up, where my dead parents are waiting for me. As I approach the house, it begins to dawn on me that no one is alive, that the house belongs to someone else, that I can never go home. Then, awake, I remind myself of something that never ceases to amaze me: I never think of 3912 Walnut Grove Road in my daytime consciousness. Moreover, I've lived with pleasure and connectedness in France, in Sweden, and especially in Providence, Rhode Island, and Block Island, far longer than I lived in Memphis as a child and teenager. But I never dream of France or Sweden or Providence or Block Island. And deep inside my psyche, locked in a room to which I have no key, is an elemental certainty that 3912 was home and that I can never get there.

There is nothing overtly about old age itself in these dreams. But how else to assess them than as some elemental, stubborn, undeniable reminder that my entire adult life is histrionic, a charade, existing in borrowed time and inhabiting borrowed space, while 3912 is rock bottom, where I belong? How can this be? I'm fine where I am. I'm at home on my range. Or so I think. Only at night, now that I'm moving toward the far side of things, does a voice tell me otherwise, notifying me that I am adrift, that there's a place I must be when it all comes to a close. I cannot help seeing those dreams as a code language for my end stage. Is there, at journey's end, a home base? Perhaps home is the inevitable target of old age: not so much whether you can stay in your house but whether your body and mind continue to house you. Dementia signals expulsion of the worst kind. Where do you go, inwardly, as you go down? Must we all end up finding that our bedrooms are hotel rooms, that our bodies are not ours, that our loved ones are only silhouettes standing in for buried others? I do not like to think about what must be coming, what must be waiting in the wings, but that is perhaps why *Out of Mind* so moves me in its portrait of descent: it respects the dignity and sheer scale of the last exit.

Virginia Woolf's To the Lighthouse

Very often in literature fathers must, as we have seen, either exit or be murdered. They wage war with their children. We call this the generational conflict about power that is both culture's and nature's plan. What about mothers? Racine's Phèdre is a mother, but you'd hardly know it, given her passion for her stepson. Strindberg muses about bearded women in one play and puts the crone Polly into a cage in another, so that she can gaze at her statue while ignoring her real daughter. Faulkner's plot arranges for the menopausal Joanna Burden's head to be cut off. Mother Courage is in the harness, by herself, at play's end, with nary a child left. None of the texts we've discussed shows us what we know to be central in life itself: a woman who can be both mother and lover, who can balance libido with nurturance, who can meet the challenge of time as bravely and fulfillingly as Hemingway's Santiago did. Virginia Woolf's *To the Lighthouse* does all these things.

Woolf's mother, Julia Stephen, died when Virginia was a young adolescent; her father, the noted British intellectual Leslie Stephen, died many years later. Virginia wrote that her father's continued life, with its incessant craving for approval, would have altogether smothered her own. I suspect there are many grown children who share her sentiment: the death of our parents is at once awful and necessary. We've seen versions of this ever since *Oedipus* and *King Lear*. But there are few of us indeed who then go on to re-create those parents in a work of fiction, writing them from the inside and endowing them—especially her—with a richness that is unrivaled in our literature.

I mention all this in order to place time and death in their proper place here: the mature child evokes the dead mother, and her portrait of Mother—full of wonder and beauty, radiant with love and, yes, power—is itself indelibly stamped by time's impress, nature's cruel scheme. Mrs. Ramsay dies in midbook, harshly, in obscene textual brackets, like a casual addendum. In that same chapter, devoted to the wreckage of Western culture caused by the Great War, other Ramsays die too: Andrew the gifted son, killed in Flanders; Prue the daughter, in childbirth. Mrs. Ramsay herself, the novel's earth mother, senses early on that her children will never again be as happy as they are when young and feels "this thing that she called life terrible, hostile and quick to pounce on you if you gave it a chance." Her husband the philosopher meditates about levels of reality, but she, the nontheoretical one, the anima of the family, is the fatalist of the group. Death and undoing haunt this book. Night must come.

But Mrs. Ramsay is the life-giving sun of this book, and like the sun's, her power is fertile, germinal, felt by all. Woolf presents her gloriously and unforgettably in the round, so as to take the measure of her radiance and aura. One of the most splendid notations comes when she is escorted into town by the book's young and insecure curmudgeon, Charles Tansley (a houseguest), and he too falls under her spell: "With stars in her eyes and veils in her hair, with cyclamen and wild violets—what nonsense was he thinking? She was fifty at least; she had eight children. Stepping through fields of flowers and taking to her breast buds that had broken and lambs that had fallen; with the stars in her eyes and the wind in her hair— He took her bag." This is vintage Woolf: this woman's beauty is a magnet that none resist, and it is powerful enough to transform a drab realist landscape and a fifty-year-old lady into something lyrical and pastoral and arcadian, replete with flower buds and lambs, so ravishing that he must take her bag. People working in the streets stop their work to look at her and pay her homage.

One remembers Blanche DuBois's fear of the light, her anxiety about the sexual game and the clock that governs it. One remembers Hamlet's disgust at his mother's love life. And I'd want to reference Hippolyte's horror at the hunger that his stepmother cannot conceal from him. Now, Charles Tansley is a foolish boor and nothing can come of his momentary adoration of Mrs. Ramsay, but it is good to see a young man smitten by an older woman, just as it is good to see the older bachelor William Bankes succumb to her aura. All respond to her. Young, old, men, women, children: it makes no difference. This is—this must be—how Virginia remembered her mother.

Gender does not bind either. Lily Briscoe, the book's spinster artist figure—doubtless the surrogate of Virginia herself—is achingly in love with her, and in one of the most spellbinding passages we see Lily with her arms around Mrs. Ramsay's knees, yearning to get still closer, imagining inside this woman chambers of mind and heart, figured as treasures in tombs, bearing sacred inscriptions, challenging the lover to read, to understand, to touch, to enter, to fuse with the loved one. Mrs. Ramsay is the novel's demiurgic figure, its outward-raying sun that illuminates and warms the family, the guests, and the book.

Loved, she also loves. The eight children are evoked with tenderness, each one seen as unique and uniquely deserving, as in the mother's decision to have Jasper and Rose select her jewels for the evening, realizing that such matters go very deep for Rose, "divining, through her own past, some deep, some buried, some quite speechless feeling that one had for one's mother at Rose's age."

What kind of a name do you put on sensitivity of this sort? How many men would be capable of it? It seems entirely right that Lily's (stalled) portrait of this mother with children would be a Madonna. There is nothing doctrinal in sight, but Mrs. Ramsay's very being tells us of the nurturance that brings life to fruition, that makes it possible for children to grow into adults. There are so many orphans in this study: Lazarillo, Pablos, Moll, Heathcliff, Jane, Pip, Huck, Joe Christmas; so many unloved children: Antoinette, Benjy, Quentin, Celie, Artie; so many characters who have to make it on their own; so little recognition of the help and love that the young must receive if they are to flourish. Above all, so little recognition that generosity—love as gift, not as hunger—is arguably the single greatest (and unsung) arena for the deeds and achievements of maturity. Mrs. Ramsay serves life in a way that few other older people appearing in this book do: she gives of herself, she seeds.

But there is only one of her, and there are so many who want to possess her heart and favor. Woolf understands the emotional dynamics of family, the fierce competition between children and spouse to be tended to, recognized, loved by the mother. I am thinking especially of the scene when Mrs. Ramsay, reading to her son James, finds herself "stormed" by her needy and despotic husband. Woolf's signature is to be seen in the stunning metaphors that deliver the violence and splendor of this moment: she pours into the air "a rain of energy, a column of spray," she is "burning and illuminating," "and into this delicious fecundity, this fountain and spray of life, the fatal sterility of the male plunged itself, like a beak of brass, barren and bare." Think back to Shakespeare's lyrical account of Romeo and Juliet's youthful passion and then contrast it to Woolf; you will see how this entire scenario is one of maturity and its conflicts, of the emotional vehemence resulting from the warring needs of loved ones, loved for many, many years, and it results in a supreme portrait of female power. She is the life source.

This sequence is followed by Mrs. Ramsay's further imaginings, further gifts, entailing the transformation of existing domestic life into something overflowing with fertility (kitchen, drawing room, bedrooms, nurseries), and it closes with something akin to sexual exhaustion as the male takes his leave and the woman folds herself together, petal after petal, still holding her son and his book of fairy tales, while there "throbbed through her, like the pulse in a spring which has expanded to its full width and now gently ceases to beat, the rapture of successful creation." *The rapture of successful creation*. It is Woolf's genius to show us the vibrant, even ecstatic, underlay of docile appearances, so that the spectacle of a man, woman, and child "doing" virtually nothing becomes a spectacle filled with exotic color and sexual tumult and ecstatic interaction. These rapturous passages coexist with others that are gentler, wryer, but no less exquisite and eye-opening in their rendition of mature love: we see the Ramsays walk together, each locked (as we all are) in his or her own mind and sensations, yet reaching out to each other, making small talk, making large talk, sometimes making no talk at all but still together, interacting. And always it is Mrs. Ramsay who initiates, nourishes, sustains, and completes these transactions, these transfusions.

This novel takes us into the bedroom once or twice, but never to witness any conjugal intimacy. One hallucinatory (orgasmic) sequence depicts the light of the lighthouse caressing Mrs. Ramsay "as if it were stroking with its silver fingers some sealed vessel in her brain whose bursting would flood her with delight," putting us on notice that ecstasy has many forms and venues, that it may connect us to the cosmos as well as to our lovers. Yet loving is also lower to the ground, more democratic, more spread out, than we often imagine. After all, its arena, its sphere of operation, is limitless; love's theater has many players and many places in it, each demanding its due. We find it, for instance, at the dinner table (!), as Mrs. Ramsay seeks to bring not only food but heat and life to her family and guests. (Here, too, ask yourself if young love could be found in such precincts—if young love would even recognize a dinner table as a site of intense emotion.) Once again it is written with a keenness and reach that astound, as we watch Mrs. Ramsay take in the scene of inert matter and infuse it with life, with her life:

Nothing seemed to have merged. They sat separate. And the whole of the effort of merging and flowing and creating rested on her. Again she felt, as a fact without hostility, the sterility of men, for if she did not do it nobody would do it, and so, giving herself the little shake that one gives a watch that has stopped, the old familiar pulse began beating, as the watch begins ticking—one, two, three, one, two, three. And so on and so on, she repeated, listening to it, sheltering and fostering the still feeble pulse as one might guard a weak flame with a newspaper.

Enduring love is the daily effort to convert insentience into sentience, silence into language, indifference into interest, lumps of flesh into people sharing food, wine, and conversation around a table. Not quite the fare for immortal romances, rarely touted as glamorous or attention-getting, this labor is nonetheless a fundamental exercise of the human heart, required countless times in a life in the service of the human family. The service of the family: not the gratification of lover or spouse. Mothers do this. For better or for worse, this has been women's work for much of history. *To the Lighthouse* makes us see that the most mundane tasks are the material of heroism and of poetry.

It is interesting to note that Woolf has inserted some sexual interest into her dinner scene, since a young couple, Paul and Minta, are among the guests and Mrs. Ramsay has helped give the young man the confidence to declare his feelings to the girl, who has accepted him, all of which confers on this scene a pagan feeling of passion's rites. Marriage is in the air. But I'd argue that the deeper and more seminal act of love is the mother's, is performed by the woman bringing these people together, so that the little miracle of "merging and flowing and creating" takes place. Yet Woolf's references to pulse, watch, and weak flame tell us that making life is never far from losing life, that a day will come when Mother disappears, when the spark goes out. And it will.

Readers of the novel are aware that the great matriarch comes in for considerable "in-house" criticism: from some of the guests, above all from the infatuated but critical Lily Briscoe, who wonders if loving too much didn't finally kill the woman who did it. Mrs. Ramsay's mantra "Marry, marry!" does not fully pass the test of time, as the collapse of Paul and Minta's marriage will demonstrate. All this is true. But it seems to me that the greatest threat to Mrs. Ramsay as mature love goddess comes from within, as if Woolf understood that we are not constituted to create a "rain of energy, a column of spray," an endless pouring out of fecundity, all the days of our lives. No person, no woman, can do this. Not because it is too exhausting and life-sapping (which it is) but because one is also, inevitably and responsibly, oneself, because one's life has its indwelling needs and integrity, on the far side of all social giving, on the far side of loving. Few writers, I think, are capable of this insight, which speaks to the demands of self versus our love for others, and in a passage of great beauty and daring, Woolf sketches out the astonishing but invisible life of self that the mother both leads and follows. The child has been put down, and we read:

> For now she need not think about anybody. She could be herself, by herself. And that was what now she often felt the need of—to think; well, not even to think. To be silent; to be alone. All the being and the doing, expansive, glittering, vocal, evaporated; and one shrunk, with a sense of solemnity, to being oneself, a wedge-shaped core of darkness, something invisible to others. Although she continued to knit, and sat upright, it was thus that she felt herself; and this self having shed its attachments was free for the strangest adventures. When life sank down for a moment, the range of experience seemed limitless.

This sequence continues into ever murkier territory, as the emancipated self leaves its corporeal base and flows out into the world, becoming the things it sees and touches, leaving even "I" far behind, as residue, as trompe l'oeil (for, had you looked at Mrs. Ramsay at that moment, in full "flight," you would have seen only a woman continuing to knit).

This celebrated passage challenges and complicates my argument for Mrs. Ramsay as a mature, loving woman. Love acquires, in my view, more rather than less significance when we realize it must coexist with so much else in life, including one's obligations to self. Remember, again, her philosopher husband, the man who meditates exploratory voyages of pure thinking, and say to your-self: this woman, who infuses the world with warmth, travels far-ther inwardly than he ever does or will, yet is never paid for it, recognized for it. Is it possible that her almost infinite sense of pri-vate, even anonymous, freedom exists in perfect harmony with her virtually infinite sense of human responsibility and love? Does one feed the other?

Mrs. Ramsay's psychic "outing," her unchartable journey into distant territories (people as well as things and places), confers an almost cosmic reach to this seemingly domestic novel and thereby stands in contrast to the grueling descent into chaos we saw in Maarten's final days. There is a splendid sense of emotional and psychic elasticity in Woolf, of our being more far-flung and ex-pansive creatures than you might think, more exploratory and questing, less bounded. Again I say: such virtues are unimaginable in the young, are the prize of age, but age understood as open vis-tas and large dominions. There is also something wonderful in gauging Mrs. Ramsay's reach and authority. There is a reason one sees her as the novel's earth goddess, for Woolf is showing us that this woman's everyday acts of body and mind—the *boeuf en daube* at dinner and the wedge-shaped core of darkness when alone— are manifestations of a *power* we must see as godlike. Her hus-band is the salaried professor, but she is the life-giving mother, the older woman who long ago birthed her children and still contin-ues to be the pulse of the family. The novel hallows her reign, her regime, her regal being.

But the watch and the pulse will stop. She will die. And the last third of the novel will consist in the efforts, ten years later, of her family and Lily Briscoe to bring her back to life. The novel is justly famous for its two versions of retrieval. Mr. Ramsay will at long last take his two now-grown children to the lighthouse, bringing parcels for those islanded there, as if to make good on his dead wife's desire. And Lily Briscoe will complete her portrait of Mrs. Ramsay, but she will do so only by dint of love and immer-sion into the depths of the past, into the still-living, unbearably painful memory of Mrs. Ramsay, alive in Lily's feelings even if dead on the earth. Art is made of blood, not paint. These are the contracts of love—husband and figurative daughter paying homage to the wife and mother—and they parallel the no-less-vital contract we witnessed at the dinner table when Mrs. Ramsay chose, as she never failed to choose, to do the "merging and flowing and creating" that life requires of its finest, perhaps of us all.

A portrait of old age? Yes and no. We never know how or why or even exactly when she died. But die eventually she must, and die she does, following time's law, carrying out nature's irreversible plot. Yet, as we saw, art, memory, and love resurrect what can be resurrected. There is something elemental and shocking about Woolf's plot: *the mother lives on.* So many of our texts—and so much of our thinking—privileges private actors and individual doing, all of which stops at death. *To the Lighthouse* suggests otherwise. Mrs. Ramsay is demiurgic. She is an energy system, and—long dead—she impacts on, indeed empowers others. Our entire model of temporal law, of waxing and waning, of rise and fall, even of growing up and growing old, is upended by this luminous story of love's power beyond the grave. Woolf seems to be saying that love is fertile beyond our wildest imaginings, that its *harvest* takes place most fully *d'outre-tombe,* in the feelings, deeds, and lives of those we've nurtured and touched. This mature woman, who gifted her husband and children and still others with her light and heat and radiance, shines still, like a beacon in the surrounding sea, like a lighthouse that never goes out. It is hard not to be moved by the portrait of a loving dead woman created by her grown-up daughter: we see this in the novel, as Lily completes her picture and has her vision, and we see this outside the novel in the achievement of Virginia Woolf, who birthed in literature the story of the woman who birthed her in life. Given the amount of conflict and friction and outright war that we've seen between the young and the old, this image of generational harmony and mutual sustenance is deeply satisfying.

J. M. *Coetzee's* Disgrace

One fine day, proud Lear stopped being king; not much later, he was mad. Ibsen's stubborn Solness was obliged ultimately to yield the stage to the young, but he died doing it. Willy Loman faced the collapse of his role and his dreams, and it killed him. The story of obsolescence is hardwired into the story of aging, and it does not, as it were, stale or wither, even if the environment and some of the givens change. Further, the shock of discovering that one has outlived one's purpose, overstayed one's time, or simply failed to exit the stage in seemly fashion, would appear to be a shock that can come to us well before we reach Willy Loman's fatigued state. It can happen while we think we are in full swing, going great guns, without any inkling that the bell is ready to toll for us, to tell us the party is over. Can wisdom be made of this? A low-to-the-ground, nonvisionary wisdom that might reinsert the old back into the march of the living? Are there late lessons that are truly redemptive?

All this is what we encounter in the depiction of David Lurie's adventures and trials, as seen in the South African novelist J. M. Coetzee's remarkable narrative *Disgrace*. This slim volume is deceptively straightforward, because its issues tend to reverberate far beyond the page, echoing for us today's still-unresolved problems of race, power, and white privilege as well as the necessity of "making friends with dying." Indeed, I firmly believe that Coetzee's novel of 1999 can be credibly and creditably compared to Shakespeare's *King Lear*. Once again, the kingdom is to be divvied up, once again the prerogatives of the seemingly powerful are to be chastened and checked, once again the story of fathers and daughters comes to stand for intergenerational murk and power sharing, and once again the overt saga of the high and mighty gestures toward the untold narratives of the weak and despised. Beyond even Shakespeare, Coetzee wants to graph what Lear would learn on the heath: the story of the "bare, forked" creature, understood at last as nonmetaphor, as the animals with whom we share the planet.

Disgrace opens in high confidence: "For a man of his age, fifty-two, divorced, he has, to his mind, solved the problem of sex rather well." David Lurie knows his needs, knows how to satisfy them, has his arrangements under control: he has sex on Thursday afternoons with the tall, slim prostitute Soraya; it takes care of his wants. On page two Coetzee limns his protagonist still more clearly and broadly: "He is in good health; his mind is clear. By profession he is, or has been, a scholar, and scholarship still engages, intermittently, the core of him. He lives within his income, within his temperament, within his emotional means. Is he happy? By most measurements, yes, he believes he is. However, he has not forgotten the last chorus of *Oedipus:* Call no man happy until he is dead." Without that last ominous Sophoclean tag, what reader would be suspicious here? Yet we will see just how time-bound and precarious David's attainments are, for he is destined to be damaged, if not undone, on all these fronts: health, mind, profession, income, temperament, and emotion. He is slated for a fall. By book's end, we are to understand all of David's achievements, balance, and equipment as the residue of privilege and luck, as overdue loans that are about to be called.

In keeping with the initial note that is struck, Coetzee locates the impending downfall in the sex department. David starts a liaison with his student Melanie, some thirty years his junior. This is motivated in part by hints that his sexual ease and authority are not quite what they used to be: Soraya has broken with him; women seem no longer to respond to his glance. But the tryst with Melanie stirs him deeply, inflames him with a kind of desire and urgency that had seemed to be gone from his life. He presses his attentions on her, beds her, is enthralled by her youthful body and by the fierceness of his wants. Melanie herself is hard to read: she accepts his overtures yet holds back, hints that she may have a lover her own age, but she does not resist him. At least not the first time. Trouble comes the next go-around: he surprises her in her flat and essentially storms her, carrying her to the bed, unstoppable, touched (as the language has it) by "the quiver of Aphrodite." But his ardor is not shared. Postcoital, he reflects: "Not rape, not quite that, but undesired nevertheless, undesired to the core. As though she had decided to go slack, die within herself for the duration, like a rabbit when the jaws of the fox close on its neck." We note not only the familiar story of power abuse but also the reference to the animal world. Registers are in play here. The voyage has begun.

David's transgression is distressingly familiar. One of his (female) colleagues does not hesitate to place him in a long tradition of abusive acts and actors, reminding us that males have been doing such things for some time now. Melanie, as I've observed, seems at least partly consenting—I've found, in teaching this book, that undergraduates resist this line of reasoning staunchly, placing all the blame on the older man, thereby giving me much to think about—and thus, when the affair becomes public and explodes into disciplinary hearings, David is certain that she has been forced into this accusation against him. Yet the book goes on to suggest that she is indeed traumatized by his behavior, given that she drops out of school and seems genuinely damaged. Now, none of this prevents David from vigorously (and quixotically) defending his behavior: not only will he not recant, as he is asked to do by the committee members, but he says that he was a "servant of Eros," that he regrets having denied such impulses in the past, adds that he was "enriched" by the experience, even to the point of (later) citing Blake's proverb "Sooner murder an infant in its cradle than nurse unacted desires." None of this goes over well. And even if Melanie is no infant in a cradle, he has inflicted damage nonetheless. Rules have been broken. The final outcome is no surprise: he is sacked.

As in *Lear*, the story of abuse is generational and political. But Coetzee wants us to understand that Lurie's taking advantage of his position as professor may not constitute his deepest misstep, his true transgression. His ex-wife, Rosalind, gives him the news: "You're what—fifty-two? Do you think a young girl finds any pleasure in going to bed with a man of that age? Do you think she finds it good to watch you in the middle of your . . . ?" On this note, the novel moves into new territory. We have seen in Molière that the spectacle of old men trying to bed young girls is a staple item of comedy, even if it can also be the source of great pathos, if we elect to read *Othello* along those lines. Coetzee, however, is drawn less to the tragicomic dimensions of this theme than to the light it sheds on a host of issues, ranging from the male climacteric to the rights of desire, seen against a backdrop not merely of institutional power arrangements but of geopolitical and racial relationships as well, extending finally to privileges that go beyond the precincts of white males and gesture toward a still-larger hubris: that of the human subject lording it over the animals who share the stage with him. But even my emphasis on power is too narrow, since the book is no less cued to how we respond to death: what are our responsibilities as well as our rights?

One's response to *Disgrace* has much to do with one's age. My undergraduates are greatly exercised by the teacher coming on to his student, but they show little interest in the meditation on aging. (Time will teach them to read otherwise, I suspect, should they happen to pick this book up again in their later years.) For David Lurie is beginning to note the temporal treadmill he is on. Leaving Cape Town and taking up with his (lesbian) daughter Lucy, David is aware of her eyes on him as he eats: "He must be careful: nothing so distasteful to a child as the workings of a parent's body." It is a stinging perception, one that Antigone must also have had in ministering to her feeble, broken-down, blind father, even if Sophocles did not think it worth writing down. David is beginning, just beginning, to see himself in the round. The warnings are coming, even if his own name is not yet attached to them.

The urbane former literature professor drives far into the country to visit Lucy, who lives on a smallholding, and we sense their estrangement from each other, a distance that goodwill and tenderness cannot easily overcome. David is game to try out a new life: he meets Petrus, a black man who now owns a portion of her land, the "dog man," who assists Lucy with the farming and the dogs she kennels; he meets Bev Shaw, a no-neck, cylindrical little woman who volunteers at the animal shelter, whose charitable labors and homely body fail to impress him. Lucy senses his general disapproval of her life, based on her failure to achieve something "higher," but she stoutly defends her choices: "They [my friends] are not going to lead me to a higher life, and the reason is, there is no higher life. This is the only life there is. Which we share with animals." David demurs, but the reader is left wondering: how does this sharing take place?

Arguably the most perfect image of David's impending crisis is located in an animal clinic, where David, searching for some way to make himself useful, has volunteered to help Bev Shaw carry out her duties vis-à-vis the sick and dying animals brought her way. In this instance it is a full-grown male goat that can barely walk: "One half of his scrotum, yellow and purple, is swollen like a balloon; the other half is a mass of caked blood and dirt." He is routinely savaged by dogs, we are told. Bev cleans his wound and discovers "white grubs waving their blind heads in the air." Certain that his siring days are over, she offers to put him down, but his owner resists. At this juncture she kneels down beside the animal, nuzzles his throat, and whispers, "What do you say, my friend? . . . What do you say? Is it enough?" This is the question that is being put to David Lurie as well, even though he does not yet know it. And whereas Coetzee cannot decorously zoom in on a fifty-two-year-old man's scrotum and testicles, he can show us a marked, wounded goat at the end, as it were, of his tether, no longer "any good." Siring is over for good. To the owner Bev says, "I can give him a quiet end. He will let me do that for him. Shall I?" We must all end. Shall it be quiet or not? Do we ever know when it is enough? How will we exit?

Literature makes its moves by indirection, so that we read the story of a male sexual end game in cross-species fashion. More, much more, is to come. David Lurie is scheduled for a crash course in altered self-perception, in gauging one's time-bound privileges, that will make the Melanie saga look tame and innocuous. Now comes the bombshell. Lucy and David are attacked by three black men—one is only a boy—and nothing will ever be the same again. Lucy is raped—impregnated, we will later learn—and David is set on fire: spirits are poured on his head and lit as he remains locked in the bathroom, unable to go to his daughter's aid. David had earlier reflected on the notion of a completed action, as conveyed by verb tense, and recalls trying to teach his students "the distinction between *drink* and *drink up*, *burned* and *burnt.* The perfective, signifying an action carried through to its conclusion." *Burn, burned, burnt* becomes a well-nigh incandescent figure for the life and times of David Lurie. He has burned with sexual desire and satisfied his need with his young student. There is more burning to come. The quasi rape that cost him his job is now followed by a much less ambiguous, much more sordid and violent rape that is going to cost him much more still.

Coetzee is out to measure the temporal curve that graphs all individual lives—the goat's, the professor's—and also the life of a country. Things are not over where you think they end. Melanie's fate bleeds into Lucy's. David's confident days as cocksman, as one who "has solved the problem of sex rather well," as a father who wants only to protect his daughter against harm, as a white man inhabiting South Africa, as a human being sharing the stage with other species: all this is seen to be inscribed in a still-moving continuum that he had never pondered, a continuum that is now entering into its final phase. Actions are being carried through to their conclusion.

We all know the expression "in the fullness of time." It has a fetching aura of mystery. Only then will all be revealed, only then will what has been sown be harvested. Whether it be the birth of a child or the moment of death, this event closes our waiting time and shows us what has been wrought. Coetzee wants us to realize that growing old obliges us to take sterner and harder measures, to recognize where we are on this curve, which moves us not only deathward but also toward a conclusion: a grasp of life's logic at last played out in its entirety, a grasp of forces evolving toward their inevitable end. Reflection is needed, but not only reflection. David Lurie must be *burned, burnt,* to comprehend the larger shape of his life. Not unlike Lear, Lurie too must be "bound / Upon a wheel of fire."

He suffers a crucible experience, a literal holocaust, which takes him forever out of the life of ease, appetite, and power he was accustomed to; partially disfigured, his hair burned off, his wounds slowly mending, he knows himself now to be "one of those sorry creatures whom children gawk at in the street." After Lucy's rape, he sees himself differently: "he has a taste of what it will be like to be an old man, tired to the bone, without hopes, without desires, indifferent to the future." In an arresting phrase that recalls Lucy's fate, Coetzee describes David as bleeding. Then we read: "His pleasure in living has been snuffed out. Like a leaf on a stream, like a puffball on a breeze, he has begun to float toward his end. . . . The blood of life is leaving his body and despair is taking its place, despair that is like a gas, odourless, tasteless, without nourishment. You breathe it in, your limbs relax, you cease to care, even at the moment when the steel touches your throat."

Again, this is cunning writing. Odorless gas, steel touching your throat: such references signal Holocaust in its other historical form—the Jews sent to the cyanide showers, the victims rounded up for the slaughter. At one point in the novel, David sees the young boy who participated in the rape, sees him at Petrus's party, and stands his ground, insists on being fully seen himself, wounds and all; Coetzee writes it like this: "He lifts a hand to his white skullcap. For the first time he is glad to have it, to wear it as his own." Large things are coming into focus, as the professor is figured Jewish, touching his yarmulke, signaling his membership in a community of victims. Lucy comes to understand her rape in comparable terms: "What if . . . what if *that* is the price one has to pay for staying on?" The story of South Africa is a harsh one of exploitation and penance, of injuries and redress, of finding oneself caught up in a history that began long ago and will end long after one's death. Privileges that seemed permanent are no more than loans that can be called, will be called.

Lucy is willing to pay the price. She will bear the child she carries, and she will enter into Petrus's African family as a kind of third wife, giving him her land, all so that the child will be protected, so that she too can stay, sheltered if not happy. It is the cost of staying, and it is total. David tells her she is mad, that this choice is humiliating. Her answer reminds us of what Lear learned on the heath: "Yes, I agree, it is humiliating. But perhaps that is a good point to start from again. Perhaps that is what I must learn to accept. To start at ground level. With nothing. Not with nothing but. With nothing. No cards, no weapons, no property, no rights, no dignity." David's reaction is harsh: "Like a dog." She agrees: "Yes, like a dog."

"*Wie ein Hund.*" "Like a dog." These are K's closing words in Kafka's *The Trial*, as the henchman of the Law plunges his great knife into him. Kafka's story is about the impossibility of finding justice; remember the man from the country who spends his life "before the Law," awaiting entry. Kafka further notes that K's murder is the source of a great shame that would outlive him. But

Coetzee has inverted Kafka's tale. Lucy moves knowingly into the sacrificial slot and lowers her head for the blade. She elects to be erased, to be brought down to nothing, to be stripped of all power. A sacrificial logic is being enacted. She feels it is what history and place require. It is the logical if hideous consequence of the life she earlier led. An action has been carried through to its conclusion.

David Lurie is also stripped of all power. But in his case, stripping has the added connotation of old age's rebuke and punishment that it had for Oedipus at Colonus, which is again why this novel is so central to my purposes in this book. Many are the passages in which Coetzee writes this chastened man's sense of an impoverished future. Sometimes they are quite down-to-earth in their material particulars: "He sees himself, white-haired, stooped, shuffling to the corner shop to buy his half-litre of milk and half-loaf of bread; he sees himself sitting blankly at a desk in a room full of yellowing papers, waiting for the afternoon to peter out so that he can cook his evening meal and go to bed." But David does not settle into the sedentary model he has fantasized. The story of privilege and power moves beyond the projected image of a stooped white-haired man with his meager milk and bread and papers, beyond even the racial and political turmoil of the changing South Africa, and opens out onto still broader themes.

"Like a dog," Lucy said. Like the goat, we might add. Indeed, like the two sheep, the black-faced Persians, which David "bonds" with before they are slaughtered for Petrus's party, causing David to reflect: "Sheep do not own themselves, do not own their lives. They exist to be used, every last ounce of them, their flesh to be eaten, their bones to be crushed and fed to poultry." Here is the routine slaughter of the innocent, a slaughter so hardwired into cultural habit as to be invisible. In a later novel, *Elizabeth Costello*, Coetzee developed a full-scale animal rights thesis, ultimately comparing the slaughter of animals to the slaughter of the Jews. He does not go that far in *Disgrace*, but that is the direction he points toward: the greatest power abuse in history, carried out on animals every single day. Is there any wonder that he invokes the German term *Lösung* to signify the fate of the animals: *Lösung*, solution, *Endlösung*, Final Solution. Do we not, each of us as we age, face a Final Solution?

Hence the fifty-two-year-old white man rebuked for sexual and racial privilege is obliged to drain the cup, and in doing so, he begins to recognize his place in a larger scene of expiation and sacrifice and death. For that is what Bev Shaw deals with all the time: animals who have come to the end of their tether; animals whose next step is to be put away. David discovers that his postacademic work is to consist of assisting in the deaths of these unwanted animals, to carry their dead bodies to the incinerator so that they can be destroyed with at least some modicum of charity. Why does he do this, he asks himself, especially since the canine bodies he carries are already dead; what, he asks, do dogs know of honor and dishonor anyway? The answer he reaches—it is an answer that requires the entire novel, the upbraiding, sacking, and burning, to reach—is an answer whose moral if not grammatical tense is the perfective, "signifying an action carried through to its conclusion":

> For himself, then. For his idea of the world, a world in which men do not use shovels to beat corpses into a more convenient shape for processing.
>   The dogs are brought to the clinic because they are unwanted: *because we are too menny.* That is where he enters their lives. He may not be their savior, the one for whom they are not too many, but he is prepared to take care of them once they are unable, utterly unable, to take care of themselves. . . . A dog-man, Petrus once called himself. Well, now he has become a dog-man.

The quasi-musical reach of this sparse but echoing novel reminds us over and over that David's own fate as aging male is mirrored in that of the animals he now cares for. It is the generic shame of mortality, the inescapable disgrace of dying, the mystery of how we leave living, that is being addressed. It is a powerful—indeed, earthshaking—issue: the curse that life itself puts us under; no Greek oracle needed. A day comes when you are "too menny," when you can no longer take care of yourself, when you start dying. In this regard, David's trajectory in the novel is no less than a Pilgrim's Progress, an ever-widening sense of the new territory he has entered, the new vistas he perceives, the new responsibilities he acquires. Coetzee takes our existential core issue—growing old—and imparts a staggeringly rich payload to it, forcing us (much as it forces David) to recognize a broader pattern of grace and disgrace, of stewardship and entropy, of desire and generosity, than we customarily assign to this theme. *Disgrace* acquires considerable pathos in this respect because David Lurie is such an improbable candidate for such a lesson: ironic, sophisticated, keen, discerning, unillusioned, unflinching, without puffery, he exerts what we'd have to call a critical gaze on all that befalls him. Much of the book's appeal derives from his intelligent good company, no matter how dubious some of his moves may be ethically speaking. Hence this man's evolution is a gripping experience for readers.

His fate becomes entwined with Bev Shaw and her activities. He makes love to this homely woman almost as a form of penance, as a recognition that his gallivanting days are over, but we also feel that whatever this man and woman do together in bed is stamped as much by kindness as it is by desire. That would be one of the lessons life teaches the old. The still-deeper lesson, however, recalls Lucy's willingness to be brought back to nothing, to be stripped of all implements of power and privilege; "Like a dog," she and her father both said. So we close with dogs. David the dog-man assists Bev in helping unwanted, superfluous, helpless dogs die. He holds them and caresses them and brushes back the fur "so that the needle can find the vein," and he supports them when their legs buckle and their souls exit, following which he packs them into bags and later wheels the bag into the flames, to "see that it is burnt, burnt up." Their canine lives have come and gone full circle. It has required the professor's help. The disgrace of dying shades into the grace of caring. Coetzee closes his novel by referencing one particular dog of which David is especially fond, an injured animal with a withered left hindquarter that loves him unconditionally, that, David is sure, would die for him. And so, one fine day, he does. He and Bev are completing their death rounds, their *Lösung*, for the day, and she asks if there are any left. The book's last lines go like this:

"One more."

He opens the cage door. "Come," he says, bends, opens his

arms. The dog wags its crippled rear, sniffs his face, licks his cheeks, his lips, his ears. He does nothing to stop it. "Come."

Bearing him in his arms like a lamb, he re-enters the surgery. "I thought you would save him for another week," says Bev Shaw. "Are you giving him up?"

"Yes, I am giving him up."

What is being given up? An injured dog? A right to life? A right to the kind of life one has enjoyed earlier and taken for granted? Male sexual privilege? White racial privilege? The privileges of our species? Giving up is all too easily construed as defeat, as humiliation (which is how David saw it with Lucy), as penance; but we can also see it as the reversal, perhaps the transcendence, of desire itself. Giving as the alternative to taking. At the end of *Disgrace*, "giving up" is the recognition that at a certain time in life appetite must be renounced, wanting must yield to something larger, giving up becomes giving. Love endures, but it must change its course, its nature. Coetzee has charted, without the least bombast or sentimentality or sermonizing, the route from eros to caritas. We are familiar with such a trajectory when it comes to religious discourse. Without any preaching or pretensions to being "wisdom literature," this novel, luminous at the close, helps us see this spiritual journey as inseparable from the temporal voyage that stamps every human life.

A final word about *Disgrace:* David Lurie may seem a most unprepossessing figure to close my study of growing old: aloof, ironic, even partially unregenerate at the end, more than a little tepid in the realm of human feeling. His fate has none of the heartbreak of Shakespeare's Lear or Bernlef's Maarten, nor does it have the rich sentience of Racine's Phèdre or Woolf's Mrs. Ramsay. Yet Coetzee succeeds in making this ordinary man's life emblematic, prismatic, as it moves into the war zone that we call old age. He is a man of privilege—as we all are in our salad days—and he will find out that these privileges can be recalled. That life's severe order requires their removal. He faces the *Endlösung*, the Final Solution, the final disgrace that all living creatures face: growing old, dying. In his dance with time, we see a replay of all our rubrics: undone fathers, exiting the stage, postsexual existence, final harvest, the good fight. He moves—grudgingly, unheroically—into a kind of generosity that I am prepared to label "enduring love." Brought permanently low, yet still breathing and going through his paces, David Lurie evinces, I believe, a bare but real wisdom about the responsibilities that we have toward our loved ones, our conflicted culture, and our vexed planet. His trajectory from noon to night encompasses both the coming of dark and the making of light.

Commencement

In calling my conclusion "Commencement," I am of course alluding to the established conceit that marks the close of the American college experience: young people complete their formal education, but instead of calling this closure event the end, we regard it as a beginning. Professors and administrators reliably and predictably hold forth on this perhaps clichéd topic each year in front of an audience of exhausted seniors (they've been partying for days now) and their no-less-fatigued families, who are waiting for the final act to be (at last) over. It is a familiar ritual. What is commencing is their postbaccalaureate life, the so-called real life that awaits them after their schooling is over. It does not seem farfetched to say that they are approaching ever more closely the noontime of their lives, even if graduate school and professional apprenticeships await them.

What never fails to stun me during these Commencement rituals is the light they shed on the two central life phases of this book: growing up and growing old. We see the young at a liminal stage of their careers. We also see the old. I am thinking especially of one of the most revered customs of Commencement at my university (and at many others): the march of the alumni classes. In Providence, Rhode Island, this is a festive and highly symbolic tradition. The mayor of the city solemnly makes his way up College Hill in order to meet, greet, and sanction the university parade that is about to begin, all to the tune of marching bands from all over the state. It has a medieval feel to it, for we see the key figures of political and intellectual culture arrayed in their various robes and gowns, celebrating a moment of high significance. The parade begins with the marching of the oldest alumni down the Hill, followed by each successive class of alums and their families, culminating with the graduating seniors, by far the youngest participants in the procession.

I look at this procession, and I see more than I want to. In witnessing the march of the very old—often in their eighties, sometimes even their nineties—moving successively to men and women slightly less old, then middle-aged, then younger, then much younger, and finally the seniors themselves, I feel that I am watching a biological countdown in reverse. Time itself is cargoed here in a stunningly visual, staggered fashion, for this succession of marching bodies (some of them with crutches, some in wheelchairs, all the way down to the youngest ones, who stride proudly, even if some of them lurch for other reasons) reads inevitably like a blueprint on aging, on entropy. Death stalks here. But memory has its part to play as well. I am invariably reminded of my own college graduation in 1962, when this parade seemed almost surreal to me, given how ancient its participants seemed, how eternally young my peers and I felt. In successive years, as professor, I have been a spectator at the parade, always alert to the look of the alumni class my age, always curious to note whether they appear older or younger than (I fantasized) I look. Each year, my own class moves ever closer to the front of the line, because we are rapidly becoming the true oldsters of the party.

What is going on in this ritual? I have described the ocular effect of the procession: we see bodies moving from age to youth, written on by time. Of course, each age group has its own spread, some seeming sprightly, others more worn, but none is unstamped by their specific place in the continuum. Why do these old people march? Why are they at college reunions? Because, at some profound level of psyche and desire, they are seeking to recapture something of their own youth, of the glorious time when they too were the graduating seniors, the stars of the show. Innocence and experience. Life itself has intervened—they are five years out, ten, fifteen, twenty, twenty-five, fifty, all the way up to seventy years out—with its lessons of experience, and they are here, I believe, to salute and revisit innocence, their own innocence, their own distant past. They are trying to recall, maybe to relive, what was perhaps best in their lives. College reunions are saturated with desire, cued to the project of a magic retrieval of the past, not all that different from what Proust's Marcel found in his tea-drenched madeleine. I may see them as old, marked by time; but their own sights are elsewhere entirely.

The graduation ceremonies close with the handing out of diplomas, conducted by each department of the university, and there too I experience a strange kind of double vision. I finally meet the parents of seniors whom I have taught. It is something I look forward to; it gives me a chance to see the seniors in a more personal and familial perspective, as I say good-bye to them after four years at Brown, as they head out into the world. A part of their growing up has happened. But the double vision is this: I see them in time, as if I were fast-forwarding; I look at their mothers and fathers and see what they are going to look like in twenty-five or thirty years. It is not always a comfortable perception, because it confers a kind of specificity, even fatality, on faces and bodies that seemed open and free during their tenure as undergraduates. Needless to say, with a little bit of effort, I also make the imaginative, perceptual trip backward, seeing what mother and father might/must have looked like at the age of twenty. Often enough, grandparents are in the picture as well—they're the ones closer to my age—and they enable me to go still further, yielding something of a triptych in time.

To be sure, I am looking only at the physical: the psychological and the moral are another story, less subject to view retinally, even if recorded in literature. That larger perspective, entailing the psychological and the moral, is what I want to explore and discuss in these final pages, for it seems appropriate to a book that has focused so intently on these two key phases of life. Commencement is a semiotic spectacle, made up of both seen and unseen elements. The young poised for takeoff. The fate that awaits them in their next phases. The old returning. The countdown of the generations graphically on show in the alumni parade. The beautiful if delirious project of recapturing the past. And my own final encounter with the young people, their parents, and their grandparents at the end of the show. How can one do justice to these segments of life? How can one go about gauging the plenitude of adventures and achievements and reversals and failures that are writ large inside this array of young and old going through their paces? How can one make the imaginative move that is so necessary, from the biological spectacle I have described on to the hidden stories of heart and mind that have their own density, truth, and sinuous reach? I have intentionally described these groups as virtually different species, for that is how I remember seeing them when I was twenty-one, and that is somehow the way I still see them, not only at Commencement but also every week in my classroom, where my white hair and lined face seem to put us in different worlds altogether.

It seems fair to say that virtually no child thinks much about growing old, other than the occasional wonderment felt at the sight of Grandma and Grandpa. I am all too aware of the allergic reactions of my students whenever I hold forth to them about issues of aging and mortality. These issues do not engage the young (other than abstractly); even to bring it up is bad form. For that reason one is surprised and moved when one does run into moments of widened child perception in literature along those lines: Rastignac's tenderness toward Goriot (*Père Goriot*), Hilda's understanding of Solness's climacteric (*The Master Builder*), Artie's need to make sense of Vladek's experience of the Holocaust (*Maus*), Marjane's dawning awareness of the suffering of her grandfather (*Persepolis*). And sometimes it can take a whole life—and then some—for us to imagine with any depth and scope the lives of our parents. Virginia Woolf's beautiful novel *To the Lighthouse* is especially stirring in this regard, for in it Virginia seeks, long after Mother's death, shortly after Father's death, to depict them as they might have been, unto themselves. How many of us are capable of this?

If children seem programmatically averse to imagining the affairs of their elders, the same cannot be said for adults, who are often obsessed with childhood, usually their own but sometimes that of others, including, of course, their own children. Why is this so? Nostalgia? Yearning to recapture what was best? Reunions point in this direction. We, the old, yearn and think backward for other reasons too. A nastier explanation might be that we are still working through the injuries of childhood, still settling scores, still tied to scenarios of long ago. Certainly Brontë's Heathcliff operates along those lines. Of course other, nobler reasons exist: our solicitude for the young and vulnerable, our role as stewards. But the most powerful stimulus is likely our certainty that our own childhood holds something of a key to who we are, what we have become, and what we have left or lost. One remembers "Rosebud" in *Citizen Kane*, a sign of a purity and beauty that fueled life but cannot be recaptured. Our own lost innocence, also that of others. Willy Loman (*Death of a Salesman*) stands in our minds as a man marked entirely by the beauty and promise of his children: it was among his prime articles of belief, it is cruelly exposed as illusory. The Blakean move from innocence to experience, the master narrative of childhood, can be a curtain going up all throughout one's life, as though disappointment or disillusionment—regarding oneself, regarding one's children or even one's parents—were a time-release punishment against which there is no immunity.

These matters can be even more punitive and coercive. You can be put into reverse gear, "childed." It was Lear's fate, according to the Fool. Strindberg's Captain (*The Father*) is systematically regressed in time, infantilized, whereas his Officer (*A Dream Play*), equipped with a doctorate, nonetheless cannot answer what two plus two makes and has his hair pulled by the schoolmaster. Bernlef's Maarten (*Out of Mind*), a victim of Alzheimer's disease, finds that his own childhood and past are usurping his life, brutally inserting themselves into current affairs, transforming everything into their terms; this is childhood relived with a vengeance. That the old become childlike is a truism that makes us smile until we begin to think harder about what is entailed. Must one end as well as begin in swaddling clothes?

Some of the works we have discussed display the longer trajectory of a human life: Oedipus's emblematic fate from cast-out infant to dying old man, Celie's curve from abused "thing" to fully realized woman, Moll Flanders's comparable trajectory through roles and partners, Faulkner's Ike McCaslin's journey from youngest hunter to old Uncle Ike, Roth's Everyman, who goes the full route and finally goes out. As I have repeatedly said, such representation remains one of the great trump cards dealt out to narrative as a genre: to package the plenitude of a life between the covers of a book. None of us possesses, on our own, that plenary vision about our own affairs.

Yet what strikes me in most of the books under discussion is how powerfully they delimit youth versus age, as if they were spheres that could never touch or interact. Who can truly imagine Blake's chimney sweep old? Jane Eyre old? Pip old? Huck Finn old? Siss old? And what of those who died: Kafka's Georg and Gregor, Faulkner's Quentin and Joe Christmas, Vesaas's Unn, Morrison's Sula? They are not to be imagined outside the arena of childhood. Still harder, I think, would be to imagine Lear or Othello young, child Goriot, Gertrude or Phèdre as a girl, Mother Courage before she became a mother, even Santiago in his youth or David Lurie coming up the ladder. Their texts are not written. Could one write them? Could knowledge of the one point us toward the other? I am quite intentionally fencing off these two phases of life as clear and distinct—even though I know there is always traffic in between, perhaps incessant traffic—because I am at pains to get at the dimensionality and reach of them both. My purpose in examining a wide swath of literary depictions of growing up and growing old is to expand, as vigorously as I can, our sense of possible trajectories for each stage, of how the voyage of these characters sheds its light on the trip that we too have made and are making.

That is why it is good to bring the golden fruits of arts and literature—stories of growing up and growing old, from Sophocles to Coetzee, dense with time and interiority—into our possession, for we are immeasurably the fuller for it, attuned to, even accosted by other voices and fates, times, and places. Here is an inheritance you can receive without anyone needing to die. Here is a fabulous voyage you can make without passport or suitcase. We

territorialize through reading and imagining, we expand our rep-
ertory. And perhaps we learn to sense the reaches and depths of
those we know and love, even of those we scarcely know and do
not love. Literature schools us in this way.

One walks into a library or bookstore and thinks: so many stories, so little time. But the truth goes the other way: each of these
stories gives time, rather than taking it. Each of these works adds
to our stock. Each one of them grows us. That is where I want to
put my final emphasis. Stories of growing up and growing old are
stories that extend who we are. Morning to noon, noon to night:
the arc of the sun and the arc of a life, from birth to death.
Human life would seem end-oriented—whether it be the route
from innocence to experience or the apprenticeship with dying—
and that is what gives the drama of growing up and growing old
its inevitable pathos. Each phase seems keyed to loss. But art reverses these matters; remember again Andrew Marvell's sweet
lines:

> *Thus, though we cannot make our sun*
> *Stand still, yet we will make him run.*

That is the propulsion of desire, but also of art. Hence, the two
phases of my study are about the continuing heat of life, not only
its eager launch or its inevitable close. One measures our coming,
the other measures our going; both measure trajectories and ve-
locities; both are kinetic. Both add to our energy and our estate.

From Lazarillo to Oskar Schell, passing through so many
other young people seeking their way—Rastignac, Jane Eyre,
Pip, Huck, Benjy, Joe Christmas, Sula, Unn, Celie, Marjane—
literature tracks the trip from morning to noon. There is nothing
servile or merely denotative here, but rather something demiurgic
and world-making. Not unlike the bear tracks that Faulkner's Ike
McCaslin learned to read, the print on the page gives birth to lives
and fates, sweeps those of us no longer young into nineteenth-
century London or onto a raft on the Mississippi. From Lear to
David Lurie, passing through so many old and not-so-old people
obeying the law of time—Phèdre, Goriot, Solness, Leopold Bloom,
Willy Loman, Blanche DuBois, Santiago, Aureliano—literature

tracks the trip from noon to night but converts it into light, our light. Art's sun never sets. It knows only birth. It is Commencement. We live other and again through the books we read and the travels of mind and heart they enable. Four-legged, two-legged, three-legged: each one of these forms of locomotion comes to us as readers, moves us as readers, even as supine readers. Art: a worthy answer for the Sphinx who interrogates us all.

Acknowledgments

This book is at once the most—and the least—professional book I've ever written. In it, I draw on more than four decades of reading, writing, and teaching, and it is not possible to gauge how many others' voices and visions are paying their way here, undergirding my own say, making it possible, at least in some measure, for me to have the ideas I have. Rather than naming any particular scholars or teachers who matter to me in this book, I want to acknowledge that utterance itself hinges on prior exchanges, a lifetime's exchanges, that find their most perfect home in the university: its classrooms as well as its libraries. That is the subsoil, the accretion of loam, that comes from a life in the academy, that nourishes a good bit of what I have come to know about literature.

"You have to rake up the leaves before you can have the bonfire," Faulkner wrote in *Absalom, Absalom!* I have been raking leaves for some time now, and I feel this book is what I have to show for it. The personal tone of this book, its seesawing between life and art, trying to discern how each illuminates the other, doubtless makes *Morning, Noon, and Night* as much memoir as literary criticism. But consciousness itself is relational, communal. So, let me acknowledge my major sources of help in this enterprise: a life of talking with—growing old with—my wife, Ann; my brother, Philip; my children, Catherine and Alexander; indeed my grandchildren, Anna and Gustav. They have all played their role. My grand topic—growing up and growing old—is scarcely a specialist's domain: not only does everything teach me about it, but it also refuses to stay in books; it leaps out at me in my life.

Nonetheless, books, as I repeatedly claim, are unique, for they capture, as nothing else does, the passing of time. Yet they do not know age, whereas authors do, and it pleases me greatly to dedicate this volume to Catherine and Alexander, each at their noontime.

Others have also played a vital, if less intimate, role in this project. Cristina Serverius has helped me with the arduous job of locating permissions, Charles Auger and Carol Wilson-Allen have graciously assisted me in numerous clerical tasks, Brown University has given me the kind of material as well as moral support I almost take for granted: writing a book is a distinctly corporate undertaking. I want especially to signal the remarkable assistance I received from Millicent Bennett at Random House: she has taken my words and ideas with the kind of seriousness and generosity that all authors hope for, helping me to transform a sprawling manuscript into a more orderly book. For all these gifts, I am grateful.

Bibliography

Anonymous. *Lazarillo de Tormes,* in *Two Spanish Picaresque Novels.* Tr. Michael Alpert. New York: Penguin, 1969.

Balzac, Honoré de. *Père Goriot.* Tr. A. J. Krailsheimer. New York: Oxford University Press, 1991.

Baudelaire, Charles. *Les Fleurs du Mal.* Paris: Garnier, 1964.

Bergman, Ingmar. *Fanny and Alexander.* Tr. Alan Blair. New York: Pantheon, 1983.

———. *Wild Strawberries,* in *Four Screenplays of Ingmar Bergman.* Trs. Lars Malmström and David Kushner. New York: Simon and Schuster, 1960.

Bernlef, J. *Out of Mind.* Tr. Adrienne Dixon. Boston: David R. Godine, 1989.

Blake, William. *Songs of Innocence and of Experience.* New York: Oxford University Press, 1990.

Brecht, Bertolt. *Mother Courage and Her Children.* Tr. John Willett. London: Methuen, 1980.

Brontë, Charlotte. *Jane Eyre.* New York: Penguin, 1966.

Brontë, Emily. *Wuthering Heights.* New York: Norton, 1971.

Calvino, Italo. *Invisible Cities.* Tr. William Weaver. New York: Harcourt Brace Jovanovich, 1972.

Coetzee, J. M. *Disgrace.* New York: Penguin, 1999.

Defoe, Daniel. *Moll Flanders.* New York: Norton, 1973.

Dickens, Charles. *Bleak House.* London: Oxford University Press, 1987.

———. *Great Expectations.* London: Oxford University Press, 1987.

Dostoevsky, Fyodor. *The Brothers Karamazov*. Trs. Richard Pevear and Larissa Volkhonsky. New York: Farrar Strauss and Giroux, 1990.

Duras, Marguerite. *The Lover*. Tr. Barbara Bray. New York: Random House, 1986.

Eliot, T. S. *The Complete Poems and Plays*. New York: Harcourt Brace and World, 1952.

Ellison, Ralph. *Invisible Man*. New York: Vintage, 1989.

Faulkner, William. *Go Down, Moses*. New York: Vintage, 1990.

————. *Light in August*. New York: Vintage, 1990.

————. *The Sound and the Fury*. New York: Vintage, 1990.

Foer, Jonathan Safran. *Extremely Loud and Incredibly Close*. New York: Houghton Mifflin, 2005.

Freud, Sigmund. *Civilization and Its Discontents*. Tr. James Strachey. New York: Norton, 1961.

————. *The Interpretation of Dreams*. Tr. James Strachey. New York: Avon, 1965.

García Márquez, Gabriel. *One Hundred Years of Solitude*. Tr. Gregory Rabassa. New York: Avon, 1971.

Grimmelshausen, Hans Jakob Christoffel von. *The Adventures of a Simpleton*. Tr. Walter Wallich. New York: Ungar, 1963.

Hemingway, Ernest. *The Old Man and the Sea*. New York: Scribner's, 2003.

Ibsen, Henrik. *A Doll House*, in *The Complete Major Prose Plays*. Tr. Rolf Fjelde. Penguin, 1978.

————. *The Master Builder*, in *The Complete Major Prose Plays*. Tr. Rolf Fjelde. New York: Penguin, 1978.

————. *When We Dead Awaken*, in *The Complete Major Prose Plays*. Tr. Rolf Fjelde. New York: Penguin, 1978.

Ionesco, Eugène. *Exit the King*. Tr. Donald Watson. New York: Grove, 1963.

Irving, Washington. "The Legend of Sleepy Hollow," in *Washington Irving: History, Tales and Sketches*. New York: Library of America, 1983.

James, Henry. *The Turn of the Screw*. New York: Norton, 1966.

Joyce, James. *Ulysses*. New York: Random House, 1986.

Kafka, Franz. *The Complete Stories*. Trs. Willa Muir and Edwin Muir. New York: Schocken, 1971.

————. *The Trial*. Trs. Willa Muir and Edwin Muir. New York: Vintage, 1969.

Laclos, Pierre Choderlos de. *Les liaisons dangereuses*. Tr. Douglas Parmée. New York: Oxford University Press, 1995.

Mann, Thomas. *Death in Venice*. Tr. H.T. Lowe-Porter. New York: Vintage, 1954.

Miller, Arthur. *Death of a Salesman*. New York: Penguin, 1976.

Molière (Jean-Baptiste Poquelin). *Oeuvres Complètes*. Paris: Garnier Frères, 1962.

Montaigne, Michel de. *The Complete Essays of Montaigne*. Tr. Donald Frame. Stanford: Stanford University Press, 1976.

Morrison, Toni. *Sula*. New York: Random House, 2004.

Prévost, Antoine François. *Manon Lescaut*. Tr. Leonard Tancock. New York: Penguin, 1991.

Proust, Marcel. *In Search of Lost Time.* Trs. Scott Moncrieff, Terence Kilmartin, et al. New York: Random House, 1981.

Quevedo, Francisco de. *The Swindler,* in *Two Spanish Picaresque Novels.* Tr. Michael Alpert. New York: Penguin, 1969.

Racine, Jean. *Phèdre,* in *Racine: Oeuvres Complètes.* Paris: Gallimard, 1995.

Rhys, Jean. *Wide Sargasso Sea.* New York: Norton, 1982.

Roth, Philip. *Everyman.* New York: Houghton Mifflin Harcourt, 2006.

Sartre, Jean-Paul. *Nausea.* Tr. Lloyd Alexander. New York: New Directions, 1964.

Satrapi, Marjane. *Persepolis: The Story of a Childhood.* New York: Pantheon, 2003.

Shakespeare, William. *The Complete Poems and Sonnets.* London: Oxford University Press, 2002.

———. *Hamlet.* New York: Norton, 1992.

———. *Othello.* New York: Penguin, 1970.

———. *Romeo and Juliet.* Cambridge: Cambridge University Press, 2005.

———. *The Tragedy of King Lear.* Ed. Jay Halio. New York: Cambridge University Press, 1992.

Sontag, Susan. *Reading the Pain of Others.* New York: St. Martin's, 2003.

Sophocles. *Oedipus the King* and *Oedipus at Colonus,* in *Sophocles: The Three Theban Plays.* Tr. Robert Fagles. New York: Penguin, 1984.

Spiegelman, Art. *Maus I: A Survivor's Tale: My Father Bleeds History.* New York: Random House, 1986.

———. *Maus II: A Survivor's Tale: And Here My Troubles Began.* New York: Random House, 1992.

Strindberg, August. *The Father,* in *August Strindberg: Miss Julie and Other Plays.* Tr. Michael Robinson. New York: Oxford University Press, 1998.

———. *The Ghost Sonata,* in *August Strindberg: Miss Julie and Other Plays.* Tr. Michael Robinson. New York: Oxford University Press, 1998.

Twain, Mark. *The Adventures of Huckleberry Finn.* New York: Norton, 1977.

Vesaas, Tarjei. *The Ice Palace.* Tr. Elizabeth Rokkan. London: Peter Owen, 1992.

Walker, Alice. *The Color Purple.* New York: Simon and Schuster, 1982.

Williams, Tennessee. *A Streetcar Named Desire.* New York: Penguin, 1959.

Woolf, Virginia. *To the Lighthouse.* New York: Harcourt Brace Jovanovich, 1981.

Index

Permissions Acknowledgments

ABOUT THE AUTHOR

ARNOLD WEINSTEIN is the Edna and Richard Salomon Distinguished Professor of Comparative Literature at Brown University. His lectures on world literature are produced in DVD and CD format by The Teaching Company. He divides his time between Brown University, Block Island, Stockholm, and Brittany.

ABOUT THE TYPE

This book was set in Walbaum, a typeface designed in 1810 by German punch cutter J. E. Walbaum. Walbaum's type is more French than German in appearance. Like Bodoni, it is a classical typeface, yet its openness and slight irregularities give it a human, romantic quality.